DAILY SWORD SHARPENING

Applying the Word of God daily to your life; keeping the Sword of the Spirit sharpened so you can Sharpen others

JOSEPH G. MISIASZEK

WESTBOW
PRESS®
A DIVISION OF THOMAS NELSON
& ZONDERVAN

Copyright © 2023 Joseph G. Misiaszek.

All rights reserved. No part of this book may be used or reproduced by any means, graphic, electronic, or mechanical, including photocopying, recording, taping or by any information storage retrieval system without the written permission of the author except in the case of brief quotations embodied in critical articles and reviews.

This book is a work of non-fiction. Unless otherwise noted, the author and the publisher make no explicit guarantees as to the accuracy of the information contained in this book and in some cases, names of people and places have been altered to protect their privacy.

WestBow Press books may be ordered through booksellers or by contacting:

WestBow Press
A Division of Thomas Nelson & Zondervan
1663 Liberty Drive
Bloomington, IN 47403
www.westbowpress.com
844-714-3454

Because of the dynamic nature of the Internet, any web addresses or links contained in this book may have changed since publication and may no longer be valid. The views expressed in this work are solely those of the author and do not necessarily reflect the views of the publisher, and the publisher hereby disclaims any responsibility for them.

Any people depicted in stock imagery provided by Getty Images are models, and such images are being used for illustrative purposes only. Certain stock imagery © Getty Images.

Cover photographed and designed by Joseph Boyd "JB" Misiaszek

Unless otherwise indicated, scripture quotations are from the ESV Bible® (The Holy Bible, English Standard Version®), copyright © 2001 by Crossway Bibles, a publishing ministry of Good News Publishers. Used by permission. All rights reserved.

Scripture quotations marked NLT are taken from the Holy Bible, New Living Translation, copyright © 1996, 2004, 2007 by Tyndale House Foundation. Used by permission of Tyndale House Publishers, Inc., Carol Stream, Illinois 60188. All rights reserved.

ISBN: 978-1-6642-8762-4 (sc)
ISBN: 978-1-6642-8761-7 (hc)
ISBN: 978-1-6642-8763-1 (e)

Library of Congress Control Number: 2022923694

Print information available on the last page.

WestBow Press rev. date: 01/19/2023

DEDICATION

I would like to first dedicate this book to my wife, Kanda, who has stood by me through it all. She helps me complete the image of God as my wife and my spiritual support, as well as being my emotional support and my best friend. She saw in me what I refused to see and encouraged me to follow God's calling even when I couldn't hear it clearly or see it and when fear tried to deter me, she challenged me to stay the course.

I would like to also dedicate this book to my kids, KaiLee and my son-in-law Jacob, JB (Joseph Boyd), Christian, James and Elise – the guiding principles in this book are what guided mom and I in raising and mentoring you – may your walk with Christ and the Holy Spirit not only deepen your relationship with God, but also may He use your faith to bring others into a right relationship with Him.

I would like to also dedicate this book to my parents, Joseph L. and Rosemary (Kitty) Misiaszek, who laid my spiritual foundation, setting the example of making God a priority and setting me on my course. They always encouraged me to follow my dreams and supported me in writing and my ministry.

Finally, I would like to dedicate this book to my only brother, Tony Misiaszek. Even though you were younger than me, I looked up to you and you challenged me to grow in my relationship with God and led me to the church that started my ministry journey and renewed my love of writing. Losing you was the hardest thing I have had to deal with on this Earth, but you read some of these devotions which sparked deep conversations between us, that I will always treasure – until I can see you again and hug you – I will continue to write and you will always be a source of inspiration.

ACKNOWLEDGMENTS

I would like to first acknowledge and thank my editor, Dr. Kelly Gehlhoff, not only for this book, but also while I was in seminary. She supported me by editing my papers – her family and my family have been church friends for a long time and they are all a blessing to us.

I would also like to thank the teachers and staff members of Pueblo School District 60 who responded lovingly when I shared my Life Journals and started asking to read them on a regular basis. Thank you for sharing them with friends and family and then challenging me to put them into print and follow my dream of becoming an author, even encouraging me when I got down to keep writing.

I would also like to thank the two life groups at *Fellowship of the Rockies* - Pueblo (Men's Wednesday Mornings and Couples Thursday nights) who asked to receive my daily devotionals, responded to the refletion questions in the devotionals, encouraged me to continue to write and also checked on me when they did not receive one.

I would like to acknowledge *Fellowship of the Rockies Church* in Pueblo where they taught us the Life Journal S-O-A-P method that eventually evolved into the daily devotionals that are printed in this book, with many more entries still being written and shared.

I would like to acknowledge Pastor Duane Arledge who saw the potential in me that I could not. He encouraged and equipped me to lead men's ministry and go into seminary and he is always there as a mentor and friend whenever I need spiritual guidance or reassurance.

I would also like to thank Barb Timock who not only trusted me to mentor and tutor her sons, but also she has been supportive and encouraging of this book and she enthusiastically helped brainstorm book titles.

FOREWORD

By Kanda Misiaszek

Joe has always had a heart for the Lord and serving him through loving others. He has also had a passion for writing. In 1990, he wrote two children's books and while unpublished as a high school student, he still aspired to publish books. After many years of having the dream of publishing a book and giving up on the dream, he did not see the journey that God had planned for him. However, Joe was faithful with being in the Word and sharing what God was doing in the lives of others because of him sharing God's Word with others. The devotionals in this book came out of learning more about God's Word and life journaling. Life journaling is writing out a scripture that stands out to the reader, observing what the passage is saying, applying it to the reader's life and praying back the words to God. Joe found the scripture and self-application to be the most inspiring to him and others. He started sharing what God was showing him with other teachers, staff, friends and family. These individuals started asking to read the inspiration daily and that set-in motion the devotionals being emailed to individuals. Then those individuals shared this Biblical wisdom with others and lead to more people asking to receive the devotionals as well. The emails began in 2013 and it led to more email addresses being added each year and requests for Joe to write a book. Here we are today and Joe is ready to share with everyone the inspiring words of God and applications that he has been able to get from God's Word. If you want to take your spiritual walk with the Lord to the next level, read this book. If you want to sharpen your spiritual sword so that you can do more for the Kingdom, read this book. If you want to be able to help others find applications of Scripture in their lives, then read this book.

PREFACE

By Joseph G Misiaszek

I have always found inspiration from and have been a monthly supporter of Pastor Greg Laurie of *Harvest Ministries*, a part of *Harvest Christian Fellowship* in Riverside, California for almost two decades now. As a result, my wife and I received thank you gifts for supporting the ministry. Two of our favorite thank you gifts were his books *For Every Season vol. I and II*. Kanda and I would read passages from these books every night together, ending the day strengthening our faith. These books had a huge influence on what would become my daily devotional practice.

Over a decade ago the church we were attending, *Fellowship of the Rockies* in Pueblo, Colorado, discovered *Life Resources* and their Life Journaling program. In that program, participants begin by praying about the verses they will be reading and for the Holy Spirit to speak to them through the Scriptures. Then the individual reads the Bible reading plan for the day and identifies the part that spoke to them most clearly. The final step is writing in one's journal about that Scripture utilizing the acronym SOAP.

> **S** stands for Scripture. The reader actually writes out the verse that stood out.
> **O** is for observation. The reader makes observations about the Scripture they read.
> **A** represents application. The reader applies the Scripture to their life.
> **P** is for prayer. The reader creates a prayer to God with the Scripture and can utilize the observation and application if they desire to.

I quickly discovered that there is nothing more powerful than praying God's Word back to Him. Soon the life journaling became so in-depth that the "life journals" we bought weren't big enough, so I shifted to using regular spiral-bound notebooks.

At the middle school, I started a morning prayer group for the teachers and we would use my classroom twice a week before the students were allowed in the building. That eventually lead to some faculty coming to me to seek spiritual advice. When one of them would indicate a personal prayer request or revealed that they had been struggling with something, I would share what just so happened to be something in my life journal that applied to their current situation. Their appreciation for the insight soon became, "Are you willing to share this wisdom daily? We love the insight you have."

By this time in my life journaling career, the O and the A became one and my journal format started resembling Pastor Laurie's devotions in his books that Kanda and I read. Scripture, personal story or anecdote and application. It felt as though I could not leave it there and began asking poignant questions at the end of the journals or devotions to challenge those who read them. How can they personalize this? How can reading this help them go deeper? So, I added questions at the end of each entry.

One teacher came and asked if they could share my devotional email with one of their friends. That led to several teachers sharing the devotions and their friends asking permission to be added to the daily email distribution list.

In 2015, we left *Fellowship of the Rockies* so I could take a part-time youth pastor position at a church in town, but the daily devotions continued to be written and shared. After three years, we left part-time ministry to return to *Fellowship of the Rockies*. Since our former life groups were now full, we joined a new couple's group and while I led a Friday morning men's group I was invited to a Wednesday morning men's group that met at a local donut shop. During the course of these life groups, my daily devotions came up in conversation and both groups asked to be on the distribution list and so my "following" continued to grow.

In the fall of 2020, I was asked to apply for the pastor's position at the *First Baptist Church of Vona* and by the end of October, I was hired to be their pastor. Through transitioning to this new full-time position of ministry, people asked if I was going to continue writing and sharing these devotions and many suggested that I should consider publishing them in a book. This book is a result of all of this effort and encouragement, plus more that I could write many pages about, but that is not the purpose of this book.

In the back of the book is an alphabetical list of the Scriptures, so you can look up a specific verse and what the Holy Spirit led me to write about that Scripture and what day of the year it is on. This book is written with the actual dates, like January 1st or July 4th. I wrote one devotional entry per day of the year and even one for February 29th, whenever it rolls around.

I understand that it is very easy to take Scripture out of context and use it for purposes that are not of God. However, my first book is written in a way to help inspire people to get into God's Word and to see how even though it was written over several thousand years and was complete about two thousand years ago, truth is truth and is always applicable. For truth to exist, there can only be one source and that source is God. I challenge you to not only read the Scriptures that are utilized for the devotions, but also to open your Bible or Bible App for yourself and read what came before, what came after and what other Scripture supports the Scripture that was written about.

It is my prayer that this book challenges you to read God's Word more comprehensively, to read it daily and to be open to the moving of the Holy Spirit as He is willing to help you apply Scripture in your own life. Ephesians 6:17-18 says, "and take the helmet of salvation and the sword of the Spirit, which is the word of God, praying at all times in the Spirit, with all prayer and supplication. To that end, keep alert with all perseverance, making supplication for all the saints." The Spiritual Sword with which we do spiritual battle is the Word of God. You must keep your spiritual sword sharp and to keep it sharp you need to use it, train with it and know it well. *Daily Sword Sharpening*, the title of this book, comes from Ephesians 17 and Proverbs 27:17, "As Iron sharpens iron, so one man sharpens another." May you not only keep your sword sharp, but also utilize it to sharpen others, encourage others and support others.

So, what is your next step? The first step is done. You bought the book. Now what? It is really simple. Pray before you read. Expect the Holy Spirit to walk you through understanding the Truth. Read the devotion for that day and then complete your own journal entry by exploring the application and taking it deeper by answering the questions.

May reading this book draw you closer to your Heavenly Father. May your walk with the Holy Spirit be deepened and may you hear His voice ever more clearly as you learn to apply what you read. Again, go back and read before, after and even search your Bible for another Scripture that teaches the same concept revealed within each daily verse. God Bless.

Pastor Joe

JANUARY 1

> Therefore, if anyone is in Christ, he is a new creation. The old has passed away; behold, the new has come. 2 Corinthians 5:17

Last year is gone - in the books! Whew! What a year! On December 31st, every year, people gather around and ring out the old year and ring in the New Year. Many make resolutions to be better in the new year; some only last a few weeks, some a few days, but some people still try. Do you have that old shirt or pair of jeans that may be stained, or has holes in it but you just can't seem to get rid of? It may not even fit anymore, but you just can't seem to let go of it. We can be that way with our spirituality. Paul tells us that anyone who belongs to Christ, anyone who accepts Christ as the Son of God and as their Savior, is a new person. The old life is gone and the new life has begun. But like that old pair of jeans or shirt, we hold onto it. It may be comfortable, but God has something better for us. We should not hold onto the old life, the sinful life. With Christ, however, we are already new. Once we accepted Him into our heart and made Him our Savior, the old died and we were made a new creation in Him. It's not something that has to happen more than once, every year, etc. We are a New Creation; the old has passed away. As we walk into this new year - we must be willing to let go of the old; the old creation, the hurt, the pain and no longer let those define us. Christ is who defines us. Live in the freedom, walk in the freedom that comes from the Holy Spirit living in you. With freedom, allow the Holy Spirit to guide and direct you and the way you should go. On this first day of the New Year, let's not get consumed by new resolutions, that we may or most likely may not follow through on, but hold onto the truth that we are already new – a New Creation. Make a commitment to see yourself as Christ sees you, created in His image, bearing His image and bearing His fingerprints. What steps can you take today to live out this truth in your life? We should be excited to live the new life in the freedom that Jesus gives us. If God says you are a new creation, how can you determine that you are not? Neither should you allow the enemy to convince you that you are not. No matter what the world says, you are not defined by your past, but by who holds your future. If God says your sins are forgiven, how can you say they are not? If God says you are loved, how can you say you are not? Lucky for us, God determines what sins are forgiven and which ones are not. God determines who is loved, not us. Are you ready to walk out of that tomb, leave the grave clothes behind and embrace your new life in Christ? Have you accepted your new identity in Christ, or are you holding onto the old? What is keeping you from walking in the freedom of new life with Christ?

JANUARY 2

"Remember not the former things, nor consider the things of old. Behold, I am doing a new thing; now it springs forth, do you not perceive it? I will make a way in the wilderness and rivers in the desert." Isaiah 43:18-19

When New Year's hits, many people make New Year's Resolutions: to be better, do more, or change. However, over 80% of resolutions have failed by February, just one month, four weeks, or 30 days into it. We fall back into old habits. We want to be new and change, but few of us have that discipline to make it happen. God, however, has the drive and the desire to do something new in us. He tells us several times in Scripture to not remember the former or consider the old things, our old life, our old bad habits. He wants to do something new in our lives and He asks us, "Do you not perceive it?" Are we so busy trying to uphold a resolution that we are not spending enough time with God to perceive the change He is wanting to do in us? The analogy here is that He is making a path in the wilderness. He is creating a river in the desert; when life seems too rough and we don't see how we can press through it, God makes a way. When we are walking in the desert and don't feel like we have the strength to make it through, He creates a river to refresh us. We need to be in communion with Him. We need to listen to and follow the directions and guidance of the Holy Spirit. We need to turn and look at Him to see the river, to see the path instead of looking into the darkness and the shadows where the enemy tries to direct our attention. How did Abraham and Sarah make it when traveling through deserts and wilderness? They had a deep relationship with God. How did Moses lead the nation of Israel through the wilderness and desert? He had a deep relationship with God. How did God create a new life for David after Goliath and being hunted by Saul and then one of his own sons? He had a deep relationship with God. There seems to be a common theme in this stream. God wants to do something new in your life, but you need to have a deeper relationship with God. Do you want help climbing that mountain? Then go to God for directions. Do you want a path out of the wilderness and into safety? Then listen to Jesus. Do you need crisp, cool water to refresh you while in the desert season of life? Allow the Holy Spirit to guide you to the waters. What are you really wanting – a deep relationship with the Living God or a prayer vending machine in the sky? Is your relationship only Sunday-deep or seven-days-deep? What steps are you willing to take to deepen your relationship with the Living God?

JANUARY 3

> Restore to me the joy of your salvation and uphold with me a willing spirit. Psalm 51:12

This is a new year and if you are anything like me, one desire you have is to do better at reading the Bible, prayer time and quiet time with God. It's not a resolution but rather a life change I want to have, but I can so easily get distracted from it. Like Paul, when he said in Romans 7:15, "For I do not understand my own actions. For I do not do what I want, but I do the very thing I hate." So, like David in Psalm 51, I have asked, "God, help me desire Your Word; make me hunger for Your presence." We may hunger for a lot of things – money, power, things like houses, cars, boats, etc., but that hunger can never be satisfied. There will always be someone else with a better job, car, house, or 401k. But when we hunger for God's Word, not only does it energize us and fuel us, but it can also satisfy us. To experience this deeper satisfaction, we have to hunger for Him and His word; we must allow Him to have power in our lives to guide and direct. It takes a simple prayer, "I hand it all over to You God, make me willing to obey You, to follow Your heart." As David continues, "Create in me a clean heart, O Lord, renew a right Spirit in me and cast me not from Your sight. Restore in me Lord, the JOY of Your salvation." No matter the trials and hardships I encounter, may I be constantly filled with the Holy Spirit and the Joy of the Lord. "Lord, I am asking because I know I tend to wander like a mindless sheep. Make me obey You, make me follow You. Help me to keep my eyes on You and prevent me from wandering and being left to my own desires." When we pray prayers like this, it can be dangerous. We are asking for Him to control our lives, control what path we take, what job we have and where we live. Are we really ready to be fully surrendered and committed to God? "Create in me a clean heart, a heart that is actively following You. Uphold me with a willing spirit. Help me to have a willing spirit to obey and follow the direction and guidance of the Holy Spirit. May the salvation I have from You be the source of joy in my life." What is the ultimate fountain or source of joy in your life? Kids, spouse, grandkids, etc. can be the typical answers, but it should ultimately be God that is the source of our joy. As you walk into this new year, what is the true desire of your heart? Are you willing to obey whatever the Lord calls you to this year?

JANUARY 4

> I will instruct you and teach you in the way you should go; I will counsel you with my eye upon you. Psalm 32:8

There was a point in my life, while in college, when I told my dad something along the lines of how smart he was or that I should have listened to him more when I was little. His comment back still brings a smile to us all every time he retells the story, "My son goes to college and I get smarter, how about that!" As a child, a teenager, or a young adult, we can dismiss the wisdom and instruction of our parents because we think, "They don't know what it's like to be a kid in this generation!" But in reality, they do. As a parent now, I do. It's the same struggles, just a different delivery method; the same sin, just a different wrapping paper. When we give God our heart and make Him Lord and realize He is our Heavenly Father, we tend to do the same with Him regardless of our age. But God promised David and He promises us that He will instruct us in the way we should go and always be looking out for us. But if we are honest with ourselves, we can believe that we know better than God; our way is better. God promises to never lead us down a path of destruction or hurt. The NLT version of this verse says, "I will guide you along the BEST pathway for your life. I will advise you and watch over you." His way is always better than our way; His blessings are better than what we think we want or need. He will lead you not down the mediocre pathway, the just ok, or even a good pathway, but promises to lead you down the best pathway. All we have to do is follow, not figure out the map or think two or three turns ahead; just follow, just trust. He will advise us and counsel us, never leaving us, but always watching over us. He is ready to speak wisdom and instruction in our life whenever we are ready to hear and recognize we need it. A year into our marriage, my wife prophesied over me saying God has a different plan for my life than being a school teacher; it would be to be a teacher, but not in a classroom and not intellectual, but rather a teacher of His. I distinctly remember telling her she was irrational; that story didn't align with my life's plan. God was patient, loving and continued to watch over me, advise me and gently guided me to His BEST pathway for my life. What is God trying to instruct you about in your life? Where is His guidance leading you? If you fully submitted to His Will, His Way, what does that best pathway look like for you? What is your first step in allowing this to happen in your life?

JANUARY 5

> and have put on the new self, which is being renewed in knowledge after the image of its creator. Colossians 3:10

As the New Year continues and people try "new things," as Christians we need to put on our New Nature, our Christ nature and continue becoming more like Him. If God provided your dream outfit for you and all He asked was that you give Him the dirty clothes with holes in them, the clothes you have on now, would you? It would be wild if you didn't, right? So, if you would take the trade, then why don't we do that spiritually? Get rid of the old identity because we are not defined by our past; we are a new creation, renewed in the knowledge and likeness of the Creator Himself. Too many of us are anchored by our past and allow it to keep us where we are instead of being free from it and going where the Holy Spirit is trying to lead us. The more we keep our new nature on, our new identity in Christ, the more we know our Creator and the more we know our Creator the deeper our relationship with the Creator will be. That should be our goal. This year, next year, every year, every day, our goal should be to learn, to know our Creator at a deeper and more intimate level so that we can become more like Him. Cut the chains off the anchor and allow your new identity to set you free! The deeper our relationship with God, the more we know Him and the more we can be like Him. Now we will never be perfect, we know that, but don't let the enemy deter you in that aspect. To be more like Him, how wonderful would that be? To be more like Him would be to love others as He loves, forgive others as He forgives, see others as He sees them; see them beyond the masks and make-up that people hide behind, to see the real person, the person God created them to be in all their gifts and imperfections and to see His fingerprints on them. To be more like Him, we would be more patient with people as He is patient with us. To be more like Him, we would be able to see more clearly the schemes of the enemy and by doing so we can prevent him from sowing tares and weeds in the garden God is having us cultivate. How are you letting your old self be anchored in the past? What can you do to cut the chains off the anchor and follow the Holy Spirit? What can you do to keep your new nature on so you can continuously be more like your Creator and know Him at a deeper level every day?

JANUARY 6

> Therefore, confess your sins to one another and pray for one another, that you may be healed. The prayer of a righteous person has great power as it is working. James 5:16

Sin is the gapping effect that separates us from God. When we sin, we must confess wholeheartedly in order for them to be forgiven. As Christians, we are told to confess our sins. James tells us here to confess our sins to one another and pray for one another. As a man and I am sure many men can testify to this, we don't like to be seen as weak or vulnerable. When we confess our sins to another person, it makes us vulnerable and in our own eyes, weak. I have a good friend, a solid young man who struggles with pornography. Whenever he slips up and fails he will reach out to a group of us men and confess how he fell short, what he did and everything. I admire his strength and courage to be not only vulnerable but also to be courageously living out his faith and this verse here. He knows that for healing to take place he must confess and ask for us to pray for him and with him. There are days when I wish I had the courage this young man has. And because of his willingness to be vulnerable, he is willing to be used by God to help other men who share in the same struggle. It is easy, no matter what the sin issue is, to buy into the lies of the enemy that they will see you as weak, less of a Christian, or a fake. The truth is, none of us have it all together and the gap that sin creates between us and God is only widened when we allow the enemy to wedge that gap more and not confess, not be vulnerable, not ask for prayer. James ends here with "the prayer of a righteous person has great power as it is working." Our righteousness comes from Christ, when we confess, we are drawn closer to Him and our prayers can be more powerful because we have been drawn into His righteousness, not pushed away by the secret of sin. My young friend may or may not know, but as a young man, he is an inspiration to those of us older men, reminding us that we need to not only confess but when the enemy is beating us down, to be bold enough to ask for prayer. In my group of solid Christian men, we ask for a spot. This comes from the weightlifting world; you never bench press without a spot, someone to help when your strength leaves you and you can't lift the bar to the rack. It can be specific or general, but when that text goes out, we all pray for that man. Even when I've been away from the group for months, if I ask for a spot, they pray and even though I am hundreds of miles away, healing takes place. Whom do you have to spot you? Who can you confess to and pray for healing? Jesus was vulnerable to come to earth and die for us; you too should be vulnerable enough to ask for prayer and confess. What is your next step?

JANUARY 7

> The Lord your God is in your midst, a mighty one who will save; he will rejoice over you with gladness; he will quiet you by his love; he will exult over you with loud singing. Zephaniah 3:17b

What causes you fear? 2020 and the COVID pandemic caused a lot of fear in a lot of people and 2021 just built on it and expanded; today it seems that fear is lingering still. Fear loves to trap you in a cage, in a sort of prison. Fear keeps you from living the life God intends for you. But there is someone whose abounding love can calm those fears. God does not use fear – it is not one of His tools, it is a weapon of the enemy. But God loves you and if you let Him, He will calm your fears. God loves you so much He wants to be able to be there for you, comfort you and calm your fears, but you have to give Him time to do it. That does not mean it takes a while for Him to do it; we just need to give Him time, which also means that we need to spend time with Him. We must go to Him, be still, be silent and rest in His Presence. We must read His word and know His word. He will not force Himself on us or force us to spend time with Him. He gives us that choice, the free will to decide for ourselves. We just need to slow down, give Him time and spend time with Him. In these uncertain times, the enemy loves to use fear to drive wedges between believers and between us and God. It's weird, I'm not afraid of the dark. I love camping and being out in nature at night, but I was walking through the church the other night and there were no lights on and for a second fear gripped my mind and the question, "What if some..." came into my head. At that moment I had the choice to let the question finish speaking and fear to take root or dismiss it. I dismissed it. But there are other times when I am not so in tune and fear consumes my mind and I can't sleep or focus. We are in a spiritual battle and we must take thoughts captive, all the ones that are not from above. Remember where fear comes from. My grandmother had an embroidered sign that showed fear as an acronym: False Evidence Appearing Real. That is how the enemy gets us with fear. It's not real, but he makes it seem real. God will calm all our fears and will rejoice over us with joyful songs if we just let Him. Don't let fear keep you from living the life that God has for you. We need to trust God enough to calm those fears and know what is real and what is not. What is truth and what is deception? The Holy Spirit brings conviction and peace, so never fear. Recognize fear for what it is and allow God to quiet those fears, still them and settle your soul. Take some extra time today to be still and know. KNOW God and feel His presence. No talking, just listen and be calmed. How are you feeling right now? What fears do you have? What is your first step in allowing God to calm those fears? What fear do you need to turn over to God for Him to calm?

JANUARY 8

"Whoever is not with me is against me and whoever does not gather with me scatters." Matthew 12:30

If you are a football fan and say you like the Broncos, you may have no feelings regarding the Vikings. They are not in our division, not in our conference and we will very rarely ever play them. So, Bronco fans may be neutral towards the Vikings. But spiritually, there is no neutral zone, no neutral feelings. We can like it, hate it, or say "It's not fair", but the fact remains that Jesus says, "If You are not with me, then you are against me." You cannot be Switzerland; there is no spiritual Switzerland. You cannot be neutral. In fact, it is better to be either hot or cold. If you are lukewarm, Jesus says, "I will spit you out." If you are not gathering with Jesus, then you are scattering with Satan. The truth often hurts and it needs to hurt for us to make a change. When people look at your life, your story, what do they see – a Sower or a scatterer? Are you a Friend or foe of Jesus? Are you a Disciple of Jesus or a student of Satan? The book of Revelation warns us that believers will wander from Jesus and chase after whatever doctrine satisfies their desires. And we can see that today as whole denominations stray away from the Word of God and not only teach what God is against, but also promote what is against God. Some say you can interpret Scripture any way you want. No, not at all. God said it, He meant what He said. The Bible is not a buffet where you can pick and choose what you like and leave behind what you don't like. God's Word is just that – God's Word, not ours. Now, as we apply God's word in our life, it may have different applications. But sin is sin. Call it for what it is. Know God's Word well enough that you can know the answer, are you a Sower or a scatterer? Are you sowing God's Word, truth and love, or do you scatter weed seeds to choke a person's soul? We need to remember Jesus' warning here, "If you are not with me then you are against me." Are you a friend of God or are you an enemy of God? Every day we need to choose to follow Him, walk with Him, talk with Him and listen to Him. And by listening to Him, His Word, His Whole Word, you can decipher what is from God and what is being manipulated and changed by the enemy to draw people away from God into chasing their own desires and plans. Are you a Sower or a scatterer? How do you know? Do you believe the whole Word of God, that it is infallible and true, or do you pick and choose what you believe? How does this verse resonate with you, with your heart and soul? How can you apply this verse in your daily walk with God?

JANUARY 9

> The Lord is merciful and gracious, slow to anger and abounding in steadfast love! Psalm 103:8

Anger can get the best of us; if we are not careful, words can be said, whether true or not, that hurt, damage, or even can kill a relationship. That is why James warns us to, "Be quick to listen, slow to speak and SLOW TO ANGER." The Lord is slow to anger when He deals with us. And, if the Lord is slow to anger – should we not also follow suit? Are we not created in His image and called to be like Him? Not only is He slow to anger, but He is full of mercy. Being merciful and gracious, He shows us mercy when we still mess up and sin, even if we sin big time. His grace covers us when we wander and desire to come back to Him; it is that grace, Christ's being gracious, that allows us to return. That is how much He loves us. He is so merciful and gracious that He is slow to anger, slow to get angry when we leave. He is also abounding in Love and not just love, steadfast love – love that is unshaken, unchanging, unending, enduring all things – true steadfast love. It is His steadfast love that is why He is slow to anger. See, Love is what causes us to be slow to anger – Love for others allows us to see life from another person's point of view, their hurt, trauma and life experiences and that God-driven empathy slows down the anger train. But the only way we can be more like Him – compassionate, gracious, slow to anger, abounding in love, is to spend more time with Him, growing the fruit of the Spirit in our life. Like a couple who has been married for 40 years and they act like each other, think like each other and complete each other's sentences – we need to spend time with Jesus Christ so we can be more like Him. The more time we spend with Him in worship, reading and prayer, the more our minds think like Him. The more we allow the Holy Spirit to guide and direct us, the more we will say and do in love. At a time when people are making resolutions, how about as Christians we resolve to spend more time in His Word, more time with Him, so that we too can be more like Him! What changes are you willing to implement to be more like Him? What can you do to slow down the anger train and see from the other person's point of view or life experiences so you also can be slow to anger?

JANUARY 10

> Create in me a clean heart, O God and renew a right (steadfast) spirit within me. Psalm 51:10

A new year brings people wanting newness in their life. Out with the old and in with the new. Americans bring truck and car loads full of old items to thrift shops to make room for buying the new. As we continue to walk in this new year, on a new path, David reminds us of a prayer we should be praying. Get rid of the old heart so God can create a new heart. As we try new things this year, we need to have a new heart, a clean heart, a heart that leans towards God and a heart that is led by the Holy Spirit. Notice David does not ask for help here. He doesn't pray, "Help me to clean my heart, help me have a loyal spirit." David goes full submission here; "God, You create a clean heart in me, create a right spirit in me, create Your steadfast love in me. God, create a loyal spirit in me. Renew my spirit so that I will be loyal to You, steadfast with You, not wandering or roaming, not distracted by the shiny new things the world tries to capture my attention with; loyal and by Your side, the whole way." Sometimes we are so weak that we need more than help. I think of the poem "Footprints" during the hard times when God carried me. Sometimes, we need God "to do" in our lives and not just provide help in our lives. We need to be able to recognize that deep need in our lives. It's been said, "God won't give you more than you can handle." But I don't believe that is true; it is bad advice, for it is only when some of us reach the point of more than we can handle that we actually turn to God. We try so hard to control and fix everything in our lives that we forget to come to Him for help and sometimes we need more than help; we need Him to clean our hearts! When was the last time you asked God to just take control and change an aspect of your life? What is holding you back? He loves you. Jesus asks, "Who when a child asks for bread would give him a viper? How much more does your heavenly Father love you and want to give you good things?" He won't give you something bad because He is a good, good Father. So, what's stopping you? What are you willing to allow Him to change? What can you pray today that just completely submits one aspect of your life over to the control of the Holy Spirit for your heart to be cleaned?

JANUARY 11

> Out of my distress I called on the Lord; the Lord answered me and set me free. The Lord is on my side; I will not fear. What can man do to me? Psalm 118:5-6

When we have an eternal perspective, we can actually ask what David is asking here, "What can man do to me?" I mean, really, what can man do to me? Men can kill the body, but not the spirit. If our body is killed, we immediately get to see God. Man can fight against me, but God, the Holy Spirit, fights for me. So actually, who will win? Paul reminds us in Romans 8:31, "What then shall we say to these things? If God is for us, who can be against us?" When we feel the pressure of the enemy, the trials feel overbearing, or we feel distressed or overwhelmed, we too can call on the Lord and He will answer us. He will set us free -- free from distress? That is up to us. He may not remove us from the situation that is causing stress, but He is there to remind us, to ask us where our eyes are focused – on the distresser or Freer (one who frees)? Are we focused on the situation or the Savior? Are we allowing the enemy to introduce fear to distract us and defeat us, or do we strike down every attack from the enemy with the promises in the Living Word of God? The Lord is on our side, the Lord goes before us and the Lord fights for us – we must not allow the enemy to use fear to capture our attention. If he can use fear to freeze us in our tracks, he really doesn't have to do anything more to win. But if we focus on the Lord, if we keep our eyes on the Lord and trust the Lord, really what can man do to us? He can chastise us, ridicule us, make life more difficult and put-up stumbling blocks. But then we have Jesus' own words in Matthew 5:10, "Blessed are those who are persecuted for righteousness' sake, for theirs is the kingdom of heaven." How deep is your faith? How much do you really believe in Scripture? If you can be honest with yourself, who do you really trust? Self or Holy Spirit? How can this Scripture change your daily walk? How can you apply His word to your life today to live more in freedom and less in the bondage of the enemy? What can you do when fear comes in? How can you counteract that fear?

JANUARY 12

> The Lord is not slow to fulfill his promise as some count slowness, but is patient toward you, not wishing that any should perish, but that all should reach repentance. 2 Peter 3:9

If you were like a normal kid and your mom like a normal mom, you probably heard her shout at one point, "My patience is wearing thin!" Well, isn't it good that the Lord's patience doesn't wear thin on us? He is the poster child for patience, for all that He waits on us for. Peter reminds us that the Lord is not slow to fulfill His promises, but rather He is patient; patient with you, with me, with your neighbor, even with your enemy. His timing and plans are perfect and He patiently waits for us to listen to His voice, follow the direction of the Holy Spirit and apply His will and plan for our lives in our life. As humans, we tend to view everything according to a timeline and we appropriate for ourselves what we believe certain timelines should be and how long they should last. But with God, He is faithful and fulfills all of His promises. The problem arises when we don't think He follows through and fulfills them according to our timeline. God promised the Israelites that He would bring them into the land flowing with milk and honey. They sinned and rejected God, so it took 40 years for that promise to be fulfilled. If God does not seem to be following through on His promises to us, we need to take a long, hard look at our own lives and see if we have done anything wrong that would prevent Him from following through. Not that we can stop God, but like a parent and a child, parents will withhold privileges while the child is misbehaving and then when the child settles down and listens, the parent follows through. Father God, being omnipotent and knowing the future, including what lies around the corner, His timing tends to be perfect; we may want or feel the need now, but God knows we need it more later on down the "timeline." Patience is needed and patience means we trust. Do you trust God to follow through on His promises? He never loses His patience with us and moves on to the next person; He is always there directing, guiding and comforting. He also patiently waits for us to go after Him and not temptation. To take it up a notch, He promises to never allow the temptation to be greater than we can handle and also to provide a way out of temptation (1 Corinthians 10:13). As the years progress and technology increases, our lives tend to get busier and we tend to get more impatient. I was in college when the internet was released to the general population. We had to wait until the phone line dialed a number and we got connected; it was time-consuming and heaven forbid someone pick up the phone to call because that meant automatic disconnection. Now, sitting and waiting for what seemed to be 3-4 minutes for connection (really 30 sec to a min), this same person who waited for that gets mad if the browser icon spins for 5 seconds (seems more like 5 minutes though). The faster the internet and technology get the less patience we seem to have. With the hustle and bustle of life, when life tries to slow down, we get upset. But look what Jeremiah wrote in Lamentations 3:25, "It is good that one should wait quietly for the salvation of the Lord." Wait, we have to wait and we have to be silent? How is that possible? We need to slow down long enough to be able to hear from the Holy Spirit. How can we expect to have a relationship with God if we are constantly in the passing lane, speeding down the road of life? God is patient and so should we be. And when obstacles come our way to slow us down, we need to take those opportunities to say, "Ok God, you got my attention, what is it you want to tell me?" instead of "God, you gotta be kidding me, I don't have time for this!" And as many times as I have said it, what it really translates to is, "God, I don't have time for You. You need to wait!" When those challenges come, don't look at them as obstacles to your plans, but as tools to develop patience and deepen your relationship with the Father, the Son and the Holy Spirit. If the Lord is patient with us and the fourth Fruit of the Spirit is patience, maybe we should slow down and use these opportunities to grow patience in our lives. How can you use people or situations in your life to develop patience like the patience God has for you? How can you trust more and be more patient with accepting God's timing, for the sake of peace reigning in your heart?

JANUARY 13

> Do not be anxious about anything, but in everything by prayer and supplication with thanksgiving let your requests be made known to God. Philippians 4:6

It's incredible what anxiety and worry can do. Some recent studies have shown that 85% of what we worry about never happens. That means, if we put it in terms of hours in a day, we worry 20.4 hours a day about something that may never happen. anxiety and worry allow your mind to dwell on difficulties and troubles; Merriam-Webster adds the image of strangle or choke to the meaning. But 85% of what tries to suffocate us and deter us from living in freedom never actually happens. What could you do with 20.4 hours a day? Or in terms of money, for every $100, we throw away $85 because we have to spend $15. Worry and anxiety happen in the mind, not the heart. The enemy has access to our minds, but not our hearts, especially once the Holy Spirit resides there. Although the enemy has access to our minds, he cannot read them; he can only throw a seed in there and hope they take root. How do they take root? His lies take root when we allow those constricting thoughts to rest in the soil of our fragile minds and take root, not replacing them with Scripture and Truth. That is why Paul told the Philippians and us to not worry and be anxious, BUT in everything by prayer. There is the weapon to defeat worry and anxiety right there, in prayer! That is how we defeat the enemy when he tries to plant anxious, fear-filled thoughts in our heads. But in everything, by prayer and supplication with Thanksgiving, let your requests be made known to God. Only 15% of what we worry about actually comes true and 100% of that God can handle, God can manage. Don't let the enemy choke you spiritually, mentally, or emotionally with what most likely will not happen. Don't let those thoughts take root, instead utilize prayer and conversations with God to pluck those lies out and replace them with the love and comfort of God's strength and love for you. Today, what thoughts are causing you to worry? What makes you anxious and unsure of tomorrow or the future? Are you worrying about other people and circumstances outside of your control? What is the enemy using to choke you spiritually or emotionally? How can you utilize prayer to remove anxious and worrisome thoughts? What can you do to make more time for God so He can help you weed the garden of your mind?

JANUARY 14

> Then when you call, the LORD will answer. "Yes, I am here," he will quickly reply. Isaiah 58:9 NLT

As a parent, several times I have called my kids and they don't respond. But if I am perfectly honest, there have been times when they called me and I was busy or sidetracked and did not respond to them. One feature I know of on the iPhone is that you can see when someone reads their text message (if they have that feature turned on). How many of us get frustrated when we see it was read but they don't reply? I know I do, especially with my kids; they don't see a need to respond. It's a good thing God is not like that. In fact, Isaiah tells us that when we call on the Lord, the Lord will quickly reply. Isaiah tells us that when we call on the Lord, the Lord will answer, "Yes, I am here!" He will promptly reply. He is not too busy answering someone else or distracted by shiny objects. He is waiting for us to call on Him. But we also have to be ready to hear Him reply. He may or may not appear in a burning bush, or shield our eyes with his hand as he passes by. His voice may or may not be in the wind. We can't think so much of ourselves that we can dictate how He responds. We must be ready and willing to hear Him, whether in the wind or in the Word. In the silence or in the praise, on the radio in the car or in the stillness of our closet, God does not, nor can He lie. He is perfect, so if he tells us that He will reply, we can hold onto that. One word of caution though, we can't read more into this than is actually there. God is not a genie that just appears at command. Scripture simply says He will quickly reply. Sometimes He quickly replies with a yes. Sometimes He quickly replies with a no. And many times, He quickly replies with a "Wait, not yet", or even "Be patient, my child". But there are also times when we call on the Lord and we do all the talking and hang up the phone without even waiting for a reply. It is in those times, in the waiting, or when we do the hanging up, that we can feel He is not there, distant, or not listening. Why is it that we feel He is obligated to answer us yes or no right away? Why do we get mad when He asks us to wait? Or is it that we are just so self-centered that we do all the talking and give God no chance to say, "Yes, I'm here my child. Let me say..." What do you have to change today and to make a habit so that when we pray it's not a monologue, rather it's a dialogue? What do you have to do to better hear from God this week? Has it been a while since you heard from Him? Are you in the midst of trials or hurt or loss? Take time, prepare your heart and call out to Him. He will reply, that I can promise!

JANUARY 15

> For the time is coming when people will not endure sound teaching, but having itching ears they will accumulate for themselves teachers to suit their own passions and will turn away from listening to the truth and wander off into myths. 2 Timothy 4:3-4

We all like good news and we all like it when things work out for us and we get blessed. But Paul warns Timothy, as well as us today, that people will turn from the truth and will go after myths. They will no longer put up with the truth and sound doctrine. While it may be nice to hear that God wants us happy, healthy and wealthy, it's not Scriptural. Jesus said many times, "As they hated me, they will hate you; pick up your cross and follow me; be like me and a servant, not one who is to be served." We have all heard the phrase, "Anything to make a buck." We should not change the Gospel message to get more people to tithe. We cannot add or subtract anything from the Gospel message to fit our agenda. In fact, we should not have an agenda when it comes to our spirituality; we should be focused on God's agenda that comes from the Word He spoke. We know His agenda when we allow the Holy Spirit to direct and guide us in our daily walk and what we preach or say to people. While some of this Guidance may be hard to hear, like forgive those and love those who persecute you, take advantage of you and have caused deep emotional wounds to you. Love them. It is a very simple command. We are created in the image of God. Our Heavenly Father does not see our sin; we should not either. While it's nearly impossible to forget, we should forgive to the point that when we see someone who has hurt us, we see them as a child of God and not their sin. Don't listen and support a pastor just because they say what you want to hear. As Christians, we have the responsibility to check everything we are taught in and out of church with God's Word. Scripture has the final say. I challenge my family, friends and church to do the same. Hold me accountable for what I say in these devotionals and in the sermons I deliver. Don't let the enemy lead you astray with false doctrine just because it is what you want to hear. Jesus loves you enough to die for you, so you should at least know what He said and taught. Have you checked what you have been taught? This week, devote some extra time in reading your Bible and allowing Scripture to be enshrined in your heart. How can you allow even difficult verses to enhance and deepen your relationship with God? How can this Scripture keep you on track with your personal relationship with the Truth?

JANUARY 16

> The Lord is near to the brokenhearted and saves the crushed in spirit.
> Psalm 34:18

Ever go through a difficult time and feel like you are all alone? I mean, in your mind, you know you're not, but emotionally you feel like you are the only person going through it? We all know what it feels like to lose someone we love. Death is never an easy part of life, but it will always be a part of it. I lost my only sibling, my brother Tony. Thanks to COVID-19, I was not allowed to travel to his funeral. While on my knees praying for his healing that didn't happen, getting the phone call that he had passed, my heart broke at that moment. This verse became more real to me at that moment than ever before. When we are brokenhearted, the Holy Spirit provides the comfort that no one else can provide for us. When our spirit feels crushed, He restores it and strengthens it. When the whole of our heart is opened, He fills it. God provides comfort because he understands the loss. Jesus felt the pain of losing a good friend. Scripture records that when his friend Lazarus died, he wept. I am sure that when Jesus was on the cross and God had to turn away from Him and remove His Spirit from Jesus so all of our sins could be poured out onto Him; with how God loves, I am sure that He wept. I believe Father God wept because He loves us so much, wept because He had to send His son to die for us and wept because He had to remove His protection and blessing on Jesus so he could do so. The enemy loves to make us feel alone, but the Bible, God's very own words, reminds us that when we face trials and tribulations the Lord is close to us when the enemy comes in. When we are alone and troubled, He will provide comfort. When the enemy tries to crush our spirit, He will rescue us. All we have to do is go to Him, call to Him and draw near to Him; we don't have to feel alone and destitute. David, of all people, knows this truth all too well. His best friend's father tried multiple times to kill him, even his own son tried to kill Him. When he was away, his entire family and the families of all the men and their property were taken and while David felt defeated, alone and crushed, he never felt abandoned by his God, our God. He simply cried out to Him and the Lord was always there and provided other men to support David and comfort him. Here in Psalm 34, we are reminded that the Lord is close to the brokenhearted. God experienced broken heartedness Himself. He sent us The Great Comforter, the Holy Spirit, as a way we can feel His presence in us when we are brokenhearted. While we all have to grieve, we don't all grieve the same way. And while it may seem that no one can understand, Jesus understands. Creator God understands. He is waiting there to comfort you, to fill the hole in your heart that is left after you lose someone you love. Let go of the pain and sadness. Allow Him time to comfort you. You do not have to walk this grief-stricken path alone. So, when, not if, when you feel like you are abandoned and alone, draw near to God. When the enemy attacks and tries to convince you of lies, draw closer to God. When your spirit feels crushed, allow the Holy Spirit to restore it. Accept the emptiness deep in your heart and let Him fill it. Combat the seemingly endless loneliness by allowing the Holy Spirit to give you companionship. How does this verse help you better understand God's Holy Presence and our blessed relationship with the Holy Spirit? How can you allow the Holy Spirit to comfort you?

JANUARY 17

> Great are the works of the Lord, studied by all who delight in them.
> Psalm 111:2

Isn't it amazing what captures our attention? How easily we can be distracted by some of the silliest things. Most people love magic tricks and many try to figure out how they pull off such illusions. How did David Copperfield make the Statue of Liberty disappear? I've even watched Penn and Teller's show when they have magicians try to stump them and when they do – it's amazing. But how much more amazing are the deeds of our Lord? He created the world, the universe with the power of His words. Darwin and evolution tried to develop a Creation Story without God, but when you look at Genesis and Evolutionary Theory side by side, Darwin copied God on the sequence; he just changed the time frame and took God out of the equation. Still the sequence is the same! He led the nation of Israel out of Egypt and through the desert by a pillar of fire by night and smoke by day. He brought down the walls of Jericho with music and shouts and saved the one family in the city that helped His people. He brought down a giant with a stone, protected men in a fiery furnace so hot that the guards fueling the fire died from the heat and He shut the mouths of lions until His enemy replaced His prophet. He came as a fully human, fully God-person, to die the most horrific death ever invented, only to raise Himself from the dead on the third day. Why? Because He loved us and didn't want anyone to be separated from Him by sin. When we accept Him into our hearts, our old self was nailed to that cross 2000 years ago. How? One of His great works, living a perfect life, when God removed His presence from Jesus, all sin, past, present and future (good for us) was poured out onto Him. In Creator God's perfectness and truth, He does not see our sin when He looks at us. He sees Jesus, His fingerprints on us. He forgives us even when we repeat our offenses. He loves us even when we don't love Him first. He forgives us whenever we ask. He sent His Holy Spirit to live in us, to guide us as we walk the path of our lives, directing us according to His Will, revealing what His Word says and how to apply it in our lives. Daily, He creates beauty in the sky, every morning and every evening, simple mathematical beauty in pineapples and roses and signs of joy in a baby's smile and a grandmother's laugh. If God has ever blessed you, ponder on His work in your life. If you feel distant from Him, what can you do to remove the scales from your eyes and heart to see His deeds in your life and draw closer to Him? How can you slow down enough to see the great works of God in your surroundings? How can you better appreciate and praise Jesus Christ for His miraculous works?

JANUARY 18

> "Tell the righteous that it shall be well with them, for they shall eat the fruit of their deeds." Isaiah 3:10

My kids tried to make a chocolate cake one time and surprise us. The cake mix called for oil, but all they saw was extra virgin olive oil, so they used it. Needless to say, it did not turn out very well and the cake ended up in the trash. We did not make them eat it. But spiritually and emotionally, we reap what we sow. Isaiah says it this way, "They shall eat the fruit of their deeds." Here, he tells those that are righteous, in right living with God, that they will eat the fruit of their deeds. They have spiritually lived a life for God, for they will have good fruit. However, the flip side is also true. If you are not living a righteous life, not living a life right with God, you are also to eat of the fruit of your deeds. So, the question for all of us is, what kind of life are we living? Is it self-serving and self-centered or is it Christ-centered and Christ-serving? To be Christ-centered and Christ-serving does not mean to sell everything and move to Haiti, Africa, or Asia and be a missionary. No, it starts with the heart. It's about listening to the Holy Spirit and following His lead right where you are today. Are you spending time with Him daily? Would it be considered quality time, truly deepening the relationship? Do you seek His face and His guidance every day? In prayer time, do you ask and seek His input on decisions you make or just ask for things? What fruit are you producing? Jesus implores us to understand, "For no good tree bears bad fruit, nor again does a bad tree bear good fruit, for each tree is known by its own fruit. For figs are not gathered from thornbushes, nor are grapes picked from a bramble bush. The good person out of the good treasure of his heart produces good and the evil person out of his evil treasure produces evil, for out of the abundance of the heart his mouth speaks." One day you will be eating the fruits of your deeds. Are they good fruit or rotten fruit? Are they figs or thorns? Grapes or brambles? Like the chocolate cake made with the wrong ingredients, while it may look good, it could be horrible inside. The world may try and sell you thorns and brambles as delicious delicacies, but they are still thorns and brambles. What fruit comes from your mouth, your deeds and your life? What change can you make today to begin or continue righteous living, right living with God? What weed, thorn, or bramble can you recognize in your life to uproot and plant a fig tree or a grape vine instead?

JANUARY 19

> No temptation has overtaken you that is not common to man. God is faithful and he will not let you be tempted beyond your ability, but with the temptation he will also provide the way of escape, that you may be able to endure it. 1 Corinthians 10:13

As we hit mid-January, we might be tempted to give up on those New Year's resolutions, promises or commitments to ourselves to be better this year. Maybe you missed a day in Bible reading or didn't go for that walk. Maybe you gave into your sweet tooth, more than once. But if we start our day with God, in reading, in prayer and in worship, we will be more equipped to face the temptations that come our way. God tells us that "No temptation has overtaken you that is not common to everyone". Not everyone faces the same spiritual battles of the flesh, but someone else has had the same temptation as you. God is forever faithful. He promises to provide a way out and He always does. He gives you the strength to overcome it. It is in His strength through the Holy Spirit living in you that you have to overcome the temptation. Are you willing to accept His strength and guidance? Are you willing to listen to the Holy Spirit as He guides you away from temptation and towards freedom? And not if, but when we fall short, have that extra dessert, skip a day in our Bible reading plan, don't get that exercise done, then tomorrow is a new day and a new opportunity to allow Him to guide us away from temptation and closer towards Him. Don't allow guilt to keep you from giving into temptation. That is how the enemy is trying to keep you from the intimacy with the Father. At any moment, God gives you an exit on that road and back onto His road, His path. How can you experience the freedom that comes from allowing the Holy Spirit to guide you and strengthen you so that when you face temptation you have His strength and His tools to fight it off and walk away from it? Do you rely on your own strength and ability, or do you rely on Him to help you break the stronghold temptation has on you? What one temptation can you allow the Holy Spirit and His guidance to help you break free from this week?

JANUARY 20

> "And it is impossible to please God without faith. Anyone who wants to come to him must believe that God exists and that he rewards those who sincerely seek him." Hebrews 11:6

It seems quite funny that the author of Hebrews says it is impossible to please God without faith. I mean, it would make sense that you would have to believe in God to try and please God, but I think many Christians only have a head knowledge of God, meaning they know OF God but do not KNOW God. Someone once said the longest distance in the world is the twelve inches between the brain and the heart and this verse speaks the truth in that. I know of Trump and Obama, but I do not "KNOW" them. The same is true with our faith. If you only know OF God, that will do you no good on your last day. Knowing "OF" someone has no benefits; it does you no good. You must "KNOW" know Him and the only way that can occur is to be in His Word and allow the Holy Spirit to connect you to Him. It's the heart knowledge of Knowing Him and not just the head knowledge of knowing OF Him. There is nothing I can do to please the President of the United States because I do not know him, I do not have a relationship with him; but God, I have a relationship with Him and I can please Him, or I can disappoint Him based on my words, my thoughts and my actions. If you KNOW God and have a relationship with Him, you also can please or disappoint Him based on your words, thoughts and actions. How is your faith in God? Is it heart or limited to head knowledge? Do you KNOW HIM or know OF him? The author of this verse says anyone who wants to come to Him must believe He exists and believe that God rewards those who sincerely seek Him. How sincere is your seeking? How active are you seeking Him on a daily basis? How can you please Him more than disappoint Him? What must you do to actively seek Him? Are you willing to start that today?

JANUARY 21

> Count it all joy, my brothers, when you meet trials of various kinds,
> for you know that the testing of your faith produces steadfastness.
> James 1:2-3

Most Christians have heard this verse, but I think they hear it wrong. Many say count it all joy because you face trials. God doesn't tell us to have joy because we face trials. Here God says "count it all joy" when you face trials. Notice the keywords there. James did not write if you face trials, but when you face trials; when you face trials, count it all joy. Let that Truth sink into your heart. This joy is not a happy dance or celebration. Joy in the Lord is having a grateful and appreciative heart for everything that God has given you, blessed you with and protected you from. Joy is having satisfaction or fulfillment in knowing that God is still in control, no matter what our chaotic circumstances are; Jesus died for our sins and rose on the third day to conquer death so we could have eternal life. Joy is knowing that we have the Holy Spirit given to us to comfort us, guide us and direct us. So, when a difficult situation comes your way, WHEN that trial in life comes even though you are actively living out your relationship with God, remember, don't be surprised that you have difficulties; remember to have joy. You can have joy because you can be confident in the one holding your heart and life through the trial. You can have joy because He never leaves you nor forsakes you – and if you have joy when the trial comes, you prevent the enemy from swaying you away from God, putting a wedge between you and Him and you can actually draw in closer to our Heavenly Father. When you have joy, it allows you and gives you the ability to look for ways God can use it for His good. Joy gives you the knowledge that when He does use it for His good, joy abounds in us even more because it was not all for not. And this verse closes with, "for you know that the testing of your faith produces steadfastness." So, when you face these trials and your faith is tested, it makes your faith stronger, your relationship with the Holy Spirit deeper and you become more aware of His voice, able to recognize His eternal voice more and more often. If your faith becomes weaker due to trials, your faith is in yourself or the world and not in your Savior. He is always eager to turn "tragedy" into powerful life lessons for us. When the test result comes back different than you prayed for, when that loved one doesn't come through the door anymore, or the pink slip arrives on your desk, how can you have joy knowing that God is holding you in the trial? How can you change your question from "Why God?" to "How can You use this for Your plan God?" or "What can I take from this to be better and stronger?"

JANUARY 22

> Finally, brothers, whatever is true, whatever is honorable, whatever is just, whatever is pure, whatever is lovely, whatever is commendable, if there is any excellence, if there is anything worthy of praise, think about these things. Philippians 4:8

We can fill our minds with lots of stuff. We can be so focused on the demands of our job, or our family, or we can even be selfish and fill our minds with our own pleasures, desires, needs and wants. But Paul tells the church at Philippi (and us) that we need to focus our minds on whatever is true, honorable and commendable. What is true? Contrary to the world's views, there is only one source of truth and that is God and God's Word. So, where do we start? We start with focusing our minds on God's Word first and foremost. Everything after that flows from being immersed in God's Word. Then it will be more natural to focus on what is honorable. That means doing what God calls us to do – love, forgive, serve and meet the needs of those around us. Think about what is pure; daydreams and fantasies are not pure. Not all fantasies are sexual in nature, but fantasizing about a new job, or the lotto, or whatever is driven by greed or insecurity and should not be what we focus our minds on. Whatever is worthy of our praise and is excellent, that is where we should focus our thoughts. Focusing our thoughts on righteousness leaves more room for us to be in the right mindset when we are present with what really needs our attention, like work, family, or even downtime. In this fast-paced society that we live in, we can be overwhelmed and so busy that sometimes we don't even know what to think. The enemy loves us being busy and overwhelmed, but Paul reminds us to think about what is true. It's not what's on the news or who is in charge, nor is it racial and economic tensions; God's Word is true! It's the only source of Truth. We need to focus on what is pure; it's not what's on TV, in movie theaters, or on the radio – it's God's love for us. We need to focus on what is honorable and just; what is honorable and just leads people to Christ, not away from Christ. Our thoughts, beliefs, actions, words and the way we handle those who believe differently than us – those need to be aligned with Christ and the way He lived His life for them to be honorable and just. We need to focus on what is lovely, commendable and excellent. We need to focus on Christ! We must focus, think about and meditate on Christ and His Word in good times and in bad times. What we spend our time on should be the things of God and not things of this world. How do we get through trials? Focus on what is true, honorable, just, pure, lovely, commendable and excellent. Don't let the world take your focus off of these things and onto what brings anxiety, fear and uncertainty. It's easy to walk downstream or with the wind, yet it takes purpose and intentionality to walk into the wind and against the current. Spend time with God today so that you too can focus on what is true, honorable, just, pure, lovely, commendable and excellent. Then and only then will you have the direction and strength to go against the current of the world swirling around you. What are your thoughts focused on? Do you daydream and fantasize about a different or better life? Are you allowing God and His Word to be the first in your mind and last thought of the day? How can you make this verse more applicable in your life to deepen your relationship with Christ and thus experience living life more abundantly?

JANUARY 23

Humble yourselves before the Lord and he will exalt you. James 4:10

Don't worry, be happy! If you are not happy, do something to make you happy. Isn't it funny how the world tells us that we need to do whatever it takes to be happy? Being humble – that is too weak, because "only the strong survive" in a worldview governed by survival of the fittest. "Take care of yourself because no one will do it for you." Or even worse, "God loves you and wants you to be happy, healthy and wealthy". These commonly held cultural beliefs create a sort of subconscious pride and vanity that often hides just under the surface. I recently saw the trailer for the 1977 movie "Oh God, you devil!" starring George Burns. Ted Wass's character finally talks to God and says he looks like the devil and George Burns (playing God) responds, "He's always wanted to look like me." Isn't that the truth! The Bible even says the devil comes as an "angel of light" to deceive. The enemy loves to twist God's words and make his own message look like God's. God says, "Humble yourselves before me and I will exalt you… Love your enemy, pray for your enemy… Look after the needs of others and make their needs more important than your desires." Jesus calls us to be like Him. He humbled Himself even to the point of death. He put others' needs before His own and we are called to be like Him. How much experience do you have at being humble? The world tells us that being humble is a weakness; if we are humble, we can never be successful and will never go anywhere in life. If we always put our desires on the back burner, we will never make anything of ourselves. But our central desire should be to be close to God, to hear His Heart and know His Will. He will be the one to provide our needs and desires if we just walk close to Him. I just asked and I'll ask again, how are you at being humble? How can you do better at humbling yourself before the Lord and following after Him?

JANUARY 24

> He restores my soul. He leads me in paths of righteousness for his name's sake. Psalm 23:3

Has your soul ever been tired? Do you ever feel completely drained? I mean to the point of being hard to get out of bed because emotionally and spiritually you have nothing left to give? Depression can swoop in and we can feel this way if we don't get restored by the Holy Spirit often. The world can try to fill that void and fill you temporarily, but only God can restore you; only the Holy Spirit can fill you up so that it won't disappear quickly. We have to be willing to walk with Him and talk with Him and listen to Him and follow Him. He should be the engine driving our life, not the caboose trailing behind and only there when we need it. His path, His Will, is of righteousness and life, while the opposite is condemnation and guilt. When we are feeling empty, we must be willing to be honest with Him. I mean, He already knows, so why do we try to hide it and fill ourselves with things of this world? He just wants us to be honest with Him and seek Him, allowing Him to restore our souls, especially when we experience any type of loss or trauma; only His restoration fills in all the holes and plugs the cracks. Allow Him to restore you. Trust Him to never leave you empty or thirsty or hungry. When we walk with Him and when people are able to see the freedom that comes from allowing Him to restore us, the glory goes to Him. Just maybe, it might be the last straw that someone needs to see why, when we've gone through struggles and loss, we can look restored. When was the last time you allowed Him to restore, refill and refresh you? What do you need to get rid of in your life so He can be the One that leads and restores you? Who might see you be restored by the Lord and filled with the Holy Spirit? How are you allowing yourself to be restored and move forward in Him? How are you desiring Jesus as Savior and Lord? How are you desiring the guidance of the Holy Spirit to help others?

JANUARY 25

God is spirit and those who worship him must worship in spirit and truth." John 4:4

What is worship? Some people think it's singing during a church service or bowing down on the knees to a statue or a king. Worship is more than body posture, more than singing and music. Jesus reminds us that since God is Spirit, we as believers must worship Him in spirit and in truth. I believe that worship extends beyond the confines of the building and is more than music and lyrics. It is more than just singing the words in a hymnal or projected on a screen. It is putting your whole heart (soul/spirit) into it, whatever the activity may be. Worship is not focusing on what the people around you are doing, but allowing the Holy Spirit to guide you in your worship. Even when the words of the song are not true in your life at the moment, these can be the most transformative, reflective moments when you still sing the lyrics anyway because you know they can be. God is faithful and He will always bring us through the trials. But limiting worship to just singing at church eliminates the truth part of the verse. I mentioned above that it is much more than that. Worship is a lifestyle that points everything back to God. We worship with our spirit in the words we use with others and about others; it's the decisions we make and how we react to what is going on in the world and what is going on in our lives. Worship is a way of life. It is walking with Him daily. It is having our hearts aligned with God and having a heart for God, which means we have a heart for others. Worship is living out what Jesus preached, Love God, Love Others. Worship is a continual prayer life and being thankful for all His blessings and Holy Presence in our lives. Worship is centered in our spirits and souls and should be a guiding factor in our lives. How is your worship looking lately? Are you like a talking statue or like David entering the city with the return of the Ark? Do you limit your worship to church services, or is it a way of life? How can you better worship God in spirit and in truth?

JANUARY 26

> For God, who said, "Let there be light in the darkness," has made this light shine in our hearts so we could know the glory of God that is seen in the face of Jesus Christ. 2 Corinthians 4:6

My little brother hated the dark, which I think he did to the end. We could always tell when Tony was home because every light in the house was on. God created light and what Paul is telling us here is that we need to love the light because it is light that allows us to see the glory of God and see that Jesus is who He says He is. It is only in accepting the Good Work that Jesus did on the cross that we have a hope for eternity. The enemy loves the darkness and tries to hide the light. He uses the world, sin and temptations, to try and shroud the light, but light always pierces through the dark. Scientifically speaking, the dark can never overcome the light. The light from a single match could be seen over 300 yards away in complete darkness – that's more than three football fields and a single match. The enemy loves to use fear to try to keep us in darkness, but God wants us to focus on the Light because He is light and dispels darkness, fear and uncertainty. When it seems like the darkness is closing in, turn around and face the light. Where is a shadow located? Opposite of the light. If what you see is darkness or shadows, the light is behind you; turn around and face the light. Are you stressed or uncertain about what is happening in the world today? Has fear crept into your heart and mind? Have you allowed the shroud of darkness to come in? Pick up His word, listen to His words to you and seek the Light. Be like Tony and turn every light on in the house to dispel any darkness that may try to surround you! Remember, when looking into the light, you don't see darkness. If you are seeing darkness, you are not looking into the light. What steps can you take to start every day looking at the light and keeping your focus on the light?

JANUARY 27

> The Lord is good to those who wait for him, to the soul who seeks him. Lamentations 3:25

When you need to go somewhere, you depend on your car, the bus, or the subway to get you there. But do any of these do good for you? No, of course not; they are inanimate objects that can neither do good nor bad, just tools. But when you depend on the Lord, depend on Him for wisdom, depend on Him for love, depend on Him for forgiveness, direction and guidance, He is good to you. When you purposefully search Him out and desire time with Him, He will be good to you. Will He say "Yes" to every prayer request? No, I am not saying that; that would actually negate being good to you. If we are completely honest with ourselves, we would agree that not everything we want is good and even some of what is actually good for us we wouldn't ask for. God doesn't promise to be a prayer vending machine or genie in the sky. He promises to be good to us. He has deposited the Holy Spirit in our hearts for coming good. But do you depend on Him? Do you depend on the Holy Spirit for wisdom? Do you search Him and His presence with reading, worship and prayer with silence built in? Do you earnestly search and desire His guidance in your life, or do you relegate Him to the guest room or dining room? How can you really know the goodness of God and what it is to you if you don't search Him out and if you don't depend on Him? If you really want the goodness of God, He has to be more than just a priority on your list. Rather Christ needs to be the central and primary priority in your life. Are you willing to spend more time this week in His Word? How much time are you willing to spend with Him in worship, prayer and silence, searching for Him? How can you depend on Him more this week?

JANUARY 28

> Be strong and courageous. Do not fear or be in dread of them, for it is the Lord your God who goes with you. He will not leave you or forsake you." Deuteronomy 31:6

The enemy loves to utilize fear. Fear can cause panic, paralyze us and push us into a dark place. But light always wins over darkness. Wherever we go, God goes with us. His light shines in the darkness that fear tries to trap us in. God commands us to be strong and courageous. Be strong and do not dread what may happen. Isn't this comforting to know that not only will God never leave nor disown us, but that God Himself goes with us into every trial in life and there is no fear if we truly trust Him? No matter the day or the trial, do not let the enemy use fear to keep you from the comfort of your loving Heavenly Father. My grandmother had an acronym for FEAR on her dining room table – False Evidence Appearing Real. That is what the enemy uses to distract us, distress us and disorient us. He utilizes false information to make his way into our heads. He may tell you God can't love you for _____ and God can't forgive _____, or if you do _____, then God won't be with you. Don't allow false information or false evidence to take root in your life. God commands us to "Be strong and courageous", so do not let lies trap you in a dungeon of fear. Don't cause fear to become bigger than forgiveness; don't let fear become bigger than love. As real as fear may seem, Truth is bigger and stronger than fear. Keep His Truth planted in your heart – you are loved, you are chosen, you are forgiven, you are created in My image, you are a child of the King. Know the truth of what God says, especially about you and firmly secure it in your heart and mind. How can you apply this verse in your life so that today, tomorrow and every day, in all that you do, you can Be Strong And Courageous?

JANUARY 29

> "For God so loved the world, that he gave his only Son, that whoever believes in him should not perish but have eternal life. John 3:16

Sometimes the enemy can make us feel unlovable or even unworthy. Certain churches can perpetuate that feeling by teaching that only those that follow dogma can make it to Heaven. God said that He so loved the world… The world. Not the nation of Israel, not a tribe or not a single denomination, but the whole world. He loved us all so much that He gave His only son so that whoever believes in Him should not perish but have Eternal Life. That means whoever believes in Him, not certain churches or denominations, but whoever loves Him. Eternal Life is easy. Jesus, Himself said it, He is the Way, the Truth, the Life, the only way to God, our Father. Whoever believes in Jesus should not perish but have Eternal Life. This is, of course, more than head knowledge; it has to be heart knowledge, because even the demons believe and they shudder and flee in fear. It's heart knowledge, intimate knowledge like a parent and child relationship. When there is that deep, heart-knowledge and a heart-centered relationship, we go to Him and run to Him in times of need and in times of celebrations. Take this verse and implant it in your heart and soul. Remove "the world" and replace it with your name. For God so loved "Joe", for God so loved "_____" that He gave His only son that if he or she believes in Him with all their heart, mind and soul that he or she should not perish but have Eternal Life in Heaven. God loves you that much. When the enemy whispers in your ear how much of a failure you are, unlovable you are, unworthy and unforgivable, recite this verse with your name in it. How can you hold onto this verse and this promise during trials or when you feel down about yourself? How can you amplify your celebrations and victories with this promise?

JANUARY 30

> Yes, what joy for those whose record the LORD has cleared of guilt, whose lives are lived in complete honesty! Psalm 32:2 NLT

How many can remember mom saying "Honesty is the best policy?" My wife and I have told our kids that if they are honest with us, the consequences will be far less severe than if they lie to us. I believe it is the same with God. We may try to hide our guilt, our lies, our sin, but He already knows all about them. God is asking for us to be honest with Him. He is not asking us to be perfect; just be honest. How can we expect Him to forgive us if we can't be open and honest with Him? What a joy we experience when we live in complete honesty with the Lord and confess to Him and He clears us of guilt. He takes away the sin. Are you living your life in complete honesty? Do you confess to God, or do you try to hide it? Do you even feel like your sin is no big deal because God forgives us? It's sad that many American Christians don't feel condemned for their sin or think it is not a big deal because of grace. But true joy is reserved for those whose lives are lived in complete honesty and their guilt is wiped clean. If you are not living a life of complete honesty, it's not too late to start! God already knows; there is nothing that is said, done, or thought of that God does not know. Just be honest with Him. Seek him and ask Him for forgiveness instead of just expecting it. Start living a life of complete honesty and receive the joy that comes from that! How can you improve the honesty in your relationship with the Lord? How can you be more honest with yourself regarding your relationship with God?

JANUARY 31

> "For you were called to freedom, brothers. Only do not use your freedom as an opportunity for the flesh, but through love serve one another." Galatians 5:13

Have you ever given someone a gift only to see it destroyed? "Wow, that didn't last long! I don't think they appreciated it!" The same is true with forgiveness. God's forgiveness is a gift and we should not abuse it. Just because He forgives us does not mean we can just go and award every desire of the flesh. No, that kind of living means we remain a slave to sin and we are not free. A.W. Tozer said, "Freedom from sin is not freedom to sin." Remember the first time you were left home by yourself? Maybe you ate cereal on the couch, turned the music way up, or even pulled a dance scene from Risky Business. Ah, that freedom! But here, Paul writes that we are not to use that freedom to sin, to satisfy the hunger of the flesh and break the rules. God didn't send Jesus to die on the cross so we could keep on sinning. He died so that when we sin, we can seek that forgiveness directly from our Father. I have heard and read stories of people who were taken captive either in war by the enemy, by terrorists, or even kidnapped. When they are finally freed, they soak up the fresh air and the sunlight and appreciate the freedom they now walk in. They don't go back and subject themselves to the abuse and mistreatment of their captors. They see each day as a gift and an opportunity. I've seen and I've read story after story after story of people experiencing freedom in Christ and the first thing they want to do is tell others and to serve others. The longer we go to church the more that feeling fades and freedom isn't even experienced anymore, it's just expected. God becomes a box on a to-do list instead of anticipation and excitement. Paul warns us the same way when we accept freedom from sin and death. Just because we are free and forgiven does not give us permission to go on and keep sinning. It's not a free license to feed the flesh and earthly desires. It allows us to come alongside our brothers and sisters, bless them, love them and help them live in freedom. We need to love others and serve others. So, in being thankful for your freedom, who can you serve this week through love? Extend the grace and love that Jesus bestows on you and love on someone who needs it. So many people are hurting right now; we need to look beyond their hurt and serve them out of a motivation of love and help to meet a need of theirs. As children of God, we have been called to freedom from sin, not to remain a slave to sin. God wants us to use His gift to give to others. As He has forgiven us, we are called to forgive others. In His forgiveness of our sins, He demonstrates His love for us. We are to use that freedom to love one another and serve the needs of others. Are you using your freedom to serve or to sin? What do you have to do to move more into the first category? That means that when we forgive, we forget what was done to us and pray for God's hand of blessing and protection for them. That is a hard idea to wrap our minds around, but Paul in Philippians 3:14 says to forget what is behind us. To forget is to choose not to remember, just as God chooses not to remember our sins. Who is it that you need to forgive this week? Or what sin issue are you staying a slave to that you need to seek forgiveness for and accept the freedom God offers? Who is it that you need to serve in Love?

FEBRUARY 1

> "Hear, O Israel: The Lord our God, the Lord is one. You shall love the Lord your God with all your heart and with all your soul and with all your might. Deuteronomy 6:4-5

What do you love? I mean, really love? I recently saw a meme of an NFL game taking place in a heavy snowstorm and the stadium was still half full, true die-hard fans, who loved their team were going to be there until the end. The meme questioned that if people who call themselves Christians loved God as much as these fans loved their team, the church could turn the world upside down again. How true of a statement is that and how sad at the same time. Football games, work and TV are more important than gathering to worship God. As a church, have we lost that passion for God? With snow outside, will we stay home and watch it on TV? Oh, the Broncos (replace with any team or sport or other form of idol) play at 11? We can't go to church today. God wants me to tithe? God wants me to serve? – Whoa, this church thing is making me uncomfortable – stay in Your lane God and Your lane is Sundays and Sunday mornings as long as my team is not playing. Moses reminds us here that we should not just love the idea of a god, or just love God, but "Love God with all our heart, with all our soul and with all our might." If we truly did that whole-heartedly, then there would never be an empty seat in church. The church would never have to do fundraisers for summer camps, missions, or building repairs. If Christians in America lived this out, people would clamor for opportunities to serve God and be willing 24/7/365 to share who God is and what He has done in their lives. Where is your love meter for God? How high is it? Do you have a sitting in a blizzard outdoors to hear a sermon and serve Him kind of love, all heart, soul and might, or has your love meter dipped down into the comfort zone? How can you rekindle your love for God today? What are you willing to do to have a passion for God and His people, His church? How can you love Him outside of your comfort zone, going all in?

FEBRUARY 2

> Little children, you are from God and have overcome them, for he who is in you is greater than he who is in the world. 1 John 4:4

Have you ever noticed that the more technology grows the more we have to recharge our devices? Yeah, my phone can take a terapixel picture, but I have to charge it three times a day. We too need to be charged and recharged every day, sometimes more often, but we need to be careful what we get recharged from. As Christians, we are of God, His children and we should be going to Him and allowing the Holy Spirit to recharge and not allowing the world to charge us up. Through the Holy Spirit living in us we have the ability to overcome trials and temptations. Because of what Jesus did on the cross, you have complete access to the God who created the universe. Don't let the enemy trick you into thinking you can do it alone or that God cannot hear you or does not want to hear from you. We need to be constantly filled with the Holy Spirit, because like a strainer, we leak. We can do all things – not some things – "we can do all things through Christ who strengthens us". But that is the clarifier here. We can't do all things. Period. We can do all things through Christ who strengthens us! Through Christ living in us, the Holy Spirit's presence guiding us, instructing us and directing us, we can do all things that God calls us to do. So how do you do that? Pray, read and apply God's word in your life. Quit falling short because you are following an envelope on a string being pulled by the world, the enemy. God is chasing after you to strengthen you and bless you, not making you chase after empty promises. Identify those, cancel those and overcome the world with the power of the Holy Spirit living in you. With the strength of the Creator of the universe living in you, what are you willing to do this week? What are you going to finally break free from? You are an overcomer; what are you going to overcome this week? What empty envelopes on a string are you chasing?

FEBRUARY 3

> "Therefore I tell you, do not be anxious about your life, what you will eat or what you will drink, nor about your body, what you will put on. Is not life more than food and the body more than clothing?
> Matthew 6:25

Some people seem to never have a worry in their life, while others worry so much, they can barely leave their house; most of us probably fall in the middle of these examples. What causes us to worry? I would suggest the uncertainty of the future. Whether it is questioning will a job continue or will pay remain constant or will benefits continue? Worry could come from being worried about myself. Do I have the ability to do, provide or accomplish _____? Jesus told his followers not to worry, not be anxious and not to worry about anything, especially tomorrow; today has its own troubles to keep attention to. He tells us to think about and be concerned about eternal things. As Jesus asked, "Is not life more than food, clothing and material status?" God loves us; He wants us to trust Him, to rely on Him. Love Him and trust Him are fundamental, foundational beliefs that our relationship with God is based on. Do you Love Him? Yes! Then, do you Trust Him, I mean really trust, even when the going gets tough and hard? It is in those times, the valley of the shadow of death walks, that we see where our trust really lies. Are you anxious or worried about someone or something? Do you want to control the situation or will you turn it over to the hands of God? You need to decide for yourself how much you trust God. How can you let go of the steering wheel, per se and trust God, trust the Holy Spirit with every aspect of your life? Start small – What is one thing you can hand over to God and trust Him with today?

FEBRUARY 4

And as you wish that others would do to you, do so to them. Luke 6:31

Life can be so complicated and as we become adults, it seems to get more and more complex as we go along, but Jesus believed in the K.I.S.S. philosophy – Keep It Super Simple! Treat others the way you want to be treated. How much more simple can we get (yes, I know I upset some English teachers with that last sentence, but I wanted that added emphasis)? We want people to be kind to us, treat us with respect, respect our different points of view and allow us to just be us. In today's society, we don't see that. We see people demanding that we allow them to express themselves and live as they see fit, but if we don't agree with them, then we are not allowed to express our points of view. As Christians, it would be easy to fall into that trap; do to others what they did to me. But Jesus flips the script – what you wish others would do for you requires you to start the process by doing that to them or doing that for them. Do we do the same with others? When driving, do you become a weaver and a honker, or do you allow others to merge politely? In the supermarket, if you have a full basket and the person behind you has one item, do you invite them to go first or do you hold the line with a "first come, first serve" attitude? When someone has a different point of view, do you allow them the freedom to have that view, or do you tear them down or mock them? Are you a helper or a passerby? See, life is really simple when we live like Jesus asks us to, but don't think I am saying it's easy; simple and easy are not equal in meaning, nor does simple equate to easy. What is easy is to expect people to treat us well; what is not easy is putting the needs of others before our own. It's simple but not easy. What is God convicting you of today from Jesus' statement – Do to others as you would like them to do to you? What change will you make and whom will you start treating differently?

FEBRUARY 5

> There is therefore now no condemnation for those who are in Christ Jesus. Romans 8:1

Ever do something foolish and then feel guilty about doing it? Yeah, me neither. If we are honest, though, we have all done stuff we are not proud of, sinned in ways we don't want to talk about and the enemy loves that – he loves guilt, because it's a powerful weapon. See, under the law we are guilty and guilt requires consequences. However, Jesus, by willingly going to the cross for us, paid for that consequence. His blood sacrifice wiped out our transgressions. So, for those that are in Christ Jesus, those who have accepted Him as their Savior, there is no guilt or condemnation. When we sin, God uses conviction, not guilt, to guide us back on the road of redemption. If you feel out of whack, out of alignment with God, or the enemy is using guilt and condemnation in your life, let it go. Run to the Father who has open arms and rest in His presence. Experience the freedom that comes from being in a relationship with Him. Let Him restore your soul. Today, give God some extra time, sit and listen to His voice and meditate on His words and His love. Do you still live under condemnation? Have you allowed the enemy to utilize guilt on you, keeping you from God, from worship and from seeking forgiveness? The thing with the crucifixion is we no longer need a priest to go before God and ask for forgiveness on our behalf; the veil was torn and we have direct access. Don't give the enemy more power than he needs. Don't let him use guilt and shame to keep you from the Father who loves you and desperately wants a deep relationship with you. Likewise, if we have no condemnation because of Jesus, neither should we leave others under condemnation. We are commanded to forgive. Jesus, in the Lord's Prayer, said, "Father forgive me as I have forgiven others." When you say that, do you mean it, or are you going through the motions? If you really meant it, would your sins be forgiven or would you be condemned? Have you forgiven those that have hurt or wronged you? What are you waiting for, an invitation? It has been given; Jesus commanded it and told us to pray for it. Who are you withholding forgiveness from? What is keeping you from forgiving them? Pray the Lord's Prayer and mean every word, every syllable and feel the weight be taken off of your shoulders. I've heard not forgiving is like taking rat poison and expecting the other person to die; no, thank you. Forgiveness is a one-person job and only one person. Free yourself from condemnation and forgive.

FEBRUARY 6

> You keep him in perfect peace whose mind is stayed on you, because he trusts in you! Isaiah 26:3

What is "perfect"? Oxford defines it as "precise, accurate, complete, free from flaw or defect and having all the required or desirable elements". What is meant by "peace"? "Mental calm and clarity; quiet, tranquility; freedom from dispute or dissension". So perfect peace would be precise tranquility, complete mental calmness and quiet with no flaw or defect. Isaiah here recognizes that those who choose to be close to God and choose to trust God will have complete mental calmness, having all the desired aspects of mental and spiritual tranquility. They will be able to live free from mental or spiritual dissension. The closer you are to God, the harder it is for the enemy to bring in disputes, wreak havoc and disturb your sense of serenity, destroying any calm you may have. Does Isaiah say that believers will be free from hurt? No. Free from trials? No. Free from attacks? No. Just when hurt, trials and attacks come, there is a mental and spiritual peace that comes from walking close to God, knowing that He has it all in His hands. Knowing that God is in control and He will work out the details brings a sense of peace and calmness that cannot be explained. Can you imagine trusting God to see you through the fire like Shadrach, Meshach and Abednego and not wavering even when the flames get hotter? Or imagine being like Job, when his friends started talking poorly of God and he remained faithful and trusted in the Lord, understanding the holiness of God and the power of God. He mourned, but he also had peace knowing God was and is still on the throne. Do you believe God is still active and has power in this world? Only 32% of Christian teens believe God is still active, but what about you? Is God still in control? Do you have an inner peace that comes from trusting and walking with the Lord? When trials or hurts come do they overtake you, or does the peace of God flow over you? What are your eyes fixed upon? What keeps your attention? The Lord or the world? What can you do today to recenter your focus and thoughts on the Lord?

FEBRUARY 7

> "But when Daniel learned that the law had been signed, he went home and knelt down as usual in his upstairs room, with its windows open toward Jerusalem. He prayed three times a day, just as he had always done, giving thanks to his God." Daniel 6:10

How are you living your life? Is it consistent with your core values and beliefs? When I was leading youth Bible Studies and mentoring youth, I would often ask them, "What if tomorrow, it became illegal to be a Christian? Would there be enough evidence to convict you of being a Christian?" A more relevant question to this passage is, "Would you still be a Christian?" See, the enemies of Daniel despised him because of how popular he was with the king, so they devised a law and convinced the king to sign a new law that people could worship no one else but the king. Daniel learned of the law but went home and worshiped the Lord anyways. He chose to still be a Christian. No law was going to stop him from worshiping the one true God. There was enough evidence in Daniel's life to convict him. The evidence was so overwhelming that his enemies had to devise a law to make his relationship with God illegal because there was really no other way to take Daniel down. Can we say the same thing in our life? This basically happened to Daniel; if anyone broke the law, they were to be thrown into a den of lions. Daniel knew of the law and what did he do? He continued to worship and pray to God. He did not let up in the least in his faith. While we are not facing the severity that Daniel faced, we must continue to draw close to God, pray, listen to God, worship God and give God thanks. Notice that even though the law had been passed, Daniel prayed three times a day, just as he has always done, GIVING THANKS TO HIS GOD. It's not giving thanks for the situation, but that God is still God in the situation. While we are called to submit to the authorities that God allows to govern us, we submit only until it violates God's law. Where are you with your relationship with Christ? Is it a Sunday event or a daily walk and relationship? When I worked with youth, I would ask them this follow-up question, "Would people be surprised that you were arrested as a Christian, or did they know it was coming?" Where does God rank in your life? 3rd? 2nd? I think if we were honest with ourselves, most of us could not say 1st and the evidence would be summed up with this question, "Most of your time out of work, is it with God and for God, or is it frivolous?" Now, as a dad, the time I spend being a God-loving husband and father is time for God, but what about the rest of the time? Am I tithing 1/10th of every day to God? That would be about 1 hr. and 36 min – just me and God. I am not there yet, but I am working on it. How about you – where are you in your time spent with God? What priority level does God have in your life?

FEBRUARY 8

> I have come into the world as light, so that whoever believes in me may not remain in darkness. John 12:46

The darkness tends to play and prey on people's minds. Look at almost every horror movie ever made –the danger happens at night. Shadows can trick our minds into thinking something is there when there is nothing or that something is bigger or scarier than it is. The funny thing with shadows is that the closer you get to the light source, the smaller the shadow is; the further away from the light source, the larger the shadow is. Spiritually speaking, I believe the same is true. The enemy loves to keep us in the dark and utilizes shadows to scare us into decisions or convince us of ideas that are not true. He loves to use fear to keep us captive to his agenda and not experiencing the freedom that comes from living in the light. However, the closer we are to Jesus, the smaller the darkness is and the smaller the shadows are. That is why the enemy loves to separate us and convince us to walk away. Satan entices us to go down the path that God does not want us to go down. There's a philosophical story I heard in high school or college psychology about two men who lived chained in a cave and only knew the fire's shadows on the walls. One day one of the men was set free and allowed to go explore the world outside the cave and experienced for the first-time color and light and the beauty of the world. When he returned to the cave to get his friend, his friend refused to leave. Fear of the unknown now was keeping him in the cave, keeping him trapped and unable to enjoy the blessings of God's creation. Jesus said He came to the world so we would no longer remain in the darkness. The choice is ours. Do we go closer to the shadows or closer to the light? Like the two men in the cave, the chains are off and we are free to choose. Do we remain in the darkness or do we go to the light? How does the dark make you feel? How does Light make you feel? How can you walk more in the Light so you can better see the obstacles and stumbling blocks the enemy has deployed?

FEBRUARY 9

> But he said to me, "My grace is sufficient for you, for my power is made perfect in weakness." Therefore I will boast all the more gladly of my weaknesses, so that the power of Christ may rest upon me. 2 Corinthians 12:9

We often hear that "God works in mysterious ways". Sometimes His ways confuse us and don't make sense to us. We know His ways are not our own and probably for a good reason. Here is another example of God's mysterious ways. He says, "My power works best in weakness". Why is that? Pride. Pride is the root of all sin and if we can say, "Look at what I did." How will people know that Christ, the Holy Spirit, is working in us if we take credit for what is done? Why would people need a God if they can do it all independently? That is why His ways are not our ways. It's not about us or on us; it is about Him and what we get and need from Him. Grace from God is all we need. How much more powerful is it when we allow God to work through us and do things that people do not think we can do? That is how the disciples and apostles turned the world upside down. He took ordinary men with no training in God's Word, "uneducated" men and brought the Light of the Word into the darkness that was being promoted by those who were supposed to be bringing God's love to people. He then used them to bring His love and mercy to everyone else in the world. When He uses the unexpected and untrained it points directly to Him, evidence that the Holy Spirit is alive and active in that person. It's also more evidence of God being alive, present and active in our world. I am genuinely an introvert. I only like small groups and groups of people I know. So doing this, being a pastor, really takes me out of my comfort zone, but then God gets the credit for doing some amazing stuff through me. It is not I but Christ in me that teaches and preaches. It is me allowing the Holy Spirit to instruct and then guide and direct my paths so that I am following Him, not me dragging Him along where I go. Through His grace and mercy, He worked wondrous deeds in my life, breaking down pride and anti-pride or extreme meekness I had in my life. I did not feel that a person like me could be used this way by God, but I have discovered, sometimes the hard way, that His grace is sufficient, His power is perfect and His way is far better than I can imagine doing. In this instance, Paul is writing about asking God to remove affliction, a thorn, in his life; but God says, "My grace, My power is sufficient for you." Are you struggling with a thorn in your side? Are you willing to allow God to use it to keep you humble and keep you close to Him? Or is God asking you to do something you don't want to? What is God trying to do in your life, but you keep saying, "No, I can't do that?" This week try saying, "God, you do it through me." How can you incorporate His grace and power in your life, in your faith walk? What is pride holding you back from? What is God calling you to do?

FEBRUARY 10

> And if I have prophetic powers and understand all mysteries and all knowledge and if I have all faith, so as to remove mountains, but have not love, I am nothing. 1 Corinthians 13:2

We know words have power; I mean, God created everything with words, but do emotions or feelings have external power? Like love, we say love has power over people. How much power does love really have? I mean, it's an emotion, right? It is just a feeling, correct? Not too much, right? Not really. The English language is such a poor language for capturing details and does not have the differentiation for different meanings of this term. Agape love, God's love, is what Paul is talking about here, the kind of love that says "Your needs are more important than mine". Look at what Paul says about love. "If I have prophetic powers and if I can predict the future and tell you what is going to happen and if I understand all the mysteries of the universe and have all knowledge and if I am the smartest person to ever live. If I have the faith to physically move mountains and destroy them, but I do not love; I do not AGAPE, then what? I am nothing." Literally, I can be the most powerful person on Earth and if I do not have love, love in my heart, then I am nothing. I can know several different languages, but it is worthless if I don't love others. I can understand all prophecies and have the deepest knowledge and strongest faith, but if I do not agape, it means nothing. I can be the smartest, richest, most powerful person in the world, even the ability to uproot a mountain and plant it in the sea; I am absolutely nothing unless agape is present in my life. Love is powerful and it's not given by a little flying fat guy shooting an arrow at you. Love moves you into action; love changes you and the way you live and the way you love others. Love conquers all things, it is the most powerful force in the universe and removes all fear and doubt. It is Agape that saved us. The real power comes from love and is shown in love. How can you grow and develop that love for God and for others in your life and daily walk as a believer?

FEBRUARY 11

Love never ends. As for prophecies, they will pass away; as for tongues, they will cease; as for knowledge, it will pass away. 1 Corinthians 13:8

Nothing lasts forever, right? I mean, we even see mountains being eroded away. But God promises that Love never ends. Agape never ends. Love transcends all things, including time, hurt and failures. There is nothing we can do to earn God's love and there is nothing we can do to lose God's Love. For God so loved us that He sent His only son to die on a cross so our sins could be forgiven and we could have a restored relationship with Him. God loves us so much that His gift to us is free will. We have the freedom to make our own decisions, make our own relationships, to fail and stop or to keep moving forward. Knowledge does not last; it dies with us, just as languages and religions disappear. Latin is no longer alive and the Greek and Roman gods only survive in mythology books on a library shelf. But Love, because God is Love, never fades, never changes and never ends. Love endures the test of time and is always there, ready to comfort during the worst of times. Love is not a feeling or an emotion – it is an action, a way of life, that takes a conscious decision to do and to continue. God loves you and that will never end nor change, no matter what you do. How can you incorporate this truth into your life and live this truth out as you interact with others, make decisions and live your daily life? Love changes you for the better. How has Agape changed you? What else are you willing to allow Agape to change in you? How can you agape others more in your daily walk?

FEBRUARY 12

> Love does not rejoice at wrongdoing, but rejoices with the truth. Love bears all things, believes all things, hopes all things, endures all things.
> 1 Corinthians 13:6-7

We are in the season that celebrates love. However, the love it celebrates is eros love, like a romantic love between courting couples and married couples. Agape love, the type of love that Corinthians talks about though, is a sacrificial, concrete, Godly love. Agape love does not rejoice in wrongdoing, meaning both that it does not enjoy doing wrong things, but it also does not make us happy when something goes astray with someone else. We don't get happy saying, "They deserve it" nor do we rejoice when someone fails. Agape love rejoices in truth, but where does truth come from? Unlike the world that says anyone can define it, truth must come from a perfect source that is unchanging and eternal. So, the Truth is only from God. His Word is the Truth, so we love and we rejoice in His Word. When we rejoice, we share His Word. Love, Agape, bears all things. It bore our sins and nailed them to the cross along with the body of Christ. So, if we are conformed to His image and bear His image in Agape, we need to bear all things, carrying the weight of others so they can survive and get their head above water. It bears the pain of when others wrong us and does not allow us to retaliate. Agape love believes all things, not falsehoods and lies, but it believes there is good in everyone, believes every word of God, believes everyone bears His fingerprints being created in His image and believes in all His promises. Agape believes that everyone is capable of love and needs to be loved. Agape hopes for all things, for all people, regardless of their beliefs or actions. Love endures all things. It empowers us to endure or to push through and survive all things and to make it through no matter what life throws our way or what speed bumps or potholes the enemy lays out. Agape gives us the strength to endure. No matter the trials we face, love sees us through it all. As you read these two verses today, what do you need to change to have more of an Agape love for others? Who is it in your life that you need to agape?

FEBRUARY 13

> Love is patient and kind; love does not envy or boast; it is not arrogant or rude. It does not insist on its own way; it is not irritable or resentful;
> 1 Corinthians 13:4-5

When driving, do you love the other drivers when traffic is bad or the other shoppers when you get in line at the grocery store with just two items and the person in front of you has a shopping cart full? Probably not and it probably shows. But we know that God is love and that God loves us with an Agape love. 1 Corinthians 13 is used in many wedding services; it was even used in mine. But Paul, in writing to the church at Corinth, was not talking about marriage, but about the love that God has for us; and if we call ourselves Christian, if we identify with Jesus, then we should love others the way God loves us. Love is patient. Back to being in traffic, are we patient? Are we patient with the ones we do love and with others? Paul tells us that one of the fruits of the Spirit after love is patience. Or another way to look at it is that the fruit of the spirit is love and love produces patience. If we have Agape in our lives, it will show up in our patience with others and in trying situations. What else does God's love look like? It does not envy. It is not jealous of what others have nor longs for what others have. Agape love is being content with what God has blessed us with. It does not boast, is not arrogant or rude, meaning love does not elevate us above others. In an Agape state of mind, we never think of ourselves as better than others and handle opposition and trials with grace. It is not rude or demeaning towards others. It does not make fun of and ridicule others. Love, Agape love, does not insist on its own way. It looks at the needs of others as more important than our own needs and wants. It says if there is a choice and a chance to meet the needs of others before filling our own needs and wants, then do it. It is not resentful or irritable when discipline happens or when things do not go our way. Think about these attributes of love in terms of God. Is he patient with us? Is he kind? Does He envy others, or is he arrogant or rude? Is he resentful or irritable? If God loves you with Agape love that does not do these things and you bear His image and call yourself a Christ follower, then should you not love others in the same way? In which of these signs of Agape are you successful? Which areas do you need to improve in how you love others? What can you do to improve those aspects you identified?

FEBRUARY 14

> So now faith, hope and love abide, these three; but the greatest of these is love. 1 Corinthians 13:13

Not much lasts long anymore. Even when things were built to last, nothing lasts forever. Rocks erode and waters evaporate and recede. But God tells us three things last forever: faith, hope and love and all three are extremely important. Faith – the complete trust in or confidence in someone or something. Hope – the expectation and desire for something specific to happen. Love – strong affection for another. These three can eradicate hate, eliminate fear and transcend the pain of our pasts. They motivate and move people and comfort people. But of these three, faith, hope and love, Love is the greatest. Why is that? God does not hope, does not have faith, but God loves. God loves us. Despite all that we do, despite all the times we walk away, even though we choose things of the world over Him, He still Loves! Agape never ends; it is unconditional and eternal. Agape drives response more than faith and hope; it calls you into action more than any other motive and is faster than faith and hope. Love is the full manifestation of the Holy Spirit living in you. And when reading the first part of this chapter, as it gives all the characteristics of love, we see why love is the greatest. God exemplifies all of those characteristics and "while we were still sinners, He sent His Son to die for our sins and conquer death so our relationship with Him could be restored". John 3:16 starts with "For God so LOVED" and says it all. Love forgives and keeps no record of wrongs – who is in your life that you need to offer a true Agape, Godly love? Do you feel how much God agapes you? If not, find some quiet time so He can remind you just how much He agapes you. No matter what you've done, He still agapes you. I pray that not only are you reminded of that but that you feel it and accept it. And it is more than a feeling; do you know how much He agapes you? What are some tangible reminders of His Agape for you?

FEBRUARY 15

> Do nothing from selfish ambition or conceit, but in humility count others more significant than yourselves. Philippians 2:3

As a kid, did you do something ill-advised to try to impress someone, or maybe as a teenager, to impress that guy or that girl? Maybe it was even as an adult! But what God wants from us is to just be ourselves. Be the person, the human that God created you to be. If we truly are a follower of Christ, then we must be humble. Here Paul gives us the double whammy – we are not to be selfish, but to be humble and consider the needs of others as more significant than our own. We are not to be selfish, self-promoting and only do something to be rewarded. We are supposed to think of other's needs as more important than ours. It does not mean we think badly of ourselves or be hard on ourselves; we are not to be our own worst enemy. It does mean doing good, even when nobody's looking. Put in that extra effort, not for the raise or promotion, but because that is what Christ calls us to do. Don't do something just to get something; don't do something just to make yourself feel better, do it because the Holy Spirit is living in you and replicate Jesus' examples and life. Paul says that we need to take care of the needs of others before taking care of our wants and needs. It also means to offer forgiveness, don't hold grudges, extend grace and be patient. Jesus himself said, "Do to others as you would like them to do to you." The only one we need to impress is God, not so that He will love us more, but because we love Him and we want to follow His guidance and His example. He thought of our need to be loved and saved, so He left Heaven to bring us back to Him. So, this week, what can you do to be humble and not selfish? Who in your life do you need to start thinking of better than yourself (their needs need to be met before your needs)? What needs can you see that God has given you the time, ability, or resources to meet?

FEBRUARY 16

> "Your love for one another will prove to the world that you are my disciples." John 13:35 NLT

People can tell a lot about us by just looking at us. For example, if I am wearing a Gronkowski jersey, people know that I am a Patriots fan (Tampa Bay now), a Pueblo West Tennis hat and they know I like PW Tennis, or even a County Soccer jacket they can assume I support PCHS Soccer. Jesus says the same thing, but it's not about what we wear. Jesus says that everyone, all people, will know that we are a disciple or a follower of Jesus by the love we have for each other. Matthew West has a Christmas song called, "Give This Christmas Away," and there is a line in it that says, "If you have love in your heart, give it away!" What good is love in your heart if you don't pour it out onto others? Jesus didn't say they would know us by the love we have in our hearts. NO! It's the love that we have for each other. A few years ago, I saw an ad where a young couple, either just engaged or just married, saw an elderly couple walking through the park holding hands. You could tell they still loved each other. I thought, "That is how I want Kanda and I to be, that much still in love so much that others could see it." Jesus tells us that everyone will know you are my follower by the love you show one another. Do we have that evidence in our lives? Are our hearts overflowing with His love because we are spending quality time with Him, in the Word and throughout the day in praise and prayer? Are we loving one another outwardly by our words and our actions so that people know we are a "Little Christ" (meaning of the word Christian)? When we see an injustice, do we step in and love the one under attack? When someone does something we don't agree with, do we attack them and pass on words of anger or do we express unconditional love? In this era of pandemics and fear, it seems as though hate, anger and frustration are winning over the idea that we can judge someone because of one decision that they make. Where is the love? Casting Crowns just released a song called "Start Right Here," and in the middle of the song they say, "What if the church on Sunday was still the church on Monday too? What if we came down from our towers and walked a mile in someone's shoes?" We are not called to just love on Sundays; we are called to love at all times, endlessly and tirelessly. Love one another. Jesus stops with this statement, keeping it simple. There were no qualifiers, no ifs, no when's. If you are my follower, love one another. What is your first step to magnifying the love that is within you? Who is it that you need to show love to? How can you show more love in your daily walk?

FEBRUARY 17

"So, flee youthful passions and pursue righteousness, faith, love and peace, along with those who call on the Lord from a pure heart." 2 Timothy 2:22

Most people like to have fun. We may differ on the definition of what fun is, but at the heart of it all, most people like to have fun. However, when the desire to have fun comes along, we should always revert back to seeing things through God's eyes, allowing fun according to God's will. It is not that God does not want us to have fun, but He has warned us and set up parameters, like a safety net for our fun. Like a loving parent telling their kid not to run out into the street, He is not withholding fun but setting up safety parameters. Here Paul is reminding a young Timothy, a pastor, to flee from youthful passions, those that would cause a barrier between Him and the Lord and eventually might cause him to be unable to lead. The Lord does not forbid alcohol, but He warns us not to get drunk, as inhabitations can fall and we can walk out of that safety net that God provides. Paul tells Timothy that the kinds of people he should allow to speak into his life and do life together and have fun with are those with a like mind, one centered on God and a pure heart. He is not preventing fun, but rather reminding us that we should do life and have fun with others that are centered on Christ; that allows the Holy Spirit to direct, guide, warn and convict us of wrong. Don't chase after empty passions. Have good, clean, fun that does not cause strife or others to sin. Don't chase empty passions that would cause you to walk away from God's side. The people you allow in your life to let your guard down around should be people with a righteous heart who seek God and will always pull you back into God's Presence when you start to walk away. Be thankful for these kinds of friends and you, yourself, be that friend to someone else. How do you have fun within the safety net guided by the Holy Spirit that God provides? How can you be that friend to someone else, one that they can have fun with and feel safe enough to be vulnerable with?

FEBRUARY 18

> We know what real love is because Jesus gave up his life for us. So, we also ought to give up our lives for our brothers and sisters. 1 John 3:16 NLT

Have you heard the song "Revolutionary" by Josh Wilson? The chorus opens boldly with, "Why does kindness seem so revolutionary? When did hate get so ordinary?" We are living in extreme circumstances where the world seems upside down in its thinking. When did hate become so ordinary and accepted? Christians seemed to fight against hate, but lately, we have become lackadaisical. Instead of fighting against it, if it doesn't affect us personally, we try to ignore it. By ignoring it, low-grade hate has become the standard, the accepted. Or we go the other extreme and hate those who think differently than us about issues like gay marriage or abortion and when we hate we don't have the love of God in us. Non-hate does not mean acceptance either. In this day and age, the questions Josh Wilson asks haunt and sadden me as I look at our country. It is more haunting when I think about myself personally, some of the words I have spoken, my actions and how I have treated others. We are so quick to judge and let our tongues run wild that we should ask ourselves, do we really believe this verse and live it out? We, as Christians, know what real love is because Jesus loved us enough to give up His life, willingly, for us. And if He loved us that much, we should be willing to live like Him, for Him. We should be willing to give up our lives for our brothers and sisters, laying aside our wants and desires for the needs of others. How do we define who really matter and who to truly love? When we are attacked, how do we respond? Do we respond without emotion, or is it more of a reaction driven by and full of emotion? Josh Wilson's lyrics continue by saying, "What would Jesus do? He would love first. He would love first, so we should love first." Jesus loved first. Do we? Do we love first and look at others as God sees them? Or do we judge first? Do we react in anger or gossip, being quick to speak and slow to listen? Or do we respond in love? Love is a Supernatural reaction. Are we Christians just as backward as the world is? This week, how can you change your outlook? How can you change the words you use and your attitude so that they are more Christ-like and not more world-like? How can you be more Christ-like in dealing with others? Whom do you need to reach out and love first before getting angry? Whom do you need to be intentional with your words and thoughts this week so you can love first?

FEBRUARY 19

> Put on then, as God's chosen ones, holy and beloved, compassionate hearts, kindness, humility, meekness and patience, Colossians 3:12

Think for a moment about the person that loves you the most. Now think of the last thing they did to show you how much they love you. How did it make you feel? Did you feel the urge to show that love back? Probably. Now, since God chose us to be His Holy people. Yes, you! He chose you to be Holy! He loves His Holy People. He Loves You! What are we to do with that kind of love? Paul tells us we are to clothe ourselves with tenderhearted mercy, kindness, humility, gentleness and patience. Why? Because that is how He loves us. He loves us with a tenderhearted mercy that forgives all of our transgressions, mistakes and failures. He is kind to us. Look at how He spoke to the woman at the well, the prostitute and all the people He healed. We should extend that kindness to others; in the words we choose and how we treat others. It is said that kindness costs nothing but means everything. God loved us so much that He humbled himself and became one of us to save us, putting our needs for a Savior over His own. Like the Good Samaritan, we are called to humility and to look at others' needs over our own. We are called to gentleness when dealing with those who cause our trials and hurts. God is gentle when dealing with us. Do we not love the gentleness that God uses when dealing with us? Should we, as His children then, be just as gentle with others? Shouldn't we love others and treat others the way God treats us? And as for patience, Peter is a great example of the patience that Jesus had. Peter has always been a sign of hope for me. If God could be patient and gentle with Peter, love him and use him, then there must be hope for me. In the speed of life and this world, it has become exceedingly more difficult to have patience. Why? What is the rush? Why is patience a dying attribute? We love the fact that God is patient with us, but in turn, we lack patience with others. This is not how God is challenging us to live. Who this week or weekend do we need to extend tenderhearted mercy towards? Whom do you need to start being kind to? What areas of your life do you need to start being humble? How can you extend gentleness to someone? Who do you need to show patience to? Look to God for the strength and wisdom to start making some of these changes this week!

FEBRUARY 20

> Many are the afflictions of the righteous, but the Lord delivers him out of them all. Psalm 34:19

Ever feel like life has you on the show "Candid Camera?" It may seem like the better you do, the more you do for God, the harder life gets. Sometimes you may think, "Man, can't I just catch a break? When are things going to go my way?" But we are reminded that the righteous person faces many troubles. The more you do for God, the bigger the enemy's target is on your back. When you don't live out your faith, when you just sit in a pew and do nothing, you are not a spiritual threat. When you are not a threat, the enemy is likely not to expend resources on you; but then again, the first part of the verse might not apply to you if this is the case ("many are the afflictions of the righteous"). Jesus said it many times in many different ways. "They hated me first... Pick up your cross and follow me." So, we are told many times in Scripture not to be surprised when we face troubles, because when we walk with Christ, we will face troubles. When we allow the Holy Spirit to guide and direct our steps, when we live our life according to God's way and not the world's way, we will face afflictions, face trials and face hard times. It's not even an If you face troubles, it's When you face troubles, so don't be surprised. Let's look closer at the rest of this verse. The Lord comes to rescue each time. Jesus promises to never leave nor forsake us. We don't get cancer because God is not with us; we get it because we live in a fallen world. Marriage's end, children pass away at a young age, not because God is on vacation or He is distracted, but because the enemy is trying to separate us from the Love of a loving Father. God comes to the rescue each time we face troubles. Each time the enemy attacks and tries to drive a wedge between us and God, the Holy Spirit is there to rescue us. The verse doesn't say He fixes everything; He rescues us. What trouble have you just come through that you can witness how God rescued you? Are you facing trouble right now? How can you spend more time with Him, get closer to God and deepen your relationship with Him, allowing Him to work and rescue you? Make a plan that allows more time with Him and allows Him to work in you!

FEBRUARY 21

"Therefore, do not be anxious about tomorrow, for tomorrow will be anxious for itself. Sufficient for the day is its own trouble. Matthew 6:34

When my brother and I were little, we would scoop up the sand in the sandbox and make a big pile, wet it down, dig tunnels and play with our action figures until the sand dried up and the tunnels collapsed. Worry can be the same way. We may be able to use it for good for a little while, but in the end, it just overwhelms and buries us. We may say it drives us, or it prepares us for tomorrow, but in the end it is overwhelming. And when anxiety and worry overwhelm us, we rob ourselves of the small blessings God sends us every day. Anxiety can even prevent us from doing what God is asking us to do today. We can sometimes be so overwhelmed that nothing that needs to get done gets done. Jesus does not say that we are not to be prepared for tomorrow. No! This is not Bobby McFerrin's "Don't Worry Be Happy". We must be prepared; He says not to worry about tomorrow. Live today for today. Make the most of today. Anxiety and worry just keep us from being close to Christ. Do we really trust Jesus, or is He just a Sunday idol? Jesus calls us to walk with Him every day. When we draw near to Him that fear and anxiety tend to leave. Who or what do you place your trust in? Is it you? Your job or your title? Or do you really trust in the Lord? Do you really trust the Holy Spirit to get you through the day and be there for you tomorrow? What are you anxious about? What are you worried about? What do you need to let go of so that the freedom that Christ gives us can be lived in and not just an idea or concept that we try to grasp? God has called you to something today – what is it? The command is clear, "Don't worry about tomorrow". What is it that God is calling you to do now? Let His peace remove your anxiety and worry. What can you do today to start leaving the anxieties and worries behind you and live a worry-free life knowing who holds today in His hands?

FEBRUARY 22

> Train up a child in the way he should go; even when he is old he will not depart from it. Proverbs 22:6

As parents, we train our children and teach them how to walk, how to talk, how to use manners and even how to ride a bike. Not only do you go over the basics, but you also go over the safety – look both ways before crossing, stop at a stop sign, etc. We do that not to crush their creativity or limit their fun with this guidance, these rules, rather to protect them and make them aware of those rules so when they get older and want to drive, they will already know some of them. The same thing goes for guiding them spiritually and emotionally. If we, as parents, don't train them spiritually and emotionally, the world will definitely step in and provide that influence for us. So as parents, we need to direct our kids onto the right path – the path of God. If we teach them early on about God and His will and love for us, how to love others and forgive others, as they practice as children it will become part of their lifestyle when they are older. If we teach them to read the Word and to pray as children, it will become second nature to them as adults. Just as we teach them to be good kids with manners and treat others respectfully, we need to do the same with spiritual issues so they can be good and godly people. These skills last throughout their lifetime. The same is true with spiritual training. If we train in the Word of God, have the Word of God planted in our hearts and souls and live out our faith, even though they grow up and move out they will not depart from it. Now, like us, when sin and temptation come, they may detour, but not depart. That is why it is so important that dads and moms read the Bible to their kids, explain what is going on and help them develop their own faith so that they live it out and not try to live the faith of their parents. I believe so many kids turn away from God when they leave for college because they have never been trained to develop their own faith and relationship with God; they've just been living out their parents' faith. But when, as parents, as mentors, we come alongside them and help them develop their faith and their personal relationship with God, though they may detour, they won't depart. For those whose children seem to have departed, hold on to this Scripture and continue to pray for them. What do you do so that you do not depart from God? What kind of example is your life to those who are younger and are watching you? How can you, either as a parent or mentor of youth, help others in the next generation develop their own personal faith?

FEBRUARY 23

> He alone is my rock and my salvation, my fortress where I will never be shaken. Psalm 62:2 NLT

Remember when you were little and you would build a fort inside your house out of blankets and pillows? While fun, in reality, it didn't provide much protection. When my brother and I were little, my dad built us an elevated clubhouse, because, well, there are not many trees in Pueblo, Colorado to build a treehouse. That clubhouse was much sturdier than the forts we had built and when I needed quiet time, I would go up there to get away from others and have it. Now as an adult, I don't have an elevated clubhouse to go to, but I do have something better. I have my God, my Savior Jesus Christ and the Holy Spirit. In this psalm, David writes that God alone is his rock and salvation, his fortress where he will never be shaken. God was the refuge that David ran to. God's Words were the foundation that when the world was against David, his foot was steady. Today, in our society, when the world seems to be turning upside down, where do you go to seek protection and quietness? When the market crashes, the pink slip comes, or the diagnosis is not what you wanted, where do you get strength from? Where is your fort, clubhouse, or strong fortress to retreat, regroup and rest in? Jesus should not be our last resort when everything fails! Jesus should not only be the first option, but our only option. He should be your fortress, a mighty fort that is strong and provides protection, shelter and safety. He should not be a Sunday event but someone you visit with, listen to, talk with and rest with daily. What shakes you to your core? What scares you? What uncertainties are in your life right now? Where do you seek refuge from those? Ask yourself, what is my foundation built on? Be real with yourself. Is it your job or your talents? Is your foundation something that can easily be swept out from underneath you? He is a rock. Immovable. Your foundation should be in Him, God. God is immovable and solid, steadfast and unchanging. If He is not your foundation, what are you willing to do to build on Him and make Him your foundation? Today, how can you move in a direction that gives God more of your time and attention? How can you allow Him to be your fortress?

FEBRUARY 24

> "The Lord directs our steps, so why try to understand everything along the way?" Proverbs 20:24 NLT

Worry – to torment oneself with or suffer from disturbing thoughts. Fear, apprehension, vexed, to cause anxiety. None of this sounds fun, so why then do we do this to ourselves? Solomon wrote, "The Lord directs our steps so why try to understand everything along the way?" In other words, how can man understand His way? If we truly trust God and allow the Holy Spirit to direct our steps and guide our lives, since His ways are not our ways, it would be hard to understand why and how He does things. When we try to control things and they go astray, it doesn't make sense to us. When things don't go how we think they should have gone, the way we would have planned them, we tend to worry or have anxiety over them. Do you really believe that God is in control and that God has this? In Matthew 6, Jesus questions the crowd, the disciples, "Why do you worry about what to eat, do not the birds of the air have food and doesn't God love you more than these? Why worry about what to wear? See the lilies of the field, even Solomon in all his glory was not as these, but these lilies die and fade. Doesn't God love you more than this?" If you are walking with Christ, allowing the Holy Spirit to direct your steps, He then cannot be your co-pilot. He has to have the wheel. If you want to encounter God fully, you must let Him lead. If you truly love Him and trust Him, why try and understand everything along the way? Does Jesus dying for our sins make sense? No! So, if God is truly good and holy, we may not understand His way on this side of Heaven, so we need to stop trying. Pray today and think about where God may be directing your steps. Pray not to understand, but for the willingness and courage to follow Jesus. He's got this! He's got you! Trust Him! Are you willing to have the courage it takes for God to direct your steps? What are you willing to let go of control of and allow the Holy Spirit to take the wheel?

FEBRUARY 25

> "for at one time you were darkness, but now you are light in the Lord. Walk as children of light" Ephesians 5:8

Why are bad habits so hard to break and good habits so hard to make? What is one of your worst bad habits? Why do you think you struggle with it so much? Even Paul struggled with this, saying in Romans 7, "I do what I don't want to do and what I want to do I don't do." It is a struggle that we all face. Paul here reminds us in today's verse that while we may have been born into sin, into darkness, we now have Christ living in us. His light shines through us. We no longer have to walk as though in darkness, when we choose to dwell in light. But why is that so hard? The world is against us. The world says if it feels good, do it. If you want it, take it. You deserve to be happy, even if that means self above others. But what was the example that Christ set for us? The example that we are supposed to follow? It was the exact opposite. Do not gratify the desires of the flesh, do unto others as you wish would be done to you; give in order to receive, the last will be first and leaders should serve not expect to be served! We are to walk in the light just as the light is in us. Light and darkness cannot co-exist. Light dispels darkness. Even scientifically speaking, light pushes away the darkness. A single, regular birthday cake candle in complete darkness can be seen over 300 yards away! That is more than three full-length football fields, end to end. The world says we are living to die, but we are actually living to live eternally. We are living or should be living opposite of the world, countercultural, counteracting the lies that the world feeds us about living. Why are bad habits hard to break? They are comfortable, known and don't take much effort. Why are good habits hard to make? They are uncomfortable, unknown territory and take a lot of effort and intentionality on our part. What can you do this week to break a bad habit that causes you to walk in darkness? What is your plan to counteract it and start a good habit that is walking in the light? How can you let the light of Christ shine through you every day?

FEBRUARY 26

> He has made everything beautiful in its time. Also, he has put eternity into man's heart, yet so that he cannot find out what God has done from the beginning to the end. Ecclesiastes 3:11

Ever watch one of those talent shows and a painter comes on and just seems to be doing nothing that makes sense and then they finish and turn the picture right side up? Or at the fair, the artist sprays paint and it seems some things look random and don't make sense until it's close to being finished or it is finished and it's an amazing work of art? God makes everything beautiful in His own time. We may see random stuff going on and not understand. Our lack of patience wants an answer right away and we can get frustrated when we don't get an answer. We may ask, "Why God?" or "How are You going to use this God?" Maybe you've even said, "When God, when will You answer my prayers?" But Solomon, when writing Ecclesiastes, asked God for wisdom. God promised Solomon he could have anything he wanted and he asked for wisdom. It is with this Godly wisdom that Solomon writes today's verse. We are created in His image, so we are created for eternity, but even though we may want to see the whole picture, we can't; just like the artist on TV painting portraits upside down and with random strokes, it's not until the artist is done and turns the portrait over that we can see the whole picture and appreciate the beauty in it. Many of us are going through trials and struggles right now, but we need to remember to take the time and see God working in it, with it and in us. We may not understand right now why we have these trials, but one day, one day we will. God's timing is not our timing. We have to be patient and trust. Without patience, I don't think we would really trust God. It is in waiting and being patient that we learn to trust. If we truly trust, we tend to see our circumstances through different lenses. We can see beauty in the pain. We can see the hand of God on us, others and the situations. Be patient, draw close and allow Him to work in and through your trials and struggles. What trial or struggle do you need to take a step back from and try to see that the Creator of the Universe is handling it? How can you slow down enough to see the beauty of where God has you covered? Can you see the beauty of your situation? How can you trust Him more?

FEBRUARY 27

He will cover you with his feathers. He will shelter you with his wings. His faithful promises are your armor and protection. Psalm 91:4 NLT

Ever get stuck in bad weather? One summer night, we were at an outdoor concert and a thunderhead unleashed. Our car was over 1/2 mile away. Needless to say, I was drenched when I reached it. But with a duck's feathers, the water just rolls right off, an aspect I wish I had experienced during that rain storm. Here, God promises us that His feathers will protect us like feathers protect a bird. He will protect us like a mother bird protects her chicks by outstretching her wing over them. Oh, how I wish I had armor or protective covering that night. But His promises are our armor. His faithfulness protects us. The Holy Spirit guards our hearts and prevents the enemy from taking up residence. God promises to never leave nor forsake us. Just that statement should bring comfort and peace to people. What better protection is there than the presence of the Almighty God, Creator of the Universe, all that is seen, unseen in the heavens and the Earth being there by our side, protecting us, providing safety for us and a place of rest? He promises to hear our prayers. All we need to do is draw close to Him. He never leaves, we do. His path doesn't change, we just exit off of it. He is always ready to provide shelter for us and protect us. This week, draw close to Him. Take time today, this week to meditate on His Word and allow Him to be your armor and protection. Armor does no good in the trunk of a car or on a nightstand; it must be worn! That stormy night we had an umbrella in the car. What good did it do us in the car a ½ mile away? His armor is the same. What good is it in the closet? Put it on. For His promises to give us protection, you need to know what His promises are. To know His promises, you must read His Word and listen during prayer. Are you willing to place yourself under His protective wing? Are you willing to be quiet so that He can speak to you and reveal His promises? How can you hear Him better? More? What are you willing to do to remain under His protection?

FEBRUARY 28

"But Martha was distracted with much serving. And she went up to him and said, "Lord, do you not care that my sister has left me to serve alone? Tell her then to help me." Luke 10:40

How many of us are good at multitasking? You can cook, clean and sew at the same time. Me? Not so much. I have to focus, because I am easily distracted and I know it is one way to worship, is to be intentional. The Lord does not want to be one of those tasks that we are dealing with, juggling and being multitasked. Jesus wants our undivided attention – and He deserves it. If Satan can distract us with sin, He can distract us with good things, like spending time with the family, serving in a ministry(ies) and helping others; these are all good in and of themselves, but if they take the place of spending time with God, then they are not. Martha was so busy DOING things for Jesus that she was not spending time WITH Jesus. I know in my own life; I tend to be more like Martha and less like Mary. I recently read a devotional by Greg Laurie, who commented, "It's good to mark your Bible, but is the Bible marking you?" You see, worship, reading the Bible and doing good things can easily become routine to us, a box to check before going off onto our next thing. I read the Bible – check, done. Next thing. Martha, Martha. Now, I am not saying Martha was bad and I am not saying don't serve. But we need to refocus, think like Mary and spend time with the Lord; let the Bible mark us so that we do what the Lord wants and not what we want to do for the Lord. Are you doing a "good thing" or a "God thing?" Who are you more like in this portion of the story, Martha or Mary? What can you do to spend more time with the Lord and not for the Lord? How do you determine the difference between good and God things?

FEBRUARY 29

"The thief comes only to steal and kill and destroy. I came that they may have life and have it abundantly." John 10:10

We can feel like God has abandoned us when we go through trials and difficult times. When he lost everything, except for his unsupportive wife, Job still worshiped the Lord. Satan went through Job's life and stole his wife's joy, killed his kids and livestock and destroyed his businesses. But Job did not sin and did not believe God caused the calamity. He had a right view of God and still believed, despite everything, that God was with him and loved him. However, in America, we can have a view of God where He is the great, big killjoy in the sky. We believe this lie and that we cannot be a Christian and have fun. The enemy says all the fun stuff is what God says "No" to. God simply calls us to moderation on some things so they don't become a god to us, while some He simply forbids. God's desire is not for us to struggle and lose our joy, but to have freedom from what can take us captive and ensnare us. Sex only within marriage is not because God thinks it is dirty, rather He sees the spiritual connection that comes with it, thus it should only be within the confines of marriage. Gambling can feed the greed monster within us and if untamed and unchecked it can kill our ability to be appreciative of God's blessings. Drunkenness can dampen our inhibitions and drop our guard, causing us to chase after and grab that sinful lure the enemy dangles in front of us. When the enemy comes in to steal our joy, God wants us to be so close to Him that He is our source of joy, so close to Him that we recognize His blessings and appreciate them. When God is our source of joy, Satan cannot steal it, destroy it, or twist it into something it is not. When the thief comes to kill our passions, desires and dreams and bury us in despair, Jesus wants us to live life, love life and live it more abundantly. When we allow the Holy Spirit to live in us and through us, the enemy cannot kill the Will of God or the dreams we get from God. When the enemy comes to destroy and crush our spirits, God comes to restore us. God knows what the enemy's schemes are, the trials and emotional rollercoasters we have faced and will face. It is not His desire for us to stay there; God prefers we draw close to Him. He can Return, Resurrect and Restore anything we allow the enemy to take or ruin. He can replenish our joy and love and resurrect our passions, desires and dreams. God can restore our spirits so we can live life not depressed and crushed, but live life abundantly. We cannot allow the enemy to convince us that our joy, happiness and successes come from anywhere but the God that gave us life and is the only source of joy, happiness and success. Job realized it. Will you remember it? How can you protect your dreams and desires from the enemy? How can you prevent the enemy from stealing your joy? What has the enemy destroyed in your life or is under threat of being destroyed? How can you allow God to reinforce and strengthen you so that you can survive and live in the freedom that God provides?

MARCH 1

> For God is not unjust so as to overlook your work and the love that you have shown for his name in serving the saints, as you still do.
> Hebrews 6:10

Remember being in school and having to do group projects? Maybe you were the one doing all the work and then someone else who did nothing got the credit. Or maybe you were the one getting the credit but not putting forth much or any effort. That's unfair, right? Life isn't always fair and we quote that a lot, especially if we are a parent, we typically say it a lot. But God is different. The God we serve, the Living God, the Creator of the universe, is not an unfair or unjust God. The writer of Hebrews reminds us with this verse that for everything we do, we do for God. He WILL NOT FORGET! God does not get dementia; neither does He forget His promises nor what we do, especially in His name, for Him. When He calls on you and you respond, He will not forget. When you act in love towards someone, He will not forget. When we forgive despite the hurt still being painful, He will not forget. When we are willing to be His hands and feet and serve when He calls us to serve, He will not forget. When you live out your faith by your words and your actions, He will not forget. We may not get recognized on this side of Heaven; we may not see what seeds we have sown or what gardens we have weeded. We may not even be rewarded here on Earth, but guess who knows? God knows and God will not forget. God doesn't believe in the saying, "I've already served (blank ministry), it's someone else's job." If God calls us to serve, He will qualify us and He will call us out when it is His timing for us to leave and hand the reins over if that time comes. We have to draw close enough to God that when He calls on us to do something, to love on someone, to sacrifice our time, talents and treasures, we are ready to do so without question or hesitation. We need to be like Samuel, "Speak Lord, your servant hears." or be like Isaiah and respond, "Here I am Lord, send me Lord. Let me go and do and serve, Lord." If we truly love God, we don't pass the buck. God who truly loves us will remember your love, your obedience to Him and your serving. So today, what is God calling you to do? Who is He calling on you to love on? Be obedient and He will not forget! What is your first step to being like Samuel? How can you prepare your heart to respond like Isaiah?

MARCH 2

> God is not man, that he should lie, or a son of man, that he should change his mind. Has he said and will he not do it? Or has he spoken and will he not fulfill it? Numbers 23:19

As a parent, when do you teach your children to lie? No one, actually. People talk about the innocence of children, but I remember Bill Cosby talking about it. His child wants a cookie and builds a massive, unstable ladder to get to the cookie and when getting caught says, "I got a cookie for you." It starts as self-preservation and is ingrained in us. You hear a glass break, run into the room and ask who broke the glass. "Not Me" did it. I am sure that every family in America has sons or daughters named "Not Me". In the garden, Eve blamed Satan. Adam blamed God because God gave Eve to Adam – a motive of self-preservation. But God is not man, so God does not lie. Neither does God change his mind. God's promises hold true for eternity. When God says He will do something, He will follow through. He does not forget as we do. How many times have you changed your mind on something? Isn't it a good thing that God doesn't? What if God was like, "Yeah, I know I said I would forgive you, Joe, but on thinking back, you have done this a lot; I've changed my mind. Sorry." Thankfully God is not like that. He promises to remove our sin from us as far as the east is from the west. He promises to never leave nor forsake us. Look at how many times His chosen people turned their back on Him and rejected Him and His ways, but He still came through all the time. While His timing is not our timing, He always follows through. I challenge you to take some time and look back at God's promises and how He has come through in your life. If you are still holding onto one of His promises, remember that His timing is perfect, He will make it happen. How has God been faithful in your life? What are some promises of God you have seen fulfilled in your life? What promise or promises are you still waiting on? What is God asking you to do while you wait on these promises? How can you hold firmly onto your faith and relationship with Him during these wait times?

MARCH 3

> Like newborn infants, long for the pure spiritual milk, that by it you may grow up into salvation 1 Peter 2:2

My wife and son can tell when their iron levels get low because they just crave beef. It's like their bodies are saying, "I'm low here, get me some iron." During summers with Sonic's half-priced shakes, they would actually prefer a hamburger over ice cream; it's what they crave, it's what their bodies need. Whether it's their blood type or just the way they are wired, like newborn babies that crave milk, they crave beef. Do we do that spiritually when we get hungry? When we are low spiritually, do we crave God's presence, the guidance of God, or do we go to something else? Electronics? People? Alcohol? Casinos? You fill in the blank. Or do we immediately grab our Bible and start reading? Do we bow our heads and start praying? Do we put on worship music and start praising? When God has been quiet, or you have walked out of God's presence when you are spiritually hungry, what do you crave, desire and turn to? In order to grow into a full experience of salvation, we must start craving spiritual milk – the Holy Spirit – the presence of God. He must be our go-to, our hamburger. We should deepen our relationship with God so deeply that when we start to stray, like when my wife and oldest son's iron levels get low and they crave beef, we should notice the distance and crave the presence of God. Like my wife and son know what their bodies need by listening to them, do you listen to your spirit when you haven't heard from God in a while? When life becomes busy, the church gets put on the side burner, Bible reading gets delayed due to higher priorities needing to be met... What do you long for, something that fills the void and brings you closer, or just leaves you hungry for more? Are you able to recognize when you are spiritually hungry? Are you listening to the Holy Spirit to know that? Have you been spiritually hungry lately? What are you doing to satisfy the spiritual hunger? How can you make sure you get full spiritually and not go to something that leaves you with stronger cravings and still feeling empty?

MARCH 4

> Show yourself in all respects to be a model of good works and in your teaching show integrity, dignity, Titus 2:7a

In James 1, James calls us to be doers of the Word and not just hearers of the Word. The song "They will know we are Christians by our Love" declares that when we live out our faith that is how they will know Jesus is our Lord. People will not know you are a Christian simply because you attend church. Paul is telling Titus here that we must be the example of a little Christ, a Christian by our works, by loving others, by doing every kind of good work that Christ calls us to do. Everything we do must reflect our beliefs. I recently saw headlines of a well-loved coach and Christian who, in picture evidence, is in an inappropriate place, treating women inappropriately. Again, Paul states that everything we do, everywhere we go and all the words we speak should reflect our integrity and the seriousness of our relationship with Jesus, showing evidence of the Holy Spirit living in us. We don't get to sin just to blow off steam; we must plant His word in our hearts and listen, not hear, but listen to the Holy Spirit and avoid areas of temptation so that we can be the example God has called us to be. This is not a call to perfection, but a call to a reality that, while we may not notice, people are watching us; the world is wanting us to fail. When my kids were getting to the age of learning how to drive, as I drove, I pointed out what I was doing. Looking both ways, checking mirrors, pulling into parking spaces, etc. Titus was an up-and-coming leader in the early church, studying under Paul. Paul reminds his student that he himself must be the example of doing good works of every kind. For if he is not the example himself, then how could he expect others to do so? Paul is writing those words to us today. How can we expect others to forgive us if we don't forgive them? How can we expect others to love if we don't first extend the love of Christ? We must first be patient, kind and gentle; then, by our example, others will learn how to incorporate those into their lives. When we start thinking of others' needs before our wants, then and only then will others start to do so. A contemporary song says, "But if we want to see hearts set free and tyrants kneel, walls to come down and our land to be healed, if we want to see a change in the world – It Starts Right Here! It Starts Right Now!" As Christians, we have to be the change we want to see. Don't give the enemy a footing in your life; don't allow him to drop seeds in your vineyard. How can you rise to the calling here to be an example by doing good works of every kind? What is it? What good work do you need to start leading by example?

MARCH 5

> I lift up my eyes to the hills. From where does my help come? My help comes from the Lord, who made heaven and earth. Psalm 121:1-2

Ever heard the saying, "When the going gets tough, the tough get going?" Ever heard that and wondered if it was actually true? Many times, it would be easier to just give up, right? Ever feel like giving up? You feel like the world is standing against you in every decision and move you make, like a chess game with few options. You may even feel like I felt at times. Many times, in my life, I felt like I was the incarnate of Murphy from Murphy's Laws or the cartoon character Ziggy with the little black cloud following him. When that happens, where do we turn to? Sometimes we can look around and see no one; sometimes, we see only the emptiness of our surroundings. But we need to look in and look up. The Creator of heaven and earth, the Creator of the universe, not only knows your name, knows your trials and knows your feelings, but He also wants to be there for you as well. For the guys reading this, we all understand that it's hard to ask for help. Not that ladies have it easy, but they generally turn to their girlfriends for help and guidance. As guys, we try to control it and figure it out ourselves; no directions or instructions are needed, we will figure it out. But Jesus is standing there asking, "Why won't you let me help? I know what comes next; I've seen the next 777 steps and decisions that you will make." If Jesus can survive 40 days and 40 nights in the desert and come out stronger, if He can look death and sin in the face and destroy them, what can't He do? What is He not able to deal with or accomplish if we just let Him in to help? His suffering and resurrection were not done for an hour or two worship service a week; it was done to have a 24/7 relationship with each and every one of us. This includes 24/7 assistance and help. I pray for those that read this today and tomorrow, to be able to hand stuff over to Him, to allow Him to be the help in your life. What do you need to let go of so He can move in your life and help you? Where do you feel you are not equipped enough to do it alone and need to ask for assistance?

MARCH 6

> Do not be deceived: God is not mocked, for whatever one sows, that will he also reap. Galatians 6:7

Ever buy one of those mystery bags at the store or online – you know, the ones that say $25 worth of items for $5 or $10? Then you open it up and try to figure out how the retailer valued those items to cost so much. God warns us that we should not be surprised by the results of our actions. A farmer does not willy-nilly blindly buy seed and throw it on the ground only to be surprised by the plants that come up. A corn farmer will not plant grapes and watermelons. He knows the seeds he plants and the crops that will grow. Jesus tells us that grapes do not come from thorn bushes and figs do not come from thistles. Good trees produce good fruit and bad trees produce bad fruit. Paul warns us here that the seeds we plant will be the seeds we harvest, so the question is, what seeds are we planting? Are we planting seeds of bitterness or seeds of forgiveness? Are we planting seeds of life or seeds of death? Are we planting seeds of love or seeds of jealousy? Is sin the bag that you are grabbing seeds from, or is Christ the one that is supplying your seeds? If you don't know, then you already know. It takes a conscious and intentional effort to go to Christ and receive the seeds He wants us to plant – seeds of love, forgiveness and life. It might be time for us to take a moment and reflect on what seeds we have been and are currently planting. If the seeds are not from Christ, dump them out, throw them away and get a new supplier of seeds! Who do you have in your life to sow seeds of love, forgiveness and life in your own life? How can you take time to allow others to sow in your life so that you have the ability to sow into others? What safeguards can you put up to ensure the seeds being sown in your life are from Christ? What seeds are the Holy Spirit trying to get you to plant and who are you being asked to sow into? In your professional life, what seeds are being sown? In your personal life, what seeds are being sown?

MARCH 7

> But, as it is written, "What no eye has seen, nor ear heard, nor the heart of man imagined, what God has prepared for those who love him" 1 Corinthians 2:9

Kids tend to have a great imagination and we can see that when they play. Many people think adults lose that as they get older, but I think adults have imaginations as well, to some extent. They dream about a bigger house or a better car. They imagine what it would be like to win the lotto. Parents and kids use their imagination to see animals and people in the clouds. But Paul tells us that we cannot imagine what God has prepared for us. In 2000, after being a guest speaker at an event, my wife told me that God had bigger plans for me, other than teaching middle school, that I would be speaking to groups of people. I told her that was outrageous. In 2010, I entered seminary and in 2020, I became a full-time pastor. I could not have imagined the life that God showed my wife. I never could see myself doing anything other than teaching math, science, or technology, yet here I am. I have led men's ministries, spoken and taught at men's retreats, led Bible studies and youth and now preach every week! That is just a small example, a smidgen of what Paul was talking about. I could not imagine what God would do in my life; how much more is that true with eternity? We can try to imagine, but we have never seen anything as beautiful as Heaven; we have not heard anything as beautiful as a choir of angels singing worship to God, nor can we imagine what it feels like to be in the presence of God, free from sin. Paul got a glimpse of Heaven and could not put into words what his vision showed him. God wants to do more things for you and in you, more than you can possibly imagine. Are you willing to allow Him to do so? You cannot imagine, just as I could not, what God wants to do in your life. You have to just love Him, draw close to Him and allow Him to do in you what you cannot yet imagine. Are you willing? What does the Holy Spirit want to do in your life that you have told Him "No" about? If you could do anything for God, what would your heart's desire be? How can you allow the Holy Spirit to guide you to that?

MARCH 8

> Don't just pretend to love others. Really love them. Hate what is wrong. Hold tightly to what is good. Romans 12:9 NLT

Growing up, we spent a lot of time outside playing. Our bikes were X-wing fighters going against Imperial forces or the fort we made was the Justice League headquarters. Pretending and using our imaginations was a good thing, but one thing we should not pretend to do is to love others. Paul says here to "really" love them. Ever meet that person who was obviously fake? Do you remember the emotions that you had with that person? Maybe you didn't trust them? Maybe you were uncomfortable and unsure? But generally, people do not want to be around fake people. Paul tells us here, "Don't show fake love to others". As Christians, we can be nice to them when we are face to face, but when they leave, we gossip, slander and speak badly of them. This does no good, nor does it accomplish anything. How terrifying would it be if Christ was that way towards us? We are called to really love them. So often, we just throw around and live by Christian cliches, like "Love the person, but hate the sin". We are called to love others as Christ loves us, as Christ loved others that He met. When someone was in sin, He loved them first. He didn't judge or condemn; He simply said, "Go and sin no more." To love people means meeting their needs where they are and seeing their needs as more important than your own. That is how Christ loves us. Our need to be saved from sin and death was greater than His need to be in Heaven and not suffer excruciating pain. But He set aside His need to meet our needs. He died for our sins and defeated death by rising again, not so that we could judge and condemn others, but so we could love them. If we truly hold onto what is good, we can do this. But you must have the right definition of what is good. Only God is good and when we hold onto Him, we can love others unconditionally. Have you been pretending? Who is it that God is calling you to show love to? What part of God's truth do you need to hold onto tightly? Really love others means to see their needs as more important than our wants. Paul continues to tell us to hate what is wrong. I've always told my kids not to use that word, "hate", because of the root meaning – hate means watching something die and being glad it's dead. But here, we have something to hate. Hate what is wrong. Let what is wrong and evil die and be glad and rejoice that what is wrong is dead. Do we hate what is wrong, or do we indulge in it? Do we celebrate it or try to make it extinct? We need to hold onto what is good. What is wrong? Sin. What is good? God. The only thing good is God; He is what we have to hold onto. We must let go of selfish desires, negative speech and wrong desires and hold tightly onto God. How do we do that? Prayer, but it may require you to pray in quiet solitude so He can speak to your heart. Worship and praise Him more than just on Sunday mornings. Daily, read His Word and be filled with the Holy Spirit. Do you really love others? Can you let down your guard and take down your masks so they can love you, in spite of your flaws? Do you really hate what is wrong? What is holding you back from living out this Scripture fully?

MARCH 9

> I rise before dawn and cry for help; I hope in your words. Psalm 119:147

There are 24 hours in a day. Most people sleep for 8 hours, which leaves 16 hours in a day to do whatever it is that we need or want to do. If we, as Christians, truly had a humble heart for God and desired Him more than anything else, we would give Him at least 10% of our day. That would be 1.6 hours or 96 minutes. We often hear in church that we are to tithe and give ten percent to God. You have probably also heard how God can do more with our ten percent than we can do with our ninety. Why tithe just on our treasure? What would happen if we not only tithed on our money, but also on our time as well by giving God 10%! That is only 96 minutes a day. In Psalm 119, David talks about how he rises before dawn to cry out to the Lord for help. What if we just start small and set the alarm earlier than we normally get up and spend those five minutes with God praying, worshiping, listening, or reading? Then after a week, increase the time by five more minutes. Every week you do it will become easier and before you know it, you will have reached the ninety-six-minute goal. You might try splitting the time into forty-eight minutes in the morning and forty-eight minutes in the evening, closing out your day; or split it even more into thirty-two minutes in the morning, thirty-two minutes of your lunch and thirty -two minutes in the evening. As we navigate the Lenten season, let us set our sights on Good Friday and Easter Sunday, Resurrection Sunday. As we commit to spending more time with God, it will help our hearts be better prepared to celebrate the love and miracle of that Sunday morning. It is easy to say that God is a priority, but it is much harder to live that way. Living out our faith requires sacrifice; I am challenging you, as well as me, to sacrifice ten percent of our days to strengthen and deepen our relationships with God. What excuses do you have or have you allowed the enemy to use to convince you to not give God ten percent of your day? What are you willing to do to commit to deepening and strengthening your relationship with Jesus? What is your first step? Can you offer Him five minutes early in the morning praying and reading a chapter of the Bible, five minutes at lunch listening to a worship song and five minutes in the evening closing your day with a Scripture and prayer? How can you do a better job of making God your top priority?

MARCH 10

> I love you, O Lord, my strength. The Lord is my rock and my fortress and my deliverer, my God, my rock, in whom I take refuge, my shield and the horn of my salvation, my stronghold. Psalm 18:1-2

Growing up, we all thought Arnold Schwarzenegger was the strongest person alive. His muscles were intimidating. His voice was intimidating. He was the iconic image of strength. It's easy as a kid to see his physical strength. Fortresses and castles were a sign of strength as well. In ancient times castles and palaces were considered strongholds and were built on hills surrounded by rock walls for security and protection. Here David is utilizing that imagery for what God is to him, what God does for him, does for us and how God should be for us. The Lord is our strength in the spiritual, emotional and daily battles that we engage in. He is our solid foundation, the rock that cannot be moved or destroyed. In His presence, the Holy Spirit, we can take refuge from the onslaught the enemy throws our way. He is the shield that deflects the fiery darts launched at us. So often, we try to do it on our own accord. As a man, I feel like this is even more true; the lies that the enemy whispers in our ear, "If you were a real man, you wouldn't need help – you'd be able to handle it on your own." But whether male or female, we have to realize that we cannot do it on our own; we need a Savior. The law proved we needed a Savior. I mean, we can't even get past rule #1 - No other gods before Him. Job, career, social status, bank account balance and extracurricular activities tend to take more precedence in our lives than deepening our relationship with our Lord and Savior. We relegate the Holy Spirit's guidance and direction to Saturday service or Sunday morning. Jesus is Lord, but not Lord over our time or treasures, just Heaven and Sunday mornings. He has delivered us; He has provided salvation – don't waste it on things of this world, but deepen your relationship with Him. Let us rely on the Holy Spirit for the strength and guidance to win the battles that are before us. He should be our stronghold, withstanding any attack the enemy could throw our way. How can you see the Lord as your stronghold? How can you allow the Holy Spirit to be the walled-up palace on the hill, providing you the strength and protection to get through your day? How can you extend that sense of safety and connection so it is steady throughout your week? How can you rely more on Him for that level of strength?

MARCH 11

> Be still before the Lord and wait patiently for him; fret not yourself over the one who prospers in his way, Psalm 37:7a

We had a dog, Nani, that was very well-trained and she was a good dog. Even though she was an excellent dog, whenever you would get a treat for her and make her sit patiently waiting for it, you could see her back leg twitch, ready to go, or her tail speed up and then when she got the treat, she was fully active. I think we can often be that way with God. Waiting patiently for Him is hard. We still twitch and try to move, all the while just waiting for the "treat" or the answer to prayer. Be still and so patient for Him that you lose track of time; you're not counting seconds, minutes, weeks, or years. Here the psalmist reminds us to be still in His presence and wait patiently for Him to act. We must be in His presence, whether it is through being in the Word, prayer, worship, meditating on a verse, or even remembering His promises. Be focused on Him and not on His action. Be focused on the awesomeness and not the answer. Don't be so ready for Him to act that you forget what He has already done for you. The first part of this psalm is to be still in the presence of the Lord. I struggle to still my mind. I have ADHD and my mind seems to always be racing and moving on to the next thought. I can relate to the dog in the movie UP and while trying to be still and patient, I chase squirrels in my mind and get distracted in prayer. The second part of the psalm is to not fret or worry over the people that seem to be successful and have no worries; your focus should stay on God and not on others. You should be patient, waiting for Him and not concerned about the outward appearances of others. God's timing for you is different from God's timing for your neighbors, yet both timings are perfect. Being still is a discipline that needs to be practiced and one that I, personally, am still trying to develop. Practice and develop this discipline. How are you with finding time to be still in His presence? How are you waiting patiently for Him? During your stillness, what is the Lord trying to teach you or show you? How can you apply this verse to help you deepen not only your relationship with the Lord, but also better appreciate His timing in your life?

MARCH 12

"not to be quickly shaken in mind or alarmed, either by a spirit or a spoken word, or a letter seeming to be from us, to the effect that the day of the Lord has come." 2 Thessalonians 2:2

One game we would play before bedtime when I was young was trying to scare each other. My brother was easily startled and scared easily, but we got major points if we could scare my dad. There was only one time in my whole life my mom was scared and I will still forever tell that story because it's such a rare occurrence. The world can try to scare us into doubting God, doubting His Word, even His Will. Paul here is telling the church at Thessalonica not to be easily alarmed or to scare easily. We need to take heed of this, especially in this day in age with all the negative news about pandemics, rare, dangerous illnesses popping up from a pandemic, wars and uncertain financial futures. We need to ensure that spoken words don't jilt us, scare us, or separate us from the love of God. The news can be scary. I stopped watching the news during the election year because of the stress and anger it was causing in my life. Despite the news being scary, we know the book's author and story and we've read the book's ending. We know who is in control and who wins in the end. Don't let our spirits be troubled. Many people are living in fear and their spirit is troubled because they don't know the story; they don't know the end. This is the day the Lord has made – let us rejoice and be glad in it. Be thankful for God allowing us another day to witness the beauty He has created. So many people today are looking at the negativeness of pandemics and inflation, wars and political and racial unrest, while only a few of us are looking at the blessing that has been granted to us. It has made us slow down. During the pandemic, it made families eat together more, be more together and do more together. By lacking or losing what we call rights, some people have realized how truly blessed they are and are now unwilling to take for granted the freedoms and privileges God has blessed us with. Are you one of those people who have been able to truly appreciate what God has blessed us with and made the decision not to take it for granted? Do you need to take some time in prayer this week and look at what is not allowed and see it for what it really is – a blessing that God is allowing us to realign our compass to Him? Have you done that? How have you seen the fingerprints of God these last few weeks? How can you protect your heart, mind and soul to not be quickly shaken or alarmed?

MARCH 13

> Know therefore that the Lord your God is God, the faithful God who keeps covenant and steadfast love with those who love him and keep his commandments, to a thousand generations, Deuteronomy 7:9

What do we really know? That the sun will come tomorrow? Now that's not a 100% for sure thing, but we believe it because we experience it every day. But do we KNOW that we KNOW that God is faithful and keeps His promises? Now, I'm not looking for the churchy answer; but do you know that as much as you know that the sun will rise tomorrow, God is good and keeps all of His promises? Do you even know His promises that He is faithful to keep? Many people confuse unanswered prayers or prayers that were answered "No" as unfilled promises. He doesn't promise to give us everything that we pray for. But He does promise to love us and forgive us. He promises that no one can pluck us from His hands. What about His love for you? Are you as certain of His love for you as you are of the sun rising tomorrow morning? The only way we can know this, know Him, is to be in a relationship with Him. We need to read His love letter to us – the BIBLE. If we truly want to know Him, to trust Him, to know His promises to us and His steadfast love for us, we need to know what He has promised and what He has to say to us. Deuteronomy 7:9 says to those who love Him and keep Him commandments, He is faithful to a thousand generations. The only way to love Him is to keep His commandments and the only way to do that is to constantly talk to Him, to walk with Him and be with Him. When you have a question, you probably ask your friends, significant other, or people you love for advice. But do you seek His advice and His answers? You know that the sun will come tomorrow; do you know His promise for you tomorrow? Don't you think you should? What are you willing to do to commit to knowing His promises? How can you apply today's verse in your daily walk with the Lord?

MARCH 14

> I, the Lord, never change. Malachi 3:6 GW

People change. You are probably not the person you were when you were in middle school, nor are you the person you were when you graduated high school. If you're married, you have probably realized that neither of you are the same as when you got married. I taught middle school for almost 25 years and every year during the first week of school, we would teach the 6th graders how to use lockers. We repeatedly told them every year, *"Do Not Share Your Combination With Anyone!"* Why? People change. We would tell them, "You may be best friends today, but that changes!" And sure enough, every year, especially with girls, I would hear, "I don't have my book, etc. it is in so-and-so's locker and she changed locks." People change. Whether it is good or bad, it is simply a fact. But God, He never changes. I chose God's Word Translation because it says I never change. That is more powerfully said than, "I do not change." He never changes! Isn't that great news? That should bring peace into all of our souls. He never changes, so it's not one day, "Joe, do this and you're forgiven." And then the next, "Oh, now do this." It's never, "I changed my mind; I am not going to love you or forgive you anymore, you simply mess up too much. You've had too many chances." That will never happen because He never changes, which means the bullseye never moves; the target is never modified. He never changes and that means His word never changes – it is always true. The bullseye, the target is being reunited and in communion with Him. He never changes, so neither does His love for us. It's not on us to be saved, only the Gift of His love for us. A whole book could be written on this topic; oh yeah, it already has been published, the BIBLE. There is no room for fear or doubt when we know that we know, that we know, that God never changes. How does this verse change or amplify your relationship with Him today? How can you help others realize the promise of this verse in their life? How does knowing that He will never love you less or forgive you less affect how you live your life?

MARCH 15

"You have heard that it was said, 'You shall love your neighbor and hate your enemy.' But I say to you, Love your enemies and pray for those who persecute you, so that you may be sons of your Father who is in heaven. Matthew 5:43-44

Jesus was radical. He went against the religious and social norms of his day. His Sermon on the Mount is the epitome of that statement. Here Jesus tells us that not only are we to love our neighbor, but also to love our enemies and pray for them. Now when Jesus said this, it was not in terms of praying for the wrath of God to be poured out onto them, but to pray for peace and prosperity and God's presence in their life, to pray for forgiveness in their life. I know, radical, right? His upside-down economy is counter-cultural to the world. No eye for an eye, tooth for tooth, but Godly love for them, agape them. Love them because His fingerprints are on them. We are called to love them not because of the value we see in them, but because of the value God sees in them. We see the shell and their actions; we hear their words, but God sees the heart. God sees the hurt that directs their words and actions and God sees their potential, the potential He gave them. If we are honest with ourselves, we are someone's enemy and it can be challenging to pray as the Lord taught us to pray, "Father, forgive me as I have forgiven". If you are truly forgiven as you have forgiven, would you still be forgiven, or would there be a litany of wrongs still against you? Pray that and truly mean it, then amplify that prayer: Lord, love me as I love others, not just those who love me, but love all others. Why? We are called to be like Jesus. We could be called children of our Father in Heaven. How well are you doing with forgiving and loving your neighbor the way God loves and forgives you? How about loving and forgiving your enemy(ies)? God tells us that Faith, Hope and Love are all good, but the greatest of these is Love. So, who can you love better today? How can you offer forgiveness to those that you have been withholding it from?

MARCH 16

"Blessed is the man who remains steadfast under trial, for when he has stood the test he will receive the crown of life, which God has promised to those who love him." James 1:12

Growing up, my parents would never let us quit. We did the same with our kids; if they started something, they had to see it through and then when the season was over or the class was over, if they didn't like it anymore then they didn't have to do it again, but they at least had to see it through. Now that they are teenagers and young adults, I can see the fruit of the "harshness" of our expectations. They have a good work ethic; they follow through and they can be counted on to finish things. So many people today are so quick to give up. Too often in Christian circles we adopt bad theology and share it like the Gospel, such as "God will never give you more than you can handle." But in fact, He will allow more than we can handle to come into our lives. He allows that so that we have to draw closer to Him. Look at Job's example. He lost everything; he broke down, but he never gave up on God. James here tells us to be like Job. Remain steadfast, steady and forward moving when we hit trials, not through our strength but through the strength of the Holy Spirit living in us. Allow Him to be the Paraclete. Allow Him to lead and when we need it, to comfort us. He can empower us when we have no power or strength left in us. Remain strong when life is tough, when the world hits you with more than you can handle. Trust Him to see you through it. When you are at the end of your rope, let go, you are already in His hands. He wants to be there for you, for us, if we would just trust Him more. Don't give up – give in; Give in to His presence. Give in to His stronghold when you are out of strength. Remain steadfast in your faith. There is light at the end of the tunnel and it's not a train or a semi. It is the glory of God waiting for you. What trial are you in that you need to remain steadfast in? If you're not, think about some of the trials you have gone through and seek God's presence there, the evidence that He was walking with you the whole way; what did that look like? How can you incorporate this verse into your life so that when you face trials and uncertainties you can remain steadfast?

MARCH 17

> Great is his faithfulness; his mercies begin afresh each morning.
> Lamentations 3:23 NLT

Faithfulness. Many times, it is discussed in terms of marriage and relationships and how and why they fail when one or more people are unfaithful to their partner. But faithfulness is a personality trait of God. As defined by dictionary.com, faithfulness is "lasting loyalty and trustworthiness in relationships". Faithfulness can be seen conceptualized as remaining unfailingly loyal. How appropriate are these definitions of God? His faithfulness is His inability to not be loyal. In other words, it is His ability to be loyal to everything He has said. He is trustworthy and can never go back on His promises. What does He promise? He promises to never leave nor forsake us. He promises eternal life for those that accept the free will gift that Jesus gave us. He promises His Holy Spirit to direct, guide and instruct us in the ways we should go and be a comforter for us when we face trials and tribulations. How great is His faithfulness? Unfailingly, remaining loyal to all of that and more. His mercies begin afresh each and every morning. Every day, we get a clean slate to follow or disobey Him. Every morning He grants us mercy and love. We do not have to be held down by our mistakes and failures of yesterday; today is a new day. While this verse comes from the book of Lamentations, Jeremiah's poetry of grief, Jeremiah reminds us that God's faithfulness is great during grief and trials. While we may not be able to see Him working right now, amidst the trial, amidst the grief, but nonetheless He is faithful. His mercies and His forgiveness renew every day, each and every morning. Don't let the enemy rob you of this truth. Every day, each and every day, God's mercies are new. Yesterday's failures do not shackle you. During times of trials and grief, when we may not be able to feel his presence, know what Scripture says, His faithfulness is great and His mercies are new. Take time and allow the Holy Spirit to speak into your life and remind you of these promises. Meditate on this promise today. Let this promise take root in your heart, mind and soul as a defensive measure against the enemy and do not be led astray by his lies. How have you seen God's greatness and faithfulness in your life? How have you experienced His mercies in your life? What is in your life that is keeping you from truly believing this verse? How can you allow the Holy Spirit to speak into your life to remind you of these promises? How much time are you willing to give Him each day to be reminded of His faithfulness and goodness?

MARCH 18

> But take care that this right of yours does not somehow become a stumbling block to the weak. 1 Corinthians 8:9

Our oldest son JB never crawled. He went from sitting to walking so he could keep up with his older sister and cousin. His younger brother, James, though, did crawl. JB would try to help him walk, but James wasn't ready and would fall over. Both boys would get frustrated. JB had freedom and was walking and wanted his brother to do the same, but it caused his brother to constantly fall. In our adult life, we can do the same. Paul warns us not to use our freedom in Christ to cause others to sin. A pastor friend I look up to refuses to have an alcoholic drink out in public and I now follow suit and incorporate that thinking into my own life. Not because we view alcohol as a sin, but as a pastor, a leader, if someone who knows us, who struggles with alcohol sees us and leads them to think, if they can, then I can; one won't hurt me. Our decision has led to tempting someone in an area of their life that they struggle with. Now that may seem like an extreme, but neither of us would want to be the reason why someone fell back into an addiction. This is what Paul is talking about here. Paul gives us a serious warning here, "where we have freedom and strength, don't allow that to cause others to stumble". This takes a conscious effort on our part and may seem unfair, but it is Christlike. It is looking at those around us and seeing their needs as more important than our wants or desires. It's making conscious decisions, knowing that as a Christian and as a Christ follower, all of our behaviors, actions and words are being viewed by others. Not that we have to be, should be, or pretend to be perfect, we can't be. But it is a call for us to check ourselves daily, fill ourselves with the Holy Spirit and allow him to be our constant GPS and pilot. We need to daily be aware and make conscious decisions and efforts with the decisions we make. Does this verse cause you irritation? How serious is your walk with the Holy Spirit? How has this changed or strengthened your understanding of this verse? Has there been a time when you viewed someone doing something that caused you to stumble? What is one step in your life that you can make a change that would implement this Scripture in your life? Why do you think Paul cautions us regarding this?

MARCH 19

> But seek first the kingdom of God and his righteousness and all these things will be added to you. Matthew 6:33

What is the first thing you do in the morning? My oldest son chooses to eat breakfast, but as a young adult male, that is no surprise. What is your goal for the day? Do you have a to-do list? What thought process goes into creating your to-do lists? In this busy society, it is all too easy to allow the world to determine our schedule and prioritize our to-do lists. Is the first thing on your list spending time with God? When you wake up, do you first seek the Holy Spirit and His presence to start your day? As you organize your to-do list, are you seeking the Kingdom of God and God's righteousness in your life first? In the busyness of life, this can unfortunately get put to the bottom of the list or buried at the bottom of the stack. But if we honestly seek Him first, we will have God's presence and the Holy Spirit guiding us every step of the way. As Christians, isn't this what we want? As we live out our faith and our relationship with Jesus Christ, we should be seeking His righteousness and His kingdom. As you start your day and your feet hit the floor, they should be followed by your knees on the floor immediately afterward. Start the day with Him in prayer and worship, allowing Him to speak to you and guide you. Start the day by asking Him to keep you on the path of His Kingdom and His Will. You seek Him first; His Kingdom, His Righteousness and everything else will fall into place. Jesus flat out tells us to seek God first; seek His presence, His righteousness and His will for your life and all of it will be added to you. Think how much better your day will be if you start by seeking the Holy Spirit's guidance for the day. How much better of a mood would you be in if you started your day in worship instead of to-dos? How full could your heart be if you started your day in His Word instead of filling your stomach? We tend to be reactionary people. We can even blame God or question Him when things go astray, but if we start the day with Him and give Him first priority, we can then handle anything that the world throws our way. It has been said that God can do more with 10% than you can do with a 100%. While that is normally spoken of regarding tithes, I believe it is also true with our time. Tithe your time, give Him your best 10%, on average 96 minutes a day and see what can happen with the rest of the day. How can you start implementing this in your own life, seeking His Kingdom first? How much time are you willing to give God to start your day? How much more will all these things be added to you and more if you seek Him first?

MARCH 20

> The Lord himself watches over you! The Lord stands beside you as your protective shade. Psalm 121:5 NLT

Do you remember learning how to ride a bike? Remember that feeling of finally being free and you turn around and your mom or dad or older sibling was there standing watching, ready to catch if you fell. The Lord watches over you as well. He gives you the freedom to ride, do wheelies and jump off ramps. But when you crash, He is already there to bandage you up and help you heal. I think we can all recall some hot summer day and then finding shade and feeling the difference between being in the scorching sun vs. the relief offered by trees. Our Lord cares and loves us enough that He personally watches over us. He stands beside us during good times and bad, trials and celebrations, plenty and famine. He is our rock and strong tower. When we feel uncertain, we can be CERTAIN that He is there to comfort, guide and protect us. All we have to do is be willing to listen and open our hearts and ears to His words and presence. When you leave the protection of the shade, the heat is more intense; the same is true with the Lord, while He will never leave nor forsake us, we tend to walk away; that is when fear, doubt and uncertainty come in. Like leaving the shade, when we leave the protection and love of the Father, the enemy is ready to snare us up. He also stands ready to protect you; all you have to do is enter His presence. When the heat of confrontation that we face comes from the world, the enemy, He is there to provide restful shade. He is our oasis to refresh and recharge us, so when we go out, we have a renewed strength to continue the path the Lord has prepared for us. As a male and an American, I find it hard to slow down and rest, especially in this rat race called life. There is always something that needs to be done – my to-do list is like the loaves and fishes, as soon as I cross one thing off, another one or two appear. But even the Lord took timeouts; Jesus took time to rest, to retreat so He could be alone and in the presence of an ever loving God. So, if you are feeling overheated or exhausted, why not stop and spend some quiet time with the Lord? Like a fresh spring, let Him renew your soul and strength. Our bodies and our souls need rest. Jesus knew it and did it as our example. Are we stronger and better than Him? Today, tomorrow and the next few days, take deliberate time to rest in the Lord. Allow Him to be your shade, your oasis in life's deserts. What do you need to do today to remain under His protective shade and take comfort in His presence?

MARCH 21

> We ought always to give thanks to God for you, brothers, as is right, because your faith is growing abundantly and the love of every one of you for one another is increasing. 2 Thessalonians 1:3

Sometimes, it is easier to remember what God does in our lives and thank Him for that, while we tend to forget to thank Him for the people He brings into our lives. Sometimes people come into your life for a short time, just a chapter, while others may leave and then reenter your story, reenter your life later down the road, or some are there for the long haul, every bump and road construction you may face. Whatever the season or reason, we need to remember to have a thankful heart and earnestly and honestly thank God for the people He brings into our lives, even those that are rough around the edges. God did not create us to do life alone; even introverts need someone in their life to experience things with, to confide in and feel understood. We need to have that attitude of gratitude for the people that God brings into our lives, especially those that bring peaceful inspiration like a refreshing mountain stream. We were created to do life together, in communion. Paul implores the church at Thessalonica that they ought to give thanks to God. Other translations say we are always thanking God. We must always thank God. We can't help but thank God for you and it is right. We can't help but give thanks because your faith is growing exponentially and not only that, the love you have for others and the way you show the love of Christ for one another is amazing. Who is the person or people in your life who encourage you with their faith? Who is it that blesses you with their love for you as well as their love for God? When was the last time you told them how thankful you are for them being in your life? Have you thanked God for bringing them into your story – will you? Who is it in your life that you can be a Thessalonian to and share your faith and your personal relationship with God? Who can you be a Thessalonian to by loving on them, walking alongside them during a rough time? Who just needs someone to love them with no strings attached, without judging or asking for anything in return? Who in your circle of influence needs pure Agape love from someone? What can you do for that person?

MARCH 22

> And he said to him, "You shall love the Lord your God with all your heart and with all your soul and with all your mind." Matthew 22:37

What do you love? See, in the English language, we have one word, "love" and we use it to say "I love pizza". "I love my dog". "I love the Broncos". "I love my wife". The Greeks, however, had several words for love: *eros* – sexual passion, *philia* – a deep friendship, *ludus* – playful love, *pragma* – longstanding love, *philautia* – love of self or brotherly love and *Agape* – unconditional love, "the highest form of love, charity" and "the love of God for man and of man for God," love for everyone, godly love. Jesus says you must agape God with all your heart, all your soul and all your mind. This is more than lip service; it is a way of life that requires sacrifice and time. Jesus said we must hate our fathers, hate our mothers, hate our siblings and hate our kids in order to be His disciple. Does He really want us to hate people? No, but He is saying that God must be a priority over our parents, over our spouse and over our kids. God must be first; we must agape Him with all our heart, all our soul and all our mind. Not part of our heart that we utilize on Sundays or even on another night of the week. All of our hearts and all of our minds. We should be thinking about Him in all we do. How would He respond? What is His will for me here? How can I do God's work where I am? "All of our souls" means He should be what we desire first in the morning to align our compasses with Him and last at night, thanking Him for all He did and all His blessings throughout the day. Do you put God first in the morning before coffee and smartphones? Does your bank statement show God before goods? If your smartwatch recorded everything you did, would we see time given to God throughout the day and through charity to others? Would your day prove He is a priority with the amount of time you spend in prayer, reading and worshiping? Do you honestly love Him more than anything else? How do you love, agape love God with all your heart, with all your soul and with all your mind? How do you show that God is your top priority, or is He third or even lower on your priority list? What can you do to start realigning your life to fulfill this Scripture? How do you love God, is it more pragma or agape? What evidence is there of that?

MARCH 23

> The idols speak deceit, diviners see visions that lie; they tell dreams that are false, they give comfort in vain. Therefore, the people wander like sheep oppressed for lack of a shepherd. Zechariah 10:2

Do you ever feel like you are just aimlessly flowing through the day, the week, the month, the year? Is the world throwing so much at you that there seems to be a lack of focus on where you are going or how you are getting there? Is the Psychic Network (lol) or Powerball getting more of your attention lately? Are you dreaming more about "what if's" than reality? The world would love nothing more than for us to follow idols, either ones we create or the ones the world does, instead of the Good Shepherd. God does not leave us, but He does allow us to choose who and what we follow, how we spend our time and what we spend our money on. Social media, technology and keeping up with the Jones' have become our most popular idols in America. Why is it that oppression feels safe, especially oppression from the enemy? It's because spiritual bondage is what is natural, sin nature is what we have inherited – freedom though – freedom from sin – freedom with Christ, that is what is unnatural, supernatural, in the world. God has an upside economy that makes no sense to the world – abundant, undeserved grace; but then again, I think that is why we can believe in it that much more. It is so contrary to the world that the only way to get it is from God. The enemy can't provide it, so he offers false security in the pleasure of sin and idols. So, if we want true freedom, we need to leave oppression behind. We need the courage to cut the ties and strive for freedom. It starts by utilizing our time intentionally and spending it with Him instead of on social media and technology. Instead, we can carve out quiet time with Him and meditate on His Word and His Will for our lives. How can we know the voice of the Shepherd if we don't give Him a chance to talk? This week, reprioritize your time. Find freedom in spending time with the Lord and quit wandering around aimlessly, but storm forward with purpose – God's purpose. Where are you currently seeking comfort from stress, anger, or disappointment? In your prayer time, are you finding stillness before the Lord? Are you quiet long enough so you can hear from Him? What goal can you make to be more silent and still and give Him some quality time today?

MARCH 24

> But I say to you, Love your enemies and pray for those who persecute you, Matthew 5:44

Isn't it easy to love those who think like you and have the same values and opinions as you? It is also very easy to love those who treat you nicely, respect you and don't come against you. But here, Jesus challenges us to love our enemies, to love those who persecute us. Whoa! Hold the horses, stop the race! What? This was revolutionary – not the revolution the disciples wanted, or the Jewish people – but revolutionary nonetheless! There are stories of martyrs, like Stephen, who not only prayed for those killing them, but some even helped those who were reluctant. Perpetua helped her executioner place the sword in her because he was hesitant. We complain and pray for pillars of fire to metaphorically consume our enemies. We pray for the wrath of God to run its course in their life, but the early church, even martyrs today, know Jesus' command. They have planted His Words in their hearts and in their souls and allowed the peace of God to grow mightier than an oak or bigger than a redwood in their souls. The command is clear to pray for those that persecute you with their thoughts, their words and their actions. Don't pray for the wrath of God or for God to teach them a lesson. While it is a prayer, it is a prayer that will not avail much and is definitely not the type of prayer Jesus was talking about. Pray for the peace of God to overwhelm them so that they might know the Love of God, not the wrath of God. Pray for God to bless them. Pray for their needs to be met and for blessings above what they need. Pray like Jesus prayed, "Father, forgive them, for they do not know what they are doing." Even if they truly know what they are doing, forgive them. Pray for God to forgive them and then bless them. In doing so, peace will have an invitation to come, settle in and heal any wounds you might have. Who is someone you might consider an enemy that you need to love and pray for God's providence and blessing to be poured into their lives? Who needs prayer in your life that you either haven't prayed for or have refused to pray for? Why do you think Jesus asks us to pray like this for those that make our lives harder?

MARCH 25

> Love means doing what God has commanded us and he has commanded us to love one another, just as you heard from the beginning. 2 John 1:6 NLT

God is Love and not just regular ole love. Agape-type love. God is Love. The New Testament has been described as God's love letter to us. In 1 Corinthians 13, Paul reminds us what love is: patient, kind, keeping no record of wrongs nor easily angered. John reminds us that love means doing what God has commanded us to do. And just so there is no confusion or place for argument or wiggle room, John tells us what God has commanded us to do – to love one another. And the cherry on top of the sundae is that John tells us, just as you have heard from the beginning. This is nothing new; you were told! How could you have forgotten already? Just as you have heard from the beginning, you, those who follow Christ, are to love one another and not just other Jesus followers. There are no membership requirements or pre-qualifiers to be loved by God. That also means there are none to be loved by us. Love means being obedient to what God has not only called us to do, but He actually commanded us to do. We are to love others as He loves us. The Lord's prayer can be very dangerous if you pray it without meaning it. Forgive my sins as I have forgiven others. Do you really want God to forgive you as you have forgiven everyone in your life? Amplify this prayer. Now add to this prayer, love me as I have loved others. Could you pray that and be confident in the amount of Love God has for you if He were to grant your prayer? I think as American Christians, first world, capitalist country Christians, we have gotten caught up in just going to church as consumers and not being the actual church, the hands and feet of Christ. We tend to only look to God so He will grant prayers, but not to be the author of our life story. If you truly believe you are a Christian, how are you doing at living out 2 John 1:6? How can you do a better job living this out to its totality? How do you love others with the Agape love God has for us? How much evidence of love is there in your life so that by your love, the world knows you are a Christian?

MARCH 26

"Bear fruit in keeping with repentance." Matthew 3:8

Living in the plains of eastern Colorado, I have a deeper respect for farmers and those in the agriculture industry than before when I was living in the city. Agriculture was a big part of life in Jesus' day. A lot of His analogies utilized agriculture so the people listening could not only understand, but also apply what He was saying in their lives. We are called to do the same, not just understand what He says, but also apply what He says in our lives. Fruit and the vine were utilized many times. To be part of the vine, we have to be grafted in. Good fruit comes from a good vine; a bad vine produces bad fruit. Part of the Lord's Prayer, the Our Father, is repentance. Father, forgive me as I have forgiven those who sinned against me. It is only when we have repentance that we can actually bear fruit. God cannot have anything to do with sin; our lack of repentance and our unwillingness to forgive others puts a wedge, a gorge between us. So, whenever we do wrong, go against what God calls us to do, sin through commission with what we do or sin through omission with what we refuse to do, God calls us to repent. If we fail to repent, then we cannot bear the fruit of the Spirit and our harvest will be lacking. When we hurt someone, we need to repent and ask them for forgiveness. When someone hurts us, we need to forgive them, whether or not they come and ask for it. Forgiveness and repentance – they are a one person job; your job as a Christian and my job as a Christian. Reconciliation may or may not take place, because it involves multiple parties. God calls us to reconciliation whenever possible, but it's not a command because He knows we cannot force someone to reconcile with us. Are you bearing fruit? What is it that you need to repent of so that your harvest may be more bountiful? Whom do you need to forgive so that you can produce good fruit? What kind of fruit are you bearing? Would others agree with your answer? Why does Jesus connect bearing fruit with repentance?

MARCH 27

> Do not remember the sins of my youth and my rebellious ways;
> according to your love remember me, for you, Lord, are good. Good
> and upright is the Lord; therefore he instructs sinners in his ways.
> Psalm 25:7-8

Memory. Isn't it a weird thing? We tease our youngest saying he doesn't remember his childhood correctly, because he will say something like, "Remember when you did this and that happened?" and we will all look at him and laugh, "That never happened!" Sometimes we can remember what we did when we were five years old and other times we can't remember what we did five minutes ago. Here, David, a man after God's own heart, cries out to the Lord, "Please don't remember my sins when I was young and rebellious like most teenagers are". Why would he ask God that besides the obvious self-reward of forgiveness? Because You God, You are good and You are upright. God not only forgives us of our sins and forgets our wrongdoings, but also, as a Father, He loves us enough to guide us and instruct us in love, truth, His way and His will. He wants us to follow Him. We should be more like David and cry out, "Abba, thank you for loving me, thank you for forgiving me and thank you for instructing me! Help me to follow Your instructions and guidance for my life!" God will instruct us if we just allow Him to. He will not force us to do anything. His gift of free will is always there for us to choose, but if we choose to allow His correction and guidance, He will; He is faithful to do that. What is your favorite memory? What do you remember more, the blessings and answered prayers or the unanswered or no answered prayers? What memory do you have of God doing something big in your life? When was the last time you cried out to God and sought His forgiveness? How can you amplify your prayer life to seek his instruction and guidance? What direction are you needing Him to lead you in?

MARCH 28

> "who saved us and called us to a holy calling, not because of our works but because of his own purpose and grace, which he gave us in Christ Jesus before the ages began," 2 Timothy 1:9

It's amazing that Christians, especially in developed nations, believe it is only the Pastor's job to preach the Word and have a "holy" calling on their life. In fact, once we accept Christ into our hearts, everyone has a holy calling on their lives. We are called to know Scripture and to know what God has to say. Not only are we keepers of that Truth, but we are also obligated to share that with other people. As Paul says, we have a holy calling on our lives. Holy means "to be set apart". We do not have the power within us to be holy. God does not grade on a curve! If the good side of the scale outweighs the bad, then we are good, or if the bad side is tipped and outweighs our good, then we must be bad. Thankfully He doesn't see it that way. The ground is level at the foot of the cross and if Jesus is the standard of goodness, then we can all agree that we will always fall short. We can try all we want, but our sinful nature always rears its ugly head and prevents us from the holiness and righteousness God calls us to. We cannot do it on our own accord, but it is through Him living through us, His Will, His Grace, His Righteousness – and His plan from the beginning. All we have to do is receive the life vest, the life preserver from Him. All we have to do is allow Him to live in us. We need to see His love for us is not based on what we do, rather it is based on whose fingerprints we bear. It is His purpose, through His grace and mercy. Remember that this holy calling is not because of what you did or did not do. Nor is it because of who you are, but who you are saved through! When you get a new car or gadget, don't you show it off and share it with your family and friends? You should do the same with the holy calling you accepted when the Holy Spirit took residence in your heart. What are you doing with the holy calling on your life? How can you share that holy calling in your life to show what God has done and is doing in your life? How do you feel knowing that we all have a holy calling on our lives?

MARCH 29

> But when I saw that their conduct was not in step with the truth of the gospel, I said to Cephas before them all, "If you, though a Jew, live like a Gentile and not like a Jew, how can you force the Gentiles to live like Jews?" Galatians 2:14

Holy Week – that is what we have entered or will be entering soon. When we hear the word Holy, probably what comes to mind is God, good, set apart; but in earthly terms, this would not be a good week or a Good Friday. What is good about death? Jesus is not only preparing for His death, but also a death that has been labeled the most horrific death penalty ever invented. Why is that good or holy? Is it because the sacrifice He made was so we could all come to experience the kingdom of God? See, when this verse was written, the Jews were trying to make the gentiles who believed in Jesus maintain their dietary habits, follow the rite of circumcision and follow the law. Jesus fulfilled the law paving the way for whoever believed in Him; no matter what they ate or drank, no matter what ethnic background they came from, they could be indwelt with the Holy Spirit and inherit the kingdom of God. Those who allowed the Holy Spirit to indwell them and guide them could and would live a life of goodness, peace and joy. Allowing the Holy Spirit to counteract selfishness so one can live a life of goodness requires counteracting fear so we can experience joy and counteracting unrighteous anger so we can live in peace. There are no hoops to jump through to get to Jesus. There are no ethnic, socioeconomic, or any other barriers that prevent the Holy Spirit from indwelling anyone that asks Him into their heart. The only thing that can prevent this is the unwillingness for someone to accept the gift of life Jesus gives, by refusing to believe and not allowing the Holy Spirit to indwell them. It is a personal choice. This week, Holy Week, what choice or choices will you make to align your conduct to be in step with the Holy Spirit or to allow the Holy Spirit to direct and guide your steps? What is keeping you from living a life of goodness, joy and peace? What do you have to do to allow the indwelt Holy Spirit to have a more active role in your life? What can you do to keep in mind what Jesus was preparing to do for us and what can you do to show gratefulness for His love for you and His willingness to lay down His life for you?

MARCH 30

> even as the Son of Man came not to be served but to serve and to give his life as a ransom for many." Matthew 20:28

When you think of the word servant, what comes to mind? For me, it's a butler or a maid in fancy clothes coming to do or give me whatever I need, want, or desire. I think the world has played a big part in that thinking and I don't think I am alone. But here, Jesus reminds us that He came not to be served, but to serve, to be a servant of God, to give everything, including His life. He calls us to follow Him, to imitate Him in our life and not the world. Especially here in the U.S., it's easy to get caught up in worldly thinking like, "I deserve this" or "I deserve that," but as we are in Holy Week, did Jesus deserve the cross? No. He chose it because He loved each one of us that much. Jesus, the night He was betrayed and arrested, stooped down and washed the feet of His disciples. This was normally the job of a slave; no good Jew would do that. But Jesus did and in doing so He taught us that if He, the Son of God, was willing and wanting to meet that need, how much more should we desire to do the same? Power and knowledge are neither good nor bad, but they can be applied in both good and bad ways. Power and knowledge can drive you to help others and improve the lives of others, or they can lead to self-promotion and self-glorification. Jesus had both power and knowledge. The power used to create the entire universe was still in Him and the knowledge of God, us, them and what He was going to do He had as well. But instead of using power and knowledge to make people serve Him, He chose to serve others. He set the example high. He raised the bar. As Christians, we are called to follow His example and shoot for the bar He set. Those that were lost, the ones the religious leaders condemned, those stuck in sin, He went to, He loved on, He served. How are we following His example? Jesus didn't just go to synagogue; He went out every day praying and serving. What are we doing on Monday to live out His example in our life? What act of service are we doing on Tuesday that follows suit? Who are we helping on Wednesday that shows the Holy Spirit is alive in us? What are we doing on Thursday to serve and not be served? How on Friday do we live out that He paid His life as a ransom for me and for others? On the weekend, besides worship and church, when we are with our spouse or kids, how do we lead in this area of faith? I understand most of these are rhetorical questions, but what if they were not? What if every day when we woke up, we prayed, "Jesus, you came to serve and not be served? Show me today, provide opportunities today, to live out your love, your life, your example. Show me how to live out my love and commitment to you." If we call Him Lord, we need to follow His example and not think of ourselves as better than anyone else. So, how can we meet the needs of those that the world would say we are better than? How would your life be radically different if you were serving others? Do you even want it to be radically different? Who is it in your life that you need to have a servant's heart for?

MARCH 31

> But since we belong to the day, let us be sober, having put on the breastplate of faith and love and for a helmet the hope of salvation. 1 Thessalonians 5:8

Have you ever heard of someone being level headed? What does it mean to be clear minded or level headed? "Keeping your mind free from distracting thoughts that lead you away from God's path" would be a good definition of clear minded. Have a clear focus on what you should be thinking about and be clear as to what you have your sights set on. The ESV version, among many others, says "to be sober". The opposite of sober is drunk; when you are drunk, you get disoriented easily. Don't allow the enemy to disorient your mind and get it drunk on fantasies, desires and dreams. In referring to his letter to the Ephesians, Paul tells Timothy, "You belong to the light; God is light." Make sure you dress yourself and protect your heart and soul with the breastplate of faith and love. Protect your mind with the helmet of hope and salvation. Let the love of our Living God and Savior protect your heart and soul – to do that you must have an active relationship with Him. Don't let the darkness come in to confuse or lead you astray. Salvation is referred to as a helmet; protecting the mind, the only battlefield the enemy can infiltrate. To be effective with our faith, we must be able to recognize the schemes of the enemy to lead us astray; you must be clear minded, clear headed and sober, not intoxicated with lies from the enemy, selfish desires, or dreams and fantasies. Keep your mind fresh and awake by being in His Word daily and praying daily. During prayer time, we must be willing to give Him talk time, so we can hear from Him and be reminded just how precious and loved we are. Take time to hear His heart and His plan for you. How can you keep sober minded and clear headed so that you can easily recognize the lies from the truth?

APRIL 1

"Father, if you are willing, remove this cup from me. Nevertheless, not my will, but yours, be done." Luke 22:42

Jesus – Fully God – Fully Human. The human side of Jesus really comes through with this prayer. Father, if this trial, pain and suffering could pass by me. If this time when You will fully remove Your presence from this human body and the experience of being fully separated from You could pass, let it please. But not because of my humanness and human desire but Your Will, Your desire be done, Father. The stress and agony of what He would fully suffer caused Him to sweat drops of blood. But He knew what His mission was, He knew what His ministry was and He knew that the only way for all of mankind to be reunited forever with their Heavenly Father without intercessors or sacrifices and the promise of eternity was to go through with God's plan. When the going is good, we tend to be aligned with God's plan, but when there are bumps and dips in the road, when it gets curvy and uncertain and hard, we tend to pray only the first part of Jesus' prayer, "God, please remove this from me", but unlike Jesus who went on, we don't; we leave it there. What if we were to continue our prayer, "God remove this, help me, but not because it's what I want, but Your will not mine be done"? We should probably continue, "If it is Your will for this, what am I supposed to take away from this? How am I to grow and be stronger on the other side of this? Strengthen me to see this through; strengthen me like Jesus when He knew what was coming to remain steadfast through the trial, pain and suffering to the glorious finish line." When you pray, do you pray for stuff you want or for what God wants? How do you pray when what you ask for does not align with God's plan for you? How content are you with an answer of "No" from God? How can you pray more in God's will? How can you change your prayer life to be more aligned with Jesus'?

APRIL 2

> For I am sure that neither death nor life, nor angels nor rulers, nor things present nor things to come, nor powers, nor height nor depth, nor anything else in all creation, will be able to separate us from the love of God in Christ Jesus our Lord. Romans 8:38-39

Sometimes miles can separate friends and family. I live in Colorado, my parents in Texas, my brother's family in Hawaii and an even more extended family live on the East Coast! While we stay in touch, nothing is like being physically present with them, sharing a meal and experiencing endless hugs. Paul says we can never be physically distant from God and His Love. He says neither life nor death can separate us. What is currently going on and what may be coming down the pike, yep, it can't separate us. He is never out of reach and His love is never too high or a depth too low to get to! Presidents, protests, viruses, angels, demons; you guessed it, none of them can keep Him distant from us. If we have the desire and choose Him, nothing can keep Him from us. 2020 and 2021 were hard years. Most of us were physically distant from friends and families and many of us have had loved ones pass on. During any pandemic, it may be a while until we can be in their presence again, but we can, every day, be physically present with the Holy Spirit, the love of God. We don't have to walk any day alone. He promises He will never leave us, even though we might. We might leave to chase after someone, or something, or some experience. But God, His Love, His Holy Spirit, never leaves us. While we may feel the hurt over losing a loved one, we can experience His Love and comfort in our grief; we just have to spend time with Him. Have you wandered away and are you feeling distant from God? There is no better time than now to return. Is your heart hurting or is it feeling empty right now? Let His Love occupy it. What are you willing to do to allow His Love and presence to be felt in your life? How much time are you willing to give the Holy Spirit to feel His presence and hear His guidance?

APRIL 3

> Have you not known? Have you not heard? The Lord is the everlasting God, the Creator of the ends of the earth. He does not faint or grow weary; his understanding is unsearchable. Isaiah 40:28

Sometimes life gets so busy that we forget what we cannot see with our eyes and cannot hear with our ears. Isaiah reminds the people of Israel and us today that our God is an everlasting God, not one that can be defeated and killed like some of the pagan gods of their day, or even those idols of today. He is the Creator of the ends of the Earth. I remember a time in my life, young and immature in my faith and relationship with God, when I thought He was too busy for me or that He had forgotten me. I also remember a time thinking I was God's court jester; that whenever God needed a good laugh, He would point His finger at me and some trial would come my way, making Him chuckle. But God is not a mean Father, purposely and forcibly pushing us into trouble; nor does His power or love grow faint or weary. His strength and power are the same today as it was when He hung the stars and stretched out the heavens. His love for us is as strong today as it was when the nails pierced Christ's wrists. Have you not heard about the love He has for you? Although satan can't force you to walk away, he can try to convince you to question God, question His Love for you, question His strength and power in your life and in the world. Have you not known or have you forgotten the power and holiness of God? Have you not heard or forgotten how much He loves you? What can you do to always remember how much God loves you? How can you hold onto your identity as a child of God? How can you apply Isaiah's words in your life for a deeper relationship with the Creator of the universe? How can you remember that God never leaves nor forsakes us even when we feel distant or don't hear from Him?

APRIL 4

> I dwell in the high and holy place and also with him who is of a contrite and lowly spirit, to revive the spirit of the lowly and to revive the heart of the contrite. Isaiah 57:15b

Today's generation is creating more words to describe situations, people, or feelings. Supposably, "adulting", "contactless" and "gender identity" are new terms in 2021 added to the dictionary. But I think we have lost the meaning of many words, especially those in Scripture, like "contrite". Oxford defines contrite as "expressing remorse or repentance". Merriam-Webster goes on to include "remorseful and sorry". Here, God tells Isaiah to tell the people, "Not only do I dwell in the holy place, but also with those who have a repentant heart and a remorseful spirit". Those who recognize that their decisions separate them from Me, I dwell with them. Why? Why would God go there? He says to revive their spirit – to revive, give new life, new breath to their spirit. When they repent, I don't want them to wallow in their sin, but to be refreshed so they can go out and be who I created them to be as well as being the testimony of my love and forgiveness. He wants our repentant heart to experience life, love and joy so that not only may we live, but also by seeing what God did in our life, others would want that freedom and revived spirit and revived heart as well. Our Holy God not only dwells in holy places, but His Holy Spirit is with us wherever we go, whatever we do and does not condemn us. He only points us back to the cross, back to Jesus, back to a loving God who wants to give us new breath, new life and to be a well of living water in us. If you feel broken down, lowly, or contrite, know that His love already knows and wants to revive you. What are you willing to do to allow Him to revive your spirit within you? The Holy Spirit is a Comforter. Are you willing to allow Him to comfort you and heal you? Where are you willing to allow the Holy Spirit to guide and direct you? How will you allow His instruction to impact your life?

APRIL 5

> In this is love, not that we have loved God but that he loved us and sent his Son to be the propitiation (sacrifice) for our sins. 1 John 4:10

This verse here is a mystery and stumbling block for some people. This is love – not that we loved God but that He loved us. God loved us first. He didn't send His son Jesus because we loved Him and were walking with Him and following Him. It was because He loved us. John 3:16 reminds us as well that God so loved the world. It starts with His love for us. In Romans 5:8, Paul reminds us that God shows his love for us in that while we were still sinners, Christ died for us. He didn't wait for us to get right with Him; He made the way to be right with Him. I believe that is why the American church needs to change its view of who it allows in; it acts more like a museum for saints than a hospital for sinners. We look down on others who don't fit in, dress like us or act like we do, when they enter a church, so they get the wrong image of God. We condemn churches like Westboro, but then may have the same attitude in our hearts. Gandhi said he loved our Jesus, he just didn't like Christians. When he attempted to attend church to learn more about God, he was told they didn't allow his type in. God loves all of us, not just those who attend your church or worship like you do or dress or pray in a certain way. He loves those who have more money than you and those who have less. He loves those with tattoos and piercings as much as those who don't. We all bear the image of God and His Love is for all of us. His propitiation, His sacrifice is for all our sins, everything from the headlining sins to the not so obvious displays of sin. When you were at your lowest, Jesus said, forgive him, forgive her, for they do not know what they do. How can you live out this verse in your life so that all may know the True Love of God? How do you experience the love of God? How do you extend His love to others? What can you do to see those that are opposite of you through the eyes of God and not through judgmental eyes?

APRIL 6

"You are the light of the world. A city set on a hill cannot be hidden.
Matthew 5:14

Light and dark are opposite. Interestingly enough, science shows that light dispels darkness; darkness cannot exist around light. Darkness is actually the absence of light. Jesus said He was the Light of the world. When we allow Him into our hearts, His light shines through us. Light penetrates the darkness and pushes it away, so a city on a hill at night can be seen for miles and miles and nothing can hide the light that comes from that city. Jesus encourages us here that when we have Him as our Savior, we are the light. When we allow Christ to work in our lives, people will be attracted to us, just like in the dark people will search for light. We should not try to hide the light. In another verse Jesus says you don't put a lamp under a basket; you let it light up the room. If we call ourselves Christians, then we should let our lights shine every day – Monday, Tuesday, Wednesday, Thursday, Friday and Saturday, not just Sunday. Not just during Bible study. At work, let His Light shine through you, at play, be the light of joy that breaks through the darkness in the world. When we go out to eat, people should see His Light and when we are driving in traffic, when dealing with those that irritate us, try us, it is then that we are also called to be the light and push out the darkness through grace. We should want people to see the real Jesus in us and want what we have for them in their lives, the peace and joy that surpasses all understanding. What are the areas in your life where you are not the Light? What can you do to start being the Light that Jesus calls us to be? How can you die to selfish desires so that the Light of God shines through you and points others to God?

APRIL 7

> When doubts filled my mind, your comfort gave me renewed hope and cheer. Psalm 94:19 NLT

What is it that brings you comfort? When you think of comfort, what comes to mind? Is it a blanket and cup of coffee by the fireplace? Is it a special kind of food, like chocolate, or a drink, like a glass of wine? Is it the ability to just sit and read a book? See, we all have different things in our lives that bring us comfort or help us relax. But here, the psalmist says, when doubts fill my mind, when fear comes in, when I question what I am doing and allow questions like who I am to enter my mind, it is Your comfort Lord, Holy Spirit, that renews me. It is the Holy Spirit that gives me hope, His presence, that cheers me up. See, things like chocolate, wine, books and technology, their effects are temporary and not always readily available; but God, our Lord, His Holy Spirit, He is always there and always waiting to fill us with His presence. He is always ready to bring comfort and hope and cheer and joy when we are down. All we have to do is seek Him first and His presence above anyone or anything else. When the enemy brings doubt into your mind, what will you do? Our mind is a battleground and that is where the enemy attacks. He has access to our minds, but not to our hearts, so he plants doubts and fears in our minds. He asks us questions so we drift away from the presence of God. When the enemy fills your mind with questions like "What are you doing?" or "Who are you?" – what do you do to settle your mind? How do you calm your spirit and renew your hope? What can you do to seek comfort and peace from the Lord? How have you experienced the comfort of the Lord? How has He renewed in you a hope that is focused on Him? How can you allow the Holy Spirit to cheer you up?

APRIL 8

"Either make the tree good and its fruit good, or make the tree bad and its fruit bad, for the tree is known by its fruit. Matthew 12:33

Ever buy a carton of strawberries only to find when you get home that some of them are rotten and no go? Kind of frustrating, huh? A tree, a plant, or a bush is known for the kind of produce it provides. When it is healthy, a good keeper will feed it, water it, fertilize it, weed around it and prune it, so it will keep producing fruit. When a bad plant continues to not produce or only produce bad fruit, it will be cut down and thrown out. Good plants produce good fruit; bad trees produce bad fruit. So, the question is this, what kind of fruit are you producing? Are you producing good fruit? Is your joy contagious, living for God? Is the fruit you are producing coming from spending time in worship and in the Word, keeping your emotions in check and looking out for the needs of others? You know, good fruit. Are you producing bad fruit? Does selfishness rule in your life? Do you allow emotions to rule, which causes you to make decisions while emotional, not being able to see the needs of others? Are you using others to get your way? You know, bad fruit. Are you producing no fruit at all? If you are not producing fruit, it might be time for pruning. Are you willing to allow the Holy Spirit to prune you so that you can produce fruit again? If you are going through a trial or life is overwhelming, pruning, if allowed to occur, could allow you to start producing fruit again. Today, take time to survey your life and your fruits (love, joy, peace, patience, kindness, goodness, faithfulness, gentleness, self-control, Galatians 5:22-23) are you producing good fruit? If yes, use your fruit to help those who are not, so the fruit basket on God's banquet table may overflow. Are you producing little to no fruit? Look for what God is trying to do with you while in the trial. Is it that you just need pruning so you can produce fruit? If so, are you willing to let God prune your soul and your life? Pruning does not feel good, but afterward, we are healthier and producing good fruit again. What are you willing to allow the Holy Spirit to cut back in your life? Do people know you are a Christian by your words, your generosity and your gracious attitude? I would ask my youth as a youth pastor, if Christianity became illegal today and you were arrested, would people be surprised?

APRIL 9

> For I know the plans I have for you, declares the Lord, plans for welfare and not for evil, to give you a future and a hope. Then you will call upon me and come and pray to me and I will hear you.
> Jeremiah 29:11-12

Have you ever felt that Murphy's laws were more prevalent than the laws of Nature? Do you ever feel like Ziggy with a little black rain cloud always following you overhead? While it may feel like the only luck we have is bad luck, God has a different message for us. He told Jeremiah to tell the nation of Israel, who was in Babylon at the time, that after 70 years they would return home. Then He said this, "For I know the plans that I have for you declares the Lord, plans for welfare/peace/good plans and not for evil, to give you a future and a hope." Now, I am not saying that He will give you everything you want; I am definitely not a believer in the prosperity gospel. But He says He plans for welfare, in a different translation, plans for peace and in another translation, good plans, to give you a future and a hope. What is that hope, the good plans He has for us? His Will – for us to be fully restored to Him, eternally with Him. When we face trials in our lives, either due to the decisions we have made or the decisions others have made, He will be there for us and see us through. When we see His presence in those times, we should then follow through with verse 12; call upon Him, pray to Him, knowing that He will hear us. He wants us to experience the peace that only comes from an intimate relationship with Him; that is His redemption plan for us. Do you feel His peace? Do you trust Him with your future, your family and your job? When life gets tough, do you find yourself distant from God or closer? How can you better apply this verse in your life, knowing God is not the killjoy in the sky the enemy says He is, but His promises He has for you? When life is uncertain, how can you be certain about God's plans for you and His Will for your life?

APRIL 10

> So whether we are at home (in this body) or away (from this body), our aim is to please him. 2 Corinthians 5:9

Remember when you were little and in school, you made a picture for your mom just so that it would make her happy, or when you did something not because you were asked to but because you knew it would make your dad happy? Paul reminds us that this is how we are to live our lives for God. Whether or not we are in this body, alive or dead, our goal is to please Him. Why would we not want to please Him? With all the love and blessings He has poured out on us, giving up His life so we can have eternity with Him, we should desire to please Him, to live our lives out as Christ did. How do we please Him, you may ask? Good question and easy answer — do His will in your life? That's not easy to know what it is, you may say. The answer is easy, but applying it in our lives is more difficult. We need to spend time with Him in prayer, in worship, in study and in quiet times so we can know Him, hear Him and have His will revealed in our lives of how to apply His words in our circumstances. Another easy way to please Him is to follow His two basic commandments – Love Him above all else and Love others as He loved us. Again, the answer is easy, but the application in our lives is more difficult. How do we love those who don't love us? It has to be the power of the Holy Spirit in our lives to do that. However, in order to love, we must first forgive. Remember, forgiveness is a one person job – yours! You don't have to talk to them, interact with them, seek them out – just forgive. When you forgive, you can then begin to love the way God loves us. I have told all my kids, my biological kids and our foster kids, that we love them not because of what they do, don't do, or say, but because of who they are and whose fingerprints they bear. They are a child of God, created in His image, bearing His fingerprints. We love them because of who they are, not what they do, just like God loves us. He loves us not because of what we do or say, but because we are His. With that being said, how do your decisions please God? What are you committed to doing to please Him? How can you please God this week with what you do? Who is it in your life that needs to hear you love them or that God loves them?

APRIL 11

> In him, we have redemption through his blood, the forgiveness of our
> trespasses, according to the riches of his grace, Ephesians 1:7

During this time of year people are gearing up for Easter, not like they do for Christmas, but maybe planning a family dinner. The whole reason for Easter was the sacrificial spilling of blood for the forgiveness of sin. What we consider the Old Testament, the priests would have two lambs; one would be slain, the blood removed from the animal and then poured over the other lamb. The spilled blood covered the sins of Israel and the priest would then lead the other animal out into the wilderness, to remove it from the people. That blood only covered their sins; it couldn't wash them away, because the lamb could not sin and did not have the ability to sin. When Jesus left Heaven, came to Earth through the birthing process from Mary's womb, being fully God and fully man, He lived His life choosing not to sin; so when He willingly gave up His life for us, His blood being poured out washed us of our sins and cleansed us as pure as the first driven snow. Paul reminds the Ephesians and us that we have been redeemed, our debts have been paid in full and we are restored to the right relationship with God and our sin and death discharged from our account. All of these meanings of redemption are done through His blood because of His grace, mercy and love for us. Do you feel redeemed? Redeemed is not an emotion, but we need to hold onto the truth, which comes from the meaning of redeemed; redeemed means to have your debt paid in full; redeemed means to restore (right relationship); discharged – our sins, debts, transgressions, even death has been discharged from our account. Bought from sin and death, freed from captivity by payment, extricated from something detrimental – death! While we may not feel redeemed, if we accept Christ as our Lord and Savior, we are – meaning we need to start living like we are redeemed. We must stop listening to emotions that change situationally and start living out our relationship and truths – we are redeemed and extricated from death and separation from God. How can you live this out in your life? How can you apply this verse in your life to walk in the riches of His grace? How can you extend the forgiveness you have received to someone else? How can you make Resurrection Sunday not a history lesson, but a lifestyle?

APRIL 12

> But the Lord said to Samuel, "Do not look on his appearance or on the height of his stature, because I have rejected him. For the Lord sees not as man sees: man looks on the outward appearance, but the Lord looks on the heart." 1 Samuel 16:7

It is amazing what the world pushes on us as to success look like. As humans, it's hard not to let our eyes influence our hearts and minds. We see someone pleasant to look at and we assume that they are a good person. We see someone that is not so pleasant on the eyes and often assume that they are not worth as much, not good enough, or smart enough. Samuel did this as well. God called him to Bethlehem to anoint a new king from the family of Jesse. Jesse brings out his oldest son, who is tall, handsome and strong. Samuel thinks this is the one, right off the bat. I mean, look at him – he is king material, surely the Lord's anointing is on this one. "Sammy, Sammy, Sammy, your eyes deceive you. He may be good-looking, tall and strong, but I have rejected him to be king. See, you guys only look at the outward appearance, but I, God, I look at the heart of a man; I see what drives him and what his heart longs for and chases after." We tend to take God out of mix, thinking we know His' heart's desire. We confuse it with the world's definition many times. The world says your beauty determines your acceptance and success in the world; if it were not so, then why would plastic surgery be a 21.1-billion-dollar industry? People pay to remain young and beautiful, hoping to maintain what the world says is beauty to be accepted, promoted and successful. But for God, your value is not in your outward appearance, rather it is based upon what is in your heart. Your ability to do things for God is not based on your bank account, your age, or your looks. All that has to be in place is that God is number one in your heart. And if God is number one, our priority, how can we not fall into this trap? Draw closer to God. Be in His word more. Pray that the Holy Spirit allows you to see people as God sees them, not by physical appearance alone. There was a movie called *Shallow Hal* where Jack Black ties women's beauty to their looks. He is hypnotized to see their inner beauty as their outer appearance. He learns this lesson. You can too and you don't have to be hypnotized to do so – have a heart after God and He will allow your eyes to see their inner beauty. Who have you judged based on their appearance? What have you learned from that? How do you think you might have prevented the work of the Holy Spirit in your life or the person whom you judged? What are you willing to do to see the inner beauty before the outward appearance?

APRIL 13

> Whom have I in heaven but you? And there is nothing on earth that I desire besides you. My flesh and my heart may fail, but God is the strength of my heart and my portion forever. Psalm 73:25-26

People tend to talk about how they can't wait to get to Heaven to see so-and-so. And while that may not be a bad thing, is that or should that be the reason we strive for Heaven? David writes, "Whom do I have in heaven but you?" David recognized that God and God's presence in Heaven were what should be desired. Nothing on Earth do I desire but you, oh God! Can we, as Christians, say that same thing? I shared this thought from *By His Grace Alone* on social media: "It's easy to look at Judas and shake our heads in disappointment; after all, he chose money over Jesus. But I have to ask myself, how often do I choose something over Jesus and do it for free?" If we are honest with ourselves and with God, how often do we do this and do the opposite of what David says? "There is nothing on Earth that I desire besides you." Notice he doesn't even say *more than you,* he says *besides you.* When our heart fails, hurt and depression move in, what do we seek, when it should be, *who* do we seek? What do we seek instead of *who* when we become weak and our flesh fails? David reminds us that God is the strength of our hearts and our portion forever. When flesh and heart fail, it is He that we should seek. His presence should be desired over anything else. It is through the power and presence of the Holy Spirit living in us that He becomes our strength. What is it that you desire more than God? What are you looking forward to more in Heaven to see, family or the Father? How can you redirect your heart, so the Father is first and allow Him to take care of the rest? What priority is God really in your life, like if you stood before Him, what would the evidence say? How can you make God your only priority?

APRIL 14

Have I not commanded you? Be strong and courageous. Do not be frightened and dismayed, for the Lord your God is with you wherever you go." Joshua 1:9

With everything happening in the world right now, it can be easy for fear to come in and take up residence. Fear is a wonderful tool that the enemy uses to keep us from moving forward, trusting God and deepening our relationship with Him. In Joshua, Chapter One, between verses one and nine, God tells Joshua three times to be strong and courageous. Joshua had just taken over for Moses, after he died. Joshua saw many things, but God had to remind him three times, "Do not be afraid or frightened, do not be dismayed or discouraged. I, Joshua, I, the Lord your God who has led you through the wilderness for 40 years, feeding you, keeping your clothing from wearing out, it is I that goes before you." Joshua was a mighty warrior and leader when they first saw the Promised Land. It was Joshua and Caleb that said, "We can take this land. God promised it to us; we can take it and take care of the giants because God is with us." This is the same man who must be reassured three times to be strong and courageous. When we are continually faced with trials and hardships and the headlines are full of doom and gloom and disparity, it can be easy to lose heart. But God is greater than giants, He is greater than wars and pandemics and His promise stands firm to never leave nor forsake us, to go before us and with us wherever we go; that fresh perspective should get the blood flowing, the heart pumping, adrenaline activating, propelling us forward. How can you plant this Scripture in your heart to remember that God calls you to be strong and courageous in any circumstances? When fear and despair try to come in, how can you keep that door and window of your mind and heart locked to keep them out? How can you live in the freedom of God's Word today?

APRIL 15

> Tell them to use their money to do good. They should be rich in good works and generous to those in need, always being ready to share with others. 1 Timothy 6:18 NLT

I heard a preacher once ask, "Do you control your money, or does your money control you?" When asked how many millions were enough, John D. Rockefeller replied, "Just a little bit more." A misconception in Christian circles is that money is the root of all evil, but that is not what the Bible says. Paul wrote in 1 Timothy 6:10 that "the LOVE of money was the root of all kinds of evil." Money is an inanimate object; without the ability to be good or evil, it is simply a tool. A tool that we can use for self-pleasure, ambitions and personal desires or a tool to do good work and extend the love of Christ to all. Paul reminds Timothy to tell his church that as "little Christs," we would be rich in good works and generous to those in need. We should be ready to keep the church and God's message going. I hear all too often from churches that only about 9% of members serve and that 9% give 90% of what is collected in tithes each week. We have no problems using this fiscal tool to buy expensive adult toys that satisfy our desires, like cars, computers, technology, entertainment, etc., but then we get defensive when the collection plate is passed around. God doesn't want us to go broke, but He does want our hearts. He knows that if we love money, if we let money control us, then it pushes His presence out of our lives and moves in to take His place of residence in our hearts. Are you generous? If you were honest with yourself and Jesus showed up in front of you right now and asked, based on your checkbook register, who do you love more, money or Messiah, what would be your answer? What would your bank statement show? God doesn't want all your money; He wants all of your heart. Does He have it? How can you be more generous, giving Him His tithe? Remember that our treasure is stored up in Heaven, so what are you storing up?

APRIL 16

> And if it is evil in your eyes to serve the Lord, choose this day whom you will serve, whether the gods your fathers served in the region beyond the River, or the gods of the Amorites in whose land you dwell. But we will serve the Lord for me and my house." Joshua 24:15

We have choices to make. Do we continue to date or break up? Do I stay at this job or look for a new one? Move or stay? Worship God or worship the idols I give my time to. Joshua had lived a long life and saw many things, including slavery in Egypt, the Egyptian army swallowed up by the Red Sea, a pillar of smoke by day and fire by night, even manna and pheasants in the desert. A golden-calf idol was created while God was leading them; Israel complained about manna and pheasants, scared of giants. Before Joshua dies, he tells his nation, who seem to easily be led astray from God, "If it is evil in your eyes to serve the Lord, then choose whom you will serve; the Egyptian gods when we were enslaved, the false gods here in this land or the one true God; but let me tell you this, as for me and my house, we will only serve the Lord!" I always thought it was weird that Joshua said, "If it is evil in your eyes, to serve the Lord." How could that be evil? Then I became an adult, a parent and society changed. Evil is glorified and celebrated; to be a follower of Christ seems wrong in our culture now. Murdering innocent lives isn't evil; following Christ is. Holding onto Biblical truths about marriage and family is evil, but vilifying Christ and His followers is not. How can serving the Lord be evil? When the evil one himself flips the script and convinces peoples and governments to love evil and hate what is good, evil becomes good and thus, good becomes evil. We all have choices to make – What is truth? God or self? What is good – God or self? What is your identity – God or self? Are you who God says you are, or have you taken control of that and decided for yourself what your identity is? Who will you serve, self or God? Who is God to you? Is it the idols we enjoy and that entertain us, or is it the one, true living God? Whom will you serve? I can quote Joshua for myself, "As for me and my house, WE WILL SERVE THE LORD?" Who will you choose this day to serve?

APRIL 17

> But he answered, "It is written, 'Man shall not live by bread alone,
> but by every word that comes from the mouth of God.'" Matthew 4:4

What is it that you desire more than anything? If you had one wish to be filled, what would it be? Is it financial freedom? Health? The ability to eat anything and not gain weight? Boy, would that be nice. What is your favorite food and meal? I tend to be a mood eater but BBQ, teriyaki, chicken (any kind) and chocolate are my favorites. Yes, we need food to function, even to survive, but Jesus reminds us here that we cannot live off of bread alone; food alone will not serve all our basic needs. We need every Word that comes from the mouth of God. When did Jesus say this? When Satan was tempting Him in the desert, "You can command these rocks to turn into bread and fill Your stomach." Jesus had to be hungry; His human body had been in the desert for several weeks and He was far beyond the kind of hunger we can understand as Americans. This was just one of the first temptations that satan tried to coerce Jesus. See, when our body is deprived of nutrients, we can lose hope and focus and we might do things or say things that we normally would not do. But, when we focus on the Holy presence of the living God in our lives, we can overcome those hunger pains. That's what happens during fasting. We deny our bodies of what they need and when that desire rears its head at us, we go into prayer, we dive into Scripture and we draw closer to Him. We long for the Holy Spirit to speak to us and guide us and allow His Presence to take our minds off of what is desired and focus on the eternal. How deep is your hunger for the Word of God? Do you have a hunger for His Word and thirst for His presence? Internalize this Scripture, pray this Scripture and desire this Scripture to be real in your life. Start desiring the Word of God in your life so much that if you miss a day, you feel starved for His sustenance. That faithful desire is the Way to finding true fulfillment in this life and intimacy with our Lord. How can you create that desire for His Word in your life? What commitment are you willing to make to keep this Scripture alive and evident in your life?

APRIL 18

> Rather, speaking the truth in love, we are to grow up in every way
> into him who is the head, into Christ, Ephesians 4:15

If the Bible could be summed up in one word, what would it be? I believe it would be *love*... "For God so *loved* the world; *love* the Lord your God, *love* your neighbor as yourself." Yet we see many Christians, some churches that spew anger and hate. God hates this, God hates that and God hates you. Many Christians feel it is their job to call out people for their sins. Paul reminds us here that we are called to speak the truth, but not just speak the truth, but to speak it in love. Paul calls us to, in every way, grow and mature in Christ, the head of the church, the bridegroom. We can get so caught up in calling sin out that we forget the love part. In today's world, with technology and social media, people feel free to say things online and attack people they don't know online because of the upfront anonymity of it. Jesus reminds us to take care of the sin in our life before we call it out in someone else's. But when the time comes, we confront a person face to face, not electronically and we do it in love. We remind ourselves and them, that they are loved by God and we can ask if _____ actions or words are conducive to a deeper relationship with Christ. With hate and unrighteous anger running wild in our lives, while there may be truth there, this judgment and lack of mercy actually separates us from Christ. Remember that Satan utilizes bits of truth to get us to sin; so, we can't utilize bits of truth to escape the trap, it must be the whole truth. Unfortunately, the whole truth can never be delivered unless it is delivered in love.

Jesus had compassion for those lost in sin, but He also condemned those who abused power, prestige and position and unjustly judged others. In Matthew 18:15-20, Jesus tells us, if a brother sins against us, go to him first, then bring others, then the church. But all this communication is to be done in love. Why then, as God so loved us, do we quickly forget the *love* part when it comes to forgiving sin and confronting sin? How do you speak *love* in truth? How can you be better at living out Paul's words here in Ephesians 4:15?

APRIL 19

> This is how one should regard us, as servants of Christ and stewards of the mysteries of God. Moreover, it is required of stewards that they be found faithful. 1 Corinthians 4:1-2

As humans, we tend to complicate things. We can let denominational labels, teaching styles, worship styles and even the size of congregations cause us to draw battle lines and attack fellow Christians. Here in 1st Corinthians Chapter 4, Paul begins with, "We should regard each other as servants of Christ and faithful stewards of the mysteries of our living God." Then he ups the ante with, "It is required of stewards to be faithful [to the living Christ and the mysteries of God that we have been called stewards of]". We are stewards of the Word, not theology. That means that we must be faithful to God's Word and not theological lines of thinking. Theological lines become battle lines. As students of God's words, not just pastors but all Christians should be students of God's Word; we must agree on what the Bible says, because those are the very words of God. What we can politely disagree on is how to implement them and the areas of faith that are not written in the Bible. It is in these unwritten areas of faith that theology comes in. We cannot allow theological disagreements to override the Scripture itself. No matter the denominational sign hanging outside our churches, we are all servants of Christ, requiring us to love God above all else and to love others as we love ourselves. If we are to be found faithful, we must adhere to what Scripture says, support each other in what Scripture says and agree to lovingly disagree with the areas on which the Bible is silent. It is already bad enough with the world attacking us, we don't need to make it worse by attacking each other and adding fuel to the enemy's fire. What area of your faith do you disagree with someone else on? How can you come to terms with these differences? How can you still love them? How can you still support them?

APRIL 20

> When pride comes, then comes disgrace, but with the humble, is wisdom. Proverbs 11:2

The world tells us that the only way to get ahead is to take care of numero uno, yourself, because if you don't, no one else will. You must see yourself and your wants first and most importantly, go get them. To be successful you have to sell yourself and boast about yourself and your talents and accomplishments. Oxford defines "pride" as "a feeling of deep pleasure or satisfaction derived from one's own achievements, the achievements that are widely admired". Dictionary.com states it is "a high or inordinate opinion of one's own dignity, importance, merit, or superiority, a dignified sense of what is due to oneself". So, when God tells us that after pride comes in, disgrace will follow, it should not be a surprise. When we have a superior view of ourselves or what is owed to us, having an inordinate opinion of our importance, we end up devaluing others. We devalue others who are created in the image of God, thus devaluing God in His creation. But with the humble comes wisdom. Humble means not proud or arrogant, having a modest self-value. When we can accomplish being humble, we can actually see the needs of others and see them as important, view others as created in His image, bearing His fingerprints. If we want to have Godly wisdom, we must be humble. Jesus Himself was humble and the Holy Spirit is humble; in order to be led by the Holy Spirit, we must be humble enough to listen. God speaks in a still, small voice so that we have to want to hear from Him. If we are so busy self-promoting and tooting our own horns, how can we possibly hear from God? How can the Holy Spirit guide us and lead us? How can we know His wisdom when we don't know Him, His Voice, His calling? If you want to hear from God, humble yourself before Him and ask Him to speak into your life and take some time to just be still and quiet and know that He is God. In what areas of your life is pride the strongest? How does God connect humility and wisdom together? Why do you think He did this? How can you kill the prideful spirit in your life to be more humble, hearing the wisdom of God?

APRIL 21

> I form light and create darkness; I make well-being and create calamity; I am the Lord, who does all these things. Isaiah 45:7

One of the things I love to do during the summer is to lay in my hammock and look at the stars at night. There is beauty in the night if we take the time to stop and look and appreciate it. Also, at night it is easier to sleep and rest. In June, parts of Alaska have very little to no darkness – can you imagine having nearly no night? They have to create it in their homes with room darkening curtains just to be able to sleep. There is a reason and a purpose for the day, a reason and a purpose for the night and its darkness. There are good times, but there is also a reason for the trouble. The best sailors, best pilots and best drivers are those that encountered bad times on the job and found a way to overcome them. Some of the best learning situations we as humans can learn from are the difficult times. God knows us and what we need. He created us with our strengths and our weaknesses. He knows what we need to be better, when we need to rest and enjoy and when we need to persevere. In my life, to deepen my relationship with the Holy Spirit, I have had to change my question from "Why God?" to "What God?" When we ask, "Why, God, am I going through this?" to be honest, we may not like the answer. Additionally, it doesn't show a deep appreciation for how powerful and all-knowing God is. God is not surprised by the trials we go through. He doesn't go to the kitchen for a snack and upon returning say, "Oh shoot, what did Joe get himself into now?" No, He knows ahead of time, like with Job. He didn't bring the trial, but He allowed the trial to occur. So, instead of "Why God," I now ask for guidance, "What do I need to learn from this? What am I supposed to take away from this? How can I be better on the other side of this trial?" Do you see a purpose in the night and in the day? Do you see the purpose in bad times as well as good times, or do you expect God to only allow blessings to come your way? Are you willing to change your questions from Why to What? Or better yet try asking How. How can I use this learning opportunity (trial) to be better? How can you change your outlook on the hills and valleys? How can you learn to appreciate the day times of life and the night times of life as well, to see God's purpose and God's hand in each and every situation?

APRIL 22

For God has not called us for impurity, but in holiness. 1 Thessalonians 4:7

I think in today's world, we have forgotten the definition of Holy and now more than ever, we should probably go back to it. Holy means dedicated or consecrated to God, set apart or sacred. I think we have all hung on that last part – sacred. God is sacred; Scripture is sacred. But here, Paul reminds us that God calls us to live Holy lives, lives dedicated and consecrated to God. Imagine what our communities would be like if Christians, just Christians, lived their lives fully dedicated to God. What would society look like if Christians were in the Holy Scriptures each day when they woke up? What if we prayed continually and always rejoiced, especially over the little blessings that most people overlook? What might change if when Christians interacted with others, their words and actions were dedicated to God? Notice that Paul does not call us to be perfect. He says God has not called us to be impure; he does not imply we are called to perfection. Impure means to contain foreign matter. We have to be without impurities, without morally wrong issues in our lives. What God calls sin we cannot permit. What breaks the heart of God we cannot bless. So, when we look at what Paul is calling us to do, it is not really impossible; living our lives dedicated to God, in the world but not influenced by the world nor controlled by its darkness. We should live lives set apart for God. We forget that God is the God of Joy and Laughter, not just valleys and worship songs. What changes do you have to make to live a Holy life, a life dedicated to God, set apart from the world we live in? How can you consecrate your life to God? How can you apply these words from Paul in your life to align with Scripture? How do you see yourself living a holy life? What impurities in your life and thoughts do you need to eliminate to live the holy life God has called you to live?

APRIL 23

> but in your hearts honor Christ the Lord as holy, always being prepared to make a defense to anyone who asks you for a reason for the hope that is in you; yet do it with gentleness and respect, 1 Peter 3:15

What in your life do you honor, regard with great respect? We hang pictures of loved ones in our living rooms or place them on coffee tables. Another definition of "honor" as a verb is "what you give special recognition to". We honor our favorite sports teams and athletes with our words, even with clothing. But in this verse, Peter calls us to honor Christ in our hearts as holy. So, when we speak His name, speak of Him, it is in an honorable way, with respectful tones. He is Holy; thus, we should honor Him with our words, actions and thoughts that maintain that holiness. Peter goes on to tell us that we are to be prepared to give a defense to anyone who asks us for the reason for the hope that we have. Our hope is in Jesus, thus this is the reason why we should honor Him in our words and deeds as Holy. When we give a defense for the reason of our hope, we do it with gentleness and respect. Telling people that God hates them, that God killed their loved ones, or that God despises them for the choices they made are neither loving, gentle, or respectful. This is the guidance within the first line of the verse: honor Jesus as holy in our hearts. If we tell people these lies about God, or that they need to change and get right with God before He will accept them, then none of us have a chance. God meets us where we are – Jesus healed and cleansed people where they were; all they had to do was come to Him with a surrendered heart. Would Jesus even be allowed in the church today, especially in America? Would we tell Him He had to clean up before coming into service? Would He be welcomed in, would people sit next to Him? Or do we see ourselves as the ones that are holy and righteous and not Jesus Christ Himself, the holy and righteous Son of God? I think we all should take a pause and examine our hearts and be honest with ourselves, especially with how we view others. Do we view them through the loving eyes of the Holy Spirit living in us, or do we view them through selfish lenses of pride and arrogance? Do we privately think, "I am better than them because, fill in the blank… ? How can you internalize this Scripture to keep a proper view of ourselves, Jesus and others? How do you honor Jesus in word, deed and in your heart? How will you give a defense to anyone who asks you for the reason for the hope that you have? How do you give a defense for your hope with gentleness and respect?

APRIL 24

> Search me, O God and know my heart! Try me and know my thoughts! And see if there is any grievous way in me and lead me in the way everlasting! Psalm 139:23-24

For the most part, people want to lead and make their own decisions, especially when it comes to life. People want to decide what to do with their lives and where to go. But in Psalm 139, David says, "Lead me. Lead me in ways everlasting!" But before David asks God to lead Him, he asks God to search his heart, to search his mind; that way, David could get rid of any sin issues, anything grievous, before allowing God to lead Him. When was the last time you asked God to search your thoughts and reveal anything that would grieve Him? Are you brave enough to ask God to do that and courageous enough to hear His answer? What about God searching your heart? What would He find? What does your heart long for before Him or more than Him? We ask Him into our hearts, but then relegate Him to the back corner so He doesn't take up too much room. We want Him to take up residence in our hearts, but we also want Him to leave room for what we desire. Do you really want God to do something in your life, to use you to build up His Heavenly Kingdom? Start by asking Him to search your heart and your thoughts. Ask Him to reveal anything that is grievous and breaks His heart. Align your thought life and your heart life with Him, His Word and allow the Holy Spirit to lead you. He took 11 ordinary men and turned the world upside down; He is wanting to turn your world upside down as well. Will you let Him? This can be such a powerful prayer. I dare you to pray this prayer. Earnestly say this prayer, but only if you want God to move in your life. What is that God wants to reveal to you or show you about yourself? What upside-down path does God want to take you down? How do you respond to God when He reveals grievous ways and sinful desires in your life? How can you be willing for them to be revealed and how will you allow God to help you defeat them?

APRIL 25

> Sow for yourselves righteousness; reap steadfast love; break up your fallow ground, for it is the time to seek the Lord, that he may come and rain righteousness upon you. Hosea 10:12

Living in an agricultural area, reaping, sowing and harvesting are common ideals. We have all heard the saying "You reap what you sow". If you sow corn seeds, you don't expect to harvest or reap wheat or carrots. What you sow or plant is what you reap or harvest. The prophet Hosea reminds us here to sow righteousness, not our own, but the righteousness of God; from that, we will reap the harvest of steadfast love. Steadfast love is love that never ends, a love that preserves through trials and hardships, a love that does not grow weak or weary, but remains sturdy and firm. Hosea was reminding the Israelites and now us, that now is the time to seek the Lord and break up the fallow ground of our hearts. Fallow ground is a farm reference for land that was purposely left untilled or sowed, allowing the soil to recover from a farming cycle and replenish its nutrients. Israel had removed God from their hearts long enough; it was time to plant the Word of God back in their heart. The same is true for America. God has been removed from the hearts of its leaders, judges, teachers, other professionals and families long enough. It is time. The soil of our hearts are ready to be dug up, trenched, weeded and have the Word of God planted in our hearts. It's time for America to sow the righteousness of God into the lives and hearts of our leaders, pastors, teachers and lawmakers. It's time for the steadfast love of God to be blooming in our hearts and souls. Our hearts are thirsty for His righteousness; it's time to let His righteousness rain and reign in our hearts again. How does your heart respond to this Scripture? What is God calling you to do to sow His Word in your Heart? What are you sowing in your professional life? What are you sowing outside of church services? How can you sow the Word of God in all aspects of your life?

APRIL 26

in whom are hidden all the treasures of wisdom and knowledge.
Colossians 2:3

There have been many great movies about looking for hidden treasure. Goonies, National Treasure and all of the Indiana Jones movies (except 3). In real life, Forrest Fenn a millionaire set up a real treasure that was recently found. Unfortunately, several people lost their lives looking for that treasure. God, though, has the treasures that really matter. Paul writes to the church at Colossi that in Christ rests all the treasures of wisdom and knowledge. These are the true treasures of Heaven that should be sought after in this world. When he was being made king, Solomon was asked what he wanted by God and God said, "Because of your father, I will grant you anything you ask." Did Solomon ask for power? No. Did Solomon ask for wisdom? Not exactly. Solomon asked for wisdom and knowledge to lead God's people according to God's Will. Because Solomon asked for wisdom, God blessed him in all other areas of his leadership and life as well. Solomon has been recorded in both secular and Biblical history as one of the wisest and wealthiest rulers to ever live. Wisdom and knowledge, especially God's wisdom and knowledge, can help us navigate the twist and turns that life throws our way and successfully determine what detours are from above and which ones are from the world. Wisdom and knowledge bring us closer to Him and instruct us on how to live Godly lives, forgiving, loving, compassionate, merciful, grace extending lives. Wisdom and knowledge for us come from a close relationship with the Holy Spirit. It comes from seeking His guidance, His direction and His instructions. Are our prayers more aligned to the world and what the world would ask for or are they aligned with Solomon's? Do we ask God to, "Grant me and fill me with your wisdom and knowledge" or do we still seek financial freedom and healing? If God spoke to you tonight and said He would grant you one thing, what would you ask for? Would it be God-driven or self-driven? How can you change your prayer life to be more aligned with Solomon's request and Paul's insight? How would seeking wisdom and knowledge above all change your relationship with God?

APRIL 27

Open my eyes, that I may behold wondrous things out of your law.
Psalm 119:18

Why is it that we think of instruction as bad? I think humans have this innate inner feeling that "I don't need instructions; I will figure it out on my own if I want to do it". At least for men, that is, right? We so often disregard the instructions that come in the box and refuse to listen to GPS or our navigator in the car. But seriously, David's prayer here needs to be our prayer today as well – "Lord, open my eyes to see the wonderful truths in your instructions." Religious people tend to see God's instructions as restrictive and joy killing, no-fun-allowed. But God has a sense of humor. He used a talking donkey to stop a prophet. He created the duckbilled platypus that scientists today cannot even figure out; it defies all logic and science. There is joy in his instruction and protection. God does not say, "Thou Shalt Not Have Fun!" God says, "Don't covet your neighbor's belongings, be joyful and thankful for what you have. Don't covet your neighbor's wife – there is a spiritual connection between sex and marriage, a unity that scientists cannot explain, but I know, I created you. Don't be driven by greed or lust; they will only leave you empty and wanting more – be driven by Me, by my Holy Spirit and as I take care of the birds of the air and the lilies of the field, I will take care of you." Love can be found in the truths of His instruction. How many marriages have been destroyed because of coveting another? How many families have been ripped apart? How many dads are not there for their spouse or kids because they work "to get ahead" instead of work to live? Don't think of God's rules as Him not wanting us to enjoy life. It is more like when our parents said, "Look both ways before crossing the street." It's not that they didn't want us to run and have fun, but rather to keep us safe. Find joy in God's truths and instructions. Look to see how you can live a fuller life. How do you view God's laws? Do you see them as restrictive or directive? How can you change your view of God and His instructions so you see the blessings and protections He has and not the killjoy the enemy is portraying them to be? How can this verse amplify your prayer life and relationship with the Holy Spirit?

APRIL 28

Light is sown for the righteous and joy for the upright in heart. Psalm 97:11

When you walk with God, you are set apart. For one, the world wants nothing to do with you and two, God is close to those who call on and draw near to Him. When you have God's Presence in your heart and in your life, you tend to see the world differently and in doing so, respond differently than those who don't walk with God. We can see things differently because His light is shining on us. When God is close to us, His light shines on us and within us. Because He is close to us, when we face trials or difficulties, we deal with them differently than those who walk without God. For example, God allowed difficulties to come to Job and having walked with God, Job responded in faith despite his suffering. In our marriage and life, Kanda and I have faced some difficult times and challenging trials in that we could have questioned or gotten mad at God, but because we walk with Him daily, His joy supersedes the trial and gives us Godly comfort. When your heart is right and trials and difficulties come your way, you can respond in kind instead of react; there is a joy and a peace that surpasses all understanding that allows you to walk through the trials and see and feel God's presence with you in it all. I am not saying that it was easy, but because we had God's light and joy and Holy Presence guiding us, we were able to go through relational trials and come out better instead of bitter. Had we not been walking with God and had His joy and peace in our lives prior to trials, who knows how or if we would have come out on the other side? That is why we need His light and joy every day, including on the mountaintops when life is going good, so we already have that relationship strong when trials come our way. Walk with Him now so that when the world tries to come in you already have light and joy to counteract it. Is your heart right with God? Is He your light in the darkness? How is your walk with Jesus – do you know of him or truly KNOW HIM? Is he a panic, 911 call or peace in the storm? How do you experience the joy of the Lord? What was the last trial you went through where you felt God's presence and control over the situation? How can you make a spiritual altar to remember how He worked in you and through you during that trial?

APRIL 29

> For the word of the LORD is upright and all his work is done in faithfulness. He loves righteousness and justice; the earth is full of the steadfast love of the LORD. Psalm 33:4-5

What in our world is completely pure? We might think of 24 carat gold, with no impurities in it. What else is pure? What is upright? Completely upright? Completely true? The only thing in this world is the Word of God. It is the only thing that is completely true, upright and unchanging. First, we have to accept that the only source of Truth is God, the Bible and it is the only thing unchanging; but when we do fully believe in the Bible as Truth, we know that He is faithful to follow through on all His promises. God is Love. God is righteousness. God is justice. FDR (Franklin D. Roosevelt) wisely said, "What do we have to fear but fear itself? What do we have to fear? Nothing! Fear is a tool of the enemy." God's love fills every corner of the Earth; it surrounds us and the Holy Spirit fills us with His love. When we allow Him to work in us we allow Him to be our guide, our protector. What do we have to do to receive His steadfast love? Accept it! Jesus told us in John 3:16, "God so loved the world that he sent His one and only Son that whoever believes in Him should not perish but have eternal life." His Word is true and upright! He is faithful to complete the work He has started in the world, in us! So that brings us back to the first part of this Scripture – the Word of the Lord is upright. What view of the Word of God do you hold onto? Do you view the Word of God as true and upright – applicable in your life here in the 21st century? Do you read, study, pray and apply His Word in your daily life? He loves righteousness and justice, but we cannot have a part of that separate from His Word. How can you take a more personal view of His Word? Are you willing to RAP His Word – Read His Word, Apply His Word and Pray His Word? What changes are you willing to commit to regarding His Word? How can you make RAP a priority in your life? He loves righteousness and justice; how can you make these values a priority in your life? How have you experienced His faithfulness in your life?

APRIL 30

The Lord is my shepherd; I shall not want. Psalm 23:1

Everyone has wants – some are realistic and some are unrealistic. So many people desire to win the lottery and hit the mega jackpot, but it is very unlikely. Most people want a new(er) car, more in the range of possibility. Having wants and being in want, however, are two different things. David, in this famous song, psalm, starts with "The Lord is my Shepherd; I shall not want." David had a Biblical view, a correct view of God and his relationship with Him. David saw God as the Good Shepherd that would provide everything His flock needed: food, water, shelter and protection. Knowing that God was right there with him, he would not have a want. The closer our daily walk with God becomes, the less want we have in our lives. He will meet our needs and when we daily walk with the shepherd, His presence erases any worldly wants we may have. Although our soul thirsts for time with the Shepherd, we tend to try to satisfy that thirst with worldly desires and things. We allow the enemy to distract us with that thirst and then we chase after shiny objects that we think will make us happy or fulfilled only to find that same emptiness or thirst that we had before we got distracted. Just one to three hours a week with the Shepherd doesn't satisfy that thirst. It is daily, allowing Him to shepherd us and guide us with His staff and His voice. Remember that the shepherd provides what we need: protection, sustenance and water – when we leave His side, we leave what He provides behind. Is the Lord your Good Shepherd? Do you have wants outside of His will for your life? What can you do to eliminate those wants and focus more on the provider, the Shepherd? How can you change your desires to want what the Holy Spirit wants for you? What is He calling you to choose not to desire or want in your life?

MAY 1

> He who did not spare his own Son but gave him up for us all, how will he not also with him graciously give us all things? Romans 8:32

How much does God love you? I mean, really love you? God loves you so much that He sent His Son to die for your sins so that you could be in a relationship with Him. Remember Abraham and Isaac? God called Abraham, whom He promised would have more offspring than the stars in the sky. He then called Abraham to sacrifice his only son, but when Abraham was faithful, God provided a substitute, a ram. God gave us His son Jesus to take our place and die to sin. If He loves you that much and gave up that much for you, will He not graciously give you the things that you need? He doesn't promise to give us everything we want. The things we want tend to become barriers that push God out of our hearts and take up residence there. He will not give us things that we would make an idol above Him or appreciate more than our relationship with Him. However, He will graciously give us what we need, to do what God has called us to do. His grace supplies us so that we have what we need when we are called into action. His Holy Spirit is living in us to guide us, direct us and help us. He gave us the Holy Spirit to help us in all things, make all decisions and in all circumstances. All we have to do is walk with Him and be open to His guidance. So, He won't give us everything we want, but He will give us everything we need and really, all we need is Him. Do you believe that – all you really need is Him? In America, it's easier to say than to actually live out, but in third world countries and in countries where Christians are being killed and martyred, He really is all they need. How can you make changes in your life so that He is all that you need? How can you fully rely on God? How can you be satisfied with what God provides and gives you? How can you change your desires to desire Him above all?

MAY 2

> Therefore, as you received Christ Jesus the Lord, so walk in him,
> Colossians 2:6

What do you do when you receive a gift? Leave it in the box or use it? I remember one birthday we got our oldest son a walking, roaring dinosaur. We put it in a big box filled with balloons. The dinosaur never got played with; he, his sister, brother and friends had more fun playing in the box and balloons. What do you do with the gift of life that Christ gave you? Another translation of this verse says you must continue to follow Him. Do you walk in Him or is He a piece of jewelry around your neck? Do you continue to follow Him or is He a weekend guest with maybe a visit during the week? When the first church received the Holy Spirit in them they were changed and they told everyone about Him and what Jesus did for us. Even today, when I am with someone and they encounter the living God, Jesus Christ and ask the Holy Spirit into their heart, they are changed. Unfortunately, with the busyness of life and the distractions of technology, we don't tend to walk with Him. Once He saves us from death, we are to walk with Him and allow the Holy Spirit to guide us, direct us and even discipline us. We must walk with Him. He doesn't save us from sin and death so we can continue to live the way we were, in darkness and sin. He saved us from sin and death so that we can walk freely on this side of eternity as well. How is your daily walk with Him? Do you feel compelled to walk with Him? I feel compelled not in the sense that I have to do it but that I want to; I long to. Like when you first started dating and are in love and you can't wait to see them again, you just have to see them. That should be the same feeling we have every morning, day and night, that we just have to have time with Him. On a scale of one to ten, how would you rate your desire to walk with Him daily? How can you increase that desire? What are you willing to do to make Him more of a priority in your life?

MAY 3

> But Caleb quieted the people before Moses and said, "Let us go up at once and occupy it, for we are well able to overcome it." Numbers 13:30

We may think that "we know more than God" is a new, twenty-first-century backslide of believers, but Israel was that way in the desert. They had reached the Promised Land. They were poised to walk in and take it. Moses sends in one man from each tribe. The single cluster of grapes was so big that when they cut it off the vine, it had to be carried between two poles by two men. What's the problem then? The current inhabitants were taller than the Israelites. Ten men said that the inhabitants would kill them, squash them. Joshua and Caleb believed in the Word of the Lord and that if the Lord promised this land to them, then the Lord would take care of the giants in the land. Caleb believed and said why waste any more time? Let us go and occupy it. We can overcome any obstacle because God is with us. Ten were afraid and didn't believe God; they believed they knew more than God did and that these giants would kill them. Even though God parted the Red Sea and annihilated the Egyptian Army, led them by a pillar of fire by night and smoke by day and provided manna, water and pheasants, after all of that, would God just let them be squashed like a grape? What giants do you face in your life? Health, money, career, self-talk? Your past, your sin, your emotions? God is bigger than any giant. If God promised you something, He is faithful to see it through to fruition. While the giants may be there, who do you place your trust in, you or God? The ten men trusted themselves more than they trusted God. They didn't believe God, do you? Who is bigger, giants or God? What giant have you allowed to stop you from God's blessing? What can you do to take hold of the blessings God wants to give you?

MAY 4

God blesses those whose hearts are pure, for they will see God.
Proverbs 20:7

To be "pure" means to not be mixed or adulterated with any other substance or material, free from contamination and without extraneous or unnecessary elements, as defined by dictionary.com and other online references. What a word picture here that Solomon draws for us. If we have a pure heart, a heart for God that is not mixed with selfish ambitions, greed, pride, lust for wealth, fame, or materialistic life, just a heart set on God, it is then and only then that we can see God. We see God in the midst of trial and suffering, in the midst of joy and success and we see God amid rest. When we set our hearts on God's way and get rid of the extraneous and unnecessary things in our hearts, minds and lives, we truly can see God in every aspect of our lives. If you feel distant from God or haven't been able to see Him work in your life lately, is it a heart issue? Do you have a pure heart, seeking after God and His wisdom, or are the crosshairs of your heart focused on worldly gain or recognition? Job had a pure heart and when Satan took everything away, Job was still able to praise God. If the same thing happened to us today, would we worship or complain? Would we pray like Job, "God gives and God takes away"? Are we able to claim, "God is Good all the time, all the time God is good", regardless of the circumstances we are experiencing? How you define blessings will determine how you respond. If you define blessings as stuff, wealth, or even family, you will not be able to live out this verse during trials. But when you see God bless those hearts that are pure as more than what you can see and touch, then you will be able to say regardless, "God is good all the time, all the time God is good". If you want to see God, start looking with your heart, not your eyes. What matters most to you – comfortable living or a deep relationship with God? How do you define blessings? How can you clean up your heart so that you have a pure heart? What elements, materials, or contamination do you need to let God cleanse from your heart so that you can see God more clearly today? How can you protect your heart from being contaminated with pride or selfishness? How can you remember this verse when you experience pain?

MAY 5

> And it is my prayer that your love may abound more and more, with knowledge and all discernment, so that you may approve what is excellent and so be pure and blameless for the day of Christ, filled with the fruit of righteousness that comes through Jesus Christ, to the glory and praise of God. Philippians 1:9-11

Notice that when we do life on our terms, our way, it tends to get messy and more difficult. OK, let me rephrase that, not just "tends to," rather it *does* get messier. Paul starts this section of verses by saying he prays that our love would "abound more and more with knowledge and discernment". Why would love need to abound with anything? Shouldn't it just abound? When we let love loose to run wild with no parameters, we get the kind of society that we currently live in. Political correctness says, "You have to love my sin and let me sin or you don't really love". But notice Paul says that he prays our love will abound with knowledge and discernment – why? So that we may approve only what is excellent, approve only what comes from God. Love will call what is righteousness "good", but love will also call sin "bad," call it for what it is. Godly love cannot love sin, nor will it call sin "good" or "natural." Notice Paul doesn't say "judge" here; he says "discernment", but discernment *in love*. So many denominations have changed the Word of God to fit into the world, thus allowing culture to cancel God's true, real love. We must let love abound in us more and more through being immersed in the knowledge of God, discerning God's Word daily so that we may be seen pure and blameless on the day of His return. Discernment comes from allowing the Holy Spirit to clarify and make clear how to apply His Word in our lives. My heart breaks for pastors who have led flocks astray, being aligned with the world and not the Word. Allowing God's love to abound in us more and more in the knowledge and discernment fills us with the fruit of righteousness. Righteousness does not come through our works, deeds, power, or strength; righteousness only comes from Jesus Christ and the Holy Spirit living in us. Righteousness points back to God so that He can get the glory. He can receive praise because He is the one that deserves it. It's easy to love the sinner and hate the sin when it's a sin issue we can relate with or have participated in. It tends to be harder not to judge on those hot topic sins that we can't relate to, but we are still called to allow love to abound in us more and more. Remember John 3:17, "For God did not send his Son into the world to condemn the world, but in order that the world might be saved through him." How do you see God's love abounding in you? How can you allow that to happen more? How do you increase your discernment?

MAY 6

> if my people who are called by my name humble themselves and pray and seek my face and turn from their wicked ways, then I will hear from heaven and will forgive their sin and heal their land. 2 Chronicles 7:14

What does God want from us above all else? It's not our tithe or our money. It is not mission trips or playing bigger, better worship sets. Our Father wants our hearts. He wants us to be humble and pray. If we seek Him first, we cannot continue in wickedness and sin when we do. God calls us to be humble. He doesn't want us to just go through the motions and only be a Christian on Sunday mornings or Saturday evenings. Time and time again in Scripture, we see God calling His people back to Him. When He does, He doesn't say, "When they start sacrificing or when they start worshiping, then I will forgive their sins and restore their land". No, reconciliation comes when they humble themselves, recognize their sin and seek Him first. Pride leads to destruction and is the sin that causes all sin – it is the sin that led Adam and Eve out of the garden. Humble yourself. Know that God really knows better than you; He is Holy, we are not. Pray continuously – speak to Him. But a common misunderstanding among Christians is that prayer involves us doing the speaking. Part of a healthy prayer life is allowing Him to speak to us. Give God talk-time by quieting your mind and soul, so He, in a still small voice, can speak directly to you. Seek Him and turn away from sin; seek Him and ask for forgiveness and God will hear you and forgive. But we must choose to seek Him! Seek His presence! Seek His guidance! Seek His peace! Seek His knowledge! Seek His love and forgiveness. When you let Him have your heart, everything else falls into place. When He has your heart, you automatically have a desire to worship. When He has your heart, you develop a desire to give. When He has your heart, you have the desire to serve. See, when He has your heart and you are in communion with Him, you see what He has done for you and the overwhelming joy that comes from that can't be contained. Then you must share the joy of your salvation with others. This morning, does He have your heart or your calendar? Does He have your heart or just your mind? Let Him heal you – your heart, your soul, your hurt. How can you humble yourself today to seek Him more? How are you humble before God? How does being humble affect the way you treat others?

MAY 7

> And we know that for those who love God all things work together for good, for those who are called according to his purpose. Romans 8:28

What is good? Who defines good? What distinguishes between good and bad? For it to be truly good, there can be only one true, one guiding factor, one example in which there can be no variance. Today's verse is often misquoted and misapplied. "And we know that for those who love God all things work together for good." God is the source of good. Many times, people will ask, what good comes from a dying child? I don't know, I am not God and neither are you. But from my heart, I feel that if someone draws closer to God for comfort through the loss of a child, that is good. An important misbelief that we have to separate out is the idea that God imposes these things. People in trauma often say, "God caused my loved one to die" or "God allowed my child to be abused." Two important facts to remember are that God does not do evil things like sexually abusing, raping, or killing people, nor does the verse say this. It does not say God does all things so they will work for good; it says God works all things for our good. He can use bad circumstances, as well as good events, for His purpose in our lives. Maybe we are so entrenched in sin that we don't even see it as sin anymore, so that when something happens like a job loss or a relationship loss, we finally realize we've walked away from God. He has open arms to welcome us back or greet us for the first time. I know for me, there is a lot I will not know on this side of Heaven, but I trust God because of His faithfulness and unchanging character. I love God. I desire God and a deeper relationship with Him, so whatever the world throws my way, I know God can use it for good if I continue to trust Him and allow Him to lead me. Remember that this verse says God works all things together for good. He can make something good come from anything. He can turn a curse into a blessing, a trial into a triumph. If we truly trust God and love Him above His ability to answer prayer, then we can hold onto the fact that He can work anything, good or bad, for good. He can make something good come from it. When you encounter a difficult Scripture, do you skip it or pray for discernment and understanding of it? How can you look at this Scripture and apply it in your life today to help you draw closer to God and deepen your trust in Him? How has God made a trial into a triumph in your life?

MAY 8

> The LORD is my light and my salvation; whom shall I fear? The LORD is the stronghold of my life; of whom shall I be afraid? Psalm 27:1

Who scares you? Some say liberals; some say conservatives. Outside of politics, who scares you? David wrote that he should not fear anyone. The Lord is my light and my salvation. Light dispels darkness and darkness is where fear resides and crawls out of. When we have light, we can walk confidently through life. Light gives us the ability to recognize unlevel ground, bumps, holes, curves in the road, inclines and slopes. What shall we fear when we have His light in us and shining before us? Whom shall we fear? Who is in control? The God I serve I know is still in control and while evil may be having a field day on Earth right now, there will come a time when that field day is over. The bell will ring, the horn will blow and God in His Holiness will bring an end to evil. We have to be patient for that day, though and keep moving forward. We need to hand over control to Him and allow Him to have the stronghold on our life; not addiction, not desires, not sin, not history and not generational traditions. God must have the stronghold in our life and when we give it to Him, He promises never to let us be tempted beyond our ability to walk away. He will always provide that secure path to walk away. If we try to do it on our own accord, we fail more than we succeed. We must trust in Him and allow His strong hand to protect and guide us. Who should you really be afraid of with the Holy Spirit living in you and guiding you? If you know who holds your future and what your future eternity holds, then nothing, no giant, can stand in your way. Fear flees like the coward it is. Fear actually has no power until we give it power. When we refuse to empower it, fear can do nothing; it cannot continue to stand, so it runs away. How can you plant this Scripture in your heart so that when fear creeps out of the shadows, you can cause it to flee and refuse to empower it? How can you make the Holy Spirit an actual stronghold in your life? How can you rely on the Holy Spirit more?

MAY 9

> "Blessed is the man who trusts in the Lord, whose trust is the Lord. He is like a tree planted by water, that sends out its roots by the stream and does not fear when heat comes, for its leaves remain green and it is not anxious in the year of drought, for it does not cease to bear fruit." Jeremiah 17:7-8

What do you trust? The weather? Not likely. Your accountant or bank? Probably. But here, Jeremiah reminds us that we are blessed when we put our trust in the Lord. He goes on to say even more when the Lord *is our trust*. The illustration is of a tree planted by a river. It doesn't fear the heat because the water is flowing nearby and during those rough trials, like a drought, it doesn't become anxious because the water will return. It continues to grow and produce fruit because where the confidence is, the trust is. What is your trust in? Your 401K? During the last recession, there was a huge increase in suicides among financial planners and brokers after having lost millions of dollars. Their trust was in the stock market and their ability to make trades and increase wealth for themselves and their clients. When the carpet was pulled out from underneath them, they had no solid foundation and in desperation they saw no way out. But when your trust is in the Lord, when life is good, you are growing, maturing and producing fruit. When the trials come, the droughts come and you are growing, maturing and producing fruit. Why is there no change? When your foundation is rock solid, you can rest in the truth that God promises to "never leave us nor forsake us"; we can continue to grow, mature and produce fruit because our trust is in the Lord. When we listen to the Holy Spirit living in us and not the fear and desperation that the world is shouting, we know the water will return and the river will flow again. We must patiently wait out the drought, not standing still and cowering in a cave, but by growing, maturing and continuing to produce fruit. How can we deepen our trust in God so that when trials, or droughts, come our way, the fruit of the spirit living in us continues to be produced as we continue to grow and mature? How can you allow the Holy Spirit to refresh you when you feel parched? How can you allow the Holy Spirit to remove anxieties from you?

MAY 10

> For the kingdom of God is not a matter of eating and drinking but of righteousness and peace and joy in the Holy Spirit. Romans 14:17

I have a really good friend who is diabetic, so that means that he, of course, cannot eat sugar. When he is around others that eat sugar, he has learned not to be tempted and when they invite us over for a meal, they still serve a dessert. Some people are not as strong as my friend and can be tempted into consuming what they should not consume. The Bible does not say that drinking alcohol is a sin, but this verse here in Romans calls us to be careful. Let me explain. It is not drinking alcohol or avoiding alcohol that brings righteousness and peace. I have another really good friend that is an alcoholic. He is recovering, but still an alcoholic. If I truly love God and the Holy Spirit is living in me, I would never think of consuming alcohol in his presence. Our actions as Christians should not lead others into temptation, sin, or questioning our faith or theirs. When we show love for those who struggle with food, bless the heart of God and stand out as firm in faith and relationship with God, led by the Holy Spirit. To deprive yourself of something you may like to support a fellow believer is a selfless act that Christians should be doing if they claim to imitate Christ. My oldest son's best friend is a Messianic Jew. Ethnically he is of Jewish heritage, believes Jesus is the Messiah spoken of in the Old Testament, reads and believes in the New Testament, but follows Jewish dietary law. When we order pizza, we order cheese or any non-pork topping pizza for him. When we love others with a sacrificial love, even with something as minor as what we eat or drink, we acknowledge that spiritual appetites are more important than bodily appetites. How aware are you of your fellow believers with their struggles? Have you ever considered text like this in Scripture in today's world and how it applies to you? How can you apply this in your life today? How can you help the Kingdom of God here on Earth? How can you help others experience the Kingdom of God in their life? What are you willing to do to love others sacrificially?

MAY 11

> In my desperation I prayed and the LORD listened; he saved me from all my troubles. Psalm 34:6 NLT

When you are desperate, what do you do? What is your go to when you reach your limit? Is it God? The Holy Spirit? God loves us so much that it amazes me some days. Yes, we are called daily to walk with Him, be in communion with Him and praise Him. But as humans we mess up and some days are so full of our own plans that we can easily forget to reconnect because we get too busy for God. Then we do something and realize we are in trouble and throw up a Hail Mary prayer – the clock has hit zero at the last minute with the ball still in the air – a "God Help Me" prayer! David, in desperation and being run out of his home by his son, threw up a Hail Mary prayer. The Lord listened to him and the Lord saved David. Would the Lord prefer that we spend time with Him on a daily basis and thus not get into desperate situations? Yes, absolutely! But He loves us so much that He will always be there for us. In good times and in bad times, He is there for you. He will save you from your troubles. Now that doesn't mean He will keep you from the consequences of your decisions. David made choices and, ultimately, he lost some of his sons due to his decisions. God saved David but still let consequences discipline him. It does not matter how long ago you turned to God, nor how long ago you turned away from God. He wants to be there for you. Has it been a while since you poured your heart out to God? Do you feel like God won't help you because of your decisions? Turn to Him, even desperate, Hail Mary prayers He hears. He would rather those than nothing at all. It is time to turn your heart back to God if you have wandered. What do you need to do to hand it over to Him today? What can you do to make God your first choice and not your last choice when you get into desperate situations? When has God answered one of your Hail Mary prayers?

MAY 12

> And above all these put on love, which binds everything together in perfect harmony. Colossians 3:14

Many people utilize their clothing to define and show who they are. Closets keep getting bigger and fashion shows keep becoming more successful, even to the point of reality TV competitions. What do your clothes say about you? People who know me, know me by my Hawaiian shirts. I wear them because they keep me cool. But here, Paul tells us to clothe ourselves with love. Wrap ourselves up in love, because that is how people will know us in our faith. People know me by my Hawaiian shirts; do they also know me by my love? Love, *Agape* love, God's Love binds us all together? I pray they do. Paul goes further to say that His love binds us "in perfect harmony" if we simply walk daily in love, clothing ourselves in love. What would it look like on a daily basis if, as Christians, we clothed ourselves in God's *Agape* Love? We would look at others past their pain, past their hurt, past their sinful pasts and see them as God sees them. We would be less quick to be angered and less quick to be jealous. If we clothed ourselves in love, we would be more grateful and more helpful. If we clothed ourselves in love, we would be more giving, both to the church and to those in need. Being clothed in love changes our vision and we see others' needs before our own wants. What are you clothed in? Are you clothed in Love? Are you clothed in Selfishness? Greed? Jealousy? What do you have to take off in order to put on and be clothed in *Agape*? What can you do today to clothe yourself in God's love? How can you change your vision, how you see, to see others' needs as more of a priority than your wants? How can you allow being clothed in unconditional love to change how giving you are? Where are you willing to serve so that others see your *agape* clothing line?

MAY 13

> "Judge not and you will not be judged; condemn not and you will not be condemned; forgive and you will be forgiven; Luke 6:37

Here, Jesus tells us that God wants us to forgive as God forgave us through Christ. We need to not judge and not condemn others unless we want the same treatment from God. How many of us have said, "I'll do it, but I'm not happy about it!"? And when we do it, we make sure to let everyone know we are not happy about doing it. Christianity has gone from a loving and serving relationship with God to, here in America and even Europe, a standard by which we compare and judge others. Our anger rises when someone sits in "our" seat; we judge others when they arrive in clothing, we deem inappropriate for God's house. Instead, we should be excited that someone new is here at church, to receive the love of Jesus and hear of His forgiveness. We hush the Holy Spirit and give the megaphone to the enemy in our hearts and minds. In order to be forgiving of one another, we need to be kind to one another; we need to be tenderhearted towards one another. These are not individual emotions or actions. No, faith, forgiveness and tenderheartedness are so interwoven that you can literally not do one without doing the others. If you are truly forgiving like God forgives us, choosing not to remember the hurt, then we are kind to those people, gentle and caring. When we have the attitude, "I'll forgive them because I have to", then we are not living out Scripture and are definitely not acting like God forgiving us. He does not have to forgive us. His Holiness keeps us separated from Him because of our sins. But because God is a God of love and God loves us, He sent Jesus to take on all of our sins so we would no longer be separated from Him. In love, He is kind and tenderhearted towards us, forgiving us. So, is our heart centered on God? Are we kind and tenderhearted to those who hurt or anger us or wrong us? Do we forgive because we have to or because so much of the Holy Spirit is rushing through our veins and being that kindness, tenderheartedness and forgiveness become second nature to us? What do you need to encompass and ingrain in your heart today to obey God's words?

MAY 14

> If we confess our sins, he is faithful and just to forgive us our sins and to cleanse us from all unrighteousness. 1 John 1:9

What can you actually count on? Ben Franklin said death and taxes are the only two certainties in life. Nonetheless, John reminds us here that God is faithful to forgive us when we confess our sins. He is just and keeps His word. Notice the unequivocal IF at the beginning of the sentence. If we confess, He is faithful and just to not only forgive us of our sins, but also to cleanse us from all unrighteousness. However, we must confess first and when we confess it should not be like Madonna's character in *A League of Their Own* where she goes to confession, not to be cleansed from unrighteousness, but to clear the slate so she can go out and sin again. The blood of Christ is not permission to keep sinning. In this first letter from John in Chapter 3, he addresses this issue further. If you are born of the Spirit, born of God, you do not desire to keep on sinning. John says if you desire to keep on sinning, He is not in you and you do not know Him. This is not a call to perfection as some would see it, but acknowledging the difference between our sinful nature and falling short again versus the desire to keep on sinning because Jesus' blood cleanses us from that sin. Paul also addresses this issue in Romans 6:1-2. "What shall we say then? Are we to continue in sin that grace may abound? By no means!" We should not take advantage of the love, grace and mercy that God extends to us through the forgiveness of our sins. Nor should we judge those when they fall. Rather we should come alongside them, help them up and inspire them to return to or introduce them to Jesus Christ. Are you consistent when you sin to ask for forgiveness, or has it become so routine that you forget about it, knowing that your sins are forgiven? I mean, God already knows, right? "If we confess, He is faithful and just to forgive." Every day we fail and sin. Do you confess every day and ask for forgiveness? Inscribe this on your heart and live it out starting today. Where have you fallen short, failed and sinned that you need to seek God and confess it to Him? How do you experience His forgiveness? What spiritual barriers can you create to prevent the same temptation from drawing you away from Him?

MAY 15

"Before I formed you in the womb I knew you and before you were born I consecrated you; I appointed you a prophet to the nations."
Jeremiah 1:5

Does Scripture apply to me, 2,000, 5,000, or even 10,000 years after it was written? I believe so. It is not just a history book. Do you believe the Bible? I believe in Scripture, I believe God. While God was speaking to Jeremiah here about being a prophet, I believe it still applies to us today as there are other scriptures that support it. Before we are formed in our mother's womb, we are known by God. Before we are formed in our mother's womb, God has a purpose for us. When God forms us in the womb, we are created on purpose, for a purpose and with a purpose. Every human ever conceived, formed in the womb by our Father God, is created for, with and on purpose. That is why every life is so valuable and we tend to take it for granted or forget how unique and special it is. Every child formed in the womb is a miracle of God. No matter how that child was conceived, he or she is still a miracle. So, no matter what trials you may face, God created you on purpose. No matter the failed relationships or job loss you face, you were created for a purpose. When the world comes in and beats you down, remember you were created with a purpose. No matter how many mistakes you make, failures you incur, or hard times that you face, your loving Father in Heaven wants to remind you – that you were created on purpose, for a purpose and with a purpose. How do you view yourself — through the lens of the world or through the eyes of God? Maybe it's time to take the lenses off and view yourself through the eyes of God and while you're at it take the time to see others through the eyes of God, too. When you look at yourself through the eyes of God, what do you see? What purpose were you created for? How does knowing you were created on purpose change your self-outlook? How can you accomplish this change of perspective today to see yourself and others through the eyes of God?

MAY 16

> For the kingdom of God does not consist in talk but in power. 1 Corinthians 4:20

Some people really like to talk. Many Christians today are Christians in word alone, title alone. Paul tells us that for the Kingdom of God consists not in talk but in power. The New Living Translation says but in living by God's Power. What does God's power do? It isn't satisfied with just Sunday worship and maybe a Bible study. The power that created the universe is not meant to be contained, but shared and spread. Fr. Scholtes' song, "They'll Know We Are Christians," reveals this truth. While inspired by John 13:35, "By this all people will know that you are my disciples, if you have love for one another," the verse speaks to this call of Paul's for us to demonstrate *agape*. Being one in the spirit and one in love is power, the power to work and change lives. "We will work with each other and we will work side by side" shows that the Gospel, the Kingdom of God, is not just to be talked about, discussed and debated, but also lived out in the power of the Holy Spirit living within us. What good would it be to go to medical school and become the best cancer-curing doctor, only to write books about cancer and go on a speaking tour about healing cancer? How much more is this analogy true in relation to knowledge of the Kingdom of God, the Messiah Jesus Christ rising from the dead on the third day and the Holy Spirit's desire to teach, lead, comfort and console us? Yes, Sunday worship and fellowship with other believers is important. Men's, women's and couples' Bible studies are important to be fed spiritually and to gain a better understanding, but we must not stop there. We must work in the power of being aligned with Heaven, showing the love of God to others so that none should perish, but all have eternal life. With all the false doctrine and misrepresentations of God, Jesus and Holy Spirit that have infiltrated American society, how much more urgent that we work in His power to allow the Holy Spirit, the true Living God, to come through? How do you reveal the Kingdom of God without talking in your life? How do you use the power and talents that God gave you for building His Kingdom? How well do your talk and walk align? How can you do a better job at exercising integrity?

MAY 17

> fear not, for I am with you; be not dismayed, for I am your God; I will strengthen you, I will help you, I will uphold you with my righteous right hand. Isaiah 41:10

Isn't it amazing how fearful people can get? Even when we witness the power of God, the enemy can come in with fear and derail us. Look at Peter, the original Rock, who experienced fear and doubts even after walking with Jesus for over three years, witnessing healings and miracles, even Lazarus being raised from the dead. Then fear sets in as the slave girl confronts him, "Hey, I saw you with Jesus, right?" Fear can be such a powerful weapon and as Christians, we must be aware of the schemes and tools the enemy utilizes to lure us away from God. "Fear not" is written 365 times in the Bible. God put it there as a daily reminder to not allow the enemy to keep us from utilizing the power of the Living God in our lives. Do not be dismayed, upset, worried, or agitated. God is with us wherever we go. He is our help and He is willing to strengthen us as long as we allow Him to. He will lift us up and hold us in His right hand, His strong, powerful, mighty, righteous, right hand. If the Holy Spirit is living in us and is willing to lead, teach and guide us, we must allow Him to speak. He will help us recognize the lies and schemes of the enemy; we just have to be obedient and listen. When fear raises its ugly head to strike at us, we must cut off its head like a snake and render it powerless. Be mature in your faith and in your relationship with Christ so that when the enemy wants to attack, he is going to have to prepare better and think of a different way to strike. We must not let False Evidence Appearing Real (F.E.A.R.) to become a reality and deter us from living in the freedom God is calling us to enjoy. It's day one hundred thirty-seven (or thirty-eight if it's a leap year) and just one of the three hundred sixty-five reminders to fear not nor be dismayed. Trust God is always by your side. How can you pray this Scripture back to God to get freedom from fear and worry? How do you become strengthened by the Lord? What can you do to recognize fear when it starts small and begins to creep in? How can you counteract fear to prevent it from freezing you in your tracks?

MAY 18

> My heart is confident in you, O God; my heart is confident. No wonder I can sing your praises! Psalm 57:7 NLT

Where do you get your confidence? What are you confident in? "Confident" means "to be full of conviction, certain, trustful". We can be confident that the sun will rise in the morning and our vehicle will get us to and from work. But what if that vehicle fails one day? What do you do? What happens to your confidence? For me, I can say, "My heart is certain in you God; my heart is trustful in you." What are we trustful of? Is it God, or do we doubt God because He doesn't answer "Yes" to all of our prayer requests? In the film *Bruce Almighty*, God gives Bruce some of His power and at one point Bruce feels overwhelmed by all the prayers, so he says "Yes" to all the prayer requests before him. Little did he know it was only part of the population of New York he was listening to and chaos breaks out because a million people win the lottery and only get like $5 each. God has good reasons for saying "No" to some prayer requests and "Wait" on other ones, but that does not mean we should lose confidence or trust in Him. He is not like our car that won't start for no reason one morning. He is not there to serve us, but for us to serve Him, to sing praise to Him because of how good and holy He is. Our confidence in Him and our trust in Him is not because He grants every prayer request, but because He has the power to do so. He has the power to create the entire universe with His hands and then use those same hands to knit us in our mother's womb. When we trust Him for everything, including hearing our prayers and having our best interests at heart, no wonder we can sing praises to Him and worship Him. What level of confidence, certainty and trust do you have in Him? What can you do to increase your confidence in Him this week? How much do you trust God with? How can you increase that? If you are honest with yourself, what is one thing you don't trust God with? How can you let Him have control of that aspect of your life?

MAY 19

> Let us hold tightly without wavering to the hope we affirm, for God can be trusted to keep his promise. Hebrews 10:23 NLT

My first time rappelling, I held on too tightly to the rope and wouldn't lean back or allow the rope to slide through. In life, everyone holds onto something. For some, it's their kids or memories of a loved one that has passed away. For some, it is a work ethic or moral standard that they hold too tightly. What is it that you hold tightly onto? The author of Hebrews says that we should hold tightly onto the hope that is affirmed, because God can be trusted to keep His promises. Throughout history and throughout Scripture, God has upheld and fulfilled every promise He made. That is an empowering hope that we can hold onto. The fact is we can trust God. He is true to His word and we never have to guess what He desires. He is unlike the idols of the Old Testament or the Greek or Roman gods, where people never knew why "they got mad," where they were, or even if they were being heard. We know that God hears and answers prayers and is true to His word and promises. We may not agree with His decisions or even desire what He says, but God is consistent and unchanging. Unlike the rappelling incident, where we are not supposed to hold too tightly as I did with the rope, we need to grip tightly to God and His Word. We can hold onto that hope as well. We never have to guess. If you have forgotten His promises, what can you do to start holding onto them? How can you allow peace to flood your mind and heart, knowing He never changes and fulfills all His promises? How can you hold more tightly onto the truth of His Word? What are you willing to commit to? How will you hold tightly to it? What promises of God have you experienced? What are you holding onto tighter than you are holding onto God? What do you need to do to make that switch?

MAY 20

> This is the message we have heard from him and proclaim to you, that
> God is light and in him is no darkness at all. 1 John 1:5

Scientifically speaking, the study of light and dark is amazing. Dark cannot overtake, consume, or dispel light. Light can overtake, consume and dispel darkness, even just a little bit of light. Jupiter is a planet and does not give off light it only reflects light. Jupiter is 484.59 million miles from the sun. It reflects light back 365.37 million miles back to Earth and we can see it unaided. As mentioned before, without the help of any device, scientists say you can see a single birthday candle 1.6 miles away with the unaided eye, ten miles away with binoculars. Amazingly, with all the advances science has made, they cannot find a way for darkness to consume light. While this may not seem like a major breakthrough for you, this was written almost two thousand years ago with a limited knowledge of the world and science. God is light. Light describes knowledge, purity, spiritual perfection and moral excellence, while darkness describes sin, lack of purity and evil with no moral compass. So, it would make sense that God could not have any darkness in Him at all. Again, while you may say that it is common sense, it was not back then. In the polytheistic world that this was written in, no god was all good. Greek, Roman and other gentile gods had raging tempers and killed people who upset them, causing cruel destruction. This was a radical view. Gods were viewed as humans with supernatural powers, living in the sky or on top of a mountain. The very idea that a god, or God, could only be light and pure, containing no darkness, was radical and incomprehensible. Science was once utilized to prove the existence of God. This scientific fact about light shared above is proven and points to the existence of God. But science has ignored this truth, trying to prove God does not exist and trying to claim that Christians steal and misapply scientific principles to prove their points. We must keep in mind when Scripture was written what the scientific and geographical knowledge, they had at the time was. God's word does not return void. God knew what scientists would be able to prove over a thousand, even two thousand years or more after it was spoken and written. Does Scripture like this bring comfort to you when reading it, or have you lost touch with the power behind a simple proclamation like this? How comforting is it to know that God has no darkness in Him, that He is pure, just and true, not given to emotional temper tantrums? How can applying verses like this in your life solidify or strengthen your relationship with God?

MAY 21

> On the day I called, you answered me; my strength of soul, you increased. Psalm 138:3

How many times do we pray and expect an answer right away? If we are honest with ourselves, probably all the time. David writes that on the day he prayed, God answered him. Does God always answer our prayers? Yes. Does He always answer them with a "Yes"? No. Do we feel that God always answers our prayers when we pray? If we are again honest with ourselves, we probably only count when He answers with a "Yes". When His answer is "No" or "Wait", those are harder times to know that He has answered them. Notice that when David said, "You answered me," he followed up with, "my strength of soul, You increased." That in and of itself is an answer to prayer. Being obedient to Him, releasing control and seeking Him in prayer – He honors that. Honoring our prayers and answering our prayers is, again, not the same as always receiving a "Yes". His answering our prayers, even with a "No" or "Wait" strengthens our souls and deepens our relationships with Him. Those are answers in and of themselves. To be strengthened by the Lord, to have our souls healed, even if the answer to the actual prayer was "No", it is a great and awesome occurrence. Are we aware of what God is doing in us and through us when we pray? Are we even being quiet enough during prayer to hear God answer our prayers? The more "smart" technology comes our way, the busier we get and the more we are on the run with a "to-do" list. Unfortunately, that lifestyle has crossed over into our spiritual lives as well, especially regarding Bible reading, praying, worship and quiet time with the Lord. How many of us actually have genuine, set apart, daily, quiet time with the Lord? When He speaks in a still, small voice, how can we hear Him when He answers if we are too busy with our to-do lists or brainless technology indulgences to focus our spiritual ears and hearts? God is faithful and answers us, but we need to stay connected to Him long enough to hear from Him and look at the blessings He gives us when we give Him more time in prayer, worship, scripture reading and quiet time. What are you willing to do to implement this Scripture in your life? How much time are you willing to give God to be still, so that when He answers you, you can hear Him? How much time do you give to just God, God alone? How much are you willing to increase that solitude or stillness to?

MAY 22

> The LORD is gracious and merciful, slow to anger and abounding in steadfast love. Psalm 145:8

Anger seems to be becoming more and more of a problem these days. Emotions tend to boil over with road rage, airline rage and pandemic-era restrictions on quarantining. Technology has seemed to replace personal interactions. So this generation that has grown up with a cellphone in one hand and an iPod in the other, now as adults, they don't know how to handle or deal with points of view contrary to their own and they let their anger get the best of them. Anger is not a sin. Anger is an emotion that leads to actions; it is those actions that can either be righteous or sinful. With people getting angry so easily these days, is it not reassuring to know that God is slow to anger? When we read through the Old Testament and Israel left God chasing after false idols, God was not like Zeus and in anger immediately punished them. No, He sent prophets and messengers to call His people back. The message was clear, "Come back and I will be your God. If not, you will be overcome by another country, enslaved and carried off, but I will eventually call you back. Come back now, though, before this happens." How much grace and mercy did He show them? How much grace and mercy does He show us when we chase after idols of careers, money and objects to be stored in self-storage lockers? He is slow to anger and rich and abounding in steadfast love. "Steadfast" means "firmly established, firm in resolute and unmoving". That is the kind of love He has for you, for me, for our neighbors and even those who hate us. When the enemy comes in to say, "How can God still love you?" you can reply confidently, "He loves me with an abounding, steadfast love". Yes, when we sin, it hurts the heart of God and puts separation between us, but His grace, mercy and steadfast love calls out to us to come back to Him. What would our country look like right now if we were all slow to anger, as James tells us to be in 1:19? Could we truly become slow to speak and slow to anger? Why was James calling us to this behavior? Because we are to imitate God in our lives and if God shows steadfast love and is slow to anger, so should we if we are allowing the Holy Spirit to live in us and to guide and direct us. What changes can you make today to live out this verse in your life? God is gracious and merciful, slow to anger and abounding in steadfast love, so should you? How do you accomplish this? What can you do to be slow to anger? How can you abound in steadfast love? How can you increase your level of implementing steadfast love?

MAY 23

> Each one must give as he has decided in his heart, not reluctantly or under compulsion, for God loves a cheerful giver. 2 Corinthians 9:7

What gets your time? What grabs your attention? I recently told a loved one that what you give your time and attention to is what you deem important, whereas what you put on the back burner and wait for "free time" to do is not that important to you. According to a recent study, 66% of Christians look at Facebook every day, 39% view YouTube and only 32% read their Bibles daily. Christians today are turning away from God and becoming part of the world instead of simply being in the world. We are called to stand out, to be the light and to be different – but we cannot do that if we are not in His Word or reading our Bibles. We are called to tithe 10%, but I believe the call for obedience in giving is about more than our money. I believe we are called to tithe 10% of our time, 10% of our talent and 10% of our treasure. 10% of our money is a given. But we should be giving God 10% of our talent, using whatever gifts and abilities He has given us for serving Him. We should be giving God at least 10% of our day. If we are up 16 hours, 1 hour and 36 minutes should be devoted to Him; but instead, we are enamored with social media and smart technology, allowing it to fill our hours. All Scripture is inspired by God and is useful to teach us what is true. There can only be one source of truth and truth cannot be changing and evolving with the times. Truth is eternal and never changing. Scripture helps us realize what is wrong in our lives. Because most Christians aren't reading His word every day, they tend to fall back on the ethical sliding scale – I'm not as bad as so-and-so, or at least I am better than them. If Christians fail to look at themselves through the lens of Scripture, then they cannot reflect and get direction on how to change and be corrected. This verse ends with, "It corrects us when we are wrong and teaches us to do what is right." Look around at what is happening in society, how good is being called bad and bad is being called good, or right is being called wrong and wrong is being called right. You can claim any belief as long as it is not in Jesus Christ, because He is too narrow minded and won't let you decide what is right and true. My closing question is as much for me as it is for you – what changes do we need to make in our lives so that Scripture becomes more of a priority? What can you do to spend more time with Him and in His Word this week? How much of your day do you spend with Him? How much of your God-given talent do you use for Him?

MAY 24

> I have told you all this so that you may have peace in me. Here on earth you will have many trials and sorrows. But take heart, because I have overcome the world. John 16:33 NLT

After the fall in the garden, God never promised an easy life, just a blessed life. He promises that if we follow and obey Him, He will meet us where we are and meet our needs. We can be strong and courageous, knowing that He goes before us. When Jesus says, "I have told you all this so that you may have peace", He doesn't mean life will be easy. He continues with, "Here on Earth, you will have many trials, many sorrows. When you follow Me, you have to pick up your cross." He doesn't say, "Pick up your easy chair, recliner, or bed and follow me", rather He says, "Pick up your cross and follow Me". He also says, "Take heart! Take heart because I have overcome the world." We have peace and our souls are not troubled because Jesus Christ has overcome the world, overcome the trials and sorrows. We have a hope and a peace that is not describable to someone who does not know Jesus. There are just no words to accurately explain the peace that overcomes you when faced with a trial or sorrow and you lean in and hunker down close to Christ. What keeps you awake at night? What do you worry about? What do you do to get rid of worry and anxiety? Jesus said that He came and taught us so that we would have peace in Him. Money and jobs do not provide peace. Homes and cars do not provide peace. Peace and joy come from knowing the Lord and knowing the Lord comes from reading His Word, worshiping Him and talking to Him frequently and personally. Jesus says right here, in John 16, that we will face trials and sorrows. Jesus doesn't say "*if* you suffer"; He says that while on Earth, you *WILL* have trials and sorrow, but take heart, have peace and be confident, because I, Jesus, have overcome the world. When anxiety and worry try to stop you in your path, have peace knowing that Jesus, a PERSONAL GOD, PERSONAL SAVIOR, is right there, ready, waiting and willing to help. Do not be surprised when trials and sorrows come; the deeper your relationship with the Lord, the more of a threat you are to Satan. Don't let him knock you off the path that God is on; stay walking with Him. While it may not be easy, there is peace and confidence that the One who created the universe is ready, willing and waiting to help by bringing peace of mind, peace of heart and peace of soul to you. How much time are you spending with Him? Maybe, just maybe, we need to increase that a little! This week, hold onto this promise that Jesus has overcome the world for us and the promise of Peace in our hearts and souls, knowing that we have a Living God that goes before us. What fears, hurts, or sorrows do you need to let go of to grab hold of His peace? How can you draw closer to the Holy Spirit to allow His peace to comfort you? When you are facing trials, how can you experience the peace of God during them?

MAY 25

casting all your anxieties on him, because he cares for you. 1 Peter 5:7 NLT

How many of you follow the directions in the box that comes with the item that needs to be assembled? How many of you actually ask for directions or use GPS? Is it me, or do we tend to make easy things harder than they need to be? I don't know why it is, but it seems to me that we humans tend to make things more complicated than they need to be. We make simple things complicated. Peter tells us that God cares about us and He cares about what worries us and what we care about. All we have to do is give it all to Him. Although we know to give Him our worries and all our cares, we tend not to. Why is that? Is it pride that drives us to say, "I can handle it, I can take care of it!" and then get to the point where we cry out, "Jesus, take the wheel"? Is it a lack of self-confidence, "I can't pray like a pastor", or "I'm no Billy Graham", or "I am not good at praying"? Is it our view of God, "He doesn't have time for the little stuff! Out of the 7.6 billion people, He doesn't have time for this little ole me." Is it our lifestyle, the fact that we are always on the move, always so busy with to-do lists and places to go and people to see and things to do that we don't actually slow down enough to take time to talk and listen to God? What is it that causes you anxiety? Anxiety is a fear or uneasiness, a dread that prevents us from doing something. What is it that causes you anxiety? Are you so busy, or do you keep yourself so busy that you don't have time to think about what causes your anxiety? Out of this list discussed, do any of them cause you anxiety, pride, lack of self-confidence or self-esteem, or skew your view of God? Do you have a small view of God or a big view of God? Peter reminds us that He cares for us, so we must cast our fears and doubts into His Holy Hands. Is Sunday the only time you take to talk to Him? Someone needs to hear this for the first time and someone needs to hear this again – be reminded that God cares about you! He cares for you! He cares about what troubles you and what makes you happy. Take some time today, just invest in your relationship with the Living God and cast your cares and worries onto Him. What causes you to be anxious? How can you give that to God? How can you trust God with your fears? How well do you know God? Is He a best friend or a Sunday visitor? What are you willing to do to deepen your relationship with Him and trust Him more? How can you apply this verse in your life to live in Christ's freedom, anxiety free?

MAY 26

> They do not fear bad news; they confidently trust the LORD to care for them. Psalm 112:7 NLT

Do you fear bad news? When you know some bad news is coming, how do you handle it? Have you conquered a fear or has fear conquered you? In seminary, I read a book on the early church and the first martyrs. They bravely faced death and torture because of their complete trust in the Lord. They knew God on a personal level; they had a deep relationship with the Holy Spirit and allowed Him to be their comfort and their strength. They could look death on Earth in the eyes and not blink, because they knew whose hands they were being held by. There is a story of one execution, where the executioner was new and since they did not die in the arena, he was supposed to impale the Christian with his sword. One of the ladies, Perpetua, saw him struggling and told him where to place the sword and what angle to thrust up on her so that she could die, so that she could be killed. How unbelievable is that? But Perpetua lived out this verse to its fullest! She did not and many like her did not fear the news of execution, because they had placed their full trust in the Lord. They refused to recant and deny Christ. While the Lord cares and loves us deeply, sin still runs rampant on Earth. Do you fear bad news? Did you get a call from the doctor's office about needing to come in? Did you get an email or voice mail from your boss stating you need to meet with them *first thing* in the morning? Are there bills piling up on your counter? Where is your confidence? Where is your trust? Are you more like the martyrs, both 2000 years ago and today, in Asia, the Middle East and the South Pacific? Today, martyrdom is still a reality. It is not a worry in the United States and many developed countries, but Christianity is illegal in or severely restricted in 59 countries as of 2022. Many Christians are still killed for their beliefs in this day and age. How do you view God? Is Jesus Christ your Lord and Savior or is he your fire insurance to keep you out of hell? How can you rely on Him for strength and courage to face the challenges that life brings your way? Where have you placed your confidence and trust? How can you allow God to be that source of confidence and trust in your life?

MAY 27

For God is not a God of confusion but of peace, 1 Corinthians 14:33a

In a day and age when peace and quiet are hard to come by, we must prioritize them. With what is happening in the news and in the world, it can seem like peace is more of a myth than a reality. But God is a God of peace; peace for the world, peace for nations, peace for states, peace for cities, peace for families and peace for individuals. God does not create confusion, because it draws people away from Him. Why would He be an author of confusion? When there is confusion and misdirection, we must realize that the enemy has had a hand in it. God wants us to experience the peace that comes from a deep relationship with Him. The kind of peace that David had when he faced Goliath. The peace Daniel had while sitting in the lion's den. The peace that Shadrach, Meshach and Abednego experienced in the fiery furnace. The peace the disciples had as they were stoned, thrown off the roof of buildings, crucified, beheaded, or boiled alive. See, the peace they all experienced had nothing to do with their surroundings or life situations, but it was based on their relationship with a Living God. They could face the life experiences with peace because they knew who the author of peace was; they trusted the author of peace with their lives and souls because He proved time and time again that He can see us through all the hills and valleys of life, all the rumors of wars and actual wars. If you need peace in your life, where do you go? How can you go to the author of peace? How can reading this verse change or amplify your relationship with God? What can you do to apply this verse in your life so you can experience the peace God wants you to experience? When you experience confusion, how can you handle it better in the future?

MAY 28

> Therefore encourage one another and build one another up, just as you are doing. 1 Thessalonians 5:11

Unfortunately, too many Christians get caught up in the "hold each other accountable" department and the "judging others" department that we forget many verses in the scriptures like 1 Thessalonians 5:11. Paul encourages the churches in Thessalonica to keep encouraging each other and building one another up. It is not that they were told not to hold accountable fellow believers, nor does Paul encourage them to build up and encourage someone who is living a sinful life. Christianity is truly about balance. When we go too far on the judging side we lose the love, but if we go too far on encouraging, we end up endorsing them living a life that separates them from God and we lose the accountability part. We must be in tune with the Holy Spirit and allow Him to guide us. After the global pandemics, wars and the hatred that is being spewed by so many on TV and social media, as Christians we should be looking for ways to encourage fellow believers and build them up, especially if they come under attack for living their lives for Christ. We forget that in battle we are to fight, but fight like the Marines, leaving no man behind. We too, as Christians, should never leave a believer behind. When they fall, or come under attack, we should be there to encourage and build them up, help them strengthen themselves, their faith and to be spiritually restored to rejoin us on the battlefield. If we are honest with ourselves, we all need to be lifted up, prayed for, encouraged and built up. I pray that, as mature Christians, we have that balance between encouragement and accountability. Who in your life needs encouragement? Who needs to be built up? Whether it's from their good decisions or bad decisions, how can we encourage and build up others? Who can you stop right now and send that text, email, or make a phone call to, that needs encouragement? How can you allow the Holy Spirit to encourage you? How can you make encouraging and building others up a priority in your life?

MAY 29

> And he said to all, "If anyone would come after me, let him deny himself and take up his cross daily and follow me." Luke 9:23

Sometimes to get people to accept Christ, Christians tell them that all Jesus wants is their heart. In some instances, that is true. That is the first step, but that is not all that Jesus wants; He wants all of us – all of our hopes, dreams, desires, successes and failures. Jesus reminds the disciples and the crowds that if anyone was to be His follower, we would have to deny ourselves, deny our dreams and desires, our wishes and life plans and pick up our cross daily to follow Him. When Jesus mentioned picking up our cross daily, it was not a good luck charm, bracelet, or necklace; it was a death sentence. The equivalent today would be to pick up your electric chair, noose, or lethal injection machine and follow me. To follow Him takes us where we would not normally go, help people we would not normally help and do things that go against our very nature. Why? Because that is what Jesus did Himself. He healed lepers, taught Samaritans, healed Roman soldiers' children, ate with tax collectors and those living sinful lives separated from God. God wants all of you and is that fair of Him to ask? Jesus gave His life, left Heaven and came to Earth, lived a perfect life so He could be the final sacrifice. He lived the example we are to follow, as Paul tells us in Philippians 2:6 "who, though he was in the form of God, did not count equality with God as a thing to be grasped." We are no better than those living a life apart from God – Jesus died for them as much as He died for you and me. Are you willing to sacrifice your dreams and desires to follow Jesus more closely? Is He the Lord of your life or your Sunday idol? And notice Jesus tells us it's going to be difficult! It is not just pick up your cross and follow; it is pick up your cross daily and follow. Every day we have the choice to live for God or live for ourselves. Every day we have the choice to follow His example and walk closely with Him or put Him aside for the weekend service or gathering. Daily we walk and daily we choose. Is ESPN, HGTV, or the latest app on our phone above or below Him in our priorities? How can you incorporate this verse in your life to deepen your relationship and walk more closely with Him on a daily basis? What do you need to start denying in your life to make God a higher priority? What are you willing to sacrifice to follow Him and make Him a higher priority?

MAY 30

> The Lord helps the fallen and lifts those bent beneath their loads.
> Psalm 145:14 NLT

Sometimes it can feel like the world is weighing us down. Life and the burdens it puts on our shoulders can sometimes feel like we are no longer strong enough to go on. If we try to continue to walk under those burdens alone, we can fall; here, it says our knees are bent under the load. Jesus, after being whipped thirty-nine times with a cat-o-nine tails, was then forced to carry His cross to the place of His execution. Even Jesus, under the burden, fell and fell not once, not twice, but three times under the load and Simon of Cyrene was forced to carry Jesus' cross the rest of the way. Jesus promised us that when He left he would send a helper, a comforter. The Holy Spirit would not come unless Jesus ascended into Heaven. The Holy Spirit is here to help us, guide us and bear the load with us, so we don't have to carry it alone. Jesus said His burden was light and easy if we would just follow Him. The world tells us, especially us men, that we should be strong enough; only the weak seek help. In fact, weakness prevents us from asking for help; it takes strength and courage to ask for help. The Lord, the Holy Spirit, is here and He already knows what we need; He already sees our struggles and sees our knees starting to buckle under the weight and burden. The Holy Spirit will not force Himself on us, but when we ask, He is there as our Helper, our Comforter. Allow Him to remove the burdens of this world, ask Him for His yoke, to carry His burden with His help and presence in your life. You don't have to be strong enough to do it independently. Jesus does not expect you to be strong enough to do it on your own. If we were strong enough, we would have no need for a Savior. Allow Him to help. Seek His help, seek His comfort. Take time and pray now; ask Him now to help you carry this burden. Start with one burden. What is one burden in your life you can remove and ask Him to help carry it with you, so you're not doing it alone? What can you do so that a situation does not become a burden? In what area of your life do you need to trust God more, to prevent burdens from being placed on you?

MAY 31

> For our sake he made him to be sin who knew no sin, so that in him we might become the righteousness of God. 2 Corinthians 5:21

Sin is an ugly thing. Not only does it weigh us down and condemn us, but it also separates us from the One who truly loves us. Sin is rebellion against God and His Word and plan for us, so it's easy to see how it could separate us. Since we were created in the image of God, rebelling against Him is serious and requires blood to be shed for that forgiveness. Today's Scripture verse is one of our faith's most important theological verses. Theologically speaking, this verse covers both justification and atonement, which are extremely important to our faith. God sent Jesus Christ, who never sinned, who knew no sin, to be sin. Jesus came to Earth so that He could be the final sin offering for us, becoming, Himself, the sacrificial lamb, so that we could become the righteousness of God. In other words, justification, being made right with God restores our relationship with God that sin destroyed and separated us from Him. We might not feel righteous, but righteousness is not an emotion, it is not a feeling, it is a way of life. When we live that life to the fullest, the righteousness of Jesus is living in us to keep us in that right relationship with Father God. God's purpose, for our good, was to send Jesus, who was tempted but never sinned, to be our final sin offering. Atonement is the paying back reparations for wrongdoing – Jesus, having done nothing wrong through sin, became our payment for our wrongdoings that we choose to do willingly. We can do nothing on our own accord to be right with God because we will just sin again. There is no limit to how many sacrifices we would have to make to ask for forgiveness. Jesus did it all for us in one divine act of surrender on the cross. All we have to do is accept this gift through our belief that becomes transforming faith. So, when the enemy comes in and whispers in your ear, "You're not good enough, God can't forgive that", or any other lie the enemy tries to tell you – remember Jesus thought of *you* when the nails were being driven. He determined *you* were worthy enough to love and accept as you are. He paved the way to Heaven; all we have to do is follow. How are you living out this theological, Biblical and spiritual truth in your life? How does this verse affect your relationship with the Lord? How can you apply this verse in your life as you interact with other believers?

JUNE 1

> But God chose what is foolish in the world to shame the wise; God chose what is weak in the world to shame the strong; 1 Corinthians 1:27

I think we all have been around people who think they are better than others; if not, you are probably that person. We know the feeling we get in our stomachs when they start to speak. For the most part, they are not walking with God. How do we know? Here, Paul tells us that God chose things and people that the world considers foolish. Look at who God chose – Moses had a speech impediment, David was the lowliest of the sons and was forgotten by Jesse, who didn't even bring him in for dinner and the disciples ranged from fishermen, tax collectors and many uneducated men. Paul was the persecutor of the believers and gave permission for Stephen to be killed, the first martyr. Because the world could only see their flaws and shortcomings, everything they said and did pointed to God. It could only be God working through them. In the book of Acts, when Peter and the disciples spoke, they astonished the people. How do these men know these things? They are from Galilee, their speech gives them away; how can they know what they know, coming from where they are from? The Pharisees, the educated men that were supposed to know about God, did they know God when He was right in front of them? They did not know it, because He did not conform to their standards or the mold they thought God should fit into. Do not let the enemy convince you that God cannot use you. God rarely uses the qualified because He qualifies those He calls. Nothing in your past disqualifies you from being called by God. Paul authorized Stephen's death and God used Him to reach the gentiles and write two-thirds of the New Testament. What do you think God can use you for? What are you willing to allow God to call you to do? How can you break the mold and allow God to qualify you where He wants you to go and serve where He calls you to serve? What have you told God "No" to that He is calling you to? What do you need to do to be more willing to follow where He leads?

JUNE 2

"The heart of man plans his way, but the Lord establishes his steps."
Proverbs 16:9

I used to like to plan things out. I wanted to know where I was going, when I was going to get there and how long it would take to get there. But in doing so, we could be so focused on the destination that we forget about the journey. In 2001, I knew God was calling me to ministry, but I had other plans. When I got enough courage to talk to someone about going into seminary, I allowed my family to talk me out of it. Why? It was "irrational". Why should I change careers midstream and leave a solid job and career? Then, I started serving in the church. As I served, I began to realize that with God I could do it, I could do anything He called me to do. In the midst of serving as a volunteer "ministry partner" as a leader of men's ministry, prayer partner and working in youth, God reminded me of that calling He had for my life. As I planned to move forward in God's direction, I replayed in my mind what my family said before. Trying to dismiss that, I mustered enough courage to move forward and I turned to friends asking them to pray for me to know exactly what God wanted me to do. After a year of the same prayer request, a really good friend had the courage to tell me to quit praying and asking for prayers and just do something. So, I finally surrendered to His will for me and enrolled in seminary. As I progressed through seminary, I took ownership of God's calling on my life and started planning. I now knew what I wanted. There was a certain church I wanted, a certain position I wanted and I tried to make my way into that; but God's path led in a different direction. Because I was making my own plans and not following His steps, I experienced some pretty deep hurt. Yes, we need to pray. Yes, we need to take the first step and do something. If all we do is sit on the couch and ask God to use us, it will most likely not happen. But if we move into action and allow Him to establish our steps, His way is always better and full of more blessings. How is God asking you to move? Are you following His steps or your own? What steps is God establishing in your life? What direction does He want to take your life in?

JUNE 3

> And whatever you do, in word or deed, do everything in the name of the Lord Jesus, giving thanks to God the Father through him.
> Colossians 3:17

We have all heard the saying, "You don't get a second chance to make a first impression." Whether or not it's right to judge on first impressions, many people do. Paul reminds us here that whatever we do or say, we are doing it as a representative of Jesus. My heart breaks when I see examples of Christians leaving bad tips. "God only gets 10%, so do you," or "My tip is 'Jesus loves you'". I have talked to many current and former wait staff and they hate working on Sundays or around the holidays. They all say that, as a whole, Christians are the worst customers. If we truly had the love of Christ in our hearts, we would actually tip something that would help them make ends meet, pay a bill or provide for medication. When I fully gave my life over to Jesus, this was one area where my wife and I were convicted. We almost always ask our server what we could pray for them about when we pray for our food and we always start at a 20% tip and go up from there. If we go out to eat on Christmas Eve or Easter, we tip 100% since we know they are away from their families. What has broken my heart is that several times we have been told that we were the first person to ever ask if they needed prayer or offered to pray for them. If Christianity is the largest "religion" in the world, how is that possible? We are not Christians only when we sit in church, during a worship service, or even during a Bible study. It should be our identity that never changes, is never hidden. As Christians, we tend to view missions as overseas work, like in Haiti, Africa, or India; but in reality, our mission field starts here at home. If we are to truly be a light on a hill, if we are truly to let the light of Christ shine through us, then we have to be intentional in every aspect of our lives and realize that what we say and what we do not only reflects us, but also reflects the relationship we have with Jesus Christ. How do your actions and your words reflect the light of Christ? How do your words reflect your relationship with Jesus, the Light of the World, the Son of God? What does the way you treat people say about your relationship with our Living God?

JUNE 4

> Always be humble and gentle. Be patient with each other, making allowance for each other's faults because of your love. Ephesians 4:2 NLT

Human nature tends to point out the faults of others. As Americans we love to laugh at others' failures or mistakes. We even have TV shows glorifying these random moments like *America's Funniest Home Videos.* Most of those videos are unplanned and capture mildly disastrous effects and mistakes. Society loves to point out the faults or imperfections of others, whether physically, mentally, or emotionally – and we have whole businesses that deal with these issues, from cosmetic surgery to memory vitamins to psychotherapy. In today's world, humility is seen as a weakness and gentleness means you have no backbone. If you are nice to someone, it is only because you are a brown noser and want something out of it or you must have a hidden agenda. But what does God say? How does God see us? He sees us bearing His fingerprints and image. He calls us to be humble and gentle. He even demonstrated those qualities while in human form with so many examples: Jesus with the prostitute, the woman at the well, the man at the pool, the blind man, Zacchaeus. He remains gentle, humble and kind even when He was on trial, or while we indulge sin. He is patient with us and calls us to be patient with each other. Paul goes a step further and tells us that God wants us to make allowances for each other's faults because of Love. What does that mean, make allowances? It means we are actively seeking to overlook and forgive a mistake or hurt. To look past their faults and to see them as God sees them. Is it easy? No! Is it simple? Absolutely. Following Jesus is not easy; the road is described as narrow and winding. But is it simple? Yes – Love God – Love others as God loves you. Simple does not equate to easy. Easy is not a synonym for simple. Simple means "not complex, not confusing". In fact, we complicate things to make them easy. But what are you doing with God's love and patience? Are you soaking it up and storing it like a camel's hump or like a sponge, ready to spread it around? How are you gentle and humble with others who are not like you? How are you patient with and gentle with people close to you? How are you at making allowances for people's faults, giving them second chances? Who do you need to make an allowance for and extend gentleness and patience to?

JUNE 5

But you will receive power when the Holy Spirit has come upon you and you will be my witnesses in Jerusalem and in all Judea and Samaria and to the end of the earth." Acts 1:8

We have probably all heard of the Great Commission. In the book of Acts, verse 1:8 is the one most often referred to regarding the Great Commission. *Great*, meaning the best, highest, or none other like it. The *Commission* is an instruction, command, or duty given to a person or group of people. The Great Commission is the best, highest command and duty given to any group of people. Which people? Christians, God-followers, including all who have accepted Jesus Christ as their Lord and Savior. When we receive this gift of eternal life, the Holy Spirit indwells us and takes up residence in our hearts. We are then called to be Jesus' witnesses in Jerusalem. Why over there? It's metaphorical. Jerusalem is where you live, your house. You must first witness to your spouse and your kids. Your first mission field is in the lives of your children, raising them in the instruction of the Lord, knowing God, not just knowing about Him, eventually guiding them to accept a relationship with our Living God. "And in all of Judea" refers to your town, your church. As a brother or sister in Christ, you must reach your city for God and that is only through a local body. I have an unpopular opinion; if you are not involved in your family and local church witnessing about Christ, I believe you have no business going on an international mission trip and I believe Acts 1:8, the Great Commission, supports that. Jesus commands the disciples to first witness at home, in the community, outside the community and then to the rest of the world. Your second mission field is the city in which you live. Through the arms of and with the guidance of your local church, you should be involved in Bible studies, youth or children's ministry, men's or women's ministry and doing outreach in your city, actively and faithfully reaching your city for God. A mission trip isn't, nor should it be, a bucket list item where you go, you serve, you come home and then back to life as normal with this bucket list item fulfilled. Mission, from the Great Com*mission*, is not a single event, not a feelgood event; your faith is not once and done and neither is the Commission. We are constantly called to the Great Commission and if your family is not engaged actively in their faith, if you are not actively engaged in your church and if you are not actively serving your community for Christ, I feel like you are not ready for going international. Men lead your wives; husbands and wives lead your kids. Serve by teaching children or youth, being involved in either men's or women's ministry, or being in a Bible Study and reaching people in your town for God. Through these actions of discipleship, the Holy Spirit will call, equip and empower you to go international. How are you engaged in the Great Commission at home? How involved are you in the Great Commission in your church? How are you reaching your community for God?

JUNE 6

> I appeal to you therefore, brothers, by the mercies of God, to present your bodies as a living sacrifice, holy and acceptable to God, which is your spiritual worship Romans 12:1

What is worship? Ask one hundred people and you may get one hundred different answers. Webster defines it as, "Spiritual devotion to a deity", but that does not mention what it looks like. Most would subscribe to worship as the singing that is done in the congregation at church. I, however, believe worship is a lifestyle; it includes singing but also incorporates prayer, Bible reading, meditation on Scripture, being silent in prayer, acts of service, forgiving, giving or tithing, obeying God and fellowshipping with other believers; all of these are forms of worship. Paul writes to us, "I appeal to you brothers by the mercies of God." What are the *mercies of God*? While we were still sinners, Jesus died for us, for our sins, to forgive us, so we could be realigned with God. Present your bodies as *a living sacrifice*. A living sacrifice can crawl off the altar; we have to choose to stay on the altar, to lay our fears, our regrets, our dreams and desires and even our life plans on the altar and allow God to do with them what He will; it requires surrender and complete trust in Him. When Jesus ascended, the Holy Spirit came. When we accepted Jesus as our Lord and Savior, the Holy Spirit took up residence in our bodies. Our bodies became a temple to the Holy Spirit, so we are to try to maintain that holiness by staying away from sin. The good news is that when we do sin and we always will, when we repent honestly, we are forgiven and then the Holy Spirit has more room in our lives, in our bodies, to lead, guide and direct us. When we follow His guidance and forgive those who have wronged us, when we spend time in prayer and listening to the Holy Spirit, when we read Scripture and ask the Holy Spirit to help us apply it in our lives, when we are careful with what we watch and listen to or put into our minds and hearts – this is worship. That is our spiritual worship. When we change the channel or playlist to something that is God-honoring instead of God separating, that is spiritual worship. When we sacrifice our likes and loves and replace them with God-centered, God-honoring choices that bring us into a deeper relationship with Him, that living sacrifice is our spiritual worship. How can you engage in spiritual worship other than during church services? What is the Holy Spirit asking you to sacrifice so that you can have a deeper relationship with Him? What do you need to do to be able to hear Him over the loudness of the world?

JUNE 7

> I am counting on the LORD; yes, I am counting on him. I have put my hope in his word. Psalm 130:5 NLT

Have you ever been let down by someone? They said they were going to be there. They said they would do something or get something and instead they left you feeling disappointed, maybe even angry? When we count on the Lord, we will not be angry, disappointed, left behind, or left high and dry. Here David tells us he *is* counting on the Lord – YES! There is absolute excitement and determination in this verse. We have probably seen some Christians moping around, thinking to themselves, "I hope God heard me; I don't know what God is going to do." David says, "I am counting on the Lord. YES! I am counting on the Lord." Not that this should lead us to think that this means we can "name it and claim it" and God will answer all of our prayers with a "Yes". God is not that way. He is not a genie in a bottle to do our every beckon call. But David reiterates here that he is counting on the Lord because he has put his hope in the Word of God! He is not trying to convince God to do his will. No, David is counting on the Lord because the Lord is trustworthy. He can count on the Lord because his hope is in the Lord, in His Word. To lie is to sin; since God cannot sin, He cannot lie. So, David puts his hopes in the Word of the Lord. He is not counting on God answering every prayer request with a "Yes", but he is counting on the Lord to be faithful in all that He promised He would be. Has God ever let you down? If you answered "Yes", what is your view of God? Is he a genie in a bottle or a prayer vending machine in the sky? Or is He holy and righteous and the Creator of everything seen and unseen? Where is your hope? Is your hope in yourself or in your abilities? Have you placed your hope in your family and friends? Who do you count on most? Count on the Lord and put your hope in Him! What is the first step you can take in doing this today? How can you apply this verse in your life so that you can honestly say that you are counting on the Lord and the Lord alone? How can His Word give you hope for what you are going through today? How can you change your view of God to have a right view of who He is?

JUNE 8

> I am the good shepherd. The good shepherd lays down his life for the sheep. John 10:11

If you ask any rancher or animal expert, they will all tell you that sheep are really unintelligent animals. And yet, God refers to us (Believers) as His sheep, thus, Jesus is known as the Good Shepherd. But the Bible tends to repeat itself, not because it doesn't have enough to say, but because we tend to be unwise and forgetful like sheep. Jesus calmed the sea with His voice and raised Jairus' daughter from the dead. Then, when 5,000 men were gathered and the disciples didn't know what to do, Jesus turned five loaves and two fish into an all you can eat buffet for the men and their families. He turned water into wine and raised a dead girl to life. He walked on water, raised Lazarus from the dead and told His disciples He would die and come back to life. After His crucifixion, where were they? Some hid in an upper room while some were already heading back home to Emmaus. They were told! How soon they forgot. How soon we, too, forget. Amid trials and sufferings, we can tend to forget the goodness of God and what He has already done in our lives. We can read His Word, Scripture and be easily led astray by the World. Even though we may be like sheep, a good shepherd will do everything to protect his flock. Our Good Shepherd did everything He could to protect us from the snares and jowls of the wolf, the enemy. All we have to do is accept His gift and allow Him to pry open the wolf's jowls and carry us from it. The Good Shepherd laid His life down for us sheep, who so easily forget what He said, did and promised in our lives, so that we may always have the ability to return to Him. Sheep know the voice of their Shepherd; all we have to do is come back to Him, which is not a long journey since He is always right beside us. Jesus paid for it all, so we don't have to. He suffered all so that we could escape the jaws of death and suffering. In a technological society, we tend to lose the significance of metaphors and analogies like the Shepherd and His sheep; but if we take the time to look historically at them, we can fully appreciate and internalize the Words of Jesus. What are you willing to do to walk more closely with the Shepherd this week? How can you internalize this Scripture in your heart, that He knew you and laid His life down for you so that you could be in communion with the Father and not separated? What are you willing to sacrifice to spend more time with your Shepherd?

JUNE 9

> but God shows his love for us in that while we were still sinners, Christ died for us. Romans 5:8

When I was in high school and we were studying Greek Mythology, I remember how vengeful the gods were, how at any moment, Zeus would launch lightning bolts. People had to try to guess why the gods were mad. Then in college, when studying ancient eastern religions, we learned how some people would sacrifice even children or whip themselves until passing out trying to please their gods. This was hard for me to relate to because we don't have to kill ourselves to get approval from God. Here is the good news about Christ! That while we were still sinners, Jesus died for us! While we were still enemies of God, God sent His son Jesus to pay the price for our sins so we would have a bridge back to Him. He didn't wait until we stopped sinning; He didn't wait until we got our life back on track or even decided to come back to Him. He didn't wait on us. He came, He died and He rose again, so that when we get tired of being separated from Him the bridge is already built, the cross already bridges that divide. We just have to accept His gift and look at the love it took to motivate His sacrifice – while we were still an enemy of Him, He came. While in opposition to Him He laid down His life for us. I think it is so easy to just read over verses like this and not take in the full weight of what God wrote. The gravity of His love is displayed here in the text if we just take a few moments out of our busy day and meditate on this verse. We need to incorporate this verse and weave it into our inner being so that when we meet people who don't know God we can share that God wants them to be united with Him. When we meet judgmental and critical Christians not loving and definitely not living out their faith, we can pray for them and over them and extend God's love to them because God wants them united with Him as well. The gravity of this verse, if we truly believe this and live this verse out, should change how we view others; it should be a reminder of God's love for you, God's love for others and how they are the same. Take some time today to just meditate on this verse and see what God is telling you through this. What sin issue keeps tripping you up? What can you do to gain victory over it? How can you allow the power of the Holy Spirit to help you break strongholds? How does this verse affect the way you see others?

JUNE 10

> And he said to all, "If anyone would come after me, let him deny himself and take up his cross daily and follow me. For whoever would save his life will lose it, but whoever loses his life for my sake will save it." Luke 9:23-24

There is a version of the Gospel that is preached in some Christian churches that does not actually follow the Bible and it is referred to as the "Prosperity Gospel." This version of the Gospel tells people that God wants them to be happy, healthy and wealthy and if they are not, it must be a sin issue in their life causing their poverty. That version of the Gospel ignores many verses like this one. Jesus essentially told His disciples, His followers and the crowd, "If you want to follow me, pick up your noose, your electric chair, your lethal injection machine and follow me." See, when Jesus spoke this, the cross was not some lucky charm, or jewelry to be worn, or even something to tattoo on the body. It symbolized death, the most horrific death sentence ever invented. Jesus says that if you try to save your life by compromising me, you will actually lose it, but if you lose your life for my sake, you will actually save it! Jesus was the inventor of the counterculture. What He said then remains true today. Christianity is no walk in the park; while the plan of salvation is simple, the walk afterward is difficult. One verse in the Bible terrifies me, Matthew 7:21-23: "Not everyone who says to me, 'Lord, Lord,' will enter the kingdom of heaven, but the one who does the will of my Father who is in heaven. On that day, many will say to me, 'Lord, Lord, did we not prophesy in your name and cast out demons in your name and do many mighty works in your name?' And then will I declare to them, 'I never knew you; depart from me, you workers of lawlessness.'" I don't want to be one of the goats that did things for Him but portrayed Him and His message so poorly that He would say, "Depart from me. I never knew you!" I want everything I write and teach to be fully aligned with God's Word and not partially aligned. Jesus promised us that following Him and living our life for Him would be hard. As Christians, we have to die to ourselves daily to follow Him. The world hated Him, so that they would hate us. We would face trials and suffering, but He overcame trials and suffering. In Romans, Paul refers to believers as living sacrifices – living means we can crawl off the altar. Do we crawl off the altar to indulge desires, or do we daily die to ourselves? If He is our Lord, do we allow Him to program the GPS of our lives? Is He driving the vehicle, or do we regulate Him to the passenger seat or even worse the back seat? How can you better live out this verse in your life? How can you allow Him to be in the driver's seat of your life? What struggle do you have that you need to die to so that you can live freely in Him?

JUNE 11

> And let the peace of Christ rule in your hearts, to which indeed you were called in one body. And be thankful. Colossians 3:15

The fruit of the Spirit is love, joy, peace. Coming in a close third is...; no, not really. I do not believe these traits are ranked, but they are sequential, building on each other. Can you truly have the joy of the Lord if you do not have the love of the Lord in you? Can you truly have the peace of Christ if you don't know the joy of the Lord? This is something theologians love to debate, but not me; this is just the way I feel. But Paul reminds us to let the peace of Christ rule in our hearts. Why? Because we are called into one body. Not Baptist or Lutheran or Catholic, but the Body of Christ. The peace of Christ frees our minds from worry, doubt, fear and unbelief. The peace of Christ surpasses all understanding. It is in His peace that we can find rest; we can have relaxation for our mind, body and spirit. We must learn to allow the peace of Christ to rule in our hearts. We must allow the Holy Spirit to speak, direct and guide us for that fruit to develop in our lives, for us to grow, mature and for fruit to ripen in our lives. When we love others as Jesus, as God loves us, we can then develop the joy and peace of the Lord. We can be overwhelmed by the joy and our hearts and our minds can be ruled by His peace. Isn't it wonderful that God told Paul to remind us to allow the peace of Christ to rule in our hearts and not the laws and legalism that people use to limit God's love? When we are ruled by peace, there is serenity and safety; that is why we can be worry-free, doubt-free and fear-free. It is in being ruled by the peace of Christ that we can dismiss those confining attitudes. When worry, doubt, or fear come in, why is that? Do you notice it when you are closely walking with the Holy Spirit or when there has been a lapse in reading, prayer and application? Is it when we are following the guidance of the Holy Spirit or when we have taken the wheel back and are driving the vehicle of our lives ourselves? When we see God's plan for our lives manifested before us, it's easy; but when it's been a while, oh, how easily we forget. How can you hand over the reins, the steering wheel, so to speak and allow the Holy Spirit to drive your life? How can you allow the peace of Christ to manifest itself and rule over your heart? Is there something or some decision you need to repent over? What changes and decisions do you need to make so that surrender can occur?

JUNE 12

> for all have sinned and fall short of the glory of God and are justified by his grace as a gift, through the redemption that is in Christ Jesus, Romans 3:23-24

People love to compare. People love to one-up someone else. We even have a catchphrase for this behavior in America, "Keeping up with the Jones." On the opposite end of the scale, we also like to see ourselves as "not as bad" as others. We formulate a hierarchy of sin in our minds. Well, I'm not as bad as Hitler, Ted Bundy, or even Timothy McVey, so I must be okay. Paul, however, tells us that we have all sinned and we have all fallen short of the glory of God. We all need our sins forgiven and we all need to be redeemed through the blood of Jesus Christ. We are justified not by what we do or did, but only by the gift of grace that is given because God loves all of us. He wants all of us to be redeemed by the blood, not just a select few, 144,000, or any other number man might try to put there or label: Baptist, Catholic, or Presbyterian. Being saved is not being within a certain number or under a particular label; it is the blood of Jesus that was poured out to not cover, but cleanse us from our sins. All we have to do is accept the gift, accept Jesus as Lord and Savior and allow the Holy Spirit to live in us and through us. All sin separates us from God. The cross of Christ is the only bridge that can traverse and forge that gap. The ground is level at the cross. Anyone who comes to the cross and accepts it is saved, even the people mentioned in the opening. All of us have sinned. All of us have the same sized gap between God and us. Some have accepted the bridge, while some have rejected the bridge, but the gap, the bridge, is all the same. There is nothing that needs to be done before the bridge can be laid. It's already there! There are no obstacles to the cross, the bridge to Heaven. God cleared all the obstacles, but we need to ensure we don't erect any for ourselves or others. The honesty and heaviness of this verse should be both mentally convicting and liberating for souls. How can you live out this verse in your daily walk? How does this verse change the way you see others? How can you walk more in the freedom of Christ with this verse inscribed in both your heart and mind?

JUNE 13

> He himself bore our sins in his body on the tree, that we might die to sin and live to righteousness. By his wounds you have been healed.
> 1 Peter 2:24

Unless you have seen *The Passion of Christ* starring Jim Caviezel, you probably don't fully comprehend the gravity and severity of the crucifixion. Sometimes, it's hard to grasp the full gravity of it, because Jesus was fully God as well as fully human. His body was fully human. He got tired. He got hungry. He got thirsty. When the weight of our sins was poured out on His body, He cried out, "My God, My God, why have You forsaken me?" By His physical wounds we are healed and those wounds inflicted severe pain on Him. Yes, while they were driving the nails through His wrists and ankles, He prayed for them, "Father, forgive them, for they know not what they are doing." But He was still in pain. Three times He fell from the scourging and loss of blood on His way to the place of crucifixion. He thirsted while on the cross. When I read Scripture like this one, I try to take in the full weight of what is being said; how did the first hearers of this verse understand it and take it in? As Christians, we understand all of this, its basic theology – but the weight of it does not always sink in, the physical pain and suffering He endured for this to happen. He didn't evoke the God card and make Himself numb to it all. In fact, while praying about it, which is the only way he coped, He sweated drops of blood because He knew He was choosing to feel everything, to take everything in so that no one, then or now, could ever doubt the sincerity of His love for us, His love for you. Have you seen the movie? If so, do you replay those scenes in your mind when you read verses like this? He bore our sin and by His wounds we are healed. Have you taken the time to assess the full gravity of what Jesus did on the cross, not just at Easter time, but throughout the year? How can you apply the weight of this verse to your walk with Him to allow the Holy Spirit to keep you close? What are you willing to do so that the Holy Spirit can guide your walk and deepen your relationship? How does this verse affect the way you view God? How does this verse affect the way you see others?

JUNE 14

> Rejoice in hope, be patient in tribulation, be constant in prayer.
> Romans 12:12

Why is it that we get everything so mixed up, rejoicing in pleasure, impatient while facing difficulties and praying only at meals and bedtimes? Really, why is that? At the beginning of Chapter Twelve, Paul tells us to "transform and renew our minds." He means to transform our minds so they are set above and not level and to renew our minds with the mind of Christ by the indwelling of the Holy Spirit. It happens when our minds are transformed on the eternal and not impermanence of life on Earth. When we transform our minds, we have the ability to rejoice in hope. Job in Chapter Six reminds us that God is our hope and Solomon, in Proverbs Ten, tells us that the hope of the righteous brings joy. We have hope in the Lord and when we have our hope in the Lord, we have the ability to be patient in tribulation. When trials come and they will, we need to see them through with patience. When an egg is laid, a cocoon is sewn, sand is deposited in an oyster, or coal is underground, it takes time and pressure, but you get birth, you get butterflies, you get pearls and you get diamonds. The final product is incomplete and not as valuable when the process is rushed. When trials and tribulations come, we must remain patient, knowing who is in ultimate control of the situation. When our minds are transformed, we desire to be in prayer constantly, throughout the day, not just during meals and bedtimes. When our minds are transformed and are focused on Him, the Holy Spirit will bring to mind people, events and situations to pray for. When you think of someone, do you dismiss it as weird that they would come to mind, or transform your thinking and pray for them? When you see someone upset in a store, do you mock their impatience or pray for them? If you see a car speeding and weaving down the road, does anger boil up or spiritual peace because you are praying for them? "Be constant in prayer" is not always about you and your needs, wants and desires; it is not about asking for others either. Be constant in prayer, thanking Him for your health, the weather, your family, friends, the sunset or sunrise and birds chirping. Thanksgiving is such an important aspect of prayer that I think we forget about it, but we should be including it daily. How can you live this out in your faith walk and relationship with God today? How can you be constant in prayer? How does this verse affect your prayer life?

JUNE 15

> Jesus answered them, "Truly, truly, I say to you, you are seeking me, not because you saw signs, but because you ate your fill of the loaves. Do not work for the food that perishes, but for the food that endures to eternal life, which the Son of Man will give to you. For on him God the Father has set his seal." John 6:26-27

The crowd searched for Jesus not because they wanted a relationship with Him, nor did they care for His teaching; they sought Him to get something. While it would be extremely easy to judge these people and be critical of them, how often do we do that with God Himself? Do we only pray when life is careening out of control in a, "Jesus take the wheel" sort of circumstance? Do we remember to pray when we've gotten ourselves in a bind? Then we tend to bargain with God, "If you get me out of this, then I will ..." fill in the blank. Maybe it's not so extreme, but when praying, we go through a litany of prayer requests either for us or for others, but that is it and we do not give God any talk time, praise or glory. Do we take time during the day for His teaching; do we really care about our daily bread or just food for our bellies? How much time do we spend in His Word every day? How much time do we spend every day worshiping Him, or is that a Sunday-only event? Do we seek Him for His guidance, direction and to have a deeper relationship with Him? It is easy to be critical when our basic needs are already met, but these people did not. Jesus cared for both their physical needs and spiritual needs. He fed them on Monday, but when all they wanted was basic needs, Jesus lovingly reminded them that there is more to life, that the spiritual is more important than the physical. On a mission trip to Haiti, people with barely anything would walk miles to church service and would devote hours. In America, we have people leave a church because the music is too loud or they don't sing the right kind of music; but those with little worship more and deeper than most Christians here in America with much. The Haitians understood Jesus' lesson here; the Bread of Life, broken and beaten for them, was more important than the volume of the music, the length of the sermon, or whether they were going back to a hut with food or not. So, we come back to the main question here, even Jesus asked 2000 years ago: Are we going after Him because He fills our stomachs or because He fills our soul? Do you worship every Sunday, like it is Easter, or just once or twice a year? How can you deepen your relationship with Him above the superficial prayer requests? How do you work for the "food" that endures until eternal life? How does this verse affect how and what you pray for?

JUNE 16

> For this is the love of God, that we keep his commandments. And his commandments are not burdensome. 1 John 5:3

When it comes down to it, Jesus reminded us that all the law and all the commandments could be summed up in two: love God with all your heart, soul, mind and strength and the other is just like it, love your neighbor as yourself. John doesn't say it is easy, he just says they are not burdensome. It is simple. God's plan and God's love are simple. It is not complicated. His love for us directs us to keep His commandments. Then why, as humans, do we always mess things up and make them more complicated than they need to be? It is not burdensome to love God, but pride and selfishness can make it difficult. He promises His yolk, His plan, His love is not a burden, not burdensome. It is really quite simple if we leave it to Him. But when we get our hands into it and our interpretations of it, we muddy the waters and add extra weight to it. Love God above all else; with all your heart, nothing before Him is a priority. Nothing should come before Him in our heart; not our spouse, not our children, nothing. He should come first in our heart so that nothing leads us away from Him. He should come first in our mind. He should be the first thought on our mind when we wake up and the last thought on our mind as we fall asleep. He should be on our mind constantly throughout the day, seeking His guidance and direction in our lives, seeking His way to make decisions. Our strength should go towards extending the overflowing love we get from Him to others; all need it, some don't realize it and some don't think they are worthy of it. But regardless of their thoughts about Him and His love, our strength should be going towards His plan and His love. If we truly live out this first commandment of His, the second is super easy to do – love our neighbors as we love ourselves. But it is only easy when we have first loved God with all of our heart, mind, soul and strength. How can the love of God be a burden? If we keep it, the love of God, it is not. Do you feel beat down and tired with your walk? Which part of God's commandments are you either not keeping or doing it your way? How can you get out from under the weight and the burden of the mess we create for ourselves and do it God's way? Why do we tend to think God's commandments are burdensome?

JUNE 17

This is the day the LORD has made. Let us rejoice and be glad in it.
Psalm 118:24

When was the last time you woke up happy and ready to start the day; I mean, actually excited to start the day? My wife would sing this verse when she would get the kids up for school, which would drive them wildly mad. The oldest and youngest are more like me and are not "morning people". They struggle to get up and get going, but guess what? Today is a new day. This is the day that the Lord has made and He has made it for you; what are you going to do with it? See, none of us are promised tomorrow. At any moment, a car may run a red light, our heart may stop, we may be in the wrong place at the wrong time and we never know when our last moment will be. When you woke up today was it with joy, a pep in your step and did you thank God for waking you up, or did you hit the snooze button, grudgingly get out of bed and your mind start racing about everything that had to be done today? We need to stop! We need to be Thankful! What I often hear from people who have lost a loved one is, "If I only had one more day with them!" Well, guess what, you do; you have one more day with people you love and to show God's love to people, it's TODAY! Don't let the sun go down before you let the people you love know you love them. Do your coworkers and bosses know you appreciate them and their leadership? Don't let the sun go down before you thank God for another day that you get to witness His mighty works. Take time today to be glad and rejoice that the Lord gave you today, no matter what is going on or what is on your calendar. Take time today to rejoice and be glad! How can you make God a priority in your day? How can you change your mindset so that when you wake up you realize the gravity of this verse? How can you rejoice in the blessing of a new day? How can you show God your appreciation for today? How can you rejoice in the day? How can you use this verse to bring comfort if you have lost a loved one? How can the Holy Spirit help you celebrate every day you are given?

JUNE 18

> I give them eternal life and they will never perish and no one will snatch them out of my hand. My Father, who has given them to me, is greater than all and no one is able to snatch them out of the Father's hand. I and the Father are one." John 10:28-30

If we go all the way back to Job, God's protection was on those who followed the Lord. Satan had to ask permission to do anything to those who followed the Lord. Jesus reaffirms this in John 10:29, "No one is able to snatch them out of the Father's hand." This is one of the Scriptures Christians who believe you can't lose your salvation refer to, supporting their beliefs. If someone truly gives their life to Christ, Christ gives them eternal life; the Holy Spirit resides in them and no one can evict Him. But if a person is just going through the motions, just providing lip service, then is their salvation real? I don't know because it really is all a heart issue. But we can hold firm to Jesus' own words: "No One can snatch them out of my Father's hand." In Arabic, it means "no one"; in Greek, it means "no one"! No one is able to take us out of the hands of God. Signed, sealed and delivered. Signed by the blood of Christ, sealed by the Holy Spirit and delivered into the Hands of God our Father. That should bring comfort to us that no matter how many times we mess up, how many times we allow temptations to overcome us, our anger to overrule us, Satan cannot, ever, take us out of God's hand. We won't be perfect and we will mess up, but we have been forgiven, eternally. Does this give us permission to keep on sinning? Paul tells us in Romans 6:1, by no means! If we are dead in sin and raised to life in Christ, we cannot remain in sin. Thus, because of God's mercy and grace, we don't keep sinning because of forgiveness. We try to avoid sin because we love Him as He loves us. So, you messed up and you stumbled. Tomorrow is a new day, this afternoon is a new beginning and tonight hasn't happened yet, so we still have time to change course. We can be confident that God, who is greater than all, holds us in His hands, so we cannot be stolen, plucked, or snatched out of them. God's love is unending and we can never be removed from His Presence. How does this truth affect how you live today? How can you use this verse to deepen your relationship with God?

JUNE 19

> For God is the one who provides seed for the farmer and then bread to eat. In the same way, he will provide and increase your resources and then produce a great harvest of generosity in you. 2 Corinthians 9:10 NLT

Why does God bless us? His love for us is, of course, the obvious reason. Paul reminds the Corinthians and us, that there is a deeper purpose for why He chooses to bless us. God blesses us so we can, in turn, bless others. He doesn't fill our storehouses so we can build more storehouses. In fact, Jesus spoke of that in Luke 12:13-21, when the rich ruler was building more barns to hold his wealth, but that very night his soul was demanded of him. God provides the seed for the farmer and thus the bread that comes from that grain. He does not provide it to make bigger farms and a select few to be richer while more go hungry. God will increase our resources so that we will produce a great harvest of generosity in our souls. Seeing the needs of others as more important than our wants and seeing the needs of others as a way to be an extension of God's hand rather than an inconvenience in our busy schedule. This cannot be read that God wants to increase our resources for the sake of increasing our resources, just so that we have more abundance to indulge in. James reminds us that pure religion, undefiled religion, is taking care of the widows and orphans. So, not only does God take care of us, but also, He wants us to show our love and appreciation to Him by utilizing His gifts and blessings He bestows to us on others. He wants others to see the Love of God through us, through our actions, thus drawing them close to Him. I recently saw a meme on a social media platform that says, "When God blesses you financially, don't raise your standard of living – raise your standard of giving!" That kind of sums up today's verse. Your love for God is demonstrated by your love for others. How appreciative of His blessings are you? Do you see blessings as a way to get something you've always wanted or a way to help someone who has nothing? How much of your prayer time is spent in thanksgiving compared to requesting? How big a harvest of generosity is God wanting to produce in your life and are you willing to allow that to happen?

JUNE 20

> The Lord is good to those who wait for him, to the soul who seeks him. It is good that one should wait quietly for the salvation of the Lord. Lamentations 3:25-26

Being patient is not an easy thing to do. In this fast paced world that we live in, we seem to grow more and more impatient with each passing day. Smart technology is training us, even the younger generations, to be more impatient. If a text or email is read and not responded to immediately, we may get anxious or even upset. I believe that this mentality seeps into our relationship with God as well. We pray and when we don't get an answer right away, we end up frustrated. But Jeremiah writes in Lamentations that the Lord is good to those who wait on Him. When we wait on the Lord, it is actually good for our soul as it causes us to seek Him and His presence more. When we wait on the Lord, it should be like Jesus' description of fasting; no one should know we are waiting on the Lord. When we complain and that is really what it is, complaining, it self-promotes us over the Lord, saying we know when the timing is right and we know what the right answer is, so we don't really need Him. That is a subtle form of pride. We should wait quietly so when someone asks us, "Did you pray about it?", we can answer, "Yes, I am just patiently waiting on the Lord" and they never knew. Patience teaches us self-control and full reliance on God. His timing is always perfect, never late nor delayed. It may seem that while we are walking through dry spells, desert times of our life, or valleys, it is hard to be patient. But look at Abraham and Sarah who wandered the land, through deserts, facing difficult people and while being patient God showed up and blessed them. When they were impatient and trusted their own plans, that is when they got in trouble. When we walk through those dry spells of life, it is then that it is even more important that we quietly wait on the Lord. He will provide "shade and stream" during those dry spells if we look to Him. Remember, patience develops full reliance on Him and a deeper relationship with Him. Why is it so hard to be patient? What is God trying to teach you when He is asking you to patiently wait on Him? What did He develop in you the last time you had to patiently wait on Him? What is He developing in your heart now as He is having you wait on Him today?

JUNE 21

> For godly grief produces a repentance that leads to salvation without regret, whereas worldly grief produces death. 2 Corinthians 7:10

The first part of this Scripture probably doesn't quite make sense upon first read – the kind of sorrow that God *WANTS* us to experience? God wants us to experience sorrow? I thought He was a loving God... But this is why reading the verses before and after (developing context) is important. Because of sin, there is grief and sorrow in the world. Since man brought sin and grief into the world, we experience brokenness and sorrow. The kind of sorrow God wants us to experience is the kind that leads us away from sin. This repentance turns us towards Him and results in salvation. We should feel sorrow when we sin, not guilt. Guilt is a tool of the enemy, but sorrow is a natural emotion that can cause us to go one of two ways. We should feel sorrow because we don't want to disappoint our dad and when we mess up, that kind of sorrow drives us to Him to ask for forgiveness. When we take time to be honest with God, despite our shame and regret, it inspires deeper healing and increases our ability to be intimate with our Savior. Worldly sorrow and guilt do not lead to repentance. These emotions generally lead to isolation and hiding instead of all out rejection of the action or admitting we were wrong. See, when we are in a real relationship with God, sin causes sorrow which motivates us to talk to Him and ask Him to forgive us. When we are in a real relationship with Him, not just a weekend service visitation, we want to restore that relationship as soon as possible because we know that sin separates us from God and we don't want to be separated from Him. Remember, guilt never comes from God, it comes from satan. Conviction comes from the Holy Spirit. Conviction should drive us to change and repent of our sinful behavior. Guilt drives us to hide or give up and the enemy gets us stuck in a sensation of denial or defeat. It is the conviction in sorrow that drives us to the foot of the cross and drives us into prayer. When we are wrong, do we know the difference between the sorrow God wants us to experience? If so, then it will bring us closer to Him and the sorrow that drives a wedge between us and our Heavenly Father. Dismiss the guilt and accept the conviction and draw closer to Him today! How can you determine if sorrow comes from the world or the Word? How do you deal with sorrow or grief over your actions?

JUNE 22

> The grass withers, the flower fades, but the word of our God will stand forever. Isaiah 40:8

In Colorado, we joke that, "If you don't like the weather, wait 30 minutes and it will change." It is constantly inconsistent, often making the weather forecasters' predictions wrong. No matter what season it is, in Colorado the cycles are only partially predictable. The grass turns a beautiful green in the spring and remains lush during the summer, but then in the fall, it withers and in winter it dies; the lushness does not remain. My wife and I bought tulips on a Saturday and within two weeks the flowers fully bloomed, the petals fell and then they were just stems – the flower faded, although once glorious, it faded into just a stem. Life on Earth is short and nothing is permanent except the Word of God. The Word of God spoke into existence everything that we can see, hear, feel and know. It is the Word of God that causes such division. Atheists have tried debunking it, other religions and their leaders have questioned it and governments have outlawed it. Why? It is the Living Word of the Living God. Truth remains. Truth does not fade. Truth does not wither or die. Truth does not change. It is the only thing that is permanent and will remain forever. So, when life throws you lemons, steers you into a valley, or brings in clouds of confusion, don't turn and run. Don't just ignore the pain, try to drown it out by taking up a bottle, or hiding from those who care about you most. Get into the Word of God, the Living Word of God that brings life and clarity. God should be our first choice, not our last. If the Word of God says to obtain guidance like in Proverbs, seek guidance from a counselor, but a godly one, one centered on the Word of God. It is not anti-Christian to seek medical help for a chemical imbalance or therapy from a professional, but seek first the Word of God. It is Truth, it is forever and it brings life. When the way is not clear, ask the Holy Spirit to make it clear, to bring divine clarity. Ask the Holy Spirit to show you the application as you read the Bible, how you can apply the verses to your life. Isn't God's love so wonderful and how intimate His knowledge is of us that He knows we can't do it alone? He knew that His Holy Word might not make sense in our unholy minds, so He sent His Son to speak it and the Holy Spirit as a Helper and Counselor to guide us and direct us in understanding His Word. Isn't it wonderful that all of our questions are answered in one book, His Word, His Scripture, His Bible and we have access to reading it? We just need to take the time to read it, understand it and apply it! How does knowing that the Word of God is *forever* enhance your walk with Christ today? How do you apply His powerful Truth and eternal promises in your life?

JUNE 23

> Love does no wrong to a neighbor; therefore love is the fulfilling of the law. Romans 13:10

1 Corinthians 13, commonly dubbed as "the love chapter", has been read at numerous weddings, mine included. It talks about what love is and is not, but the verse is ultimately not about the love between a man and a woman. It's more about the love God has for us and how we should share that love with others. Paul, who wrote both Romans and Corinthians, reminds the Roman church that Love does no wrong. Love does no wrong in the words we speak, the actions we take and the decisions we make. Paul continues that thought, saying, "Therefore, love is the fulfilling of the law." If you want to obey the law, fulfill the law, then Love. If you want a deep relationship with God, then surrender to Love. If you want blessings and protection, then choose to be in His Love. If you want God to use you as a lighthouse, a beacon for His presence, His love, His peace, His mercy, His grace, His forgiveness, then be Love. Jesus, when asked what the greatest commandment was, He responded, "Love!" Love the Lord your God with all your heart. Love the Lord your God with all your soul. Love the Lord your God with all your mind. Then He added, "Love your neighbor as yourself." See, if you love your neighbor, you will honor and obey your parents, you will not lie, you will not kill, you will not steal and you will not sleep with someone else's spouse, nor desire what your neighbor has. When you love your neighbor as God loves you, none of those desires happen, thus fulfilling the law. God so loved the world that He sent Jesus for us. God so loved the worlds that when Jesus ascended into Heaven, He sent the Holy Spirit to guide us, direct us and to plant, sow and nurture love in us so that we can love God and love others. Danny Gokey has a song out featuring Michael W Smith called *Love God, Love People.* The lyrics explain how we rush around so much, checking boxes, getting caught up in our own life's details, we forget the simplicity of God's law: Love God, Love People; Love God, Love your neighbor as yourself. How much simpler of a plan can be devised? Think about what the world would look like if even just the self-proclaimed Christians lived this out in their daily lives. Love does no wrong to anyone, thus fulfilling the law. How much different would your life look if you lived out this Truth? What steps can you take to do so, starting today? How does love fulfill the law of God? How do you love those who do not love you?

JUNE 24

Be strong and let your heart take courage, all you who wait for the Lord! Psalm 31:24

The Bible is written for everyone. However, some scriptures have specific, targeted audiences. Some verses are written to everyone while some are written to fellow believers as the target audience. Today's verse is one of those examples. To those of you who put your hope in the Lord, "Be Strong and Courageous". Why should we be strong and courageous? Because we put our hope in the Lord. The Lord goes before us and fights for us. The Greek word for Holy Spirit was *paraclete*, meaning a back-to-back fighting warrior. Literally, His back is to your back. When you get tired, He goes first and you switch and you cover the back is the word picture for *paraclete*. The Lord has our best interests at heart. But notice that it does not say, "Rest easy all who put their hope in the Lord". No, He says, "Be strong and courageous". Why is that? Because God knows that when we put our Hope in Him, we will face trials and troubles. When we are saved and the Holy Spirit moves into our hearts, we put a large target on our backs. The more we obey the Lord, follow the instruction of the Holy Spirit and allow Him to direct and guide our lives, the target gets bigger. The enemy of God will try to persuade us to leave Him and leave His protection so he can attack us. So, when we put our hope in the Lord, we must be strong and courageous to face the coming trials. His plan is simple, but not easy; that is why we need to be strong. "Be strong in the Lord" means we must allow His strength to be our strength. His plan is clear, but the enemy hides and will try to use who and what we love to cause fear. So, we must be courageous, that way we can stand with God and not be led astray. While we wait on the Lord, we must remain strong and watchful for attacks and schemes of the enemy. While we wait on the Lord, we must be courageous and not allow the lies of the enemy to convince us or trick us into walking away from what God is doing. God's timing is not our timing and because we can be impatient, in that waiting the enemy can use fear and doubt to question if we heard God right or even if God will what He says He will do. God gives us courage to fight the fear and doubt and kill it where it starts. God knows what the schemes of Satan are – that is why He is constantly reminding us to be *strong* and *courageous*. What area of your life do you need to increase your strength of faith? Where is God calling you to be courageous, realizing that God has that part of your life in His hands?

JUNE 25

> And it is my prayer that your love may abound more and more, with knowledge and all discernment, Philippians 1:9

Imagine the impact if our love were to "abound more and more", even if just professing Christians exhibited love in the way they treat each other and non-believers. Would that make a difference in our society? Absolutely it would. There is no doubt that Love changes everything. Thirteen ordinary men turned the world upside down and it's never been the same. The NLT version says it this way, "I pray that your love will overflow more and more and that you will keep on growing in knowledge and understanding." Are you walking so closely with the Lord, with the Holy Spirit, that the love He is pouring into your life is overflowing, like a gallon jug under an open spicket? Are you allowing Him to pour Love into your life so that it just oozes out in everything you say and do? Not only that, but Paul adds that you will keep growing in your knowledge, discernment and understanding. Knowledge, discernment and understanding of what? His Love, His Word, His Will. Understanding how to love your neighbor and enemy, knowing what the Bible says, what God says, then discernment on how to live out Scripture in your life. In fact, an easy way to love your neighbor and love your enemy is to pray this over them, "May the love of God abound more and more, that God's love would overflow more and more. May the knowledge and understanding of God and His love, His Mercy, His grace be continually filling and never ending." May we pray the same for ourselves, our children and our family. One of the most powerful prayers you can pray is the praying of God's Word back to Him. In leadership and counseling, we are taught to repeat and rephrase what the person said to show active listening and understanding or help clear up what we didn't hear or understand. How much more powerful is that when we do that with God? When we do, it's called prayer, but it shows our intentional and active listening, the importance of Him saying it and if we got the meaning wrong, He will let us know. If you have never prayed Scripture back, try it and you will see the power in it. Start with something simple yet powerful, like Philippians 1:9. Are you willing to change up your prayer routine? What does your prayer life look like? Do you pray for discernment? If not, why not? How does this verse deepen your relationship with our Living God?

JUNE 26

> "The LORD is my portion," says my soul, "therefore I will hope in him." Lamentations 3:24

How did Jesus survive in the wilderness for forty days? The same way Moses did on the mountain; the Lord, God, was their portion. They fully relied on God. When I started in youth ministry in the 1990s, jelly bracelets were big and the Christian commerce caught on to that making FROG and WWJD bracelets a popular fad. While great in concept, they soon became a cliché. But if we Christians could get back to the heart of the clichés, we could go deeper with our relationship with God. FROG stands for "Fully Relying on God", meaning the Lord is my portion, the Lord is enough for me, the Lord will provide my needs and therefore I will have hope in Him and have no fear. WWJD stands for "What Would Jesus Do?" If we would just stop for a moment before we speak, before we act, we might actually live out our faith more and shine more of His light in our lives. As Christians, we need to stop the enemy from making clichés of our faith and stand firm in Truth given by Scripture and the Holy Spirit. This passage, "The Lord is my portion, says my soul and therefore I will hope in Him", should not be just historical, but the belief should be alive in our souls. Instead of desiring the latest tech or streaming service or instant fame, we should be satisfied with the portion God gives us and be directed by the Holy Spirit to use the portion God gives us not only for our survival, but also to bring others the Gospel Message, the Good News. Our hope should be in the Lord and not in our talents, our 401ks or our jobs, not even in our spouses or kids. Our hope comes from the Lord and thus should be in the Lord alone. He is our portion, so when the enemy attacks and the dark night of the soul arrives, your hope is not drained, you don't forget the portion provided to you to get through it; you can turn back to the light. Where is your hope centered; where is your hope anchored? Is the Lord your portion? Do you trust Him to be enough to meet all your needs? How can you start living out this Scripture in your life and experience the hope it describes? What changes in your life do you need to make so that the Lord is your portion, demonstrating trust that the Lord is enough for you?

JUNE 27

> And he said, "Naked I came from my mother's womb and naked shall I return. The LORD gave and the LORD has taken away; blessed be the name of the LORD." In all this Job did not sin or charge God with wrong. Job 1:21-22

When life goes sideways, we go down a path we didn't see coming, or when life throws us a curveball and hits us unexpectedly, what is our typical response? Do we shake our fists at Heaven like the lyrics in the Matthew West song "Do Something" or do we get mad at God? All in a day, Job lost everything. His entire business was wiped out, his home destroyed and his children killed. Job was a righteous man, a devout man, following God. If anyone had the right to be angry at God, it was Job. But what did Job do when his world was turned upside down? He fell to the ground and worshiped God. His wife, in her despair, just cried, "Curse God and die," while Job responded in love: "Naked I came from my mother's womb and naked shall I return. The Lord gave and He has taken away, but still, blessed be the name of the Lord." In his hurt, despair and tragedy, Job did not sin; he did not "charge" this "injustice" to God, but he had a deep understanding of his relationship with God. When our dream job gets taken away, we lose that loved one in our life, or when nothing seems to be going in our favor, is our response similar to Job's response? Do we drop to the floor and worship? Worshiping through the pain is the only way I know to relieve the suffering. Sometimes during the process of worship, I can't vocalize the lyrics because the tears are steadily flowing, but it is then that my heart has a chance to deeply worship. I've learned in my life to stop asking God, "Why?" but change it to, "What?" "What, God, can I learn from this?" Or "How?" "How can I use this life lesson and pain to be a better person, husband, father, son, brother, or employee?" "How can *we* use this to deepen our relationship, Lord?" "What do I have to do to draw closer to you during this?" It was worshiping during the pain and hurt that got me through the loss of my brother and gave me the strength to officiate his funeral. God is good and perfect and He loves us, but because of sin we all suffer on this side of Heaven. It doesn't negate His holiness, but amplifies it since He is right there in the pain to carry us. In our daily walk, in pain, do you have the ability to say, "Blessed be the name of the Lord?" Like the song by that same title by Matt Redman, "When I'm found in the desert place, when I walk through the wilderness, on the road marked with suffering, or when there's pain in the offering… Blessed be your name." How can we strive to have the faith and endurance of Job? Remember God's love for you was demonstrated by Him sending Jesus on a mission for you. How can today's verse help you to always remember to bless the name of the Lord?

JUNE 28

> no weapon that is fashioned against you shall succeed and you shall refute every tongue that rises against you in judgment. This is the heritage of the servants of the Lord and their vindication from me, declares the Lord. Isaiah 54:17

Sometimes we think we are not strong enough to do what God calls us to do. But we don't have to do it alone. The Greek word for the Holy Spirit is *paraclete*; if you recall, it refers to the idea of two soldiers fighting back-to-back, so when we get tired the Holy Spirit fights for us. God told Isaiah, "No weapon that is fashioned against you shall succeed and you shall refute every tongue that rises against you in judgment." Jesus promised that no one would be able to pluck us from His hand. The enemy may attack us, but God defends us, protects us and the Holy Spirit fights for us. Remember the definition of *paraclete*? It is back-to-back. We have to be walking with Him daily in order to experience this level of support. We can't go off on our own course and choose not to follow His directions. Now, this does not mean that the Lord will not protect us when we wander, but if we want His full protection, we need to be in an intimate relationship with Him. By doing so, we know His Word, His Will, His Way. When we are intimate with Christ, we tend to wander less and return faster when we do. We can be assured that no weapon, whether physical, spoken, or that another person fashions against us, will succeed. That truth should ground us and encourage us to live boldly for the Lord. No tongue that raises a judgment against us will be successful. So, speak the truth in love, share the Good News that our Lord lives – His grave is empty! He walked out of it so we could walk into eternal life with Him. The Lord says that no weapon shall succeed; it does not say that no attack will be formed. Attacks will come when we live out our lives for God. Untruths will be spoken, but what do we have to fear? Nothing! We must be strong and courageous! God commands us, Joshua 1:9, "Have I not commanded you? Be strong and courageous. Do not be frightened and do not be dismayed, for the Lord your God is with you wherever you go." Why can we be strong and courageous? Because the Lord our God goes with us. Why will no weapon succeed or words of judgment prevail against us; because the Lord our God goes before us, He is with us and He wants us to trust Him to fulfill His words and His promises. How does this verse encourage you? How can you be bolder in living out your faith knowing this verse?

JUNE 29

> And you will feel secure because there is hope; you will look around and take your rest in security. Job 11:18

Where does your hope come from? Where does your security come from? Job's friend Zophar tells him, "If you prepare your heart, then…" implying he did something wrong to cause his own suffering. When we are in a right relationship with God, there is security in knowing that He is in control. Here, Job had actually done nothing wrong. But when we sin and we don't allow conviction to turn us to repent, we allow the enemy to use guilt to keep us from feeling that security that comes from the Lord. Guilt can be a hope and security killer, but we have hope in Jesus Christ. David writes in Psalm 121, "I lift up my eyes to the hills. From where does my help come? My help comes from the LORD, who made heaven and earth." He who made the heavens and the Earth is there to help us; look around and see His goodness. Look around, including in the mirror and see the wonderful work He is doing and has done. We can rest because the Lord is our help, our Savior. He sent the Holy Spirit to not only be a Comforter, but also as a Helper. We just have to be willing to allow Him to help us, to be our Helper, to give us the help we need (not just answering prayers the way we want). We can rest and have security knowing that He will never leave nor forsake us. He is always by our side, even when it feels like we are alone. Don't listen to the world, the enemy and put your hope in your job, because it can disappear overnight. Don't put your hope in your 401K or your health, because they may be gone tomorrow. Your hope is in your salvation; your hope is the Lord and because of that you can rest secure that no weapon formed against you can succeed – the war is already won. Look around, take a rest. If the Lord rested on the seventh day and He commanded that we keep it Holy, the Sabbath was created for man, so prioritize taking a Sabbath and rest. During your Sabbath, look around and count your blessings, take hold of your security and praise Him who is your ever-present help in times of need. Acknowledge Him for being a strong tower built on steadfast love, mercy and grace. How secure do you feel? How well do you rest? What blessings have you taken for granted in the busyness of life?

JUNE 30

"The Lord will fight for you and you have only to be silent." Exodus 14:14

In the absence of prayer, in the silence of our minds, worries tend to arise. What is "worry"? Other words for worry include disturb, fret, oppress, fear, vex, distress and despair. We know that for those that believe in Christ as our Savior, the Lord fights for us. The NLT translation of this passage goes "The Lord Himself fights for you; just stay calm." Again, it brings to mind how simple God's plan is, but how humans tend to complicate things. Remember that simple does not equate to easy. In the midst of spiritual warfare, we can easily become overwhelmed by the loss of a loved one, a medical diagnosis, or the loss of a job. In every circumstance, the Lord will fight for us. We have to remain calm and be silent. This is Joe, not the Bible, but I think the "you have to be silent" means that we need to quiet our minds. We have to stop playing out all the possible outcomes. We have to limit the talk time we have and that we give the enemy and be silent to hear that still, small voice, the Voice of God. We can allow the enemy talk time in our minds and then he complicates situations and allows fear to reside in us. If we limit Satan's talk time and only allow the Holy Spirit to talk, when we face these situations, His peace that surpasses all understanding can envelop us and give us the strength to move forward in the confidence that the Lord is fighting the battle for us. We tend to do all the talking and say "Amen" at the end where we never give God time to respond. You only have to be silent. You only have to remain calm. What battle is overwhelming you that you need to hand over to the Lord and allow Him to fight for you? How can you make sure you remain calm and silent so that He can speak to you? Are you allowing His presence and Word to comfort you?

JULY 1

> but they who wait for the LORD shall renew their strength; they shall mount up with wings like eagles; they shall run and not be weary; they shall walk and not faint. Isaiah 40:31

Ever feel like your strength is just drained from you? Ever feel like you have nothing left to give and nothing you seem to do can fix that? Are you waiting on the Lord or trying to do it all yourself? The verse before this one says "youth will faint and young men will become exhausted… but". Verse 31 starts with a big word, *but*. It means there is something different, a contrast, that it doesn't have to be that way. What is different? But those who *wait for the Lord* shall renew their strength. See, God's timing is always perfect. Wait for the Lord, allow the Holy Spirit to lead and He will renew your strength. Those who wait for the Lord shall mount up with wings like eagles and soar above the storm as they wait for the Lord. Ever watch an eagle in flight? Its gliding seems almost effortless. When we wait for the Lord, the Holy Spirit will renew our strength so that as we move forward it will seem effortless to others. We will run and not grow weary like the young men who run and do not seek the Lord. We will walk and faint like the youth who do it on their own ability. Recently, some commercials have been released regarding mental health and not seeking help. One shows a man bench pressing a huge weight by himself and struggling. In that commercial, a man walks up and asks if he can help him. He's worried about what others might think of him if he can't lift the weight himself. I think we can do the same thing with our spiritual walk. We think we have to do it alone, by ourselves, not asking for help. But one of the titles of the Holy Spirit is the Comforter and another is Helper. He has specific tasks in our lives, but we must allow Him to do that in us. We must wait for the Lord and allow Him to renew in us His strength; allow the Holy Spirit to be the Helper He is designed to be and help restore and renew our souls. How do you wait for the Lord? What steps can you take to allow Him to be the Helper in your life, advancing your walk with Him?

JULY 2

"Jesus answered and said to him, 'If anyone loves Me, he will keep My word; and My Father will love him and We will come to him and make Our home with him.'" John 14:23

Can you remember a time when you did not follow your parent's advice or did the opposite of it and did not work out in your favor? Remember that feeling? For those of us who have a good relationship with our parents and love and respect them, that feeling of disappointment is magnified. Jesus reminds us that just like with our parents, we will keep His word and obey if we love. What does His Word say? "Love the Lord, your God, with all your heart, with all your soul, with all your mind and with all your strength... Love your neighbor as yourself." Simple but hard. It's not complex, but it is difficult to follow through on. It's easy to say, "Yeah, I love God," but then, are you at church when the Broncos (or any favorite team) are playing? Is church or Bible reading the first thing to be removed from a list to make room for something else? What else does He say in His Holy Word? "Take up your cross and follow Him", meaning to die daily to your wants and desires and live out God's will and desires for your life. Simple, yet hard. It is not complex in His words. His Word is easy to understand, but when it comes to dying to self, killing personal wants and dreams to allow the Holy Spirit to guide us down His path, that is more difficult. If your spouse asks you to love them and you do, would you not put their needs before your own? To truly love someone is to sacrifice your wants and dreams and place their needs in higher priority. Love is patient, love is kind, love does not envy or boast in itself. Love is not arrogant, love does not insist on its own way; it bears, believes, hopes and endures all things. Do you Love Him? Of course. Or perhaps a better question is, do you love Him according to His definition of love? How can you apply His Word in your life and what life change are you willing to make according to His Word? This week and as we progress through this new year, how can you keep His Word better than you did last year?

JULY 3

Rejoice in the Lord always; again I will say, rejoice. Philippians 4:4

Rejoice means "to take great joy or delight". What do you rejoice in? My family makes fun of me because when the Denver Broncos won their first Super Bowl with John Elway at the helm, when Terrell Davis ran in the winning touchdown, I jumped off the couch and accidentally punched a hole in the ceiling tile of my parent's basement. A few years later, when we switched churches and attended a nondenominational church which had worship that was not hymns, but contemporary music, I was convicted about why I didn't rejoice in the Lord like I rejoiced in watching my team win a football, soccer, basketball or baseball game. What do you take great joy in? Why is there more excitement in professional athletics than in worshiping the Lord? *Israel and New Breed*, in their song, "Again I say rejoice," their lyrics resound with "Come bless the Lord, draw near to Him in worship." Paul tells us to rejoice in the Lord *ALWAYS*; again, I say rejoice! Remember that this is joy in the Lord, not happiness based on circumstances, but joy in the fact that God still reigns over darkness. He is King when times are good and still King and in control when we face trials and troubles. Rejoice in the Lord always reminds us to replace anxiety, worry and fear with the great joy and delight that God never leaves us nor forsakes us. There is contentment in knowing that no matter what choices we make and where those choices take us, the Holy Spirit is living in us and is willing to guide us back to God if we are simply willing. "Again, I say rejoice" is important because neither your past, nor your current choices, define you. You bear the fingerprints of God, you are Chosen, you are Loved, you are Forgiven, in fact, you are a child of the King! Rejoice? Why? Because you are a child of the King, a child of God, adopted into the family and given Spiritual guidance to always lead you back to Him. How do you worship the Lord? What do you rejoice in? How do you embody this verse in your life? What can you do to live it out better, with all that God has blessed you with and done for you? How can you rejoice joyfully in the Lord always?

JULY 4

> Now the Lord is the Spirit and where the Spirit of the Lord is, there is freedom. 2 Corinthians 3:17

Today we celebrate the birth of our nation, the birth of freedom, freedom from the tyranny that enslaved us from across the pond. Yet that is only physical freedom. With what is going on in our nation these past few years, it seems as though those freedoms are being chipped and whittled away so that we are dependent on the government for everything, which only enslaves us to the government. However, spiritual freedom is not something we can lose; it can't be taken away. "Now the Lord is Spirit and where the Spirit of the Lord is, there is freedom." The Holy Spirit, when invited in by accepting Jesus as our Lord and Savior, comes into our hearts and protects our souls from the enslavement the enemy is trying to put on us. We have freedom from condemnation; we are not condemned to hell and we are free from the judgment of sin, no matter what the enemy tries to whisper in our ears. We are free from guilt. The guilt of our sin was poured out on Jesus as He hung on the cross. Guilt is another tool the enemy utilizes to try and place a wedge between God and us. Since you are free from guilt, do not allow guilt to separate you from God. We all fall short; none of us have it all together. We sin and that is why we need a Savior to save us when we fall short. We have freedom from the spiritual consequences of sin. Our sin was nailed to the cross with Jesus; death was overcome when He walked out of the grave. Death lost its power over us. We have freedom from the heavy burden the enemy tries to weigh us down, slow us down with. But the yoke of the Lord is easy and His burden is light. We have the freedom to go to God Almighty, Creator of the Heavens and Earth directly. No more need for a high priest to do it for us. Freedom from the Holy Spirit gives us direct access to His Love, His Forgiveness, His Mercy and His Grace. As you celebrate the freedom you have as an American, take time to celebrate the eternal freedom you have as a Christian. What freedom has the enemy been trying to steal from you? How can you maintain access to that freedom? What are you willing to do to show appreciation for the freedom you live in as a Christian?

JULY 5

> He gives power to the faint and to him who has no might he increases strength. Isaiah 40:29

When you get tired and worn out, what do you typically do? I get grouchy and depressed. Generally, I turn to high sugar foods to try to feel better. But God is a better choice – mentally, emotionally, spiritually and physically, choosing to lean into Jesus as a source of comfort or release from stress is a healthier, better choice. God does not suffer setbacks. He does not fail or mess up. He is always in control. His love for us is so great that when we get tired, lonely and depressed, when we don't have the desire to go on, He gives us power. He gives us strength. Our endurance comes from the Holy Spirit living in us, His power, His strength to go on. He increases our strength so we can continue moving forward, continue living for Him. He privileges us with the ability and opportunity to be a walking, living testimony for others to see His love and power in real life, real time. Human strength, even at its best, gives way, fails and is unable to maintain integrity; but spiritual strength comes from a Living God. The Holy Spirit living in us never fails, never grows weak, never leaves us and is always present when we need it. In 1992, Derek Redman was the favorite to win the gold medal in the 400m race, but shortly after rounding the curve his hamstring tore. On his own strength, he hobbled towards the finish line; but his dad, his earthly dad, broke through security and helped him across the finish line. Our Heavenly Father will do the same for us. He will break through any barriers the enemy erects around us to prevent us from getting to Him. Nothing stops God! There are no physical or spiritual barriers that will prevent the Holy Spirit from helping us. The Holy Spirit loves providing us with the needed strength, encouragement and assistance to finish whatever God calls us to do. If you are unaware of the Olympic event mentioned above, I recommend you Google it and watch it. It left an indelible and permanent impression on me as to what the Holy Spirit is willing to do for me at a much higher and deeper level than I ever understood before. How does this Scripture empower you to follow God without fear or hesitation? How can you use this verse to delete any fear or question the enemy tries to plant and grow in the garden of your mind?

JULY 6

> O my son, give me your heart and let your eyes observe (take delight) in my ways. Proverbs 23:26

What do you take delight in? For me, one thing is the sound of a child laughing or excitedly shouting "Momma" or "Daddy" and seeing their eyes light up when they see their parents. That unfiltered, unwavering love that the child has for their parents will always bring a smile to my face. In this verse, Solomon reminds us that we should take that delight in following God and His ways. Does your walk with Christ, with the Holy Spirit, bring you joy that is as contagious as a child's laughter or their excitedly shouting "Momma"? We should be unfiltered, unwavering in our following the ways of God. His ways are simple, not complicated! It may not be easy, but it is simple. Love Him, Love others and forgive as He forgave us. Simple, but not easy. All God wants is your heart. When your heart is set on God, it fills with the things of God, but when your heart is set on the world, it fills with things of the world. If you give Him your heart, allow Him to reign there, He will show you how to do the rest. He doesn't just send you off to do His Will on your own. He sent us the Holy Spirit to do that, to show us, guide us and direct us in how we should obey and follow. He will give you peace that surpasses all understanding, a love that is indescribable, joy that is abounding. His Way is always better. His timing is always perfect. Just give Him your heart, not just on Sundays or Wednesdays, but every day. He created it, He knows what it needs and He knows how to protect it. We just have to trust Him. Do you want unspeakable joy? Give Him your heart and trust Him. Want to get rid of paralyzing stress? Follow Him and His path, His Way. My prayer for you is to take delight in following God and His plan for your life. Starting today, how can you do that? What is one step you can take to make this happen?

JULY 7

> "All Scripture is inspired by God and is useful to teach us what is true and to make us realize what is wrong in our lives. It corrects us when we are wrong and teaches us to do what is right." 2 Timothy 3:16

Why do I have to read this old book anyway – isn't it over 2,000 years old? How can something that old have any relevance today? Well, to answer this question, we must first see what beliefs we hold about the Bible. Do we believe it was written by man, or was it Scribed by man? Well, isn't that the same? No, no it is not. "Written by" means the writer came up with it. "Scribed by" is like a court transcriber, writing down the words that are said, in this case by God Himself. If it was written by man, then you are right; it probably holds no relevance to us today. But if you have a high view of the Holy Bible as God-breathed, God-spoken, then man only recorded what God said to record. Then it is timeless, meaning its relevance transcends time and is always applicable. Here, Paul is telling Timothy that we need to remember that God's Word is truth and is profitable for teaching. If we want to learn, then we need to read the Bible. It is the source of truth, life and inspiration. For reproof, the Greek word *elegchos* means proven or convicted. God's Word has been proven correct many times and it can cause us to be convicted with our choices and decisions if we allow the Holy Spirit to lead and guide us. With reproof comes conviction; the Holy Spirit convicts, while Satan condemns and induces guilt. Conviction makes you want to change; guilt makes you want to hide. God's Word trains you up in righteousness and completes you. It equips you for whatever God calls you to; you are never unprepared nor unequipped if you are daily in His Word. It is the only source of truth and the only way to be prepared to do all things that God wants you to do; whether it is as a missionary to Haiti or a missionary at your job, feeding the hungry in Africa or in your neighborhood, or telling whoever you meet that the God of the Universe loves them. Who has more of your time, Pinterest or Jesus? Instagram, TikTok, YouTube, or Scripture? How much time are you spending in Scripture? According to a recent study, 66% of Christians look at Facebook every day, 39% are on YouTube, yet only 32% read their Bibles daily. Christians today are turning from God and becoming of the world instead of simply being in the world. We are called to stand out, be the light and be different, but we cannot do that if we are not in His Word, reading His Bible. We are called to tithe 10%, but I believe this commitment requires more than our money. I believe we are called to tithe 10% of our time, talents and treasures. We should be giving God 10% of our talents, using whatever gifts and abilities He has given us for Him. We should be giving God at least 10% of our day. If we are up 16 hours, 1 hour and 36 minutes should be devoted to Him. But instead, we are enamored with social media and smart technology. All Scripture is inspired by God and is useful to teach us what is true. There can only be one source of truth and truth cannot change and evolve with the times. Scripture helps us realize what is wrong in our lives. Because most Christians aren't reading His word every day, they tend to fall into comparing themselves to others as a sense of worth or righteousness. They fail to look at themselves through the lens of Scripture and get direction on how to change and be corrected. This verse ends with, "It corrects us when we are wrong and teaches us to do what is right." Look around at what is happening in society; good is being called bad, bad is being called good, right is being called wrong and wrong is being called right. You can claim any belief as long as it is not in Jesus Christ because he is too narrow minded and won't let me decide what is right and true. My closing questions are as much for me as they are for you. What changes do you need to make in your life so that Scripture becomes more of a priority? What can you do to spend more time with Him and in His Word this week?

JULY 8

> For freedom Christ has set us free; stand firm therefore and do not submit again to a yoke of slavery. Galatians 5:1

Freedom is the power or right to act, speak, or think as one wants without hindrance or restraint. It also represents the idea or the state of not being imprisoned or enslaved. Jesus set us free and broke the shackles of slavery; why would you want to put them back on? In Matthew 11:30, Jesus said, "For my yoke is easy and my burden is light." The enemy wants to weigh you down in guilt and shame, but Jesus has set you free from that. Stand firm in His Word. Stand firm in His promises. Stand firm and guard your mind against the lies and burdens the enemy wants to enslave and burden you with. Allow the Holy Spirit's voice to be the voice that guides and directs you. He will help you keep the shackles off and identify the lies for what they are. To stand firm is to refuse to change direction, refuse to change your mind, refuse to accept imprisonment when you are granted a pardon – so, exercise your freedom. But how do you stand firm? In order to refuse to change direction, you must first know what direction God is calling you towards. That is only done by being in the Word daily, praying daily, worshiping daily and allowing Him to speak into your life. In order to refuse to change your mind, you must first firmly plant your mind on truth, which only comes from one source. God is the only source of truth. In order for the truth to exist, it must come from somewhere, someone who does not change; truth has to be eternal in order for it to be Truth. Jesus' yoke is easy – he invites us, "Be my disciple and follow me". Jesus' burden in light. So, forgive as you want to be forgiven, love God and love others. It is simple really, but the enemy wants to convolute The Good News and make it harder, more difficult and heavier than it needs to be. Stand firm on the rock of the Gospel that you will not be swept away by false gospels, false teachers, or false teachings, but remain strong under Jesus' yoke. If Christ set you free, why would you want to return to bondage? What can you do with the freedom Christ has given you? This is not freedom to continue to sin because you are covered by His Grace and Forgiveness. This is another lie, another tactic of the enemy. But truly, what is God calling you to do with your freedom? What shackles have you put back on? How can you permanently remove them? How can you apply this verse in your life today?

JULY 9

> Live as people who are free, not using your freedom as a cover-up for evil, but living as servants of God. 1 Peter 2:16

The ESV Study Bible defines freedom in Scripture as a devotion to doing what is good; in other words, freedom in Christ is devotion to doing God's will in our lives. Freedom from sin is not permission to keep on sinning. Paul asks us in Romans 6:1-2, "What shall we say then? Are we to continue in sin that grace may abound? By no means! How can we who died to sin still live in it?" The author of Hebrews in 10:26 states, "For if we go on sinning deliberately after receiving the knowledge of the truth, there no longer remains a sacrifice for sins." So, Peter, like Paul and the author of Hebrews, states that freedom in Christ is not permission to keep on sinning or to use that freedom and forgiveness to cover up evil. Why would you keep on sinning just to seek forgiveness? As a parent, how would you feel if your child did the same thing every day and when asked why they respond, "I want you to forgive me." How would you feel? Frustrated, most likely. But if the Holy Spirit is in us, He wants us to follow His guidance and His direction. He wants us to be vessels to live and serve God, a loving God. He wants us, His children, not only to seek forgiveness, but to live in the freedom that comes from His forgiveness and live out His Will for our lives. If we are truly free from the judgment of sin, why put on the shackles, yoke and burden that sin brings just so Jesus can take it off of us repeatedly? Isn't once enough? Twice maybe? But every day? How much do you truly love God? How grateful to God are you, really, that your sins are forgiven? Do you show that by living in His grace? Can people see your testimony to that? "Live as people who are free" – refuse to pick up the shackles of sin and the slavery that comes with it. Use your freedom to live for God, a living servant, following the direction and guidance of the Holy Spirit. How can you exhibit this freedom in your life? How are you living as a free servant of the Living God?

JULY 10

> A person standing alone can be attacked and defeated, but two can stand back-to-back and conquer. Three are even better, for a triple-braided cord is not easily broken. Ecclesiastes 4:12 NLT

We were not created to be alone. Even the Boy Scouts know that being alone is not an ideal situation. If one gets hurt, you need someone else to give aid. When alone, you are an easy target; but when there is someone with you, you are less likely to be attacked. Two can fight better than one can alone. The enemy loves to isolate us because then we are alone and there is no one to help us fight the temptation. The devil knows that you are less likely to fall and less likely to fail when you are with other believers. But he can tempt you more successfully when you are alone. Nevertheless, a rope twisted of three cords is a rope that is not easily broken. We are not created to be alone. God created woman to be a helper to man, so he would not experience life alone. The husband and wife stand arm in arm and fight the good fight that lies ahead of godly couples. Who is the third? God. The Holy Spirit. When a marriage is God-centered and God is the third strand of the cord, that marriage bond is not quickly nor easily broken. As a married couple, when a man and woman enter the marriage union, we complete the image of God. In order to maintain that unity and that completion of His image, He must be the third strand. He sends His Holy Spirit to us so that we have an added layer of protection, guidance and direction over our marriage. There is no *No-Fault Clause* in marriage when the Holy Spirit is intertwined in the lives and souls of the man and the woman as husband and wife. Although American society attacks the sanctity of marriage, when we allow the Holy Spirit to be our third strand, we are able to stand strong together, our union more solid. Couples should pray together. Couples should read and study the Bible together. Couples should worship together. The more they are connected spiritually, with the Holy Spirit being their third strand, the more they will be witness to the goodness and the image of God in all aspects of their lives. If you are married, what will you do to take the time to pray and study Scripture together? How can you make it a priority to worship together and both seek the guidance of the Holy Spirit?

JULY 11

> No unbelief made him waver concerning the promise of God, but he grew strong in his faith as he gave glory to God, fully convinced that God was able to do what he had promised. That is why his faith was "counted to him as righteousness." Romans 4:20-22

I could never be a marathon runner. I am too much like the dog from the movie *UP*. I can easily get distracted and experience chase after "squirrel" moments. Especially when my muscles start to burn and I see how far I still have to go, or when I realize I am at the back of the pack, I want to quit before the race has even begun. Running is just not a passion of mine. Although I have friends whose passion is running, it is not contagious. When Kanda and I got married, we both agreed that no matter how much the muscles burned, how far we still had to go, or even if it looked like we were at the back of the pack, we would always strive forward and push through the hurt and burn to protect our union and finish the race of life well. Marriage, our relationship with each other and God, are all that important to keep us motivated beyond the discomfort. We made a commitment to be unwavering in our marriage, our promise to each other, the covenant we made before God. Abraham had that same determination, especially when it came to the promises of God. No matter whether it looked like it was possible or not, Abraham, as Paul says here in Romans 4, "grew in his faith and gave glory to God, fully convinced that God was able to do what He had promised." Abraham had doubts, probably struggled with the length of the race, being passed by others (other people conceiving and having kids), wandering through the desert, but Him and Sarah just faithfully followed God, knowing that God cannot lie, God would fulfill His promise to him and Sarah. Did Abraham stumble sometimes? Yes. Did he fail sometimes? Yes. Was God still faithful after the stumbles and failures of Abraham and Sarah to bring His promise to fulfillment? Yes! See, God's promise is not determined by our steps, more successes than failures, or anything in our control. It is about His holiness and love for us. Despite being sinners and separated from Him by being born humans, He loved us enough and promised a Messiah to bring us back to Him. What is it in your life that you are willing to fight through the burn and pain to keep striving forward no matter how much more there is or how many have passed you up? What is it in your life that you are unwaveringly committed to? The hill you will die on? Your spouse or kids? Your job? Or your Savior? What promises have you forgotten because God did not complete them on your timeline? What causes your faith to waver, even just a little? Is God good enough, holy enough, to fulfill His promises to you, or has He become a little "g" god in your life because of disappointment? What marathon are you willing to run for God, for the sake of building up His Eternal Kingdom?

JULY 12

> I will walk in freedom, for I have devoted myself to your commandments. Psalm 119:45 NLT

Many people feel that freedom means that they can do whatever they want; however, it also means not being imprisoned, enslaved, or the state of not being physically restricted (by a particular undesirable thing). Here the psalmist says that because he has devoted his life to the commandments of God, he walks in freedom, not imprisoned or enslaved, not physically, mentally, or emotionally restrained; he walks in freedom. What about God's commandments? What do they say? Not to serve any other gods but Him, keep the Sabbath, honor your mother and father, do not kill, lie or steal. Basically, if you put God first, love God, love others, then there is no way for the enemy to enslave you. Simple, right? Easy? No. Loving God includes keeping the Sabbath. As a man, we can easily fill our 7-day week with enough stuff to keep us so busy that we don't have time for God. Keeping the Sabbath was extremely important to God because He knew we would never stop if it weren't important. It was so important that the penalty for breaking the Sabbath was death. That is why when Jesus healed on the Sabbath, they wanted to kill Him. When His disciples walked through the wheat field and broke wheat heads to eat, it angered the religious-minded. God created the Sabbath for man – to take time and rest. We should be taking time with Him and resting in Him. Today we make excuses for the Sabbath. Crops need to be harvested and there is not enough time; remodeling the basement is not work, it is a stress release. Or we can go to the other extreme, for example, the Broncos are playing at 11 and since church is at 1030, I can't make it today. Do we really love God and trust God when we treat the Sabbath this way? We must take time to spend with Him, hear from Him, worship Him, thank Him and praise Him. All of that is covered by the commandments, but we must keep a Sabbath holy to have time to do this. Devote yourself to loving God and loving others, so you can experience the same freedom that the psalmist is talking about here. What is preventing you from walking in this freedom? How do you keep a Sabbath? What day of your week is devoted to resting in the Lord? How do you utilize your Sabbath? How much time is given to God and prioritizing rest for your mind and soul?

JULY 13

> Oh, magnify the Lord with me and let us exalt his name together!
> Psalm 34:3

What is your definition of "good"? What is pleasing and acceptable? We all have different definitions or thoughts on what good is or what is good. But a bigger question is, "Is the Lord really good?" I mean, look around you and what do you see? Hate, destruction, greed and death? We must realize that neither the condition of the world, nor the condition of a man's heart, has anything to do with how good the Lord is. The Lord is good, eternally. Creator God being good is defined by His character and His heart. He is good because He is faithful to do everything He promised and said He would do. He is good because He created all things seen and unseen. However, Satan came in and convinced man through corrupting his heart to try to be like God. By doing so and following Satan, people have infused this world with sin. That is why the world is in its current condition. It has nothing to do with the goodness of God, but more to do with the rejection of God by those created in His image. His goodness comes through this broken world like a lifeboat, a rescue vessel from this chaos and destruction – we just have to decide to get on board. No matter our past decisions or actions, in His love and goodness, He still has the lifeboat right next to us for us to get in. So, come, let us tell of the Lord's greatness and of His love for us and how He forgives us. Let us praise and exalt His name so that others who have been lied to about God's greatness can see the truth and accept the lifeboat that is our rescue, our Savior, Jesus Christ. How are you exalting His name and telling of His greatness and goodness? How do you do that outside of church? How does your soul magnify the Lord? How do your words and actions magnify the Lord? What can you do to change so that you magnify the Lord more with the way you treat people and talk to others?

JULY 14

> Why should a living man complain, a man, about the punishment of his sins? Lamentations 3:39

Why do we complain? We complain because we don't get something we think we want, need, or deserve. We complain because things didn't work out the way we wanted them to! When we sin, when we mess up, why do we complain? We can sometimes see God's discipline as an attack from the enemy, a trial, or a cross to bear. We don't like to think that there really are consequences for our sins, especially if we are Christians. Jesus said He would forgive our sins, but He did not remove our sins' consequences. For those that are parents, when we discipline our kids, we don't remove the consequences – if that were the case, there would be no discipline then. God says He disciplines those whom He loves. As parents, if we truly love our kids, we discipline them and allow consequences to have their full effect. Because we love our kids, we discipline them with love and allow consequences in their lives. If we who are evil do this, how much more will the God that is love do this for those that He loves? In any trial or hardship, we should reflect and identify what it is – is the circumstance really an attack, or is the hardship a result of our own actions or consequences that God is allowing for His discipline to occur? It may feel that He has left or turned from us, but that is not true. He promised He would never leave nor forsake us – there was no qualifier on that promise. He did not say that I will never leave nor forsake you… as long as you do as I say, as long as you don't sin more than x-number of times, etc. It's just that plain and simple – He will *never* leave nor forsake us. In all hardships, whether discipline or attack, don't ask, "Why God?" Instead, look closer and ask any of these deeper questions to gain insight and wisdom: (1) What can I learn from this? (2) God, what do I need to know, change, or do differently? (3) How can I be a better person, a better Christian after this? (4) How can this deepen my relationship with You, Jesus? As you boldly ask these questions (and listen) in your quiet time, hold onto His undying love. Don't complain like a child when they get caught with their hand in the cookie jar. Allow His discipline to take its course. Learn from His love, His mercy and from His discipline, so that you can be a better person, a better Christian, as a result of seeking answers directly from Him. Taking time to confess and ask for forgiveness is one aspect of our relationship with God worth investing in. As a follower of God, you can have a deeper relationship with Him after experiencing this vulnerability and tenderness of His Grace. What can you do to change your heart regarding His discipline? What can you do to change complaints into the right questions?

JULY 15

> Nor do people light a lamp and put it under a basket, but on a stand and it gives light to all in the house. In the same way, let your light shine before others, so that they may see your good works and give glory to your Father who is in heaven. Matthew 5:15-16

Light is defined as, "The natural agent that stimulates sight and makes things visible," "illumination", or "not dark". Light is one of the most powerful sources around – nothing can extinguish it. Jesus says people do not put a lamp under a basket, but on a stand. Why? To illuminate the house, to stimulate sight and make things visible, not allowing things to be hidden. Jesus said He is the Light of the World. His light shines on everything, illuminating the physical, emotional, mental and spiritual aspects of our lives. Nothing is hidden from His light. When His Holy Spirit is living in us, we radiate His Light from our words, our actions, our responses and how we treat and talk about others. Do not put your light under a basket when you go to work. Do not put your light under a basket when you go out on the athletic field or into a classroom. Do not put your light under a basket when suffering trials or loss. Do not put your light under a basket when you are on vacation, at a restaurant, or doing your taxes. If you own your own business, do not put your light under a basket as you conduct business or choose how to treat employees. Like the Sunday School many of us learned as kids, "Let your little light shine!" Let your light shine so that your good works may be seen, witnessed and encourage others, while the glory and praise go to God. Do not put your light under a basket; do not let the enemy convince you that "just this one time…" We should always be on guard and watchful of the enemy's tactics, also remembering that whether we realize it or not, we are always being observed. How we treat a poor or neglectful waiter or waitress, a slow checker at the store, or the homeless person on the street… We should always be ready to build up and not tear down someone, to do the good works that the Father brings our way. Is your light on a stand, hanging from the ceiling, or hidden under a basket? How can you protect yourself from being tempted to put it under a basket? How can you hang it from your ceiling so that there is no way for it to be covered? How are you shining God's light in a dark world?

JULY 16

> You will say in that day: "I will give thanks to you, O LORD, for though you were angry with me, your anger turned away, that you might comfort me". Isaiah 12:1

Any loving parent knows what it is like when a child does wrong and gets into trouble. We get angry and disappointed that they got themselves into that situation. I think of when I got into my first auto accident; it was a pretty big one. While my parents were probably angry at me, they refused to show it because they knew I needed comfort and reassurance. I remember my mom decided that what she cooked for dinner would be the next day's meal and we went out to eat. I was so shaken up that I refused to drive; in fact, I said I would never drive again. My parents took my brother and me to dinner, we got a CD and came home. I never knew how angry or how disappointed they were, because their love and care for me were more important and deliberate, just like God's. Steadfastness and longsuffering are words used to describe God's love for us, remaining strong and lasting through times of rejection. Isaiah 12:1 reminds us that, "In that day, 'I will give thanks to the Lord, for though You were angry with me, Your anger turned away that You might comfort me.'" While we still have to face the consequences of our sins, He will turn His anger aside so that He can comfort us. One of the names of the Holy Spirit is *Comforter*. We have to allow Him to comfort us. When we do, when we submit to Him and allow Him to comfort us, it allows us to see His ability and desire to comfort others in the way He comforted us. As we receive His comfort, it challenges us to love and comfort others, turning our anger aside to do so. That accident was over thirty years ago and while I had to go to traffic school because of it (the consequence of my sin), I remember the grace and love that my parents had for me. Despite how distraught I was and attacking myself, in the end I only remember the love they had for me and the comfort they gave me. Also, I remember days when I just wanted to give up, when I royally messed up, but God simply said, "I still love you." I submitted to the Holy Spirit and allowed His comfort to envelop me. I try to hold onto that feeling of trust and surrender, remembering that so I can extend it to others and provide encouragement that God wants to do that for them as well. Are you afraid of God's anger so much that you avoid Him? He wants to remind you that His love for you is based on Him and not what you do or don't do. He wants you to know, "I still love you." How can you hold on to this truth and allow the Holy Spirit to comfort you? When was the last time you thanked God for turning His anger away from you? How do you apply that level of grace and forgiveness to others in your life?

JULY 17

> Or do you not know that your body is a temple of the Holy Spirit within you, whom you have from God? You are not your own, for you were bought with a price. So glorify God in your body. 1 Corinthians 6:19-20

Contrary to what society is screaming, our body is not our own. At least for believers, it is not our own. Our bodies are the temple in which the Holy Spirit resides and is on active duty, waiting to be called on by us when we seek His direction, guidance, or teaching. You were bought for a price and with a price. David knew God personally, understood His Holiness and desired to build Him a temple in which to reside. That request was denied but later granted to his son, Solomon. Eventually, the temple was destroyed and rebuilt several times until its final destruction in 70 A.D. at the hands of the Romans. Before this, the curtain in the inner sanctuary was torn at the death of Jesus, removing any barrier between God and us. With the Veil being torn, those of us adopted into the family of God became the temple for God to reside in, His Holy Spirit. He goes where we go. I used to joke about my weight saying I give more room to the Holy Spirit than skinny people, but over time I have been convicted by this verse. If the Holy Spirit truly resides in me, my body is His temple, then I should be taking better care of it. Paul charges us with being good stewards of our bodies and taking care of our bodies, not for our own good, but because the Holy Spirit of God resides in you and me. Glorify God in our bodies, with our bodies. Does this mean we all have to look alike and match what society says is good looking? No, but we should be mindful of what we consume physically, mentally and spiritually. We should be watchful with what we allow our eyes to view, our ears to listen to, what information we allow to occupy our thoughts. We should be mindful of the nutritional value of the food we partake in and the exercise we do to keep our bodies running. The blood of Christ purchased us from the grips of death and destruction so that we could bring Glory to God. In every aspect of our lives, we should be a witness to the goodness of God, even taking care of our bodies so that God can continue to have His will accomplished in and through us. How do you view this Scripture? How do you plan to live out this verse in your life? How does it or will it impact your life? How can you glorify God in your body?

JULY 18

> And these words that I command you today shall be on your heart. You shall teach them diligently to your children and shall talk of them when you sit in your house and when you walk by the way and when you lie down and when you rise. You shall bind them as a sign on your hand and they shall be as frontlets between your eyes. You shall write them on the doorposts of your house and on your gates.
> Deuteronomy 6:6-9

If you are a parent, you know how important it is that we teach our children right from wrong. To start, we must first identify and communicate what is right, what is true and what is wrong. God is the only source of truth, what is right. Here God commands us as His children to teach His Word, His Way, to our children and not just in a school setting – when we sit and when we walk away, when we lie down and when we rise up. We should be so focused on God that when we sit, we think of Him, His Way. When we walk, we should meditate on His Word and His Will for us. He should be the first thing on our minds when we wake in the morning and the last thought we have when we fall asleep. In other words, He should be our first priority. Jesus said that whoever did not love Him and hate his mother, father, brother, sister, etc., would not be His disciple. These are harsh words that I struggled with when I was younger, but now I understand. God should be our first priority and if our loved ones try to talk us out of following God's Word or God's will for our life, then we should love, listen, follow and obey God over family. We should inscribe His Word on our hands, our hearts and the glasses we look through. What we put our hands to do should be directed by the Holy Spirit. What our heart longs for is the presence, guidance and instruction from the Holy Spirit. Through the truth of His Word is how we should view the world and see others. Like the blood of the lamb that was spread on the doorposts to instruct the Angel of Death to *pass over* the households of Israel, so should the Word of God be inscribed on our doorposts. His Word should be what is holding up our houses, our homes. His Word is what we should pass through, coming home and going out into the World. 3 John 1:4 says, "I have no greater joy than to hear that my children are walking in the truth." That will only happen when, from the youngest age, we as parents instruct our children in the Ways and Love of the Lord. We started early; while still in the womb, I read the Bible to my kids, prayed over them and it has been beautiful to see as they grow up they all have a heart for God. I live 3 John 1:4 every day to see their love and devotion for the Lord; there is nothing more that I could ask for as a dad. It's never too late to start teaching and modeling a relationship with the Lord and His Holy Word. How do you live out this verse? How has this verse caused trials in your life? What blessings has this verse brought to you in your life?

JULY 19

> "Therefore I did not presume to come to you. But say the word and let my servant be healed. For I too am a man set under authority, with soldiers under me: and I say to one, 'Go,' and he goes; and to another, 'Come,' and he comes; and to my servant, 'Do this,' and he does it." When Jesus heard these things, he marveled at him and turning to the crowd that followed him, said, "I tell you, not even in Israel have I found such faith." And when those who had been sent returned to the house, they found the servant well." Luke 7:7-10

Why is it that we make things more complicated than they need to be, especially men? When we buy anything that needs assembled, as men we can complicate the assembly process. Comedians always talk about how men don't read the directions until everything is messed up and we have several spare parts left over and the object has a slight lean to it. Men are also infamous for not asking for directions until they are completely lost. In the verse above, this Roman soldier kept his faith simple. Let us not confuse the words simple and easy. His faith was simple, not easy. His faith was taking him out on a limb and nothing like what he was asking had been done before. Healing from someone many miles away from the sick? Not easy. Simple. Jesus, by Your word, no matter how many miles there are between Your and my servant, I have faith and know that You can do it. Like directions to get somewhere or put something together, we can make faith more complicated than it needs to be. It's simple. Go to Him and ask. Then, when you ask, believe. Don't make the mistake of believing that this is a say-it and claim-it idea. NO! Understand that God will not answer every prayer with a "Yes." But we don't have to complicate it either. We tend to try to control and make things work the way we want them to work. But God's way is always better. God's way is higher. This centurion believed and trusted, so he simply asked. The belief and trust were already in place when he made the ask. He kept it simple. He understood the authority that Jesus had and trusted in the power that came with His authority. Are trust and belief already in place before you ask? When you pray, are you hopeful, or are you bold? How can you increase your faith, like the centurion had, when you pray? How can you better align your prayers with the will of God?

JULY 20

> Ascribe to the Lord the glory due his name; worship the Lord in the splendor of holiness. Psalm 29:2

Commandment #3, "You shall not take the name of your Lord, God, in vain." Now five to ten thousand years later, "God" and "Jesus Christ" seem to be used more as a superlative and swear word than anything else. But here in Psalm 29, it says to honor the Lord for *the glory of His name*. His name is glorious; His name is power. By His name we cast out demons and spirits and principalities. In His name we pray and ask for forgiveness. His name irritates. those who don't believe in Him and reject God. Look around, if you mention Allah or any one of the thousands of Hindu gods, people don't usually bat an eye. But mention God or mention Jesus and people tend to get defensive, irritated and lash out. It is because His name is Holy and His name has glory. We need to return to seeing the holiness of God and His name and not viewing Him through the 21st-century lens as some far-off deity used only to bless us and answer our prayers. We need to return to true worship for the Holiness and Perfection that is God. The Jews held His name so Holy that to even spell it out would be considered unholy, but today we throw it around like any other word and use it in frustration and even to show displeasure. Blasphemy is thought of as funny in our mainstream media and there is little understanding of true reverence with the younger generations. If you are honest with yourself, what is your view of God? How do you view the sanctity of His name? How can you exalt your view of the name of God? What do you have to do to exhibit your belief that His name is holy and righteous? How can you better glorify God's name in your life?

JULY 21

> I have no greater joy than to hear that my children are walking in the truth. 3 John 1:4

What legacy are you instilling and leaving in your children? Is it a strong work ethic? That's not a bad thing. Is it respect for all life? Not bad, either. Personally, I agree with the disciple John. I have no greater joy than knowing that my children are walking in truth, living out their faith actively in their lives. The fact that they are not hanging on my or my wife's coattails of faith, but have developed their own personal faith, a personal relationship with Jesus Christ, allowing the Holy Spirit to guide and direct them, makes me one proud papa. Seeing how my children's relationships with God are exhibited in how they treat others, have a heart for kids, study Scripture, respect and love people and work as if they are working for the Lord, is a reward with immeasurable value. They have caught the love bug; Love God and Love others. You can witness their faith in what bothers them, how they stand up for others and serve others and how they see the needs of other people as important. They are not blind to the needs of others, nor do they self-promote over others, but with their peers they walk side-by-side. As they mature, I hope they find a spouse who is also living out this verse, living out his or her faith and is a faithful servant of Christ, being guided, directed and instructed by the Holy Spirit. It is an eternal legacy that will continue to be passed on; I received it, my wife and I demonstrated it and taught it to our kids and now as young adults they have taken the proverbial faith-football and are making touchdowns and scoring goals. So many young adults have only the faith of their parents and when they leave home and are confronted by the world, they easily fall away from the faith, because they never made it their own; they only lived in the shadow and protection of their parent's faith. Over two-thirds of Christian teens leave the church while away at college. In a 2022 study by Barna, only 61% of Christian teens believe Jesus was crucified and only 50% believe He was raised from the dead. No matter how old our children get, they are never too old to witness us living out our faith. They are never too old to be encouraged to deepen their understanding of Scripture and personalize their faith with our Living God. What is your greatest joy? Mine is being lived out in front of my eyes. How does this verse resonate with you? What are you doing in your life as a child of God to bring your Heavenly Father joy? What does *walking in the truth* look like for your life?

JULY 22

> Blessed is the nation whose God is the LORD, the people whom he has chosen as his heritage! Psalm 33:12

When Israel was faithful and the god they worshiped was God, was Yahweh, there was no sword that could come against them; but when they chased after and worshiped other gods, the protective hand of God was taken off. Slavery, destruction and loss of the Promised Land resulted in them desiring to be like others and worship other gods. Looking at the history of the United States, we have overcome many extreme hurdles; defeating a well-trained and large army for independence, invading French and Spanish armies, the succession of southern states and sneak attacks in the Pacific Ocean. The country was founded on "one nation, under God," with a capital G, the Living God of the Bible, Heavenly Father who sent Jesus Christ the Messiah for the world. As a nation, His blessings, prosperity and hand were upon us until we decided to remove God from the country. Since the fight to remove God from schools and now government buildings, to the point where praying in public in His Name can be seen as hate speech, we have fallen and are no longer His heritage. We have formed other gods to worship. Post-modern American worship includes a gender god, the sexual-freedom god, the god of indulgence and allows biblical spirits like Jezebel to control our society, our laws, or norms and even define our values. As a truly God-less culture, God is forbidden to enter our country; a country, like Israel, we as a nation are doomed. Was Israel doomed forever? No! When they returned to the Lord, the Lord returned them to the Promised Land, restored His Hand of blessing, restored His Hand of protection, returning as His heritage. So, is it too late for our country? No! We must turn from our sinful societal norms and turn back toward Him. We must invite Him back into all the areas of society from which we have excluded Him. We must ask Him to be our God, our Lord and allow us to be His heritage with His hand of protection, His blessings pouring out for us and on us. As Christians, we must not stand idle anymore. How do you publicly live out your faith? What can you do to bring God back into our society? How do you lovingly stand by your Christian values and morals when confronted with hate and intolerance?

JULY 23

> but as servants of God we commend ourselves in every way: by great endurance, in afflictions, hardships, calamities, 2 Corinthians 6:4

The early church saw affliction and persecution as a blessing, a sign that meant they were living their life according to the words of Jesus and how God would want them to live; the Holy Spirit was alive and active in their life and they were actively following His direction, instruction and guidance. When a Christian responds to affliction, hardship, calamities and trials, it reveals what is really in their heart. Do they respond with vengeance or love, with retaliation or steadfastness to continue? If the Holy Spirit is active in your life and you are actively following Him, you outlast longsuffering and continue to push through, allowing the light of God to shine forth from you in your grace-filled words, actions and reactions. When you are able to endure, your testimony gains strength and power because you are giving glory to God. You give honor to the Holy Spirit for seeing you through it, giving you the strength to continue and come out the other side; you testify to the power of God and show that He is still active in the twenty-first century and His power has not been diminished nor diluted. His power is made perfect in our weakness, so when we allow His power in our life to guide and direct us, we become a living message and testimony to God and His power and presence. However, nowadays, it feels as though Christians, especially here in America and in other industrialized nations, when the fiery trials come, most leave the kitchen and get out or quit. Even today, Christians in third-world countries with less to spend live out their faith stronger and better than most American Christians. Unfortunately, many of them are still being martyred even today. The nonprofit *Voice of the Martyrs* tells their stories. We must have a full and complete understanding of God and understanding of His Word. Yes, He wants to bless us, but He also said that we would face persecution and hatred. Of the eleven disciples that were still present after the crucifixion, ten of them were martyred and they all accepted it as a badge of honor. How do you handle people questioning your beliefs or faith? How can you go deeper with your relationship with Christ so that when trials and afflictions come you are prepared to handle them with the power of the Holy Spirit guiding and comforting you? How do you let the light of God shine through you when others mistreat you?

JULY 24

> When I am afraid, I put my trust in you. In God, whose word I praise, in God I trust; I shall not be afraid. What can flesh do to me? Psalm 56:3-4

Growing up, my younger brother was afraid of the dark. When anyone would get home, we would know that either Tony was home or Tony had been at home because every light in the house would be on. When he was afraid, his solution was to turn on every light and leave it on. That way, if someone entered the house, he could see it. Tony put his trust in the light and what He could see. But here we see the true strength of a Christ follower. When I am afraid, *I WILL* put my trust in you. Not in lights, not in a security system or guns, but trust in the Lord. I trust the God whose Word I praise and write on my heart. My God whose word says, "I will never leave you nor forsake you," I trust. When the doctor gives you the diagnosis that you have been dreading, you can still trust in the Lord. When you are left without a job, pray and trust in the Lord. Truly, what can man do to me? If we truly believe in the Lord, leaving Earth would mean we are in His presence. The antidote to fear is trust. The Lord knows the schemes the enemy uses and He provides the solution, the antidote, the only true cure to fear – TRUST! Trust Him and Trust in Him. When the enemy tries to use fear to drive a wedge between you and the Lord, trust deeper than the lies, for He is Good! Think, pray and meditate on the characteristics of God, how He is our: Provider, Shelter, Strong Tower, Good Father, Lord of Mercy, Lord of Love and Lord of forgiveness. Use the cure, the antidote that God gave us and turn fear into trust and hold onto the One that holds the universe in His hands! What practical ways can you turn fear into trust? How can Scripture like this one help you when fear rears its ugly head? When our prayers are answered with a "No", how can we prevent fear from driving that wedge between God and us? Where do you put your trust?

JULY 25

> Charm is deceitful and beauty is vain, but a woman who fears the Lord is to be praised. Proverbs 31:30

In this day and age of cosmetic surgery and doing whatever it takes to look younger, it is even more true that looks can be deceiving. The writer of this proverb tells readers that charm is deceitful and beauty is in vain. Words mean nothing. Most of this proverb from King Lemuel is about the qualities of a godly woman and it concludes here with "a woman who fears the Lord is to be praised". A woman whose heart is focused and centered on God is a treasure to be cherished and admired. Charm is defined as "the power to please and attract people or distract them, power over people" and if indulged in, it can lead you down a path of destruction and separation from God. Charm can be deceitful and used as a weapon to lure you away from God to follow after false idols. Charm is the allure and can captivate or enchant you, even take you captive; charm can be harmful if not godly. Charm can fool us into believing that bad is good and that good is actually bad. American culture has turned charm into something to be desired, Prince Charming comes to take away a young woman to be his princess, but we must be aware and remember that actions speak louder than words. Beauty, along with charm, is fruitless and will fade. While they may fill a temporary need or desire, it is not long-lasting. If beauty was permanent, there would be no cosmetic industry. Beauty does not last and while many today try to utilize modern medicine to make it last longer, it does not. Unfortunately, beauty is often "only skin deep". I am not a Jack Black fan, but the movie "*Shallow Hal*" is a good one. He plays a man lusting after an outwardly beautiful woman, but he gets hypnotized to see the inner beauty of people. It reminds us that true beauty is on the inside and not manipulated by outward appearances. When selecting a new king, Samuel thought he found the right one by outward appearance, deceitful and vain appearances, but God told him and us in 1 Samuel 16:7, "Do not look on his appearance or on the height of his stature, because I have rejected him. For the LORD sees not as man sees: man looks on the outward appearance, but the LORD looks on the heart." True beauty is how one loves and serves the Lord, following the instruction, guidance and direction of the Holy Spirit; how they treat others in word, deed and thought. Thus, a woman who fears the Lord is a blessing to her children, her family and her husband. Fear of the Lord is foundational to any believer's faith. Not fear, like being scared, but fear that is a deep respect for the power and holiness of God, Jesus and the Holy Spirit. There is no better blessing for a man than to find a woman who has this foundational faith principle in her life – God first, above all else and everyone else. For when she fears the Lord, she follows Him out of love and gratitude and treats others accordingly. She loves God, loves others and her beliefs are shown through her words and actions. This foundational principle does not fade like beauty and it can deepen and improve her relationship with everyone, unlike charm and beauty. Do you know of anyone who has used charm or beauty to get their way or like a weapon against someone? What is your definition of beauty? How do you define and understand the fear of the Lord? How do you live out your fear of the Lord?

JULY 26

> Why am I discouraged? Why is my heart so sad? I will put my hope in God! I will praise Him again— my Savior and my God! Psalm 43:5 NLT

I used to love watching the news, knowing what was going on in the world. Even if it was bleak, I at least knew what was going on. Then, in August 2020, I stopped watching the news. I felt myself getting more depressed, more overwhelmed and my joy was completely gone; needless to say, I felt discouraged. "Why am I discouraged? Why is my heart sad?" I became overwhelmed with the world. I did not do what the psalmist did after the first part of the verse. I did not put my hope in God. I needed to, as well as praise and worship Him in my discouragement, in my sadness and in my overwhelm. The author reminds us that the Lord our God is our Savior. He is our source of hope. When the world is bleak and overwhelming, we need to turn to God; we need to allow the Holy Spirit to comfort us, settle our souls and ease our hearts. The enemy would cause us to be so overwhelmed that we separate ourselves from God, from other believers and get lost in despair. His attacks can be more successful when we isolate ourselves. If the COVID-19 quarantine taught us anything, it showed how isolation and separation from others could be detrimental to our mental and emotional health, which strains our spiritual health as well. We were created to be in community, in communion with God, with others, especially other believers. That is why corporate worship is so vital to our mental, emotional and spiritual health. Watching via live stream is a temporary solution and should not become *Modus Operandi*. In addition, we need to remember what the author says here, as well as Job's example. No matter what happens, we worship God with all we have. Praise Him for who He is, His Holiness and His power, not just because He answers "Yes" to our prayers. When Job lost everything, he fell to the ground and worshiped. We worship in joy as well as in sorrow. We worship God, not our circumstances. The Holy Spirit will speak for us, pray for us and worship for us when we are at a loss for words. Worship, even if it is through sobs, even when it doesn't make sense. I lost my brother to COVID, even though I prayed so earnestly for his healing. Even though God did not answer "Yes," I still worshiped Him. Although I did not understand, I still worshiped. Even though my heart was shattered, I still worshiped. Through sobs, brokenness and not understanding His purpose in it all, I still worshiped; sometimes, I had to rely on the Holy Spirit to do it for me. How do you respond when life takes the floor out from underneath you? Do you still worship God? How can you deepen your worship during times of discouragement and depression?

JULY 27

> Do you not know that in a race all the runners run, but only one receives the prize? So run that you may obtain it. 1 Corinthians 9:24

When I was a middle school teacher, as a staff we had many discussions about intrinsic value and extrinsic value. The debate was about whether we should reward students for doing good, doing what they should do, or whether they should care more about the intrinsic value of being pleased with themselves for a job well done. While it is honorable to appreciate intrinsic value, we must realize that people are naturally geared towards seeking extrinsic rewards, working to earn something. As adults, we don't go to work to feel good about ourselves, we work to earn a paycheck. Paul reminds us here that runners in a race run for the prize: the wreath, floral crown, or nowadays the gold medal. Only one wins the gold medal, but all give it their full effort to win it. We are called to run so we may obtain it, the prize. What's the prize? The crown of righteousness. We earn it as we walk out our faith and relationship with Christ, teaching and living out by example what Scripture says about being a Christ-follower. Is there enough evidence in our lifestyles to convict us of being a Believer? The idea here is not to live out our faith for the crown, but as if we are trying for it. We should be so dedicated in our relationship with Jesus and to following the direction and guidance of the Holy Spirit that our dedication should mirror that of a runner running for the prize, striving for first place. Run the faith race, where running is building your relationship with God and run it so that you will achieve the prize (eternal life). Push yourself, like a runner in a marathon when their legs start to ache, they push through to finish it. Push yourself in the race of life, in the race of faith, so that fatigue and stress don't make you quit, but challenge you that much more to keep pushing forward. Racers run for a prize that is temporal, it will not last, they cannot take it with them. But Christians run for a prize that is not temporal, rather it is eternal. We will not receive a prize here on earth but an eternal, heavenly reward. We all want to hear at the end of our lives, "Well done, good and faithful servant, you ran the race well!" How deep is your relationship with your Savior? How do you allow the Holy Spirit to challenge you and encourage you to continue the race? How can you turn challenge into encouragement to continue down God's path when you feel like quitting? What is your goal, to barely squeak into Heaven or to run full force across the finish line like a runner going for the gold? How can you step up your race to achieve the next level of your faith?

JULY 28

> The name of the LORD is a strong tower; the righteous man runs into it and is safe. Proverbs 18:10

When you were little and scared, where did you run to? Where did you go? Who made you feel safe again? Like many, I'm sure, I ran to my parents. My mom and dad were my safe place and I knew they would stick up for me. But parents aren't always there to protect us. As a father, now I realize that there is only so much I can do to protect my kids; but the Lord, He is *always* there. He can *always* protect and guide. The Lord is a strong tower. A tower was built for defense and to see dangers and enemies coming from far away. They were also a tactical advantage to strike against the enemy. The Lord is our strong tower. He can defend us and fight for us. He can see the enemy coming and warns us, but do we listen? The Holy Spirit has been sent to us to guide, direct, instruct and comfort us, but we must listen to Him when He is offering these gifts. He warns us when we are headed down a wrong path or opening a door for the enemy, but do we just shrug him off and ignore the warnings? He defends us when we are in His presence, but we need to be in His presence. Solomon writes that the righteous man runs into the strong tower and is safe. A believer runs into the presence of the Lord, seeks Him and His guidance and is protected by the Lord. This does not mean protected from the consequences of his decisions, but protected when the enemy comes to attack, steal, kill and destroy. God is ready and willing to fight, defend and protect us, but we need to let Him. He is not going to force His protection on us. We have to metaphorically get out of the driver's seat and allow Him to drive, to control. That can be a scary place for people, especially when God is calling us out of our comfort zone and we know that when we leave the comfort zone, the battle will begin… but remember, if we allow it, He fights for us. That means we cannot survive the mental and emotional battles alone, without the foundation of Truth backing us. The Greek word for the Holy Spirit, *Paraclete*, references the idea of fighting back-to-back, not leaving any one side exposed – when the one in front gets tired, they rotate and the one defending the back takes the lead. Jesus Christ is willing to take the lead fighting position if we let Him. What battle do you need to be defended from? How can you allow the Holy Spirit to fight with you and for you? How can you find safety in the strong tower that is the Lord?

JULY 29

> "Be still and know that I am God. I will be exalted among the nations,
> I will be exalted in the earth!" Psalm 46:10

What do you do to slow down? Do you do anything to slow down? I'm ADHD, so my mind is always going, going and I am always on the move or moving; even on vacation, my kids tell me I walk too fast. Here the sons of Korah record what they heard from God, "Be still." Stop talking, stop thinking, stop doing, just be still. "Be still and know that I am God!" I think so often in life, especially our spiritual lives, we are so busy that we just run from task to task, making and checking off our to-do lists. Pray, check. Pay bills, check. Read my Bible, check. Drive the kids to practice, check. God is so holy that He is to be exalted among all the nations, exalted throughout the entire Earth, the entire world. He is not an item on our to-do list to just do and move on to other things. We need to be still and know that He is God, in awe and purposeful reverence. We need to be still in our minds so that we actually listen to Him, soak up His presence and power, letting the Holy Spirit just flow over us and through us, bringing His peace to us. We need to be still and honor God with our time, giving Him time, not looking at our watches and getting impatient to go do other things. We need to be still in our talking and not consume the entire conversation with God, but allowing Him talk-time to speak to us. We need to return to a time when God was not only worshiped in church, but also in all aspects of our lives. We should give Him at least ten percent of our day. That is 1.6 hours on average, one hour and thirty-six minutes of devotion to Christ. We need to take that time to be still and know that He is God, He is in control, He and He alone is the creator of everything seen and unseen. For the full ninety-six minutes, we don't need to be still and silent – I would fall asleep doing that! But we need to take some of that time to worship, to pray, to read, to focus and meditate on His Word. We need to work in time to be still, be silent, to rest in His presence and allow Him to minister to us, to fill our hearts, our souls and our minds. We must have the discipline to be still and be silent, so He has permission to speak into our lives and give us the direction and guidance we need, even the comfort we need. Are you like me and always on the run? What can you do to slow down? How can you incorporate being still into your time with God? How can you step up this commitment and increase your quiet time with Him? In our family, with our tithe of money, we have witnessed how God can do more with 10% than we can do with 100%. The same is true with our time; allow Him to do more by giving Him 10% of your day. What can He do with that multiplier effect in your life? How much time are you willing to give God every day? How can you see the difference and feel the impact of exalting Him in your life, so He can demonstrate His love and power?

JULY 30

> You are my hiding place and my shield; I hope in your word. Psalm 119:114

One thing that has always fascinated me with my love of science fiction is the idea of forcefields or shields. Whether it's a shield for a spaceship or a base, the idea is that it can deflect any type of attack, similar to a shield that a warrior would carry to defend from a sword or arrow attack. The Roman shield was almost full length and could deflect arrows, even flaming arrows. When soldiers were lined up, they would put their shields up like a wall and the second row would raise and tilt theirs to form a wall and roof-like structure. It must have been amazing to see! Here David is instructing his son Solomon and even us now, describing how God is his "shield and hiding place". Like two rows of Roman shields create an impenetrable wall, God is ready to be our shield, spiritually protecting us. David continues, "I hope in Your word." God is the only true source of hope and we can remain in His hope by being in His Word. We need to read it; we need to pray and meditate on it. Like what you are doing now by reading this book, you need to apply His Truth in all aspects of your life. When you feel vulnerable and weak, run to Him and allow Him to protect you. When that desire to give in to temptation and do something sinful, run to Him. Seek His presence to allow Him to defend and protect you. This calls for humility on our part. We must recognize that we cannot do it on our own, we must seek help. When that temptation comes to go to that website, or drive to that place, or whatever sin is tempting you, open His word. Pray His word and meditate on His Word. Allow the Holy Spirit to talk to you, guide, direct and protect you. As we know from the life of David, when you don't do that, you can give into temptation and sin. Now, don't misunderstand what I'm saying. I am not insinuating that by being in His word, we will never sin. I am just reminding us that God always gives us a way to escape. His escape route is through His Word and His Holy Spirit. When you feel under attack, rest under His shield and choose to worship under His shield. How do you rest? How can you rest under God's shield? When feeling down, where do you look for hope? What are you willing to commit to doing to make God your source of hope?

JULY 31

"Behold, God is my salvation; I will trust and will not be afraid; for the LORD GOD is my strength and my song and he has become my salvation." Isaiah 12:2

Salvation is defined as, "preservation or deliverance, a source or means of being saved from harm, ruin, or loss". What is your source of salvation? What saves you from harm or loss? Prior to September 11, 2001, the U.S. believed it was safe from harm and loss, because we had the best military in the world. While our military protected us from outside threats, we didn't see the threats coming from inside our own borders. When we believe that we are safe through our own strength and ability, we widen and enlarge the bullseye, the target on us. King Ahaz believed in his ability as king to lead and be safe, but Isaiah replied to the king, "Behold, God is my salvation. I will trust him and not be afraid." Isaiah's faith was so strong, because his relationship with God was so deep. The Lord is my strength and He is my song being played as I march forward in His name. He and He alone is my salvation. For centuries, armies would play music to not only intimidate their enemies, but also to encourage their soldiers. We are engaged in spiritual warfare daily; what music or song is being played daily as you go out into battle? Are you even going out into battle or do you relegate that to other Christians? We are called to be His light in this dark world, to love others as He loved us. This doesn't mean permitting people to live in sin, or validating their sin, but loving them into a relationship with the Lord. We are told to, no, we are commanded to go into the world and tell others about Jesus. We are called to let the Holy Spirit be our compass, our General of military operations. He will give us the words to speak and instruct us on the actions to take if we are just open to His leading. We cannot do it on our own accord. We speak His Word and do His Will off of His strength living in us. We just have to be courageous enough to take those first couple of steps and trust that He fights for us. His strength is what gets us through. His song is playing, intimidating the enemy. Can you hear it? Does it encourage you or frighten you? His song of victory plays as we march out into this mad, mad world. The enemy plays his song too, to intimidate us. What song are you going to listen to? What shall we fear? The God that raised Lazarus and Jesus from the dead goes forth and fights for us. We are guaranteed victory if we follow His song, His directions. What song are you listening to? Are you willing to be used by God to defeat the enemy or are you content just staying in the base camp? My prayer is that on my last day, I hear, "Well done good and faithful servant." That is all I want to hear! What about you? How can you live out this verse in your daily walk? What is God calling you to follow Him through as you confidently trust the sound of His victory song?

AUGUST 1

For God alone my soul waits in silence; from him comes my salvation.
Psalm 62:1

I am sure we have had, at times, been asked to prioritize people in our life and if we think we are a good person, a good Christian, we put God as our first priority. But if we are honest with ourselves, is He really first in our lives? Is He the first thing we think of in the morning? Do we engage in His Word first thing in the morning? After being in His word, do we follow up with worshiping Him first before we do anything for ourselves in the morning? Do we give in or give it to Him when we face temptation? Do we hold our tongues when we are angered or feel disrespected? David writes, "For God alone, my soul waits in silence." Do we wait on Him patiently? Take it up a notch – do we wait for Him in silence? Is it God and God alone that we thirst for and wait on? Or do we have our own agenda, our own idea of what life is to look like, the path we should walk down, the people who need assistance and help – do we decide that? I wish that my testimony aligned with David's words, but I would be lying. I am impatient when it comes to me waiting on God's timing and several times I told God, "No, you have the wrong person here!" But as I continue to grow in my faith and my relationship with Him, I am starting to allow the Holy Spirit to guide and direct me more with less questioning. I am becoming more patient when it comes to God's timing. Have I arrived there yet? No and probably not until my last breath leaves me, but it is something that I am striving for; it is something that all believers should strive for. Waiting in silence, but not inaction. We continue to move forward, but in our prayer time, we become more silent so that He can speak more. Do we occupy all the talk time, or do we allow Him time to speak? He and He alone should be what we wait for, our first priority of the day and the last thought of the night. What does your soul wait for, long for? How can you realign it so that you wait for the Lord and wait in silence for Him? What can you do to increase your desire for Him and spend more time with Him?

AUGUST 2

> "For who is God, but the LORD? And who is a rock, except our God? This God is my strong refuge and has made my way blameless.
> 2 Samuel 22:32–33

Who is God? That is a question that continues to be asked and has been asked for countless generations. The answer for current world society is that god is whatever or whomever you believe in; truth is what you make of it. But capital G *God*, not so! God is the living creator of the universe, by which His hands, everything that is seen and unseen, has been created. Capital G *God* has walked the Earth and ate and talked with Abraham. He was born of a virgin, lived a perfect life, died for our sins and rose alive from the grave after three days to conquer death. His Spirit is still with us, directing, guiding, instructing, counseling and comforting us in our daily walks. He never leaves nor forsakes us. He is the rock on which our faith is built. Being that rock, that solid foundation, He has also made Himself for us a strong refuge, a mighty tower. In Him, we can seek refuge and find safety. In His presence, we find rest and comfort. When we follow Him, obey His words and live out His will for our lives, He makes our way blameless. So, when we face battles, spiritual or otherwise, do we fight on our own, or do we allow the Rock and the Refuge to protect us and fight for us? When we are living out His will, He will fight for us and He will be that Rock. When we wander off and do our own things, follow our own pursuits and indulge our own desires, He won't fight for us. He will, however, leave the door open and the lights on for us so that whenever we come back to Him, His strong refuge is available to us. He won't bless us in our phases of disobedience, nor eliminate the consequences of our disobedience, but will be there to restore us and refresh us. If you want to walk blamelessly, you need to get out of the driver's seat and follow and be willing to go wherever God directs you. But now, back to the original question: Who is God? Is the God you create in your life the one who wants you happy, healthy and wealthy and answers only "Yes" to prayer requests, or the God of Scripture, the God of the Bible? Is He the God who says, "Pick up your cross and follow me"? If you want a solid foundation, a strong refuge, you must seek God with a capital G and not a lower-case g; the capital G *God* is only found in the Bible, so study and read Scripture for yourself. Who is your capital G *God*? What little-g god(s) have you intentionally or unintentionally put in His place? How can you make sure you know who God is? How can you personally thank Him for being an everlasting source of safety?

AUGUST 3

> The counsel of the LORD stands forever, the plans of his heart to all generations. Psalm 33:11

Author Sidney Sheldon is credited as first saying, "Nothing lasts forever." As children, we are told this truism. The world also tells us this and that since nothing lasts forever, if we want our life to matter then we have to decide it and make it so. But life does matter and God says all life matters. He also says that His counsel stands forever. The New Living Translation says today's verse this way, "But the Lord's plans stand firm forever; His intentions can never be shaken." God is forever, eternal, always has existed, is existing and forever will exist. His Counsel for us, His plans for us are firm, forever, eternal. His intentions for us, for all generations, cannot be shaken, broken, changed, or terminated. His plans, His heart was not just for a moment or a specific group of people, but for all generations. He wants all generations to know Him, love Him and receive His grace and forgiveness. He wants to bless us and be in communion with us. His plans to bless us, forgive us and His love for us will never change. He is the source of Truth and in that, He does not change. For truth to be true and remain true, it cannot change; it cannot be interpreted differently nor applied differently. Truth in and of itself is eternal, Truth lasts forever. So, when we read His Word, whether it was written 10,000 or 2,000 years ago, it is still applicable. Sin is sin, love is love and no matter what the world tells us, it does not change. Since He is truth and His counsel stands forever, we can be confident in His Will and not allow fear to come in and deter us from following His counsel, His advice. His heart is always willing to receive us, no matter our thoughts, words, actions, or the sinful desires we gratify. As long as we return to Him and seek His forgiveness and His counsel, He stands ready to extend those to us. Have you ever considered this verse before, "The counsel of the Lord stands forever, the plans of His heart to all generations, His plans are forever, His intentions can never be shaken"? How does this affect your life, today, in the twenty-first century? What fears does this verse help you release?

AUGUST 4

> Submit yourselves therefore to God. Resist the devil and he will flee from you. James 4:7

How often do you give in to the devil and follow him? Never? Often? Daily? I think it's easy for Christians to say we resist the devil. No one wants to admit that they give in to him. James says to first submit ourselves to God. The only real way to resist the devil is to submit your will and your life to God. The closer you draw near to God and walk with God on a daily basis, that causes the devil to flee. It is when you stray from God, go out on your own and leave His presence that, like a prowling lion looking for someone to devour, the devil pounces or one of his minions' attacks. It is so easy to take Scripture out of context and many false doctrines have developed because of that. We have to look at what comes before and after this verse for full context. James doesn't just tell us to resist the devil and he will flee from you; he says you must first submit to God. Submit to His authority in your life. Submit to His will for your life. Submit to the lifestyle He is calling you to. Love Him, love your neighbor, forgive others, extend mercy and grace and speak His Word correctly and with love. We also need to be aware of the temptation that the enemy will try to distract us with and lure us away from the presence of God. I love the word lure because it is like a fishing lure that attracts a fish to the hook that leads to its demise and the enemy does the same. While he can't destroy those who have the Holy Spirit living in them, he can lure them away from His teaching and His guidance. His voice can be louder than the Holy Spirit, so we must pay attention to it instead of the still, small voice that God uses; the Holy Spirit uses. Be aware of the enemy's schemes, be vigilant and be intentional with your relationship with God, Jesus and the Holy Spirit. Make sure you are in Scripture. Make sure you are worshiping where you are. Make sure you are in prayer and that your prayer time includes listening time. Submit yourself to the power and presence of the Holy Spirit in your life. What are you willing to commit to doing to submit more to God, more to the Holy Spirit? What is it in your life that you need to submit to God to make the devil flee?

AUGUST 5

> I will meditate on your precepts and fix my eyes on your ways. I will delight in your statutes; I will not forget your word. Psalm 119:15-16

What do you spend your time doing? With smart devices, our attention is fought over non-stop and I think we rarely stop and think about how much time we spend on our devices, whether smartphones, tablets, laptops, or watches. The author of Psalm 119 states that in this part of the psalm, they will meditate on God's precepts and fix their eyes on the Lord's way. Another translation says, "I will study His commandments and reflect on His ways." How much time during our busy lives, busy days, do we spend meditating on God's Word? Not only should we be meditating on His Word, but also we should take time to think and reflect on the ways of God. If God were here with me now, what would He want me to do? In the 1990s, youth groups took on Rev. Charles Sheldon's phrase, "What Would Jesus Do?" and turned it into a movement. It quickly became a cliche and lost its intended power, but what if we returned to it? What would Jesus do in this situation? In order to know what Jesus would do, we need to reflect on the ways of God and meditate on His Word, know His Word and inscribe His Word on our hearts and souls. The author goes further and says, "I will delight in your statutes and I will not forget your word." What do you take delight in? Is it a larger portion of dessert? A bonus added to your pay? The laughter of a small child? None of these are bad, but do we delight in the Word of God as much as we delight in these other worldly things? I have heard people say, "I can't memorize Scripture," yet they can sing the theme song to *Cheers* or *Gilligan's Island* or they can remember obscure movie quotes or sports statistics. Why do we memorize meaningless information but make excuses for forgetting God's Word? Is it a heart issue or a priority issue? What is it that we really want? Do we want a genie in the sky or do we want a trusting relationship with God? I mean, do we really want God?! What can you do to make memorizing Scripture and having a deep relationship with God more of a priority in your life? Realistically, how much time are you willing to start putting into meditating on God's Word, studying His Word and taking more delight in His Word?

AUGUST 6

> Behold, the LORD's hand is not shortened, that it cannot save, or his ear dull, that it cannot hear; but your iniquities have made a separation between you and your God and your sins have hidden his face from you so that he does not hear. Isaiah 59:1-2

I think many times when we find ourselves in tight or difficult situations, we can turn our frustrations and anger towards the wrong person. Sometimes when God doesn't "rescue" us right away, we can become mad at Him. The problem is that a lot of the time we put ourselves into those situations. Isaiah reminds us that God's arm is not so short that He cannot save us. He has not gone deaf and cannot hear us, but our sin has caused the problem, caused the separation between us. When we don't see or feel God's presence in our lives, we need to check ourselves and ask: "Have we walked out of the presence of God?" and "Is there a sin issue in my life that is blocking the communication between Him and me?" Sin separates us from God. That is the whole reason why Jesus died on the cross. He died for our sins and made a way to restore that relationship with God, a permanent bridge to the Father. No more sacrifices, no more priests to make atonement for us; Jesus did it all and *it is finished*. Jesus' death and resurrection do not prevent us from sinning, although I wish it did; it just makes a way for us to come back to Him. When we confess our sins and ask for forgiveness, it is like us walking back into the Garden of Eden after hiding behind the trees. God is there, not hidden, just waiting for us to return to Him. In sin, we hide and put up barriers between God and us, asking, "Where are You God?" In reality, He has not gone anywhere. We are the ones who have wandered, left, or are hidden. Pride, the original sin, the root of every sin, tends to prevent us from seeing that we are the problem, not God. How strong is your connection to God? Has it been a while since you heard from Him? How long has it been since you felt His presence? Check yourself. Do you have any unconfessed sin? Confess and repent, turn back around to go back; God never left. He is waiting for you! How can this Scripture help you in your daily walk?

AUGUST 7

> A soft answer turns away wrath, but a harsh word stirs up anger.
> Proverbs 15:1

Irish, Italians and redheads all have one thing in common. They are joked about for having hot tempers and short fuses. Something we all need to remember is that words are powerful. We are created in His Image; we bear the image of God. God created everything with the power of His words. While we may not be able to create by speaking, our words are still powerful. When we are faced with certain situations, a soft answer can turn away wrath, or as the NLT translation says, "a gentle answer can deflect anger." Whether you are one of the stereotypes mentioned at the beginning or not, you have probably done something or said things in anger and made a situation worse; we all do it. But when we are confronted, we can deflect and turn away wrath and anger by maintaining control of our emotions and controlling our tongues. As we continue with the verse, harsh words make tempers flare or stir up anger. When we react instead of respond, it is generally done emotionally and not logically. When we are harsh, we speak in anger or disgust, it makes matters worse and a bad situation easily becomes worse. It can stir up anger in others, cause tempers to flare and words to be said that cannot be taken back. Reacting is done emotionally and generally with little control and is not done in discipline with a clear mind. Responding and not reacting allows us to maintain control of our emotions, speak logically and speak the truth, whereas reacting and speaking emotionally, we generally exaggerate as a defense, which in turn becomes a lie when we exaggerate. In all my studies, Jesus responded to people without reacting. Were there times when Jesus was angry? Yes, He grabbed a whip and ran people out of the temple. But in that anger, He still responded instead of reacting. His anger was righteous because the people were defaming the house of God. He called the Pharisees a "brood of vipers" and "white-washed tombs", but not in an emotional rant, rather in responding to their lack of faith and knowledge of the God they were supposed to be serving. Emotions are not sins and not wrong; it is what we do with emotions and being emotional that can step over the line into sin. When we face confrontation, may we allow the Holy Spirit to respond for us and not prematurely react in the flesh? How can you respond and not react when confronted? How can you control your emotions and not allow your emotions to control you?

AUGUST 8

> Finally, be strong in the Lord and in the strength of his might.
> Ephesians 6:10

What does strong look like? What does it mean to be strong? The world tells us that, especially as a man, we need to be strong and endure, but then the world tells us that we are weak when we cannot handle the pressures it throws at us. So what makes us strong? Is it dead lifting weights? Is it working until you have nothing left to give? If we look to the world for an answer, we will be left with unhealthy, unrealistic expectations. But Paul reminds us here that we need to be strong in the Lord, not strong in our own power. Our faith and who we put our faith in is where our strength comes from. It's not us. As much as the enemy wants to try to convince us that we are our own source of strength, it will never be true. While we have our part to do, God is our ultimate source of strength; He *is* our strength. When we try to control everything and be strong by ourselves, we will fall short and fail. But when we put our full trust in the Lord, when we have a deep relationship with Jesus, we know the voice of the Holy Spirit and can rely on Him to make us strong and give us the strength to successfully pass through any trials and hard times the world throws our way. With Christ we can successfully come out the other side more than a conqueror. It is not outward strength, not muscle strength, that makes us able to fight the battles that come our way. It is the Holy Spirit living in us and through us, that is our strength. When we allow Him to equip us and strengthen us, then and only then can we come out the other side successful. Allowing Him to be our strength is not giving up, but it is how we make it through our Job-like trials. Remember, you have your part to play; you still have to walk the path in front of you. You just don't have to do it alone or on your own accord or from your own ability. What is God asking you to allow Him to be your strength for? How can you rely on His strength and not your own will? How can you surrender your heart to experience His strength more purposefully and powerfully in your life?

AUGUST 9

> Put on the whole armor of God, that you may be able to stand against the schemes of the devil. For we do not wrestle against flesh and blood, but against the rulers, against the authorities, against the cosmic powers over this present darkness, against the spiritual forces of evil in the heavenly places. Ephesians 6:11-12

People tend to believe in *karma*, the type of energy you send out into the universe will be the same returned to you. Others believe in luck, that some people are lucky and some are not. Many professional athletes believe in luck. For example, baseball players are some of the most infamous athletes to believe in luck, using lucky socks or rituals to get ready. Some believe that all there is to life is only what can be seen and touched. Some Christians believe in the devil while others do not. Satan is a metaphor for evil. How can a God of love create a devil? Well, Paul warns us believers to prepare for battle as we fight Satan, demons and spirits. The devil is a real entity. The evil spirits Paul is speaking of here are not what we think of come Halloween time or a way to scare kids into obedience. Rather they are forces of evil that are not to be taken lightly. If we are to believe the Bible – it's either an all-or-nothing scenario. Either God speaks the truth or nothing can be believed. Jesus spoke of Satan. The Old Testament speaks of him. Paul warns us of him and he even tempted Jesus in the desert. Paul reminds us that we need to put on the full armor of God to fight not against flesh and blood, but against the rulers, authorities, cosmic powers and spiritual forces that are at work in the world. We can't just put on a piece of armor, but the full armor to be ready for battle. Don't use the devil as an excuse to be weak and sin, giving him more power and credit than he has. God will not allow us to be tempted more than we can resist and He will provide a way out. Satan cannot make you do anything; that is the gift of free will that God gives us. You choose to follow him or follow Christ. How can you strengthen your walk with the Holy Spirit so that you are better prepared for each day? What do you have to change in your life so that you are not giving Satan credit for power he really doesn't have? How do you spiritually prepare for every day? What spiritual battles do you see happening?

AUGUST 10

> Therefore take up the whole armor of God, that you may be able to withstand in the evil day and having done all, to stand firm. Stand therefore, having fastened on the belt of truth, Ephesians 6:13-14a

One good thing about losing weight is your clothes start to be looser and you need that belt to keep your shorts or pants up. That was the first item I bought when I lost twenty pounds – a new belt to hold everything up and in place. The belt keeps the pants up so you don't trip on them. Paul uses the Roman soldier, an image very familiar to the people he was writing to, as an icon for what armor is needed for battle. The Roman soldier had a leather belt around his waist that not only kept his tunic up above the knee so he could run, but also housed the sheath to carry his sword. The spiritual belt is TRUTH. There can only be one source for truth and it has to be unchanging for it to actually be *the truth*. Today people try to say, "Well, that is true for you, but that is not true for me." That cannot be. For truth to exist, there can only be one source. The Bible is the source of Truth. Jesus is Truth. He said it Himself – He is the Way, the Truth and the Life. The Bible is the reminder that Jesus is our foundation that holds everything together and keeps everything in place. The truth holds our weapon (and our armor), so when it is needed, it is there. It is in knowing the Truth that we are able to decipher the lies of the enemies. In order to stand in battle, ready to fight, we need to be anchored, held together by truth, by Jesus alone. It is in our daily relationship with Him that we have the ability to stand and face the enemy in both defense and offense. Most of the soldier's outfit is basically useless without the belt; the breastplate and the sword are dependent on there being a belt. It is just another reminder of how fruitless life can be without our foundation being in Jesus. Without Him holding everything together for us and without Truth in our life, we are truly building on sinking sand. Make sure to begin your day securing your foundation in the Truth, in Jesus. How do you see Truth and determine what is true? How do you let Truth guide your direction in life and what you do? How can you apply God's Truth more in your everyday life?

AUGUST 11

> Therefore take up the whole armor of God, that you may be able to withstand in the evil day and having done all, to stand firm. Stand therefore, having fastened on the belt of truth and having put on the breastplate of righteousness. Ephesians 6:13-14

Righteousness means "morally right, justifiable, virtuous". As people, we tend to grade on a curve and compare ourselves to others, whether we know them personally or not. We tell ourselves, "I'm a more moral person than so-in-so." In society now, due to globalization, we have this concept of moral relativism, that cultures have different definitions of truth and morals; what is true for you does not have to be true for me and what is moral for you does not necessarily make sense to me. You might tell yourself, "I am a better person than Hitler." Ok, but are you a better person than Mother Theresa? Take it up a notch, are you a better person than Jesus? We try to justify ourselves, but we constantly fall short in terms of God's example of righteousness. When we spend time in His word, we realize there is no need to compare ourselves as God's children and we don our armor and allow God to provide us with strong spiritual defenses against the enemy. The breastplate protected the vital organs of the Roman soldier, his heart, lungs, kidneys, liver and stomach. Like the Roman breastplate, God's breastplate of righteousness protects what is most vital, our hearts and souls. It is His righteousness, the righteousness of Jesus that protects us. The breastplate was held in place by the belt, the belt of Truth. When we start to work off of our own righteousness, we take off the metal breastplate and put on a holey, dirty, torn, thin, cotton shirt. That will not protect us, nor can we be righteous on our own accord. We need to remember that as sinful people, we need the Holy Spirit to live in us to have His righteousness in us. We need the Holy Spirit to protect us in the spiritual battles and help us face the temptations that come at us on a daily basis. Where do you seek your protection – in yourself or in the Lord? How "good" of a person are you? How can this verse help you understand why we need Him? How can you be more intune to what spiritual battles we actually face?

AUGUST 12

> and, as shoes for your feet, having put on the readiness given by the gospel of peace. Ephesians 6:15

We may not think of it, but shoes are really important. As a middle school teacher, many places required closed-toe shoes when we would go on field trips. Why? To protect the feet, because feet are challenging to protect as the farthest body part from the brain. With racers, shoes are the most important feature or equipment to run a race. Some professional runners, like Olympic athletes, have custom made shoes to make them run faster and more efficiently. For a Roman soldier, his shoes were just as important as the belt and breastplate. He needed to be able to stand his ground and maintain stability and agility. They were generally thick leather sandals with metal spikes in them to grip the ground and hold tight. These metal spikes gave the soldier the stability to fight in battle. We are called, as Christians, to be ready to share the Gospel and share the reason we have hope. That is done through the *Gospel of Peace – The Good News*. The Good News is that Jesus loves us enough that He gave His own life for our sins and rose from the dead on the third day so we could have eternal life with Him and have direct access to the Father. Jesus said he did not come to judge the world but to save the world. The sandals of peace, like Romans' sandals, have sharp grippers to hold us firm. Jesus is the only way – the Way, the Truth, the Life. His Bible is all true, not just parts of it. We share the Gospel in love, the peace that surpasses all understanding, but we don't dilute the Gospel either. It is His Good News, His Gospel, not ours. That is the Gospel we need to be grounded in, firmly rooted in and relying on. Do you walk more in peace or frustration? Do you walk in peace or regret? What do you need to change to put on the shoes of readiness and peace? How can you walk in the protection of His holy peace? What do you need to do to be more firmly grounded in peace?

AUGUST 13

> In all circumstances take up the shield of faith, with which you can extinguish all the flaming darts of the evil one; Ephesians 6:16

Do you remember how we started this week, by putting on the full armor of God? Don't forget even one piece. Today we look at the shield of faith. What is a shield? An object used for protection. The Roman shield was about four feet tall and two feet wide layers of wood glued together and then covered with leather. When the Romans lined up and put their shields together, they formed an impenetrable wall. Our faith is the same way. When we put our faith in Jesus, He forms an impenetrable wall to our heart and soul. A shield is only good when we bring it with us; it does no good unless we use it to defend ourselves. The enemy loves to create doubt in our minds with a million questions: "Are you really saved? You just did what? Said what? And you call yourself a Christian? Are you sure this is really a sin? God wants you happy; doesn't He love you?" Satan likes to recreate the original lie, asking us, "Does the Bible/did God really say that?" But when you utilize your faith and allow it to protect you from the fiery lies of the enemy, they become useless, like an arrow shot at a wall of Roman shields lined up. Even with our proverbial Roman shields lined up, we need to come together in the faith and form that wall, not letting other believers become isolated, trying to defend and hold the ground on which they stand alone. Neither can we be that Christian who tries to do it alone, not recognizing the importance of fellowship and working alongside the body of Christ. No one is called to be a Lone Ranger Christian; we were created to be in community and unified under the banner of the name of Jesus Christ. How have you let your guard down, lowered your shield of faith and allowed fiery arrows to enter? Who do you have in your life to help you remember your shield and will align their shield with yours to offer more protection and help? Who can you come alongside for extra defense, benefitting both you and them?

AUGUST 14

and take the helmet of salvation, Ephesians 6:17a

Football players wear helmets to protect their brains from injuries involved in playing the sport and they are constantly improving the design of helmets to limit concussions and brain injuries. With baseball pitchers hurling baseballs, sometimes close to 100 miles per hour, baseball players wear helmets while batting to protect their heads from fast, wild pitches. Construction workers, steel workers, road workers, etc., all wear helmets to protect their heads and their brains from injuries from heavy equipment in the workforce. Some states even have laws requiring you to wear a helmet if you ride a motorcycle. Roman soldiers also wore helmets that covered part of the shoulders, neck and most of the face to protect them from flying arrows and spike driven clubs. Spiritually speaking, we need to put on our helmets as well. Since the enemy cannot access our hearts or souls, demonic forces can only speak into our minds. When we put on the helmet of salvation, it reminds us that once we are saved by Grace the enemy has no power over us. Salvation is through our accepting the sacrifice of Jesus and the gift of Eternal Life; He is our only Way out, our only protection from the lies of the enemy. He has won the spiritual, emotional, mental and physical battles for us. When we forget the helmet, the enemy can easily convince us that our faith is not strong enough with questioning attacks like, "Are you really saved? Are you really forgiven? A real Christian wouldn't do or say those things." Protect your mind from the lies of the enemy. Temptation starts in the mind with a thought. This is the last defensive piece of armor, but in order to protect us fully, our defensive line must be complete – belt, breastplate, shoes, shield and helmet. When even one part of the armor is not utilized, it opens up ways for the enemy to infiltrate and wound us, causing us to become ineffective and incapacitated. When doubt and fear enter your mind, check and see if your spiritual helmet is on and secure. How can you readjust your spiritual helmet to better protect your mind when you face trials and doubts? How do you take thoughts captive? When enemy thoughts infiltrate your mind, what do you do? How can you secure your helmet of salvation on a daily basis?

AUGUST 15

> and the sword of the Spirit, which is the word of God, praying at all times in the Spirit, with all prayer and supplication. Ephesians 6:17b-18

As we have walked through and reflected on Ephesians 6:10-17a, every part of the armor of God has been defensive. You may be wondering, "When do we get to the warrior part of the armor?" A soldier is only as good as what protects him, but the Holy Spirit does give us an offensive weapon – the Sword of the Spirit, which is the Word of God. Don't underestimate this weapon; God's words are powerful. In Genesis, He created all life by speaking it into existence. Satan had no way to influence Jesus in the desert and had to depart at the spoken word of God. Demons were cast out, healings never heard of since Elisha's time, a man raised from the dead by the Word of God. But in order to use this weapon, you need to know about it. Law Enforcement and military personnel are not just handed a gun and told, "Go for it." They learn how to load, hold, carry, aim, fire and clean it first. To use the Sword of the Spirit, you must know the word of God, meaning you must read it, learn it, study it and plant it in your heart, mind and soul. You cannot rely on someone else to teach you the Word of God. You must read it for yourself and internalize it. Then and only then will you be able to utilize the Sword of the Spirit. Paul tells us that with the Sword of the Spirit, the Word of God, we need to be praying at all times in the spirit with all prayer and supplication. Some of the most powerful prayers you can pray are when you pray the Word of God back to Him. By praying His Word back to Him, it helps engrave those words in our own spirit. What do you do when you face a trial, a hardship, or a difficult time? Do you complain or cry out? That is fine for a moment, but when you get through the initial emotion, do you dwell there? Do you throw yourself a pity party or do you pray and read God's Word? As you go through one of these challenging circumstances, try to utilize the armor of God to be able to stand your ground and defend yourself and your family. Don't get emotional, get armored up. How can you implement this verse in your life today? How much time do you spend in the Bible and in prayer? How much are you willing to increase your commitment to reading His Holy Word, so that you can be better prepared for spiritual battles? What can you do to stick to adding that time in every day?

AUGUST 16

> To that end, keep alert with all perseverance, making supplication for all the saints and also for me, that words may be given to me in opening my mouth boldly to proclaim the mystery of the gospel,
> Ephesians 6:18b-19a

I have heard that being a pastor is one of the loneliest jobs out there. People have higher expectations of you than others. Pastors tend to not have people pouring into their lives like people want pastors to do for them. Pastors also find it hard to trust people, so it's hard to find a trusted confidant when they need someone to talk to. I think so often, as Christians, that we get so caught up in our prayer requests that we forget to pray for those in service of the Gospel. Whether it be the senior pastors, worship leaders, or kids' area workers, it is easy to think that if they are serving, they have everything together. In reality, they are no different from everyone else sitting in the pews weekly. They know they don't have it all together; they just want to play their part in the body of Christ and be obedient to what God has laid on their hearts. Here in Ephesians 6, Paul exhorts his church at Ephesus, as well as us, to pray for all the saints and those working to make the Gospel available to everyone. But then he says, "and also for me," that words may be given to him so that when he opens his mouth, the "mystery of the Gospel" will be revealed. Have you prayed this for your pastor that the Holy Spirit would give him the words to be bold? This week, in your prayer time, include prayers for your pastor, the worship team and kids' ministry workers. Pray for them to be blessed for remaining obedient to the Lord, pray for protection from spiritual attacks against them and pray for them to be able to receive rest. Many won't ask for it, so it's up to us, the church, to be intentional in praying for them. Pray for those who make church happen by being the hands and feet of Christ. Pray for your pastor and for him to be the microphone through which God speaks. How can you pray this week for your pastor and those who are serving the Lord every week? How can you apply this verse in your life to deepen your Christian walk?

AUGUST 17

> Let the one who boasts, boast in the Lord. For it is not the one who commends himself who is approved, but the one whom the Lord commends. 2 Corinthians 10:17-18

It can be annoying being around someone who is always patting themselves on the back. There is not much room for God when you are constantly putting the spotlight on yourself. I honestly believe this is the reason why Jesus chose the 12 most unlikely men to be His disciples. They could not boast of being a disciple of Gamaliel, another renowned Pharisee or Sadducee. They were not schooled in Scripture or taught how to lead. They were outcasts, fishermen, tax collectors and laborers from the impoverished section of Galilee, nonetheless. When Paul was Saul, he could boast about being a disciple of Gamaliel, but when he met Jesus on the road to Damascus, all of that was wiped out. At that point he realized that he could do nothing, say nothing, know nothing, without the wisdom and indwelling of the Holy Spirit. Jesus himself taught us to look at the Pharisee, how he stands in public and lifts up lofty prayers, for he has already received his reward. Do you do what you do for God or for the approval of man? You have received your reward when you want man to think highly of you, like this Pharisee. But when we allow God to work through us, He can accomplish what we could not do. So, He gets the credit and our reward is in Heaven. When we fully surrender to Him and allow Him to be our guide, He will have us do things, say things, know things that we wouldn't know, say or be able to do on our own accord, so we can only say that is God speaking, working through me. We want to lead people to know Jesus, not to know us, to have a relationship with the living God and to follow Him, not to follow us. Boast in the Lord, don't let the world drag you into seeking temporary recognition when you can get eternal recognition from the Creator of the Universe. So, when it feels like no one sees what you are doing, know that the Father sees it. How can you modify your outlook so that it is commendation from the Lord and not from the world that you seek? How can you realign your priorities to be more closely aligned with God?

AUGUST 18

> Seek the Lord and his strength; seek his presence continually! Psalm 105:4

The English language is so poor compared to other languages. We have limited words that we use over and over again. The love I have for my spouse is the same word to describe how I feel about pepperoni pizza. Many times, throughout Scripture we see, "Seek the Lord" or "Search for the Lord," like He is lost or hiding from us. God has gone nowhere; it is us who have wandered like mindless sheep away from Him. The problem is that these verses are saying more that we should return to the Lord, or seek His presence, ask for His guidance and desire His presence in our lives. Search for the Lord and for His strength. Look into your heart, is there room for Him? Do you desire His strength in your life? We need to be continually conversing with Him and have a conversation with Him, not always talking, but allowing Him sincere talk time. Continually, we must make time for Him throughout the day, not just at meals and bedtime. We should continually desire Him and His guidance, instruction and wisdom. We should be willing to continually return to Him when we stray. If we truly love Him, we should continually read His Word and continually apply His Truth in our life. The Lord never leaves us. We tend to exit off of His path, but He is always providing an onramp back onto His will, His way, if we just desire and want to return to Him. His strength will allow us to walk through any trial; through His strength, He carried the sin of the world, past, present and future on His body as He hung there on the cross. His strength is more than enough to get us through any situation the world may throw our way. How are you seeking or desiring His presence in your life? How can you return to His strength to help you walk the path you are currently on?

AUGUST 19

> Again Jesus spoke to them, saying, "I am the light of the world. Whoever follows me will not walk in darkness but have the light of life." John 8:12

Have you ever experienced complete darkness? I have. I have been to Cave of the Winds and Glenwood Caverns and they always shut off the lights so you can experience total darkness underground. When that happens, you cannot even see your hand in front of your face. I have also done the more advanced tours and experiencing the contrast of lighting a single match, it's amazing how much light it actually puts off in complete darkness. I have heard it said that a single match could shine as far as one thousand feet in complete darkness. That is more than three football fields stacked end to end. Darkness and Light cannot coexist. Scientifically speaking, darkness is actually just the void of light, so light dispels darkness. Jesus says, "I am the light of the world… if you follow Me, you will not walk in darkness because you will have the light that leads to life." Walking in darkness can mess with your balance, throw off your equilibrium, shake your confidence and inhibit your peace. But Jesus says we won't walk in darkness if we follow Him; if we accept Him as the Messiah and allow the Holy Spirit to guide and direct us, then the light will be in us and will guide us and dispel darkness while lighting up our path. He doesn't promise that the light will show us every curve in the road ahead of time, just that we will have the light that we need to navigate life. When we feel like we are being consumed by darkness and that is all we see, all we have to do is turn around with our arms uplifted to Him. Light pushes the shadows and the darkness away. So if you are facing it, turn your back to the darkness and face the Light, face Christ. How can you make Scripture so intertwined in your DNA that when the enemy is trying to convince you that darkness has won? How can you remember God's word and use the Sword of the Spirit to dispel and destroy the lies that the enemy tries to convince you to consume? How can you increase the light in your life? What avenues do you have open that allow the darkness in?

AUGUST 20

> I have set the Lord always before me; because he is at my right hand,
> I shall not be shaken. Psalm 16:8

What is your faith based on? How solid and strong is it? What can shake your faith will determine what your faith is in. So, what can shake your faith? An unwelcome diagnosis from a doctor? Could it be job loss in uncertain markets, or financial loss with no assurance of recovery? Family tragedy and the unexpected loss of a loved one(s)? When these things happen, what are you looking at? What is before you? Do you have your eyes set on the Lord or on medicine? Is your security found in your job or 401K? Did you have faith because you had a family? David is writing in Psalm 16 that he is focused on the Lord and wherever he goes he stays close to the Lord. David makes sure the Lord is always at his right hand. He doesn't exit off the path of the Lord; he stays in God's will so that the Lord is always at his right hand. This is how he can face the Goliaths in his life. This is how he keeps his faith from being shaken. Because David is connected to the Lord. No matter what happens, no matter what comes his way, he knows that he is walking with the Lord; no matter his mistakes, he is walking with the Lord so he will not be shaken. Now was David perfect? No. Did he flee when King Saul was trying to kill him? Yes. God did not want David, nor us, to stay in physically dangerous situations. But while away from Jerusalem, David did not fear for his life. He had many and ample opportunities to kill Saul and take the throne that was promised to him, but he didn't stray from the Father and was patient while God worked out the complicated details. Doubt, fear, uncertainty and the unknown cannot have a seat at your table if you have Jesus sitting there. How can you stand firm and not be shaken when the Goliaths of fear, doubt, worry, or uncertainty come knocking at your door or calling your name? What giants and Goliaths are invading your life? How can you kill your giants, your Goliaths?

AUGUST 21

> We were buried therefore with him by baptism into death, in order that, just as Christ was raised from the dead by the glory of the Father, we too might walk in newness of life. Romans 6:4

Remember the thrill of getting that brand new toy or brand-new car, or if you were like my family, "brand new to me"? Remember the pride we took in it, taking care of it and the joy we got in using it? Mine was a light blue Pontiac Sunbird. Every weekend I washed it, *ArmorAlled* all the seats and dash and vacuumed it out. I loved that car and even put in a new stereo on my own. Are we that way with the new life we get when we are born again? When Christ came into our lives, our hearts, He gave us a new life! Not a life tied down with sin and sorrow, but one of joy and of life more abundant! He gave us a new identity with freedom. When you were baptized, the old sinful nature was washed away; when you came out of the water, it symbolized that you were raised to new life. You were given a new life in Christ. The enemy loves to try to keep us shackled and weighed down by our sinful nature, our past. He loves to use guilt and condemnation on us to try to prevent us from living in freedom, living in that new identity. But God wants you to live in freedom from guilt and condemnation. He wants you to experience the joy that comes from living with Him. Like the pride and excitement you have when you get a new car or new toy, aim to experience the same pride and excitement you have in the new life Christ has given you. Enjoy the freedom that comes from Him living inside of you. Allow that glorious power within you to challenge you to live as Christ did. What is God calling you to do today? What do you need to let go of in your past so that you can hold onto the new life that Christ is giving you? How have you experienced the newness of life Paul is talking about? How do you enjoy the freedom that the Holy Spirit brings us?

AUGUST 22

and he died for all, that those who live might no longer live for themselves but for him who for their sake died and was raised. 2 Corinthians 5:15

Carpe Diem! Seize the day! The world tells us to live for ourselves and in the moment. Take care of *numero uno!* When we talk about or think of a religious fanatic, we think of religious terrorists, regardless of religion. Islam and Christianity both have people who do harm in the name of their God. But a fanatic, someone who goes beyond reason, could be said of the disciples, the apostles and here Paul. Christ died for all, that those who live should no longer live for themselves. Wait! What? Everything around me tells me to satisfy my needs, my desires, live for myself and take care of myself, because no one else will. You want me to follow this Jesus dude and stop living for me? You want me to live for Him? Well, Paul says, He died for you and was raised on the third day to conquer death. How can you repay that? We can't. But we can live for Him. Live in His will and His desire for our lives. Yes, it is counter-cultural, but would it really be from God if it was cultural? Since the expulsion from the garden, we have been at odds with God because pride has entered us and pride takes care of self-first and foremost. When God saves us, the Holy Spirit comes into us. He lives in our hearts and is there to direct us, to instruct us in His ways and guide us, so that we follow God and His direction. We can't do it on our own. While created in His image, we are born with a pride issue, a sin issue. So we need to seek Him and allow Him to help us in all things. We need to stop living for ourselves and live for Him, which means loving others, all others, not just some. To stop living for self means to let go of hurt, forgive and love and serve those who hurt us. A harsh reality we don't like to contemplate is that we are nothing without Him, truly! So, if, in fact, we are truly nothing without Him, then we should stop living for ourselves and live for Him. Again, like many things with our walk with the Lord, it is simple but not easy. We tend to forgive but not forget, yet He does. Because the blood of Christ cleanses us and separates us from our sins, as far as the east is from the west, like God, we can choose to forget, to not remember. Live for Him and not for ourselves. How do you live out this verse in your life? What is the most difficult aspect of this verse? What steps can you take to improve in this area of your life?

AUGUST 23

> Not only that, but we rejoice in our sufferings, knowing that suffering produces endurance and endurance produces character and character produces hope, Romans 5:3

When I was in the Boy Scouts, I went for national training to be the Nature and Ecology Director. Then, while I taught middle school math and science, I also received more training. One lesson from both arenas was in the field of forestry. The strongest trees in the forest were the ones that went through rough years, trials so to speak. After enduring fires, trees develop stronger and thicker bark. In years of drought, their roots have to go further to find a water source. Those trees that never go through drought, their root systems stay close to the surface and can easily be knocked over. The same is true in our lives. No one likes going through trials, but Paul reminds us here that we can rejoice, not that we have problems and trials in life, but we rejoice in the knowledge that they help us develop endurance. As we develop spiritual endurance, the further we can run, the further we can go and the more we can handle the stress and friction of the spiritual warfare and keep moving. When runners prepare for a marathon, they don't start by running 26.2 miles. They start with less, way less. They begin running a few miles during practice sessions, maybe five to ten. Then, when they have that down, they add a few miles to their run and continue to do so until they hit the bigger goal of 26.2 miles. Then as serious runners build up endurance, they work on speed and form. If you are not experiencing trials and problems, how can you prepare your spirit and your soul to be able to rejoice through any and all circumstances? That is where true freedom can be found, like when Paul and Silas sang to the Lord in faith and the prison doors forcibly opened by the hand of God. Suffering of any kind produces endurance. Endurance, once we have developed that, produces character. It is your character that people witness and view from afar or close. As you continue your walk and endure, your character develops hope. When we have hope, we can endure much. Without hope, small trials can be crippling. If you are in the midst of problems and trials, remember to rejoice. Remember it's not praising because you have trials, but because God has something better for you on the other side. Allow the trial to deepen your prayer life, enhance your reading life and strengthen your relationship with God our Father. Why is character first and then hope is developed second? Why does Paul connect suffering to endurance? How do you endure trials when they come your way? Take a moment and remember a trial you successfully endured. What trial have you allowed to produce endurance in you, then character and finally hope?

AUGUST 24

> Those who listen to instruction will prosper; those who trust the Lord will be joyful. Proverbs 16:20 NLT

How many of us remember our mom saying, "If I told you once, I've told you a thousand times …" Many of us, I'm sure. As kids, we didn't want to listen to mom or dad; they're old and out of touch with reality, they don't even know what they are talking about. But as we got older, somehow our parents got smarter! How many trials, hurts and disappointments might we have avoided if we had only listened to them in the first place? My youngest son, after he turned 18, told me that he learned when he wants to do something and if he does it his way, it doesn't work out, but if he listens to me and his mom, it seems to always work out. He was younger than I was when I realized that. Solomon reminds us here in Proverbs that those who listen to instruction will prosper. God wants us to prosper and be successful; all we have to do is listen to Him, His instruction and be in His will. When we do that, we can learn to trust Him more; the more we trust Him, the more joy we will have! Where is your joy level? I don't mean happy and giddy, joy. If it's not high, then maybe God is trying to give you some instructions and you are responding internally like, "What does he know? He's too old to know the right way," like when you were a kid, or, "God, that doesn't apply today. Can you get with the times?" Instead of being childish, can you open your heart, mind and soul to hear His instruction, heed His knowledge and trust that He knows what He is doing? After all, He did create everything with the power of His words! If you fully trust in the Lord, the joy of salvation is a byproduct of that. What God-spoken, spiritual instruction are you needing to hear? What do you need to hand over and trust the Lord with? How can you increase your joy level by following the Holy Spirit's instructions?

AUGUST 25

> And who can win this battle against the world? Only those who believe that Jesus is the Son of God. 1 John 5:5 NLT

In today's society, fighting is glamorized. Underground Fight Rings, UFC, MMA. Champions in these arenas can become idolized and we may think, "Man, I want so-so on my side if we are walking down a dark street." We tend to see physique and muscle as strength, which, if we were fighting flesh and blood, we would need to succeed. But to overcome the world, the ruler of this world, it matters not our physical strength nor muscle mass; it is in the fact that Jesus Christ overcame the world and those of us who have accepted Him as Savior and Messiah can win the battles of this world. When Jesus went to Heaven, He promised a Helper for us believers left behind, the Holy Spirit. Through the power of the Holy Spirit, we would be given the tools to win the battles, spiritual battles. It is He who fights for us, helping us utilize the Sword of the Spirit, which is the Word of God. It matters not our muscle mass nor strength, but we can count on the Holy Spirit's strength to win these battles. To overcome the battles that we face in this world, on this side of Heaven, we can only do it with faith in Jesus and by the power of the Holy Spirit. For those who do not believe but look like they are winning the race of life, appearances can be deceiving. They have a hunger they cannot explain and a hole in their souls they are trying to fill with the world. But the world only leaves them emptier than before as nothing can fill a God-sized hole except the presence of God. So, when we face trials or hardships, we know that we can because the power of Christ, the Holy Spirit, is living in us. When you are facing trials, how can you remember to utilize the power of the Holy Spirit living in you and not try to win on your own accord? What spiritual battles are you facing? What is the enemy using to trip you with? How can you overcome these obstacles and win the battle?

AUGUST 26

> Since, therefore, we have now been justified by his blood, much more shall we be saved by him from the wrath of God. Romans 5:9

What is the hardest thing that you have ever done? Between rappelling off a cliff, participating in a search and rescue for a learning-disabled kid stuck on the side of a waterfall and standing up for myself to a family member, all stand out in my memory as a pretty close tie in difficult things I've had to do. No matter what it is for you or me, what is even harder is trying to get your good deeds to outweigh your bad deeds. Someone I loved dearly, before they passed, told me they were scared. They didn't think their good deeds outweighed their bad deeds, so would God let them into Heaven? They were a believer and born again, so I reminded them there is no way our good deeds outweigh our bad deeds, but when they accepted Christ as their Lord and Savior, they were justified by His Blood. *Justified* means to be made right in the eyes of God and that we are saved from the wrath of God and will one day be in Heaven with our Heavenly Father. See, sin is like yeast; once it's put in the dough, it's contaminated and can't be removed no matter what we try. There is nothing we can do to be made right in God's sight. Paul reminds us here that it is only through the blood of Jesus Christ that we are made right in the sight of God, because it is His blood that cleanses us from any and all transgressions. The cross removed our sins from us as far as the East is from the West. His blood cleanses us from all unrighteousness. He will certainly save us from the wrath that is promised to those who are enemies of God. We can try all we want, but God's plan is simple. His offer is clear, "Let me restore our relationship; let me pay your price for sin. All that I ask is that you accept this gift and allow me to live in your heart. Let me create in you a clean heart, to desire good, not bad." He did just that in my brother's life and I know he was at peace when he passed because he was restored by the blood of Christ to full relationship with God. How has the promise of God to save us from condemnation changed and impacted your life? Have you ever felt like my loved one? How have you come to terms with that internal conflict to find peace with God?

AUGUST 27

> But blessed are those who trust in the Lord and have made the Lord their hope and confidence. Jeremiah 17:7 NLT

I remember when we were little, we always hoped and prayed for a snow day whenever the weather was getting bad. Who am I kidding? As a teacher, I still hoped for these unexpected days off. However, when we put our hope in something so unpredictable as the weather or circumstances controlled by people, we are often disappointed. But here in Jeremiah, we are considered blessed and even called blessed when we put our trust in the Lord. When He is our hope and our confidence, we can be sure and strong. See, God is not extinct, nor is He controlled by people. So, unlike snow days or lotto numbers, we can place our trust and hope in the Creator of the Universe. Why is it that in 3rd world countries people with the least economically and having less materialistic things can be the happiest and have the strongest faith? It's not because they don't know what they don't have, as some would expect; it's because they know what they have, a relationship with the Author of Creation and our salvation! They have placed their trust in the Lord. Their hope and confidence are in something that cannot be taken away. Houses, retirements and bank accounts can all be taken away, but the love and strength of the Lord cannot. I just watched the movie about Philippe Petit, the man who walked between the Twin Towers while they were still being built. He is quoted as saying, "Trust your feet; they know where they are going." But do they really? Do you trust your feet, your eyes, or even your heart? Jeremiah reminds us that blessed are those "whose trust is in the Lord." Blessed are those who have made the Lord their hope, their confidence. Our own desires and wants can lead us astray. If we trust in ourselves, we tend to fall back into our sinful desires. When we trust in the Lord, we don't always know the way or the why; but the peace that comes from living with faith, in faith, is overwhelming. In life, we can hope someone gets better, we can hope our finances get better and we can hope for better weather (or snow days) ... but when we place our trust in our hopes, we almost always end up disappointed. When our hope and confidence is in the Lord, then we can trust whatever paths He leads us down. He will never leave nor forsake us, nor lead us down paths of destruction. When our hope and confidence is in the Lord, though we may not be able to see over the hill or around the corner, we can trust His word that He will be there for us and that He can work all things for the good of those who call on Him. We may not see the good on this side of Heaven, but we must remember that it is His Holy definition of *good* and not our selfish humanistic definition of good. He always was, always is and always will be in control. He is eager with open arms to receive you whenever you seek Him. Where or whom do you put your trust in? Where or whom do you put your hope in? Where or who drives your confidence? This week, how can you take time to reevaluate your faith and trust the Lord? How can you worship like believers who are content with all they have because Jesus is enough for them?

AUGUST 28

> Every word of God proves true; he is a shield to those who take refuge in him. Proverbs 30:5

I remember in middle school, all my brother and I really wanted was a dirt bike for Christmas. It was all we talked about and all we wanted. When we got it, we were thrilled! Every spare moment I could find, I took that bike out into the prairies behind our house and rode my heart out. Now that I am an adult, what I really want has changed. It has changed from material things to nonmaterial things. Now I will be the first to admit that I would like a new house, to go on a cruise and to have the ability to buy the things my kids really want, but these are not the things that get me truly excited. What I really want to do is to follow God's direction and will for my life, no matter what it is or where it leads. There is peace and joy in doing what God has called you to do and when the world rears its ugly head and strikes, there is peace in knowing that God is in control. Now, please don't walk away from reading this thinking that I am some super-Christian or super spiritual person. I am not. I sin and I suffer and struggle as anyone does. I suffer from depression, especially when I am not in the place of refuge that God provides. Daily, hourly, by the minute or even second sometimes, we have to choose how we respond to the world. We have to daily, hourly, by the minute, or even by each breath and thought be filled with the Holy Spirit because we leak. Sometimes I see my heart as a colander, constantly needing to be refilled. But that's where the love and grace of our loving father come into play. He knows that we leak and the Holy Spirit is always there, ready and willing to fill us with His Presence when we ask. I strongly desire to do God's will, but constantly fall short. However, I don't use that as an excuse and shift my desires to worldly goals; I just need to try harder to do what He places in my heart and reveals as His will in my life. Without spending quiet time dedicated to listening to His guidance, it can be challenging to know what that is for you. What is it that you really want in life? I mean, deep down, what is it really? If it's not God, then do like me and shift your focus – be in the Holy Word more, develop a hunger for His presence and His will and it will be easier to sense His protection.

AUGUST 29

> But I do not account my life of any value nor as precious to myself, if only I may finish my course and the ministry that I received from the Lord Jesus, to testify to the gospel of the grace of God. Acts 20:24

What do you value most? Is it what you have built for yourself? We can't take money with us and even if they name a building after us, people will soon ask, "Who was that?" What do you value most? Is it your family? That is a legacy that will continue, especially a spiritual legacy. But again, about the third generation after you, will your descendants even know any stories about you? What do you value most? Is it that path God has set before you and the Will of God in your life? That lasts an eternity. Paul says here that he counts nothing of value in his life. He views nothing as precious except to finish the race God set before him, the will of God for his life and the path God led him down. The ministry that he "received from the Lord to testify to the Gospel of the grace of God." It is the same ministry that we are called to do. Do you see that? Jesus told us all to go out, to go to Jerusalem, Judea, Samaria and the rest of the world. Your life may be the only testimony that leads someone to the knowledge of Jesus Christ and a saving relationship with Him. When you go to your version of Jerusalem and live out your relationship with our loving, living God and you allow the Holy Spirit to guide, direct, instruct, comfort and heal you, then your actions actually testify to the Gospel and what God is doing in your life. If you are not sharing your testimony and your God story in your Jerusalem, you should not be looking to go out of town, state, or country to do so. If you are not interested in local missions, what are you interested in? What do you value the most and how is that lived out in your life? Do others know you are a follower of Christ because you told them, or do they see you in church on Saturday night or Sunday morning? Do they know you are a Christian, a little Christ, a follower and disciple of the Living God, Emmanuel, by your choices, the words you use and the decisions you make? Do they know your faith by how lovingly you treat others who are not like you, less fortunate than you, or even those who mistreat you? Do they know you value your relationship with Jesus above all else, because even though you are not perfect, you try to model your life off of His teachings and His calling on your life? What do you value? How is that demonstrated in your daily life through your words, actions, decisions, etc.? What can you do to be more aligned like Paul, where you value God's commands over your own selfish desires and dreams? What is God calling you to do? Who is God calling you to share with? Who are you choosing to hit the mute button instead of telling them about what God has done in your life?

AUGUST 30

> Do not be conformed to this world, but be transformed by the renewal of your mind, that by testing you may discern what is the will of God, what is good and acceptable and perfect. Romans 12:2

Kids are funny and imitation is one of the best ways they learn. Oscar Wilde once said, "Imitation is the best form of flattery." I saw this when I was a teacher and had my students present and teach a lesson to the group. As I watched the students present their projects or their lesson, I quickly realized that there were certain catchphrases that I said often and didn't realize it. I also noticed that they imitated me with certain physical gestures that I made while teaching. I never realized I made these gestures and said certain catchphrases a lot until watching them teach and then me taking over and teaching again. In Romans 12:2, Paul warns us not to flatter the world, not to imitate or copy the world. Instead, we need to imitate God and allow the Holy Spirit to transform our minds to be more like God's. Paul says that when we do this, we will learn God's will, which is good, pleasing and perfect. Are you struggling to know God's will for your life? If so, ask yourself, are you being transformed and conformed by the world or by the Holy Spirit? Stop for a moment and be honest with yourself. Are your choices self-serving (worldly driven) or selfless (Holy Spirit driven)? Our hearts and minds are like clay that is being molded and conformed by a potter's hand. The real question is, who is the potter? God or satan? As harsh as that may sound, those are really the only two choices. Who are you allowing to transform and conform your mind and your heart to? Who do you flatter and imitate, God or satan? If you are struggling to hear from God, look and see who you have allowed to sit at the Potter's Wheel… It is up to us to only allow the Holy Spirit to transform our minds into the likeness of Christ. What changes can you make so that you only allow God to transform you? How can you renew your mind so you can be aware of who is sitting at the Potter's Wheel? How do you discern and know the will of God for your life?

AUGUST 31

> Why are you cast down, O my soul and why are you in turmoil within me? Hope in God; for I shall again praise him, my salvation and my God. Psalm 42:11

How are you doing mentally, emotionally and spiritually? How healthy are you in each of those areas? With everything going on in the world right now with pandemics, economic collapses and war, even secular psychologists and counselors are encouraging people to find something that brings them joy, to find something good in the midst of these trying times. But David, who was literally being hunted by his best friend's dad, asks and declares, "Why am I discouraged? Why is my heart so sad? I will put my hope in God. I will praise Him again – my savior and my God!" When David couldn't make sense of the world around him, he knew where to find hope. "I will put my hope in my Lord, my God!" If we put our hope in things of this world or in things we think we can control, we will only be disappointed. But when we put our hope in the Lord, we also hand over our worry and anxiety. Then David did something we should all do. While feeling discouraged and sad, David praised God. He didn't praise God for what he was going through, but he praised God for who God is. So, when we get discouraged and sad, overwhelmed or scared, we need to put our hope in the Lord. Not hope that He will make everything right, but a hope that knows He is in control and will praise Him no matter what. We need to praise Him despite our circumstances. In a world of unknowns, uncertain jobs, health and family members, we need to praise God continually. Just by lifting our voices, we can join the angels in Heaven singing, "Praise God, Praise God, from whom all blessings flow." Praise God for who He is, not because of your current situation. The band Casting Crowns has a popular and meaningful song entitled *Praise You in the Storm*. The chorus goes, "I will praise You in the storm, I will lift my hands for You are who You are, no matter where I am." We can praise Him in our storms, not because of where we are, but because of who He is. Where do you find hope and rest? How do you praise God in the storms of your life?

SEPTEMBER 1

> And which of you by being anxious can add a single hour to his span of life? Matthew 6:27

When we worry, we essentially give anxiety and unease a roadmap and permission to drive. Another meaning of worry is "to allow your mind to dwell and focus on troubles and difficulties." The world gives us so much to worry about. If you have nothing to worry about, watch the 5 o'clock news! The Stock Market, wars, famines, pandemics, crimes and rumors of anything that will instill fear – you will never run out of reasons to worry if you look for them. I have discovered that worry is a symptom that we are not trusting God or trusting in God's Word. The enemy loves to make us worry because when we worry, it causes us to take our eyes off of God and causes us to focus on whatever he places before us that is the source of worry. Jesus told us not to worry, that the birds of the air have food and the flowers of the field neither spin nor sow. In the midst of this, He asks us, "Can any one of you add a single hour to your life by worrying, by being anxious?" The answer is, of course, NO; but more importantly, it actually takes away time from your life that you cannot get back. We have to trust in God. Now, I am not promoting a feel-good gospel or a Name-it-and-Claim-it gospel. God is not this great big vending machine in the sky that just dispenses answered prayers. But I have trusted God to cure my child or wife and I trusted God to bring me a source of income. God does not answer every prayer with "Yes". But we still have to pray and trust that His will be accomplished. Worrying about it won't change His answer, nor will it change the situation or make it go by faster. God wants you to live life and give you life to the fullest, but when you live for Him, trials and troubles come. When they do, don't worry because you know the Creator of the Universe is still in control. What worry is the enemy trapping you with? How can you draw closer to Him? How can you know and surrender to His will so intimately that the worry can be dispersed and you can rest in the presence of the Holy Spirit?

SEPTEMBER 2

The earth, O Lord, is full of your steadfast love; teach me your statutes!
Psalm 119:64

Men generally don't like to be taught. How do I know? Where are the instructions that come in any box once it is opened? When driving, how many men actually ask their wives to give them directions and tell them where to go? But if we humble ourselves and read the directions, it gets finished more quickly and without mistakes; if we follow directions, we don't get lost and arrive on time. Here David's prayer is, "teach me Your statutes" – I ask God to give me directions on how to live my life, give me direction on what paths to take so that I am on the ones that lead to Him and not away from Him. As I read this verse, I acknowledge the Earth is so "full of Your steadfast love"! I cry out to Father God in gratitude. Your remaining love, unchanging love, Lord, I want to be a part of that, so teach me how to live. I want to experience Your love to the fullest, so I am willing to follow Your directions if You give them to me. In prayer, I ask for help to release the fear that the enemy is using to keep me from doing so. I know there will be no unused parts and it will work perfectly; we just need to follow His directions, His statutes! Are we as hungry for God's statutes as we are for our paychecks or 401ks? Do we desire His love and statutes, or do we desire what pleases our eyes or our fleshly desires? If we are not feeling full of the Holy Spirit, we need only ask in prayer, "Lord, fill me like You fill the world with Your steadfast love, so I am so overwhelmed by Your love and presence, I desire to die to self and live for You!" Is this a prayer you could actually pray and mean it? Do you desire *His* GPS and *His* assembly directions so you can build your life according to his directions? Are you on His road and path and not your own? What do you have to let go of so that you can build your life according to His directions? How can you pray David's prayer to change the direction of your life? What statutes and directions is God trying to give you? How can you do better listening to and applying His statutes?

SEPTEMBER 3

> The purpose of my instruction is that all believers would be filled with love that comes from a pure heart, a clear conscience and genuine faith. 1 Timothy 1:5 NLT

Why is it that we send kids to school, or go to school as adults, besides it being required to get to the next stage of life? I mean, some kids hate school while others love it. The main goal is to learn, to get instruction and to gain knowledge and skills. Paul was helping Timothy, a young pastor and explaining what the purpose of his letters and instructions were. Paul wanted to make sure that all believers, existing and new, old and young, would gain knowledge and access to love. He was describing a pure love that comes from a relationship with Christ, a love that does not love because of who someone is in the world, or what they can do for you, or who they are related to. It's a pure love for them because of who their Father is! My wife and I have told our biological kids and later we told our adopted kids as well, that we love them, not because of who they are, but because of who their Father is; we love them because of whose fingerprints they bear and who they were created in the image of. So, that means they can do nothing to lose our love, nor can they do anything to be loved any more than they already are — that is the pure *agape* love that comes from God. Yes, we may get angry and yes, we may be disappointed, but that cannot, nor does it, affect our love for them or how much we love them. Having access to that pure love develops a more genuine and deeper faith and relationship between us and Christ. By reading the Bible every day and seeing how you can apply the verses in your life, you develop a clear conscience when the enemy tries to come in and nudge you off the path that God has you on. It also deepens your faith and relationship with Jesus. Take time every day this week to read a chapter out of the Bible and see how God wants you to apply a verse from there so that you can love purer, have a clearer conscience and have a deeper, more genuine faith! Hopefully, these questions have helped you apply Scripture to your own life and faith walk. How can you create a daily habit of reading the Bible? How can you, on your own, memorize and apply verses in your life? Why is applying Scripture in your life so important?

SEPTEMBER 4

> Be watchful, stand firm in the faith, act like men, be strong. Let all that you do be done in love. 1 Corinthians 16:13-14

What does it mean to act like a man? Is it knocking down doors, kicking butt first and taking names later? Is it being able to play any sport that you want? I would say no. Jesus is the only example of what a real man is and Paul reminds us of this fact here. A real man is watchful, being prepared for whatever the enemy decides to bring our way. When Jesus was in the desert and Satan tried several times to tempt Him, Jesus was watchful and prepared. He had God's word written in His heart and on His tongue to be able to rebuke the devil. A real man has faith and is not afraid or ashamed to show it. Every day and every encounter, Jesus was pointing people, Hebrews and Gentiles alike, to Father God. Jesus was strong and not just physically. He was physically strong, don't get me wrong. But although he was physically strong, He was beaten to a pulp and then had to carry His cross as He did. He was also mentally strong, emotionally strong and spiritually strong. He loved more than anyone. With His mental strength, He did not let people trick Him or trap Him. He never lost faith and was always kind. Everything Jesus did was in love. Love – it's the one word that could sum up Jesus' life and ministry. Real men love. Real men think. Real men act. Real men respond out of Love. Do you need to be watchful? Watchful of what you allow into your mind? Watchful and prepared so you are not trapped or snared. What is an area of your life that you need to be strong in – physically, mentally, or emotionally? Do you need to show more love? What is it that God is calling you to do today? What is one thing you are going to do this week to be more like Christ? Who do you need to show love to? What is something you have not been doing in love that the Holy Spirit is prompting you to change and do in love?

SEPTEMBER 5

> If any of you lacks wisdom, let him ask God, who gives generously to all without reproach and it will be given him. But let him ask in faith, with no doubting, for the one who doubts is like a wave of the sea that is driven and tossed by the wind. James 1:5-6

When he was appointed king, Solomon was offered the opportunity by God to ask for anything and God would grant it to him. Now, Solomon could have asked for power, prestige, or riches. Instead, Solomon asked for Godly wisdom so he could rule righteously and according to God's will. Because Solomon asked for Godly wisdom and rejected any of the worldly desires, God granted him both wisdom and made him the wealthiest king to ever live. James reminds us in the very first chapter that if we lack wisdom, all we need to do is ask God for it. Father God will reveal it to you and not rebuke you or get mad at you for asking. This statement comes after James saying, "Count it all joy when you face trials, remain strong and steadfast during trials and that your steadfastness will become complete." Yes, we always need God's wisdom and should seek it when making decisions and living life, probably even more so when we face times of trials; that's when we really need a firm foundation of godly wisdom. We need to see the light at the end of the tunnel and realize it is not a speeding train! We need His wisdom to get ourselves through trials and make sense of the life lessons. We need a prayerful and surrendered heart to dissolve our doubts and fears into trust. Even when we do our best, the world will still attack us and bring us into trials and battles. We need God's wisdom and direction in our lives; thus, the Holy Spirit has been sent to reside in the hearts and souls of those who are born again of the spirit. James continues with this – he doesn't stop in verse five, but continues with verse six pleading, "But ask in faith without doubting!" Why is that warning written there for us? How many times have we thrown up a Hail Mary prayer, just hoping God might hear it and answer it? James says to abolish doubt because doubt is "like waves being tossed to and fro by the wind". If we truly want wisdom, we must simply ask God and the Holy Spirit will grant it without being mad at us for asking. Just ask! Seek His wisdom above all else and don't doubt that God will grant it. Why would He not want you to have Godly wisdom? The Holy Spirit is here to guide and direct us according to His wisdom. Seek it, ask for it, trust it and trust that He will grant it! When was the last time your prayer time included asking for Godly wisdom? Why is it not a daily request for most believers? How can Godly wisdom help you with a current situation you are in?

SEPTEMBER 6

> Why, even the hairs of your head are all numbered. Fear not; you are of more value than many sparrows. Luke 12:7

What does God value? What part of creation brings Him the most joy? Us. We do. At the end of each day of creation, God says, "It is good." But on day six, when He creates man, God says, "It is very good!" We are the only part of Creation that was created in His Image. We bear more than His fingerprints; we are valued and placed above all creation because we were created in His image. Sometimes we think and even allow the world or the enemy to come in and devalue us. We can begin to believe that we are less than what we really are. Human nature, worldly nature compares, but God does not compare; He loves everyone, because everyone is created in His image. Regardless of what the world says, our value does not come from the job we do, the family we have, or the talents we were born with or developed. Our value comes from the Father, our Heavenly Father. It is because He is Your Father that you have worth and value. Jesus refers to Psalm 139, where God intricately knits us together, so He would know the number of cells that make us up and how many hairs are on our heads. So, if God knows you that intimately, why do you have fear? Why do you allow False Evidence Appearing Real to take the place of God's Word in your life? Look here at the sparrows, Jesus said. The cost is two copper coins, fairly cheap, but the Father knows each of them; if one of them falls dead, the Father knows it. But you, aren't you much more valuable than the sparrows? Where do you find your worth? Is it in character qualities like honesty and hard work? There might be value there, but mean people can be honest and a hard worker without being righteous! Like a prince or princess, who does not have worth in and of themselves; it comes from their parents, so you as well, as a son or daughter of the King of Kings and Lord of Lords, your value is found in your Father. Your value is not found in what you have done or can do – it is in being a child, an heir of the King, that your worth is determined. Look at your spiritual birth certificate. Are you a child of God? Then your worth, your value is in Him. As His child, as Christians, we need to start living that truth out in our lives. Not flaunting wealth, but living in the freedom of being a child of God. When the world questions your wealth, pull your spiritual birth certificate out and remind yourself and the enemy whose child you are! How can this verse affect the course of your life? What freedom can you gain from this truth? How can you walk in freedom and love this week, knowing God cares for every little detail?

SEPTEMBER 7

When I think on my ways, I turn my feet to your testimonies; Psalm 119:59

A lot of us think we are pretty smart and we know our way around. I was born and raised in Colorado, but I have a lot of family in Massachusetts. When I got married, my wife and I would visit my family back there and I would take her to the house and property my dad grew up on. I would show her different places from my family history and I was able to drive from the airport to my grandmother's house without help. This was, of course, before smartphones and Google maps. I impressed her and my parents with my knowledge of an area I actually never lived in and only visited about a dozen times in my life. In life, though, if we have that philosophy where we think we know everything, we can actually separate ourselves from God; this attitude will automatically put a wedge between us. The author of Psalm 119 says that when he thinks about his own ways, he turns his feet to God's testimonies. On one visit to see my family a new bypass was put in and my "normal" route from the airport was changed. I was initially devastated that I didn't know how to get to my grandmother's house anymore. The world has changed and continues to change, but the Word of God never does. His Word will never get us lost, never deceive, nor confuse us. When we think we know what to do and where to go, we should check in and see what God's Word says and attempt to discern what His Will is. We should always check our motives and our intentions against God's Word. We should always be willing to allow the Holy Spirit to direct our feet and set our path before us, to be our moral compass. We should check our thoughts and decisions against the Word and Will of God. To do that, we have to be open to the movement of the Holy Spirit in our lives. The only way to hear from the Holy Spirit and allow Him to direct our feet and set our path is to be in the Word, reading Scripture every day. We need to be praying every day and allow the Holy Spirit talk time in our prayer life. It's hard to hear from Him when we do all the talking. We need to be worshiping every day. If we leave even one aspect out of practicing our faith, we can easily get distracted and led down the wrong road. How do you apply this piece of Scripture in your life? How often do you check in with yourself and reflect on the Word and Will of God? What has the Holy Spirit spoken to you through this verse?

SEPTEMBER 8

> Blessed is the one who finds wisdom and the one who gets understanding, Proverbs 3:13

Did you ever play along with *Jeopardy*, *Wheel of Fortune*, or *Family Feud* while watching TV? I do this with many game shows and some days I feel really smart, like I could be the next Ken Jennings. Other days I feel like, "Don't I know anything at all?" especially with *Jeopardy*. However, James says 3:13, let Your humble works and Your good conduct show how wise You are. See, intelligence and wisdom are not the same things. One can be extremely smart and not wise. For example, someone may be able to solve a Calculus III equation in his or her head, but not know how to solve a moral dilemma. Intelligence can be formed and learned, yet wisdom comes from God. Someone who may have trouble balancing a checkbook can have the wisdom of God overflowing through them. Who is wise and understanding? Those who walk with the Lord know the Lord, seek His guidance and know His word. These people are wise and understanding. They are also humble and meek. Don't confuse meek with weak. These are not even close to being the same. Weak means giving up whereas meek is choosing the best for the other person. To be meek is to be righteous, humble, teachable and patient under suffering, longsuffering and willing to follow gospel teachings; it's an attribute of a true disciple. When you are humble, you are imitating Christ and are working in His wisdom. When you are teachable, you are wise. When you are patient, you live out your trust in God, thus being wise. It's not possessions or careers or even degrees that show wisdom. It is through living out your faith and serving, worshiping the God of Creation, the God who saved you. Based on this week, on a scale of 1 to 10, how wise have you been? Based on the Biblical definition of meek and wise, how do you guess others would rate you? If you rate six or above, keep going and keep developing that deeper relationship with God. If you rate under a 6, what are you willing to do to become meeker, wiser, to grasp Godly wisdom? It is never too late to start that journey. So today, commit to becoming wiser, meeker, more teachable and more patient under trials. How can wisdom help you with something you have been struggling with? How teachable are you?

SEPTEMBER 9

> Such things were written in the Scriptures long ago to teach us. And the Scriptures give us hope and encouragement as we wait patiently for God's promises to be fulfilled. Romans 15:4 NLT

Do you have a personal reading plan for the Bible? Is Bible reading really a priority for you? I mean, that's the pastor's job, right? Read it, teach it and help us digest the truth. Paul reminds us here that Scripture was written for us, not the priests and rabbis. It is given to us for hope and encouragement. It is for us to draw near to Him as we wait patiently for His promises and plan to be fulfilled. We all have the duty to be in Scripture, the Word of God, so we can see when the enemy loves to twist it and sway it to try to convince us that God meant something else. That's how he tricked Eve in the garden. He asked, "Did God really say that?" It is how he tempted Jesus. God said you would not stub your toe or go hungry. That is how we have pastors preaching a theology that is not in the Bible, like, "God wants you happy, healthy and wealthy – all you have to do is name it and then claim it in the name of Jesus. If you don't get it, you don't have enough faith." The enemy has swayed whole denominations to believe this or worse. Some denominations leave the teachings of the Bible incomplete, perverting the truth to be interpreted as, "God didn't say homosexuality was a sin", or "having an affair was only a sin in Biblical times; it's no longer a sin now, since everyone makes that mistake." You and you alone are accountable for what the Word of God says and how you apply it. We cannot say, "But Pastor Joe said this," or "Pastor Greg taught that." We have to know; you have to know! The Holy Spirit will bring understanding if you desire it. Think of the Bible as an anthology, not a chapter story. You don't have to start on page 1 and read to page 2033. But do read it, meditate on it, pray it back to God and apply it to your life. If you have questions or are confused, then call on a pastor, but not until you have tried to read it first yourself. Know what God is saying to you! How can you start to incorporate reading the Bible into your daily routine? How have you applied Biblical truth in your life so far? What are you willing to do to increase your time in Scripture?

SEPTEMBER 10

> It is the Lord who goes before you. He will be with you; he will not leave you or forsake you. Do not fear or be dismayed." Deuteronomy 31:8

Fear is one of the favorite weapons of the enemy. If he can keep us fear filled and afraid, we will not be able to do what God has called us to do. But when we are Spirit-filled and confident in the Lord, we can do all things through Christ, through the Holy Spirit. God promises to personally go before us and will never leave nor abandon us or fail us. The enemy tries to convince us of the opposite, but in these trying times, when the world is throwing doubt and fear at us from all directions, where do we look? Inward or upward? Secular psychologists tell us that to find one's inner strength he or she must look inward for wealth and value. But we need to look to the Lord for our worth! Take captive the thoughts and lies of the enemy, the fear and concerns about what may or may not happen. Trust in the Lord with all your heart, all your might and surrender. We can walk down any path, any road He directs us to, because He has already been there and He knows what lies ahead. He has also promised to be there to walk the path with us so we never journey down a road or path alone. As long as we seek His presence and seek His guidance on what road to go down, He will journey with us. Hold on to the promises that He gives you. Do you want to be fearful or full of the Spirit? Do you want to be fear filled or filled by the Holy Spirit? Do you want to listen to the voice of maybes or the voice of promises? We have a choice in how we walk each and every day. We can walk in the Spirit or walk in the ways of the world. Don't let the enemy imprison you; don't give him the power to replace courage with discouragement. Fear is a nasty seed that if we let take root, it will spring forth as a strong weed that chokes out everything else. So, don't allow that seed to take root. Be strong and courageous. How can you be strong and courageous in these trying times? Inscribe this verse on your heart; how can it bring you comfort?

SEPTEMBER 11

> GOD, the Lord, is my strength; he makes my feet like the deer's; he makes me tread on my high places. Habakkuk 3:19

I remember in school and, in particular, science class, watching films and seeing mountain goats climbing rock cliffs and deer running and turning on a dime. The surefootedness of these animals is amazing. This final prayer recorded by Habakkuk reminds us that he is surefooted, that God is still powerful and that his confidence in God cannot be shaken. He knows that his strength comes from God and even in uncertain times and extreme circumstances, God will keep him firmly planted in his faith. His circumstances and uncertain times do not determine, nor do they affect, his relationship with God, nor do they lessen God's effect or His strength and power. We have been living in uncertain, uneasy times and the world, the enemy, can make it feel like God has left us, God has abandoned us, or at least His power and influence have diminished. Habakkuk encourages us to keep a right view of God. The world does not affect the power and presence of God in our lives. We have the choice and free will to decide how much power He has in our lives. Is He truly God of all, whom we fully submit to, or a god of Sunday that we take off the mantle each week to worship and pray to, hoping he will grant us answers to our prayers? Yes, He is an all-powerful, all-knowing God and while we don't limit His power, He allows us to choose how much power we want in our life. Unlike angels and spiritual beings who do not have a choice, we are created in His Image and His final and very good creation. In His love, He gave us free will to choose. He does not force, nor coerce, us into a relationship with Him. Habakkuk had a deep relationship with the Lord, allowing the Lord to guide and direct his life. In that, he can say the Lord made his feet like the deer. "He makes me tread on my high places." Habakkuk is fully relying on God to keep him steady when trekking the high places of life. At what level of confidence do you have in the Lord? While living in uncertain and difficult times, how have you seen the power of God still at work in your life and in the world around you? How have you witnessed God do this in your life?

SEPTEMBER 12

Iron sharpens iron and one man sharpens another. Proverbs 27:17

Have you ever tried using a dull knife to cut something? It isn't very useful, is it? Sometimes we really need a sharp knife, or we can't do what we need to do. A knife is sharpened by sliding it against another piece of metal. Swords are the same way. They need another like object and the strength of friction to become sharpened. They scrape off the knicks and dings in the metal, making it sharper. In our spiritual walk, we are the same. We need another person, another believer, so that when we get dull or our faith becomes stagnant, we have someone to help us up and to become sharp again. We need the roughed-up parts taken off and smoothed and sharpened so that we can be useful again. In the Bible there are many examples of this: Moses had Aaron, David had Jonathan, Paul had Silas, Timothy and Luke, etc. We are created to be in community and not to do life alone. Jesus demonstrated this – He had three in his inner circle of close confidants, nine in His bigger circle that He kept close and then hundreds of followers that would fluctuate in size depending on His teachings. We cannot let pride or insecurity keep us from either offering our faith to help those who need to be sharpened or asking for someone to help us be sharpened. We should not be content to float through life dull and unused. God created you and no one else is exactly like you. You have gifts and talents that God wants you to use to share His Love, Grace and Mercy. So, whether you are sharpened and need to mentor and sharpen someone else or you are the one needing sharpening, reach out and let God use you as a blessing to others. Are you a Jonathan (a loyal friend) to someone? Who could you act like a Silas (who encouraged Paul) or a Timothy (who learned from Paul what it took to live faith out in their daily life) for? If you are in a valley, who is your Luke or your Aaron? What special gifts has God given you to help you sharpen other believers?

SEPTEMBER 13

> Let the words of my mouth and the meditation of my heart be acceptable in your sight, O Lord, my rock and my redeemer. Psalm 19:14

Are you like me and sometimes get so caught up in life that we don't always check the words coming out of our mouths or even taking our thoughts captive? Have you ever told your child they need to think before they speak, or has someone told you that? We have (or act like) a child who says whatever comes to their mind without filter and without checking if it is actually true or not. As parents, we work with our kids to understand that our words have power and as adults God reminds us that we must be careful as well; our words can build or destroy people. God created all of Creation with His Words. We are created in His image, so our words are also powerful. I often use in my preaching the example of the "Sticks and Stones" saying we teach children who feel bullied and how much of a lie it is. Broken bones heal much faster than hearts that are broken over words said to them. David's prayer here is a reminder to me that the words I speak are powerful and they should be a blessing to God and not a curse on someone. By my words, others should know that I am a child of God, a disciple of the Living God. The desires of our hearts and the longings and wants that they have should be pleasing to God, like fragrant aromas, pleasing to Him. But often enough the desires of the world creep into our hearts and we don't weed them out; our 401ks, popularity, paychecks, jobs, or personal relationships, they can become the focus of our lives and not the Word of God, our relationship with Him, our praise for Him. These should be the desires of our hearts and what we meditate on. Like David says here, "He is our Rock and our Redeemer." When the Lord is our Rock, we are on solid ground, not to be shaken. As our Redeemer, He has paid for us to be adopted into His family, into eternal life in Heaven. Are the words you speak a pleasing aroma to the Lord? Are the desires of your heart, what you focus on, pleasing to the Lord? How can you change your words and desires to be more aligned with the Lord and your Words and Desires be a pleasing aroma to Him? How has this verse convicted you? How are you receiving grace as you allow the Lord to redirect your thoughts, passions or desires?

SEPTEMBER 14

> Don't use foul or abusive language. Let everything you say be good and helpful, so that your words will be an encouragement to those who hear them. Ephesians 4:29 NLT

I remember growing up and when we were first able to get cable TV, you had to stay up late at night and be on a cable channel to hear swearing words less profane than the worse profane; but nowadays, cursing seems to be common language, especially the worst profanity. It may be heard in line at McDonald's, in the doctor's office, or even just walking down the street. In schools, students and adults alike use it like it's an everyday, commonplace word. Paul tells us here, "Don't use foul or abusive language." Let *EVERYTHING* you say be good and helpful. Paul doesn't say let some things you say be good or even let most of what you say be helpful. Let *every word* that comes out of your mouth be good and helpful. What would our world, our society, look like if every person who professes to be a believer lived this way, only speaking good and helpful words? But if they are to be truly "helpful," they will also be an encouragement to those who hear them. We tend to forget that we are created in the image of God and that God created and spoke most things into existence. There is power in His words and since we are created in His image, there is power in our words. We have the power to uplift and affirm others and ourselves. In contrast, hearts and souls can be permanently damaged by abusive words and hurtful words spoken to them. We must be careful with the words we allow to come out of our mouths. This requires a conscious effort on our part as believers to be in control of our tongue and not let it run rampant on its own accord. It requires us to respond to people and not react out of emotion. Yes, we have to hold each other accountable, but it is supposed to be done in love and when we use foul and abusive language, the love is absent. How can you change your speech to better resemble Christ in you? How can you start responding in love and not reacting from fear? How can you control your tongue, so you think before you speak?

SEPTEMBER 15

> Therefore the Lord waits to be gracious to you and therefore he exalts himself to show mercy to you. For the Lord is a God of justice; all those who wait for him are blessed. Isaiah 30:18

Patience, if I had it, I wouldn't need it. I can't tell you how many times in my life I've prayed, "God, just give me patience. Stop giving me situations so my patience will grow and develop. I need patience now!" In the Bible, it often says we need to be patient. I mean, it's the fourth Fruit of the Spirit to be developed. For a fruit to grow, it takes time and it takes nourishment. It is in that time to grow that patience is developed, but we want immediate results most of the time. As I've matured in my faith and relationship with God, I have learned that God's timing is always perfect. Do I always remember that during the trials? Not always, but sometimes. The times I do remember to ask God for patience, the trials are much easier to endure, because I can see Him working in the small aspects of it all. We need to be still in the presence of the Lord; all too often, we do all the speaking and then we are on the go again. Be still, wait *patiently* and don't worry. Especially don't worry about evil people who seem to scheme and prosper while they go against the will of God. He is still in charge. Jesus told us these things would happen before He came back, so why am I always so surprised by corruption or abuses of power? Why are you so surprised? I think we get so busy living our lives that we forget to stop, be still and *know* that He is God. We can think prophecy is so far off that it won't happen to us, but by being still in the presence of the Lord, we allow Him to remind us of the depths of His word. This is not a call to try to predict the end times or identify the Antichrist; it is simply a call to be still in His presence and not be surprised when prophecy happens. He said this would come. He has it under control for His plan, so be still and wait for Him to act, to respond to our continual prayers. Keep grounded in the Truth of His Word. One way we can spend more time with Him and allow Him to speak to us is through a process called Life Journaling. You use the word SOAP as an acronym. S-Scripture, O-observation (what is this verse saying), A-application (how does this apply to my life), P-Prayer (write a prayer to God utilizing the actual Scripture verse. These devotionals sprouted and grew out of Life Journaling, except now instead of prayer, I have Digging Deeper questions to help my friends and readers go deeper with the application and their relationship with Jesus. How can you be still in His presence and wait patiently on Him in your life? What are you willing to do to spend more time with Him and give Him more talk time?

SEPTEMBER 16

> We should help others do what is right and build them up in the Lord.
> Romans 15:2 NLT

Have you ever heard, "Help yourself, 'cause no one's gonna do it for you"? That seems to be the wisdom of the world. Somehow the wisdom of the world always seems to contradict the Word of God. Paul reminds us of what Jesus said, "Love God, then Love others." As Christians, we are called to not just love others but *agape*-love them. *Agape* love is an action, a verb, not based on an emotion. As we *agape* others, we should be helping them do what is right and only God's way is right. By loving others as God loves us, we build them up in the Lord. As part of God's family, we are meant to build them up in the love of the Lord, the wisdom of the Lord and the grace of the Lord. Wisdom of the Lord that is instilled in us and passed on to others from us is an invaluable gift. It is by being immersed in Truth by reading His Holy Word daily, worshiping the Lord daily and allowing the Holy Spirit to talk to us daily that we will learn the Wisdom of the Lord. Then we can build others up in the Lord. We are not called to tear down others, whether they are believers or unbelievers. We can hold other believers accountable while still communicating in love. Being held accountable and tearing them down are two different things. In fact, if you hold them accountable to Biblical standards you are actually building them up, helping them draw closer to the Lord. So, our tongue is like a double-edged sharp sword; we need to be mindful of the words we use. Our words should help and build others up, not tear down and destroy. Even criticism can be delivered constructively, kindly, gracefully, or compassionately versus out of an offended or fearful heart. How can you start helping others do right in the eyes of the Lord? Where can you be humble before God in prayer about any areas of hypocrisy in your Christian walk that could use increased integrity or discipline? How can you start building up others in the Lord with your intentional, loving words and by being a positive example of someone in love with Christ and dedicated to sharing the Gospel? Who, right now in your life, needs words of encouragement and needs to be built up?

SEPTEMBER 17

> Who is wise and understanding among you? By his good conduct let him show his works in the meekness of wisdom. James 3:13

Have you ever seen an episode of "Kids Say the Darndest Things" or something similar? I bet it is true in every culture, how hilarious it is with what comes out of the mouths of babes. Children can speak authoritatively about topics they have absolutely no knowledge of, but somehow, they still have the confidence to speak about them in detail. Maybe you have seen an episode of a show where they go out in public and ask some common-sense type questions? Isn't it funny when people try to sound smarter than they really are, or isn't it sad when everyday citizens have no idea about important historical facts? Wisdom, true wisdom, is more than mere intelligence; it is a gift given by God that cannot be self-attained or learned. It is similar to common sense but includes the ability to understand God and discern His voice to guide you to moral decisions. We can all have it; we just need to seek it and ask God for it. It is in His wisdom that we can understand and apply His Word in our lives. Having wisdom is not something that needs to be bragged about; if you have it, people know it. Ironically, if you have to brag about it, you probably don't have it. James reminds us here that our works and our attitudes will show wisdom. How we treat others and how we love others are indicators of Godly wisdom. In meekness, wisdom shines. Meekness is the quality of your heart to willingly submit to the will of God, resisting selfish desires by replacing them with the needs and desires of others. This shows a true understanding of the love and character of God. By living your life according to His will, He provides the wisdom that so many seek and desire. Do your conduct, actions and words speak of wisdom or ignorance? Your source of confidence is revealed – where is it, in God or self? How can you make changes in your life so that God's wisdom is displayed in you?

SEPTEMBER 18

> Keep your life free from love of money and be content with what you have, for he has said, "I will never leave you nor forsake you."
> Hebrews 13:5

My family loves Chinese food. Although we get a lot of food for the money, I noticed that as full as the kids seem after eating it, they are soon hungry again not too long afterward. The meal is quickly burned up and the fullness doesn't remain. I think we can be the same way with God's provisions. While He is pouring out we are satisfied, but when He's not, we are hungry for more. In America, especially, we tire ourselves out trying to get bigger and better things in life without being satisfied with what we have. Where is our desire for God if we constantly only desire the next biggest thing? If we love money and are trying to always get newer, bigger and better, where does our love for God fall among our priorities? Here's the truth of the matter, if we truly love God, we appreciate all the blessings and all the good things He gives us. We cannot have a love of money and a thankful spirit simultaneously. The love of money kills a thankful spirit. Remember that the love of money is the root of evil. It is not money itself, but the love of money that is full of corruption. If you love money, you cannot love God. We are to love God with all of our hearts, all our souls and all our minds. We need to learn to be content in any and every circumstance; we need to be satisfied with the blessings of God and the protection that God provides. God promises never to leave us, nor abandon us, so we need to seek His presence before all else. We need to love Him above all else. We need to be thankful for what He has blessed us with and hold onto His promises to never fail us or leave us behind and so much more. We must be content and satisfied with whatever God brings and everything God gives us. What is occupying your heart in place of God? What desire do you need to let go of to allow Him His proper place in your heart?

SEPTEMBER 19

> for it is God who works in you, both to will and to work for his good pleasure. Philippians 2:13

When we face trials and walk through valleys, the enemy loves to make us feel like we are all alone. Do you ever feel like you are all alone and you are left to figure something out on your own? Well, you're not. God is with you and working in you and in your heart. If we would only slow down long enough to listen to His still, small voice. He is giving us the desire and the power to do His Will, to do what pleases Him and to be His hands and feet in this broken world. Even in our relationships, He gives us His desire and power to do His Will. We have to let go of our selfish desires long enough to see what His desires are for us. As a man, a lot of the time I often feel like I have to do things on my own. I have trouble asking for help from others and even from God… but He is working with me and on me for improvement in that area. In addition to being humble enough to ask others for help, I also need to humble myself before Him and ask Him not only for help and help that He desires to give, but also to know His will and His desires. His desires for us are simple, not easy, but simple. Our part is to love Him with all our strength, all our hearts, all our souls and all minds. Love others as Christ loves us. It's a simple plan, to put the needs of others before our own and it comes easy when we are working with His power and presence. Again, while simple, a lot of the time, it is not the easiest to do. The enemy loves to whisper things like, "When will your desires and needs be a priority for others if you keep putting them first?" or "When will your needs be met?" or "Take care of yourself first, because no one else will." But God will! In His time and in accordance with His will and plans. He is not only giving you His desires to do His will for you, but also the power to do it; all you have to do is hold onto that power and let the Holy Spirit guide your steps. What desire of His is He asking you to work on right now? What desires do you need to let go of so you can start meeting the needs of others?

SEPTEMBER 20

> How beautiful upon the mountains are the feet of him who brings good news, who publishes peace, who brings good news of happiness, who publishes salvation, who says to Zion, "Your God reigns." Isaiah 52:7

Do you ever feel like Ziggy or Charlie Brown with that little black storm cloud that follows you or having someone like Lucy always take the football away when you get ready to kick it? The good news is that during times like those when we feel that way and the enemy is trying to get us to ask, "Where are You, God?" is that He is still there. He is still on His throne and nothing takes God by surprise. Peter doesn't run to God and say, "Hey, look at Joe, there is that little storm cloud over him, should we do something about it?" God knows. Nothing happens without God knowing it already. So, with that in mind, what are we doing about it? Do we get mad at Lucy for grabbing the football away again? We know she is going to do it, so we need to do what Charlie Brown never does; we need to stop asking her to hold the ball for us. When the enemy wants to bring in a storm cloud to hide the sun, we know that the sun *(Son)* is still there and is still shining. We don't stop living; we grab the umbrella and the raincoat and still go and do what God calls us to do. So, when we see someone who has that little storm cloud or a Lucy stealing the ball when someone tries to kick it, we need to bring them the Good News that God still loves them and He is still in control. We need to remind them to take comfort in the Peace that comes from being in the presence of a Loving Father. We have a hope and a peace that this world cannot take away and we need to share it! The Good News is that God is still in control, so remember that! Are you like Ziggy and Charlie Brown, who need to be reminded of this? Is there someone in your life who needs to know this truth? Who is it that you need to share that hope and peace with?

SEPTEMBER 21

Little children, let us not love in word or talk but in deed and in truth.
1 John 3:18

I am sure we have all heard the expression, "Actions speak louder than words." Here the apostle John reminds us of that fact. Jesus has called us to love one another, friend and foe, as He loved us. He doesn't put qualifiers on love, like, "love those who love you" or "love those who can give back to you". *Love others!* But we must ensure that our words and our actions parallel each other and not contradict each other. Our love for others must be shown and not just spoken. Anyone can say the words and not mean it, but it is much harder to show love and not mean it. Because Jesus loved us, we are called to love others as He loved us. How did He love us? Did he merely say, I love you? No, He loved through His actions. He was compassionate. He was forgiving. An old adage I try to live by is, I believe St Francis of Assisi said something along the lines of, "At all times preach the gospel only, when necessary, use words," and another is, "If Christianity became illegal today, would there be enough evidence to convict you of being a Christian? Would there be witnesses on the accuser's side, or would people be surprised you were arrested?" Do your beliefs extend beyond the four walls of your church? Does your relationship with God, with Jesus, with the Holy Spirit, extend beyond church services and Bible studies? Are you living your life so that you love in deeds and truth? By your actions and your words, people know whether you are a disciple of Christ or not. How can you go deeper in your relationship with God today, so these become even more evident in your life? How can you put love into action? How is God calling you to do just that? Who is it that you need to love that the world would wonder why? How much evidence are you giving the world to convict you of being a follower of Christ?

SEPTEMBER 22

> Set a guard, O Lord, over my mouth; keep watch over the door of my lips! Psalm 141:3

We probably all know someone whose mouth is faster than his or her brain. We can recall the many moments when their words got them into trouble. You can probably see it happening in slow motion, too; you see it pop into their head and you think, "Don't say it, don't say it", but by the time that thought ends, they have already said it out loud. When we have the Holy Spirit living in us, we should pray something similar to, "Lord, Holy Spirit, take control of what I say." I pray, "Holy Spirit, control my tongue so what I say brings people to you and that words are only from you; please hold my tongue when I go to say something against your will." Words are powerful tools and words can become powerful weapons. If used properly, they can be the tool that heals wounds and hearts, strengthens the weak, gives hope to those who worry and love to those who feel dejected. If we, however, go off of self and allow the world to influence our words, they can be the weapon that destroys a heart, tears down hopes and dreams and crushes those who need to be loved. I also pray, "Holy Spirit, guard my lips prevent me from speaking against your will." When I would remember to pray these words, "Holy Spirit, take control of my lips, guard my words and let me speak only what you want to speak and guard my lips and prevent me from speaking against your will." There would be days when anger would try to get me to say something, but because I had prayed, the Holy Spirit protected the other person and me from such destructive drama. I wish I could say I did this every day; it's difficult, especially when going through trials and hardships. Join me in making this a daily prayer. How might you change your life, your family, your job and your sphere of influence, if you were to earnestly pray this every day? What is your prayer to help you only speak the words God wants you to speak?

SEPTEMBER 23

"Oh, taste and see that the Lord is good! Blessed is the man who takes refuge in him!" Psalm 34:8

Refuge is defined as, "shelter or protection from danger or trouble." See, Jesus never said following Him would be easy. He didn't say, "Sit on your throne or easy chair and follow me." No! Jesus promised us that we would see troubles and have trials. The world tries to entice us to find shelter and protection in the emptiness that it provides, but there is actually no protection to be found in the world; it is like taking shelter in a rattlesnake den or bear cave. While it may provide shelter from the wind or rain, the danger lurking inside is much worse and could lead to death. *Taste and see* – these terms have been used more than once and in more than one sense to know that God is Good. While Jesus foretold of the trials we would have on Earth, He also promised us that He would never leave nor forsake us, that when He ascended into Heaven, He would send the Helper, the Holy Spirit in His place, so that we would never be alone. We just have to draw close to Him and His presence. The only way to escape the world is through the Holy Spirit living in us and allowing Him to guide us and remind us of God's goodness and love that He has for us. He is our strong tower; He is a mighty warrior battling with us and going before us. If you need to take a time of refuge, take it in His presence. Listen to worship music so you can worship and thank Him; thank Him for the blessings and protection you have seen and not seen. Take time to thank Him that while trials may be hard, He is in the furnace and lion's den with us. Through worship, we are drawn closer to Him. Read His Word and allow Scripture to bring peace and comfort into your life. Be still and quiet so you can allow Him to speak to you. Just remember that no matter what you are going through, the Lord is Good. How do you take refuge in the Lord? What has the Lord sheltered you from? How have you tasted and seen that the Lord is truly good?

SEPTEMBER 24

> "You're going to wear yourself out – and the people, too. This job is too heavy a burden for you to handle all by yourself." Exodus 18:18 NLT

Some people are really good at delegating, while some people like me, well, we're not. We feel like if we want the job done right, to do it ourselves. That is a dangerous thought process if we really consider what that means. Moses had a loving and caring father-in-law. He knew what God had called Moses to do. He also knew that God did not tell Moses that he had to do it all himself. We can see this in what he tells Moses, "This job is too heavy a burden for you to handle all by yourself." He then instructs Moses to find honest, God-loving, God-fearing men to help him. If we are not careful, we can allow our jobs, caring for others and ministry to wear us out. God Himself, on the 7th day, rested. He took a complete, whole day of rest. He considers taking an entire day of rest, a Sabbath, so serious that breaking it was punishable by death. Now, while we may not be able to enlist the help of others, we can and we must delegate it to another day. We have to be able to refresh our bodies and our souls, or we will be no good to our family, friends and coworkers. We have to come to the point of saying, "This can wait until Monday", or "These can wait until tomorrow." Moses was tasked with a serious task, but God didn't say he had to do it alone. In fact, God's plan is that we live, work, play and worship in community. Are you being worn down, laden with burdens? Are you delegating tasks to someone else or at least to another day so that you can be the best version of yourself, or are you wearing yourself out? God wants you to rest and be refreshed, but you must be willing to do so. Don't allow the enemy to guilt you when you take time for self-care. Don't go overboard with self-care where you stop making progress altogether. Make a plan – how will you delegate this next week and how will you refresh yourself so you can be the best version of yourself on Monday? How has the enemy used self-care (or lack thereof, as is the case with many moms) to interfere with God's plan? How do you find balance with self-care? Who has God placed in your life to help with self-care, sharing the burden and taking a true, entire day of rest?

SEPTEMBER 25

> Don't forget to show hospitality to strangers, for some who have done this have entertained angels without realizing it! Hebrews 13:2 NLT

I'm part Italian and while I don't have a lot of money, one thing I do know is that I can cook. Whenever we have friends over, even if it is just for a visit or to play cards – I put out a full spread. The Italian meme of "I've prepared a few snacks," and it's showing an entire banquet table of food, is not much of an exaggeration. That is how we are called to be with everyone — not just friends and family. When we see a need, we are called to meet the need, but like in the parable of the Good Samaritan, as American Christians, we often take on the role of the Priest or the Levite and cross to the other side of the road thinking someone else will come along and meet this need… we are too busy, they got themselves into this mess, or we fear that our giving them money will be used to just get drunk and not get better. We allow the enemy to dump a lot of garbage into our minds to help us justify why we should be like the Levite and the Priest. I mean, doesn't God tell us to be good stewards of the resources He has given us? Why, yes. Yes, we do need to be good stewards of His love, we need to be conduits of His blessings so that where we see a need, we can meet it. We shouldn't be the ones deciding and making sure the beaten man on the road uses what we give for God's purposes. We are called to be more like the Samaritan; when we see a need, we simply and gracefully meet the need. It is really that simple. Sometimes it can be as simple as a friendly smile and, "I hope you have a great day." Maybe someone needs to hear that God really loves them despite their past. However, some people need help with basic needs (food, paying bills, home or car repairs). Someone may just need a hand-up, not a hand-out, but we don't determine what they use it for; we just need to be obedient and open to the Holy Spirit's prompting and don't dismiss Him with, "Someone else can do that!" Who is it that you need to be hospitable towards this week? How can you be more ready to meet the needs of others?

SEPTEMBER 26

"A fool despises his father's instruction, but whoever heeds reproof is prudent." Proverbs 15:5

My dad loves telling the story of how I went off to college and he and my mom got smarter. I would come home and tell him things like, "Now I know why you and mom said…" or "You and mom were right when you said…" Solomon reminds us that we need to be open to instruction. Teenagers are notorious for rejecting instructions or help. They are in the in between stage, not a kid but still not an adult and they are trying to figure life out on their own. My wife and I have told our kids we've lived a while and made mistakes, so learn from our mistakes and don't repeat them; instead, make new ones. God does not treat us like sea turtles; once they hatch, they are left on their own to find their way to the sea. No, God walks with us and tries to instruct and guide us, but we have to be open to receive it. We cannot constantly be like a typical teenager and think we know everything. God is not an old man who is out of touch with current reality. His instructions are still as relevant today as they were 10 to 20,000 years ago. As a loving Father, His desire is not to let us flounder and fail, but for us to be successful and blessed, not necessarily monetary-wise, but in life. He wants us to come to Him and seek His guidance and instruction. He wants us to accept reproof when needed and not be "sour" when He needs to show us reproof. He sent us His Holy Spirit to direct us, guide us and give us instruction, as much as to also be our comforter and our helper. Remember, discipline is not to harm or embarrass us, but to help us not make the same mistakes repeatedly. Pray for His instruction and discipline to be clear and be open to Him and His loving guidance! Today, what are the Holy Spirit's instructions and guidance for you? Where in your life has the Holy Spirit been trying to show reproof and you resist it?

SEPTEMBER 27

> A fool takes no pleasure in understanding, but only in expressing his opinion. Proverbs 18:2

I had heard that when I was younger, there were words that I could never pronounce correctly. Try as my parents might, they could not understand me, even though they tried. They didn't just ignore me, they truly tried to understand. I saw a meme of a number painted on the sidewalk, one person at each end of the number. One person says it's a six, the other says no, it's a nine. The idea is to try seeing from the other's point of view and although our viewpoints are different, they are not necessarily right or wrong. Solomon here reminds us that we must try to understand God's Word and plan and understand other people's opinions and where they are coming from. A fool is more impressed with his own opinion than understanding where someone may be coming from. Like the number meme previously mentioned, we can't be so enamored with ourselves and our point of view that we don't try to see the other person's point of view. We need to seek first to understand rather than to be understood. That is how we love others with *agape* love, understanding them and not making them understand us. We need to be slow to speak, but quick to listen. While we may be right, if there is a right and wrong, the other person may just need to be heard. Too many people's voices have been silenced and people are not heard because of many different factors: history, income, education, career, ethnicity, etc. Jesus did, however. He listened. He understood where people were coming from. Look at the Pharisees – they held themselves up in high opinion and were quick to share, so much so that they did not even realize who was right in front of them. They delighted so much in themselves that they had no room for God's wisdom to be planted. This week, can you slow down and notice where it is that you are quicker to speak and share your opinion? Who do you need to listen to and try to understand where they are coming from? In what areas of your life do you need to seek God's opinion over your own opinion?

SEPTEMBER 28

> "Enter by the narrow gate. For the gate is wide and the way is easy that leads to destruction and those who enter by it are many. For the gate is narrow and the way is hard that leads to life and those who find it are few." Matthew 7:13-14

Ask most people if they will choose hard or easy and easy will be the majority vote. You don't have to put in much effort, time, or even thought. That is what makes it easy. I need to make an important clarification here, simple does not equate to easy, as they are not synonymous with each other. Jesus' path, His way, is simple, but not easy. He warns us here that easy is the path that "leads to destruction". I think many of us Christians confuse the two, as well as some pastors preaching about the easiness of Christianity. But we can see Jesus' own words here, "The gate is wide and the easy way leads to destruction… Those who enter it are many." Why is that? To follow Christ, we must die to ourselves and live for Him. We must resist and fight against what the world says is good and what the world tells us we should do. We could be like lemmings and easily follow the others off the cliff towards sin, but God calls us to follow His ways and allow the Holy Spirit to lead us, direct us and guide us. It takes strength and self-control to fight off fleshly urges and desires; it takes self-control to fight temptation and not give in to sin. Jesus reminds us that the gate is narrow and the way is hard that leads to life and those who find it are few! That scares me. Few find it? Why? A little pushback from society and people tend to cave. They rank sins as worse or better than other sins; they have taken what the world says and believe that God said, "You should be happy and wealthy and if you're not, something is wrong with you!" They change the Word of God to conform to what society says is right instead of standing on the foundation that is the Word of God. Jesus' way, God's way is simple, just follow the ABC's of faith: Accept Jesus as your Lord and Savior, Believe He is the Messiah, Confess your sins to God and ask for forgiveness. Accept the gift of Jesus Christ, which sounds simple. But the walk afterward is hard, not easy. Living out your relationship with our Living God, allowing the Holy Spirit's presence and power in our life to guide, direct, confront and convict us, is not easy. Loving those that don't love you and praying for those who don't even like you is difficult. Offering them the other cheek and forgiving them as they slap it a second, a third, or a fourth time, is not easy. Not easy, but worth it! How do Jesus' words in this verse resonate with you? How does this affect your walk and your outlook on life? What fruit do you see from living this verse out?

SEPTEMBER 29

> For you did not receive the spirit of slavery to fall back into fear, but you have received the Spirit of adoption as sons, by whom we cry, "Abba! Father!" Romans 8:15

The enemy loves to use fear to keep us from the Godly potential that God our Father has instilled and installed in us. While we may not be a member of one of the tribes of Israel, we have been adopted as children of God through His son Jesus Christ. The enemy hates for us to experience the freedom we have inherited from God. You don't have to be a slave to sin. You can overcome temptation if you remember that when the temptation comes to draw near to Him. The enemy loves to isolate us emotionally and spiritually. He loves to use depression and lowering our self-esteem to get us to engage in sin, but God has set us free. Not free to sin, but free from the condemnation that the enemy loves to turn on us when we do. When your self-esteem lowers, look at yourself through the eyes of the Father – remember you were worth dying for. When the enemy overwhelms you with depression, remember your worth is not determined by what you do, but by who your Father is. Jesus says He will not allow us to be tempted beyond our ability to reject it; we must do our part not to put ourselves in places where it is greater. Also remember that even when we fall short, tomorrow is another day. If the enemy is successful today, draw closer to God and be in Scripture and worship Him more so tomorrow the enemies' tools will be deemed useless. We must remember the power of prayer so that when the enemy wants to put chains on us, we can pray and allow the Holy Spirit to guide us to truth and away from fear. When fear, depression, low self-esteem and the concept of not being "good enough" come to bear, what Scripture do you need to write on your heart to help you climb out of the pit the enemy puts you in? How does this Scripture help you with having a healthier sense of self-worth and identity? How does being a child of the Living God affect your life and your decisions?

SEPTEMBER 30

> A peaceful heart leads to a healthy body; jealousy is like cancer in the bones. Proverbs 14:30 NLT

Right around January 1 of every year, people talk about getting healthy. They buy gym memberships, supplements and diet plans, go at it hard for about a month and then fall off the bandwagon. One problem is their starting point. Where they really need to start is not in the gym, but rather in the Bible. This is the source of our commitment, motivation and inner peace. Solomon reminds us that the beginning of a healthy body is a peaceful heart. Long before modern day medicine and science proved that negative emotions caused harmful health side effects, Solomon knew it. God revealed it to him. Jealousy is like a cancer in the bones that will grow, multiply and destroy. Unforgiveness is like depleting calcium from the bones, leaving us in a weakened state with no strength. You need to have a peaceful, peace filled heart in order to have any sense of longevity. That is the beginning of healthy living. Everything is connected. Your mental health, emotional health, social health, spiritual health and physical health are all connected and when one gets pulled out of shape and is unhealthy, it strains and pulls on all the others. When the peace and joy of walking with Christ is in you, you are spiritually and emotionally healthy, which must occur if you want physical and mental health as well. While a cough is contagious, so are spiritual and emotional health symptoms. The flu is passed on to others as much as a friendly smile, loving service to others, or just praying for someone. True health in all aspects only comes from walking daily with Christ. What is it you need to let go of today to have a peaceful, peace filled heart? What can you do to increase and magnify your spiritual health and sense of belonging in the Body of Christ? How can you improve your emotional health? How can you improve and maintain your mental health?

OCTOBER 1

> For everything there is a season and a time for every matter under heaven: Ecclesiastes 3:1

When things are going well, we don't want them to change, but when things are going bad, we want change immediately. Isn't it good that neither happens? So often, we learn more from struggles than times of no struggle. Many scientific discoveries were discovered because of a "failed" experiment. When we overcome a challenge, we learn how strong we really are and how good God really is. Solomon tells us that there is a season for everything under the sun. There is a time to plant and a time to harvest. With sin in the world, good times can't and won't last forever; but on the flip side of the coin, when we go through trials, they won't go on forever either. Because sin is in the world, bad things happen to good people. God doesn't cause harm on purpose. These things happen because there is sin in the world, but we can take hope that God is in control. Could God cancel all the bad things until we have no more sin in the world? Yes, He could. Oh, wait, He did and we messed it up. He loved us enough to give us the gift of free will; we have the choice to make. Because of sin, life is not fair and God never promised it would be. We can be doing everything for God and still go through trials. While it may seem that those who don't even believe in God are prospering, we must stay the course. This, too, shall pass. Trials only happen for a season. A forest fire burns off the dead wood and fertilizes the ground; afterward, it can actually be a healthier forest. It just takes time to grow. No matter what season you are in, it is only for a season. If it is a time of peace, enjoy the rest; if it's a time of blessing, take the time to enjoy His blessings and be rested for when that season ends. If it's a time of trials, it is only for a season. If you are in a season with a trial, can you identify what is the dead "stuff" that God is trying to burn off so you can have a healthier "forest" (life)? How can you use this trial to equip yourself to help others and serve God? What tools is God developing in your life during the trial to help others? How can you see God's power in your trial? How can the trial better conform you to His image?

OCTOBER 2

> As a father shows compassion to his children, so the Lord shows compassion to those who fear him. Psalm 103:13

I was lucky as a child, because I had a father who was loving and compassionate and made me want to be a dad. I wanted to carry on family traditions like having a son named Joseph, various ethnic foods, family values and rituals and beliefs of the faith. I love making my sauce for people (for spaghetti and meatball subs), having pierogi with kielbasa as well as family days, family outings, praying together as a family to name a few. I know that everyone was not as lucky as me to have an earthly dad as great as me, but Scripture reminds us that God is a good, good father to us. He is tender and filled with compassion, not mean-spirited. He is loving and compassionate, not abusive. Many of us try to view God through the lens of our earthly fathers. Whether we had an awesome dad like I did, or an angry, abusive, or neglectful father, we cannot pass those views onto the likeness of God. We have to view God through getting to know Him in quiet time, who the Bible says He is and who He has proven to be, not through expectations based on what we had as a dad. The last part of this verse is "for those who fear Him." This "fear Him" is not referring to fear like being afraid, but a deep respect and reverence for the power that He has. We do not have to be afraid of our Heavenly Father, but respect Him for who He is and His power. He is all-knowing, all-powerful and always present. He is a good, good father who loves and is tender and compassionate to His children. How is your view of God this week? Do you need to go back to your childhood and see yourself as a child of God, the child of a tender and compassionate Father? Pray this week and meditate on the tender and compassionate side of your good, good Father. How has God shown you compassion? How have you received God's love in your life? How has your understanding of the fear of the Lord changed your relationship with Him? How do you allow His omnipresence in your life?

OCTOBER 3

> bearing with one another and, if one has a complaint against another, forgiving each other; as the Lord has forgiven you, so you also must forgive. Colossians 3:13

I am sure we all know people who all they do is complain and we really don't like spending much time with them. But then we can often find things to complain about as well. Why is it that when we complain, we need to do it in front of others? Misery loves company, right? Maybe if we are honest with ourselves, we want other people to have a complaint against the same person to justify ourselves and be on a team instead of sitting alone with that fact. Jesus tells us that if we have anything against our brother before we come before God to sacrifice (worship), to go to them. Paul reminds us of that here; if we have a complaint against someone, we are to forgive them. Why? Because God has forgiven us, so we must also forgive. In the Lord's Prayer, Jesus said the same thing: "Forgive us our sins as we forgive those who sin against us." WOW! Powerful. When we say the Lord's Prayer, do we really mean it, or are we just saying it as a ritual? If we mean the words, how many of our sins are actually forgiven if we meant what we said during the prayer? We must forgive as the Lord has forgiven us; why is that so important to God? God knows that unforgiveness hardens the heart and kills the spirit. I have heard that not forgiving is like trying to kill someone else by drinking poison. God knows the health benefits of forgiving others. Then there is the fact that we are called to be like Christ; He forgave, so we follow and forgive. Complaining accomplishes what? Nothing but getting the wrong emotions stirred up. Forgiveness actually heals the heart, heals the hurt and can restore relationships, if not with the other person, at least your relationship with the Lord. If you haven't heard from the Holy Spirit in a while, maybe unforgiveness is blocking the channel. If you feel distant from the Holy Spirit, is it unforgiveness that has become a wedge between you? Why is forgiveness so hard to give, but so desired for ourselves? Who do you know, dead or alive, that forgiveness needs to be extended to? Who do you need to seek forgiveness from? How can you mean every word in the Lord's Prayer when you pray it?

OCTOBER 4

For you, O Lord, are my hope, my trust, O Lord, from my youth.
Psalms 71:5

What heritage are you leaving your children? Sometimes as parents, we might not think about it often. One morning, my friend and I were reminded when his five-year-old daughter ran her bike off the porch, "This is just ridiculous!" she said. We both looked at each other and laughed; we knew exactly where she got it from. Later that day, I was reminded when my twenty-something-year-old son told me what he wrote in his life journal from his Bible reading plan. The best legacy we can leave our kids is love for the Lord. Not our love, but demonstrating and living out how to love God, so they, in turn, develop their own love and relationship with the Lord. When they have their relationship with the Lord, children tend to remain faithful with that relationship and are not tossed to and fro by society and end up leaving the church. They end up planting themselves on the solid foundation of Christ and allowing the Holy Spirit to be their guide and teacher. They can say for themselves, "You alone, Lord, are my hope, my strength, my salvation." Nothing is better than being able to say, "Lord, I have trusted you from my childhood; since I was a child, I have personally known you." When they see the Lord working in our lives and how we trust Him, when we follow the teaching and guidance of the Holy Spirit and how He comforts us when life throws us curveballs, they will want that relationship too! Just like key phrases we tend to say and don't realize until our children repeat them and repeat them appropriately, they will trust in the Lord and accept the Holy Spirit into their hearts and souls to direct, teach and guide. Eternal legacies are priceless. Inheritances and traditions can disappear, but a spiritual legacy of trusting in the Lord and following the Holy Spirit is beyond measurable; it is invaluable. What spiritual legacy are you intentionally and faithfully leaving your children? How can you encourage, not force, but encourage your children to walk in the Lord, trust the Lord and follow Him? How do you show your relationship with the Lord to your family?

OCTOBER 5

Seek the Lord and his strength; seek his presence continually! 1 Chronicles 16:11

When my brother and I were young, the neighborhood kids would get together and play hide and seek and we had rules like no hiding in backyards, no one in vehicles and you could go from this house to that house. While we had fun, I remember that no one ever liked being the seeker, whereas everyone liked to hide. The good thing for us is that the Lord does not play and seek, nor does He hide from us; all we have to do is seek Him. Unlike childhood hide and seek, where no one wanted to be the seeker, here we actually have to choose to be the seeker, to seek Him. Since He is not hiding, seeking Him is not hard either. Many, though, like when we were kids, do not like to be a seeker and unless God follows our rules, revealing Himself our way or how we want Him to reveal Himself, or we have no desire to seek. The irony is this; we will seek after financial strength, emotional security and other things the world promises to make us feel fulfilled, but we don't want to spend the time or energy to seek God. We need to turn our hearts' desires instead to seek the Lord, seek His strength and seek His presence. We need to have a proper view of Him; He is not there for our wants. We are here to bring Him glory and praise. If we continually seek His presence and strength, then our wants change and His presence is made ever more real. God is not hiding, but when we run to things of this world, we are not seeking Him either. We need to turn back and seek Him. What is it you seek strength, security, or purpose from in this world? How can you turn those into seeking Him first and seeing those areas filled with His power and presence?

OCTOBER 6

> For to set the mind on the flesh is death, but to set the mind on the Spirit is life and peace. Romans 8:6

We have to be careful what we allow our eyes to see and our ears to hear; we also have to be careful what we think about. Even secular psychologists state that what we focus on affects our mindset. Paul tells us here in Romans 8:6 that to set your mind on what the flesh wants leads to death, but to concentrate on the Holy Spirit leads to not only life, but peace as well. The NLT version says that letting your sinful nature, your flesh, control your mind leads to death. Self-Control is a fruit of the Spirit and is evidence of the Holy Spirit in your life. Letting the Holy Spirit control your mind leads to life and leads to peace. Self-Control is extremely difficult, but even more so when we don't have the guidance of the Holy Spirit in our lives to help with developing that fruit. There are tons of scriptures that discuss controlling the tongue, lack of control with our anger and how those show lack of wisdom. It actually takes wisdom and inner strength to control our tongues and not say everything that comes to our minds. It also shows respect and love when we are actually quick to listen and slow to speak, not thinking about what we will say (quick to speak), but actually listening. Setting our mind on the Holy Spirit and allowing Him to direct and guide us brings forth the fruits of the Spirit. Lack of self-control allows the flesh and its desires to take over and control and as Paul states here when we allow the desires of the flesh, our wants to control our minds, that leads to death. Self-Control, a fruit of the Holy Spirit, squashes the flesh, puts it in its place and keeps it tamed. To be in tune with the Holy Spirit and to set our minds on Him, we need to spend time with Him, reading, listening and worshiping; but even more so, we need to be careful as to what we also allow into our minds through our phones, computers, TV and movies. During the 2020 election year, I decided to stop watching all news sources. As a result, my mental health improved. I love crime dramas, but I had to stop watching one of my favorite shows, because I could actually feel the mental and emotional strain it was having on me. Now, I am not hiding in a cave, nor oblivious to what is going on in the world, but I have to be more intentional about what I allow my mind to be set on and what I allow in my mind during my downtime. What do you set your mind on? Have you paid attention to what you allow in through your eyes and ears? How does it affect your emotional health? Your spiritual health? How can you be more intentional in setting your mind on the Spirit, the Holy Spirit?

OCTOBER 7

> for God gave us a spirit not of fear but of power and love and self-control. 2 Timothy 1:7

Fear – anxiety, despair, dread, uneasiness, worry, aversion, distress; the list goes on and on. These words describe fear, the tool used by the enemy. Remember the acronym for fear? (False Evidence Appearing Real.) But God did not give us a spirit of fear; the opposite of fear is calmness, assurance, confidence, encouragement, faith, joy, trust, contentment, courage and love; this is the spirit that God gives us. So, when fear is trying to drive a wedge between you and God, you and Jesus, you and the Holy Spirit, recognize what he is trying to put into your life and what he is trying to take out of your life. He wants to replace assurance for anxiety, confidence for despair, courage for dread, contentment for worry and uneasiness, love, joy and trust for distress. The Spirit of God gives us power in His love. When fear rears its ugly head in your life, chop it off like you would if a rattlesnake reared its head at you. Don't give fear the ability to rob you of the peace that comes from being in communion with the Lord. Don't wait. Once fear attacks, you must respond immediately; don't let it drop seeds that can take root and choke out the fruit producing vine that God is growing in your life. When he wrote the song, *"Fear, He is a Liar"*, Zach Williams hit the nail on the head. It says, "He will take your breath, stop you in your steps; Fear, he is a liar. He will rob you of rest, steal your happiness; Cast your fear in the fire, 'cause fear, he is a liar." What is fear trying to rob you of? What is fear trying to replace it with? How can you replace that with a promise of God? How can you kill the fear in your life to experience the joy and peace of the Lord more fully in your life?

OCTOBER 8

> And do not grieve the Holy Spirit of God, by whom you were sealed for the day of redemption. Ephesians 4:30

As kids, I am sure many of us heard from our parents, "Now don't embarrass us," when we would go do something or go out with friends. There is also something to be said about our last name," Keep our last name pure, clean, honorable." With a last name like Misiaszek, people know who's related, people know the parents, the siblings and even grandparents and cousins! Similarly, Paul here is saying, "Do not grieve the Holy Spirit." In the NLT translation, it says, "And do not bring sorrow to God's Holy Spirit by the way you live." We are a walking, talking testimony, especially if we are vocal about our relationship with Jesus, the Holy Spirit and God. When we are born again, the Holy Spirit indwells us, identifying us as His own, sealing us for the day of redemption. We should be grateful for that and live it out. We should not go on indulging in sin and every fleshly desire, because we have been saved and redeemed. The words we use should build and encourage, not destroy and tear down. If we own a business, everything we do should be "above water," honest and transparent. It hurts my heart when I hear about waitstaff saying they hate working Sundays because of the "Church crowd" and how demeaning and demanding they are, stingy with tips and ungrateful. For almost two decades now, when at a restaurant, we ask our servers if there is anything we can pray for them. A few we never saw again, but it was only a few who never came back. On the other hand, many stayed and prayed with us; we have even had many say we were the first person in their life to ever ask if we could pray for them. We also leave a minimum 20% tip regardless of service, knowing that Christians have a bad reputation in the food industry. We have even had people come up to us at McDonald's or Wendy's and thank us for praying over our meal, as it was encouraging to them. We never know what a person is going through and what they are dealing with in their life outside of work, so how you treat them can encourage them or dishearten them, either build up or tear down. How do you treat the slow checker at the grocery store or the waiter who forgets to check if you need refills? With the person racing down the highway, is your anger fueled, or do you pray for them? How do you live out your relationship with God outside of church and Bible Study? How do the words you use either confirm or confuse others about the Holy Spirit living in you?

OCTOBER 9

> Buy truth and do not sell it; buy wisdom, instruction and understanding. The father of the righteous will greatly rejoice; he who fathers a wise son will be glad in him. Proverbs 23:23-24

When we buy, we gain and we take possession. When we sell, we let go and we give it away. Solomon tells us to buy *truth*. In order to buy, we work, we earn and we use what we earn to buy something of value. To buy truth, we must be working for it, towards it and earning our way to get it. Truth, though, has to be eternal, never changing, remaining constant. Real truth surpasses all time. So, the source of truth must also be eternal and surpasses all time and the "thing," the only One that fits that criterion is God; God the Father, God the Son (Jesus) and God the Spirit (Holy Spirit). We don't see truth or peddle it to people to gain a following. When confronted with truth, it generally makes people take a step back, think and consider it. It is not something that can be handed out willy-nilly, nor can we sell it to profit from it. Since it is not from us, we cannot commercialize it, especially since it is not ours to begin with. Solomon also tells us, in addition to truth, to "buy wisdom, instruction and understanding." Like truth, wisdom must be worked for and earned, especially to understand it and share it. It is our duty as children of God to earn and acquire truth and wisdom. We should be listening to and following the instruction and guidance of the Holy Spirit. Through Him, His presence and power in our lives, we get understanding – understanding of God, understanding of wisdom and understanding of His Will for our lives. As a father myself, I rejoice when my kids take ownership of their faith and relationship and listen to the Holy Spirit. It is exciting when they start to understand God's Will for their lives or begin to hunger for His direction and guidance in their lives. My heart leaps when they understand God's truth, incorporate it into their lives and live it out! How much more does our Heavenly Father rejoice and is glad when we do that, when we understand His truth, gain His wisdom and submit to His Will? Are you a buyer or a seller? Are you gaining or giving away? As you continue your walk, what are you working for? What are you buying? What are you doing with what you purchase?

OCTOBER 10

> Trouble and anguish have found me out, but your commandments are my delight. Psalm 119:143

In this world, there can be a lot that weighs us down. For instance, Bull and Bear markets, mortgages and interest rates and the price of gas acting like it's always on a rollercoaster. Then, there are more personal pressures, like marriages, kids, careers, health and family. The enemy would love to weigh us down, because it's an easy way to break us. Here the author of Psalm 119 tells us his solution; it is like he wrote it this year – as pressure and stress bear down on me, weigh me down, it can't take away my joy, because my joy is in you, in your commands. Why are His commands his delight? Remember what Jesus says in Matthew 11, "Take my yoke upon you and learn from me, for I am gentle and lowly in heart and you will find rest for your souls? For my yoke is easy and my burden is light." In Luke 10:27, Jesus affirms, "You shall love the Lord your God with all your heart and with all your soul and with all your strength and with all your mind and your neighbor as yourself." His commandments are there to protect us and guide us. The Lord knows the emptiness that can come chasing after the empty promises of the world. He also knows that nothing stays hidden; the truth always comes to light. Trouble and anguish that you have sowed eventually find you. When they do, how do you react? When you chase after and pursue sin, you create separation from God. When you act in ways against His commandments, trouble and anguish find you. The enemy loves to tempt you away from God with a shiny lure, but then he is quick to condemn you and fill you with guilt. When we take delight in His commands and take joy in His yoke, life becomes easier to bear. When our joy comes from the Lord and we can find satisfaction from living within the guidelines the Lord puts before us, then we also get to experience His peace which is supernatural and beyond explanation. The NLT translation reads, "As pressure and stress bear on me, my joy is in your commands." How do we, as Christians, find relief from the stress and pressures in life? Where do you go to find joy when stress and pressure bear down on you? Where is your joy found? How do you handle stress and pressure? How can you allow the Holy Spirit to step in and provide that for you?

OCTOBER 11

> Let not steadfast love and faithfulness forsake you; bind them around your neck; write them on the tablet of your heart. So you will find favor and good success in the sight of God and man. Proverbs 3:3-4

As I get older, I am finding that my memory is not as accurate as when it was young. David and Solomon are great Biblical examples of when they got old, they forgot what God had done for them, through them and how He had blessed them with His teachings and His wisdom. Solomon writes and warns us in Proverbs 3:3, "Let not steadfast love and faithfulness forsake you; bind them around your neck and write them on the tablet of your heart." God is steadfast and unmoving; His faithfulness to His promises is unmatched. New believers are often "on fire" over their salvation and can become an unstoppable force in sharing God and His attributes with others and what God saved them from and did for them. But then, like a fire that is not kept, it eventually burns down and just smolders. Solomon is telling us not to let that happen – don't let the fire burn out. Bind the promises of God around your neck, so you're reminded every time you look in the mirror. Let His yoke be your yoke so that when the world tries to hand you its yoke, there is no room to take it on because God's yoke is already there. Write on the tablet of your heart the faithfulness and steadfastness of the Lord so that your heart is secured and impenetrable when you walk through the valleys and trials. When you do this, Solomon continues, "... you will find favor and good success in the sight of God and man." It pleases the heart of God when we live out our relationship with Him, when we hold onto His promises and walk in His statutes. When we do this, we say, "God is more important than the others. God's way is better than the world's way!" Men will want what you have; what you have is the Living God and His Will in your life, His Word instructing you, His Holy Spirit guiding and directing you. Don't let the fire, the passion, burn down and just smolder. Stay on fire for sharing the joy of your salvation! Remember all that God has done for you. Remember all the promises that God has fulfilled in your life. Remember His blessings on your life. Remember His Word, His Way, His Will. How is your spiritual memory? How are you living out this verse in your life? How have you seen verse four come to fruition in your life?

OCTOBER 12

> Come and see what our God has done, what awesome miracles he performs for people! Psalm 66:5 NLT

2020 – What a pivotal year 2020 was. COVID-19. Presidential Elections. North Korea. In years like that, we can easily get overwhelmed by the fear and negativity blasted at us every day in the media and news. But when was the last time we stopped and looked to see what our God has done? Do you notice the fingerprints of God all around you? In the miracle in the face of a baby sleeping or smiling? In the leaves changing color on trees? In the beauty drawn in a sunrise or sunset? In the creativity of God in the clouds floating by? In the joy in the laughter of children? We too often forget to appreciate the small miracles that God performs all around us, because we allow ourselves to be overcome and consumed by the world. We want big miracles, like a pillar of fire coming down from Heaven or a multitude of angels delivering a message. Maybe we want God to part traffic on the Interstate like He parted the Red Sea or to save and heal a loved one, as Jesus did. You know, a Big Miracle. But what about the miracle of life, the miracle of conception, the miracle of birth and the miracle of God's love and eternal life? We forget about these and chalk them up to science or just the natural flow of life; these processes are hard to conceptualize and grasp, so we mentally dismiss them. What about when you paused when the light turned green and a car flew through the intersection? Do you consider that luck or a miracle? Have you ever run a stop sign or red light because you were not paying attention and luckily no was around to get hurt? Have you ever lost something valuable only to find it in the most unusual place? Small miracles happen every day if we just take the time to see and acknowledge them. Today we don't want to give God credit for the miracles He does, because they are not big enough or don't fit our definition of a miracle. Instead, we disguise it or explain it away as luck or just a coincidence. However, I truly believe that in life there is no luck, there is no such thing as a coincidence; it's God's presence exercising miracles in our lives. What miracles has God shown you that you have not thanked Him for lately? How can you be more observant of His miracles and working in your life this week? How can the small miracles help you in your walk with Him?

OCTOBER 13

> Hear, my son, your father's instruction and forsake not your mother's teaching, for they are a graceful garland for your head and pendants for your neck. Proverbs 1:8-9

What would you consider something you are proud of that you would want to wear a medal around your neck for or a pendant pinned on your jacket or shirt? I was not very popular in high school. In fact, I was quiet and introverted. When I lettered in the shotput and discus, I suddenly became a little more popular and wore my jacket year-round, even through my freshman year in college. Solomon says what we should wear with pride, like a crown or pendant, is a father's instruction and a mother's teaching. As we continue to progress through time, we see more people, especially students in school, choosing not to listen to their parents or teachers and flat-out disrespecting authority. As I taught middle school, the more time I spent there, the more it seemed children were running the household and telling the parents what to do. As a parent myself, I have had to reiterate to my children to trust my instruction that while I am not of their generation, I still have wisdom to pour into them. My wife and I would like them to learn from us and not repeat our mistakes, but learn from them and make new ones. The struggles are always the same; just each generation has a different avenue to bring or usher them in. If you have God-fearing, God-loving parents, no matter how old you get, your parents have still lived longer and have more life experience than you do. So, it is a blessing when you give them the respect of still speaking into your life. What advice did your parents give you that you thought they were out of touch, but in hindsight you see that they were right? How can you let your parents know you appreciate the wise counsel and teaching they raised you with? What is something your father or mother taught you that sticks with you the most?

OCTOBER 14

> For the mountains may depart and the hills be removed, but my steadfast love shall not depart from you and my covenant of peace shall not be removed," says the Lord, who has compassion on you.
> Isaiah 54:10

My wife is notorious for losing things and she hates it when she can't find something. You can probably relate. Don't you just hate it when something you need to have right now seems to have disappeared? The older I get, the more things seem to do just that, disappear, like sunglasses, keys, my wife, etc. But with the Lord, mountains and hills may disappear, but He never will. His love will never disappear from us, nor leave us. His love for us will always be there. We may try to disappear from Him, or hide from Him; lucky for us, neither He, nor His love will ever depart from us as believers. His covenant with us is always there; even when we try to run and hide from Him, when we come to our senses and return, He is there with open arms to welcome us back. He is the Father in the Prodigal Son parable; with open arms He ran to welcome His son returning home. He took Him back no matter what, although nothing had changed. His love is not like a club or organization. When you leave and come back, there are new terms and policies to agree to. His covenant will never be broken, nor will it be modified or changed. Since God is unchanging, so is His love for us and His covenant with us. No matter the thoughtless decisions we may make, He doesn't change the terms or conditions on us. He just wants us and our love. He wants our whole heart, not just part of it. How can you hold onto this truth so that His words can dissolve any lingering fears or questions? What can you do for God to show that you understand His love for you? How can you help others come to understand God's love for them?

OCTOBER 15

> so as to walk in a manner worthy of the Lord, fully pleasing to him: bearing fruit in every good work and increasing in the knowledge of God. Colossians 1:10

What is the first thought you have when you wake up? Do you wish the alarm clock would shut up? That is my usual one, or asking where is the snooze button? Do you wake up and immediately start going through your mental to-do list? With your first thought of the day, do you ever ask God to show you your steps for the day? Do you ask Him what fruit He is asking you to bear? Do you start by asking Him for His guidance to make godly choices? Paul reminds us that we are to walk in a manner worthy of the Lord, but we cannot do that without being in communion with Him, allowing the Holy Spirit to guide us and allowing Him talk time in our hearts and minds. In the verse before this, Paul states that the whole group was praying for them to receive spiritual knowledge, wisdom and understanding. By gaining that spiritual knowledge, wisdom and understanding, we, too, should be able to walk in a manner worthy of the Lord. What does your daily walk look like? Are you walking in the spiritual knowledge, wisdom and understanding of the Lord? Do you start your day with Him and then not stop there, but do you continue your day with Him and finally end your day with Him? When we do, we can bear good fruit. Bearing God's fruit in our life not only blesses others, but also increases our knowledge of God, so when trials come we can have the endurance and patience to have joy through them (Colossians 3:11). The Christian walk is not an easy or leisurely walk. Jesus tells us to pick up our cross to follow Him. Jesus said the world hated Him first, so it will also hate us. Paul talks several times about endurance and pushing through. As you push through, how can you walk in a manner worthy of being called a Christian, a little Christ? How can you bear fruit in your works, so you can increase your knowledge of God? How can you increase in your spiritual knowledge, wisdom and understanding so that the light of Christ can shine through you throughout your day? How can you change the first thought of your day to be focused on the Lord? What spiritual fruit is the Holy Spirit trying to get you to produce? How can you seek His knowledge to know His steps for you to walk this day? What about Tomorrow?

OCTOBER 16

> Fathers, do not provoke your children to anger, but bring them up in the discipline and instruction of the Lord. Ephesians 6:4

What is the hot poker or pet peeve that really gets you mad? For me, it's when kids ask reckless questions while I'm cooking like, "Is the stove hot?" It drives me to sarcasm, dryly answering, "Nope, I'm cooking at room temperature." But seriously, for me, being lied to is what ignites my anger. Paul is saying, "Fathers, do not provoke your children to anger," meaning they are young and impressionable, so being thoughtless or not in control of your words, emotions and actions could plant the seeds of resentment, anger, or bitterness. Those abusive experiences can cause our children to lose the desire to please their parents. It also causes resistance to the follow up statement, but fathers, "bring them up in discipline and instruction of the Lord." A neglectful or abusive father, whether verbal, physical, emotional, or any other way, is building barriers to the kids knowing God. Yes, they can overcome these barriers, but why place them there to begin with? Don't our children already have enough trouble the world and society are throwing their way, beyond the barriers between us and God we need to break down? To be a godly father, we must lead by example. Our lives, our words, our actions, how we treat people and how we conduct business must be led by the Holy Spirit and we must live out our faith and our relationship with Christ. No matter how young or old our children are, they are watching. It is never too late to start living a godly life; it just starts with one step. When our children see us repent and ask for forgiveness, even from them, it displays the discipline of the Lord. It is humbling for a father to ask his son or daughter for forgiveness when he messes up. We can't just assume our kids will forgive us because they love us; we must display the very same actions and attributes we want them to have. The instruction of the Lord includes prayer and meditation. Do they see these disciplines in your life? His instruction includes forgiveness and loving our enemies; how have your children witnessed this in your life? The Lord's instructions state, "Love God, Love others." Is there visible evidence of this in your life so that you can bring them up in faith and instruct them in Lord? It's caught, not taught – our walk and words must match and actions speak louder than words; however, you have heard it, thus it is true. If we want them to walk with the direction and guidance of the Holy Spirit, they have to see how that looks in our lives first as parents. If you have intentionally provoked your kids to anger, have you gracefully sought forgiveness and reconciliation? How have you lived out the discipline of the Lord in your life? How have your kids witnessed you being transformed and matured by receiving the instruction of the Lord?

OCTOBER 17

> Remind them to be submissive to rulers and authorities, to be obedient, to be ready for every good work, to speak evil of no one, to avoid quarreling, to be gentle and to show perfect courtesy toward all people. Titus 3:1-2

When I was growing up, my mom would say, "If you can't say anything nice, don't say anything at all," which, being part Italian, is really, really hard to do. But here, Paul reminds us that we, as Christians, are called to be kind to each other. It is righteous to be submissive to the rulers only to the point that it does not violate God's law and is ready to not only do good work, but also be ready for every good work. During times of the global pandemic and election years, it is even more so that we need this reminder. We need to be tenderhearted, loving, forgiving, speaking evil of no one. We need to not only speak evil of no one, but also as Christians, we are called to avoid quarreling and show perfect courtesy to everyone. That means not just fellow believers, but all people. As Christians, we are called to forgive as Christ forgave us, fully and completely. You cannot name one sin that God will not forgive of yours, so there is not one sin you cannot forgive someone else from. Today, is there someone that comes to mind when you are told to be kind, that you typically have a hard time being kind to? Why is it hard to be kind to them? As you start to name off the reasons why, ask why is it that they are that way. Look at them through the eyes of Christ and not through worldly lenses. Being gentle and tenderhearted means that just because you are right does not mean you can force feed that truth to someone. As a follower of Jesus, you may have to lay aside your "being right" for the sake of being kind and tenderhearted. Christ was right and the Pharisees were wrong; Christ was crucified and the Pharisees mocked him. Jesus rose from the dead, yet they did not. So, in the scope of eternity, is being right, right now, more important or less important than allowing the Holy Spirit to work His will in you? Are you ready for every good work God wants to bring your way, or are you too busy quarreling and arguing your point, proving you are right, to the point of refusing to be obedient? Who do you need to be courteous to, especially if they have a different political view than you? Who is it that, being as hard as it may be, that you need to be kind and tenderhearted towards? How can you show them the heart of Christ this week?

OCTOBER 18

> Therefore we must pay much closer attention to what we have heard, lest we drift away from it. Hebrews 2:1

I remember in a sitcom I was watching as a kid, the wife yelled at the husband, "Did you hear me?" and he replied back, "Yes, I just wasn't listening!" While this may be funny, or even confusing for some, there is a difference between listening and hearing. Hearing is an automatic sense that your brain activates, whether or not you realize it. Your brain even hears while you are sleeping. Listening, however, requires an active response on the hearer's part. To listen, you must pay attention and apply all your attention to the one speaking. I believe we also need to apply this application in our spiritual lives as well. The longer we are Christians, the less we may listen to a sermon, worship song, or Bible story, because "I've already heard this one." Don't allow the enemy to come in and steal an opportunity the Lord wants to speak to you by deceiving you into believing you don't need to hear it again. I truly believe that the Bible is the living Word of God. That means every time I read it, the words may speak to me differently, depending on my circumstances in life. I may listen to a part I never really paid attention to before. The writer of Hebrews warns us to listen carefully to the truth that has been told, *The Bible*, or we may drift from it. If you look around society, you can see the impact it has had on our country as it has drifted away from being founded on principles from the Scriptures. Churches and whole denominations are drifting away from Biblical truth to be relevant to the world and increase attendance. Our spiritual lives can end up like this if we do not listen to the Truth, the Bible and the Holy Spirit. Have you allowed the enemy to convince you that you don't need to read or listen to that one again? How can you rid your heart of that lie and begin to eagerly desire to listen to Him, His Voice, His Truth? How can you pay closer attention to every Scripture you read? How can you set up spiritual guard rails, so that you don't dilute or deny truths found in the Bible?

OCTOBER 19

> Whoever pursues righteousness and kindness will find life, righteousness and honor. Proverbs 21:21

With everything going on in life, it's easy to see how it can be referred to as a rat race. Chasing dreams and jobs and peace, we have to ask ourselves, what is it that I am pursuing? It's amazing what the world tells us to pursue to find happiness and fulfillment. After centuries and centuries of these lies, people still fall for them. A better job, better house, nicer car, a bigger bank account, or a 401K at a certain level. But by chasing these lies, there is always one more to try to gain. You never reach the top; it's like walking an escalator in the wrong direction, the top is always just out of reach. Solomon reminds us here to pursue God, to pursue righteousness and unfailing love. As Solomon says, if we pursue righteousness and kindness, those two pursuits will bloom into three rewards: righteousness, life and honor. Remember that righteousness is defined as acting according to a divine or moral law, being free from guilt and sin. If you act according to God's divine and moral law, being free from guilt and sin, you become righteous. When you pursue God and His unfailing love, you find life and righteousness and honor. In essence, you find your purpose in life, which there is a peace about that, a confidence that withstands fear. Pursue God and His attributes. Weave His attributes into your mindset so that your decisions are based on what you are pursuing – God. Let the light of God shine through you, like a lighthouse on a hill. By pursuing unfailing love and righteousness, it changes your heart, not just towards desires, but how you treat other people. The problem is that we cannot transform our heart on our own accord. The only one we can pursue righteousness from is the one righteous person, Jesus Christ. We get righteousness from being in Him and having the Holy Spirit deposited in us. But the more we pursue the righteousness of God, the more we will have it deposited in us. We cannot be morally correct or justifiable on our own accord, regardless of what the world says. The problem with the word *moral* is that the world tells us we can define truth and morality; how did that work out for Adolf Hitler? There can only be one source of truth, thus one source or definition of morality. So, as Solomon says, we will find life, honor and righteousness when we pursue God, righteousness and kindness. Jesus himself said, "I am the Way, the Truth, the Life." What is it that you are pursuing? Are you pursuing God's kindness and righteousness, or are you still pursuing and participating in the rat race called life? What changes can you make to pursue God more? What are you pursuing in your life? How can you recalculate your spiritual and personal GPS to start pursuing God's righteousness and unfailing love?

OCTOBER 20

> But I discipline my body and keep it under control, lest after preaching to others I myself should be disqualified. 1 Corinthians 9:27

It is difficult to be self-disciplined. I show little self-discipline in certain situations, especially with hot, gooey brownies or freshly picked berries. It takes a lot of inner strength and focus to stay disciplined. You have to determine that the long-term goal you are working towards is more valuable than the short-term desire is. Paul is stating here that he disciplines his body to keep it under control, so he does not disqualify him from the service God has called him to. How many pastors have we seen fall because they gave in to their short-term desires and disqualified themselves? Whether it be an affair, skimming money off the top, attacking other believers for something they don't personally believe in, lack of self-discipline, or keeping their bodies under control, moral trials led to their fall and failures. No one is free from sin; we all sin. All pastors are under more scrutiny than anyone else in the church, so they have to be careful. But as believers in Christ, we must all heed Paul's words and examples for ourselves. We must be careful with the words we choose when speaking to someone or about someone. We must be careful what we allow in our minds through media, social media and print. We must be careful not to allow ourselves to be put into situations that could cause us to lose integrity and the ability to be God's microphone. James tells us how dangerous the tongue can be. Even though it is one of the smallest muscles in the body, it does the most damage. He compares it to a rudder on a ship; though small, it controls the ship's direction. Like a small spark that can cause a great fire and immense damage, so too the tongue can cause great damage. Jesus warns us that if our eye causes us to sin, we should cut it out. If we look lustfully at a woman, we have already committed adultery with her. If our hand causes us to sin, we should cut it off. We must control our bodies, whether or not we are a preacher or a Sunday school teacher. If you are a Christian, a capital "C" Christian, you must keep your body under control lest your actions destroy your testimony, pushing others away from Christ instead of drawing them near to Him. You never know who is watching how you treat others with words and actions. Do your words and actions towards others testify to the goodness of Christ or evidence of self-indulgence? How do you discipline your body and your desires? What area of your life needs more discipline? How can you stay focused on God's Word and God's Will for your life?

OCTOBER 21

> Then David said to the Philistine, "You come to me with a sword and with a spear and with a javelin, but I come to you in the name of the Lord of hosts, the God of the armies of Israel, whom you have defied." 1 Samuel 17:45

In this day and age of social media, with texting and apps like Snapchat that delete messages after they are read, people have become more and more brazen. When I was growing up, it took a lot of courage to confront someone, especially publicly. Bullying someone took some level of confidence, even if your confidence came from others going with you. How confident are you? Here we see a small shepherd boy walking the ranks of the Israeli army, decked out in full armor, facing another army larger and stronger than them. The Israelites, looking at their enemy, allowed fear to overpower them; they lost their confidence because they put their confidence in themselves and not in the fact God went before them. David told them, "Even at my age and size, I've killed bears, lions, any enemy that attacked our flock." King Saul tried to give David his armor when David decided to confront Goliath. With Saul's armor being too big for David to wear, David does what he does best; he goes out with the confidence of the Lord. Goliath defied and reviled God. David called him out, "You come at us with a sword and a spear, manmade weapons and self-confidence, but I come to you in the name of the Lord, the God of our army and it is through Him you will fall." David's confidence was in the Lord, not himself. He was not concerned with what his brothers said, what the soldiers thought of him, or even the size of the enemy standing before him. He knew the God he served was bigger, stronger and mightier than any army. He trusted that God would not only prevail, but also equip him with what he needed. The story of David and Goliath reminds us of God's upside-down economy and way. He doesn't call the qualified; He qualifies those He calls. He uses the unlikely to accomplish the impossible so that we can see His Power and His Presence in the outcomes. David could not or did not take credit for taking down Goliath, because he knew it was God using him to do the impossible. What is God calling you to do that is out of your comfort zone? Where is your confidence – in your Self or your Savior? Are you more like Saul, his army, or David's brothers, afraid to confront the gigantic task God has called you to, or do you really trust God and His judgment of you? Which is stronger, fear the enemy tries to fill you with, or trust in God, knowing He knows better and His Will, His Way is better? What giant in your life does God want you to kill and demolish so He can be bigger in your life?

OCTOBER 22

> He has told you, O man, what is good; and what does the LORD require of you but to do justice and to love kindness and to walk humbly with your God? Micah 6:8

Isn't it amazing how short our memory gets? I mean, as a dad, I will tell my kids what to do and not even five minutes later, they are doing something else, "Oh, I forgot, Papa." As a teacher, I saw the same thing; you would tell students, show them and help them, but then they would immediately forget. Micah reminds the nation of Israel and us today, that the Lord told us what to do and what He wants from us. What is good and what does the Lord require of us? *Require* is strong verbiage, but as his children, there are still things He requires us to do. Is it difficult, hard and confusing? No. He requires us to "Do justice, to love kindness and walk humbly with our God." Do justice; how hard can that be? It is not our justice, but His justice. It is to act justly, rightly, reasonably, honestly, truthfully, honorably and righteously. Treat others based on the character of God. We are called to love kindness, so that it oozes out of us through our thoughts, our words, our actions and the way we treat others. We are called to walk humbly with God. We need to have a humble heart, knowing that without God, we are nothing, we can accomplish nothing. It is God who gives us talents, skills and gifts. He gives us intelligence and gives us the ability to think through and solve problems. There is no "I deserve this" in the vocabulary of a humble person. They have a right view of self and a right view of God. Before sacrifices and tithes, God first wants us to live just lives, love in kindness and walk humbly with Him. Notice Micah says *with* God, not before God. God wants us to walk with Him, not before Him, not after Him and not going after Him. He wants us to be humble and walk with Him. So, we walk His path, follow His will for our lives, which develops a deep trust in Him, His Word and His Way. Looking at that list of what it means to do justice and act justly, how are you doing in your spiritual walk? How are those characteristics evident in your life? Do you extend kindness or just want kindness extended to you? How humble is your walk with God? Are you walking with Him or after Him?

OCTOBER 23

As in water face reflects face, so the heart of man reflects the man.
Proverbs 27:19

I remember late in my thirties looking in the mirror and seeing my first gray hair. I plucked it out, asking myself, "How can I be getting old?" Now I'm in my forties and more gray hairs have joined the party, but they are not the majority yet. We can look in the mirror and think things like, "How did I get old? How did I get here?" The mirror reflects back only what is in front of it. Looking into clear water shows us that same reflection. Solomon says, like clear water that reflects the face, so does your heart reflect what you are truly made of, what is at the root of you. From your heart flows what is in it, including things you may try to hide with smiles or work ethic. Is it greed and success or love and forgiveness? What is in the heart can only be hidden for so long; it eventually comes out. Who resides in your heart? Is it self and selfish desires, or have you accepted Christ and allowed the Holy Spirit to come in and take up residence? If you have, do you relegate the Holy Spirit to the couch in the family room, or do you give Him free access to all? Is Jesus the Lord of your life or your Lord on Sunday? The words you use with people reflect what is in your heart. Your actions and decisions reflect what is in your heart. As a youth pastor and small group leader for youth, I would often ask, "If Christianity were to become illegal today, would you get arrested? Would there be witnesses to condemn you, or would people be surprised that you were in court?" When you see someone in need, do you stop and help or make excuses why not to? Do you serve in your church, or are you too busy? Do your words build people up or tear them down? Jesus told the Pharisees they were like whitewashed tombs, beautiful on the outside but full of dead bones on the inside. What is in our hearts comes out. Are you full of the Holy Spirit or dead man's bones? How much control do you give the Holy Spirit over your life? What does your life testify to? How much evidence is in your life to show that the Holy Spirit is living in you?

OCTOBER 24

> For we are his workmanship, created in Christ Jesus for good works, which God prepared beforehand, that we should walk in them.
> Ephesians 2:10

The Mona Lisa. The Sistine Chapel. The Statue of David. All are masterpieces of great artists and are known all over the world; even if they haven't been seen in person, people have seen them. God, however, is the greatest artist of all time. You, me, we are His workmanship, His masterpiece. Like the Sistine Chapel and the Statue of David were created for a purpose, to tell a story, so were we created in His likeness. We were created for good works and God knew beforehand what we would need to do, how to do it and who to do it for. The NLT says He created us anew in Jesus Christ. We are a new creation in Christ Jesus. The old sinful nature is gone and we are made new in Christ. The Holy Spirit now rules in our hearts, so we should walk according to His directions and His guidance. In a world where people and life are devalued, we need to hold onto this truth; you need to hold onto this truth, this word. You are a masterpiece, created new in Jesus to do good things, good works. Go. Do them! Don't let fear of people, fear of judgment, or, most of all, fear of failure, deter you from doing what God created you to do. You have natural gifts and talents; you have spiritual gifts and spiritual fruits to do the good works God has prepared you to do. You are enough. You are equipped. You are not alone! The Holy Spirit goes with you and before you. God has prepared ahead of time for you. Be strong and courageous, do not fear; your value is not of this world, in this world, or from this world. Your worth is determined by your Father, the Creator and Master Craftsman, who knitted you together and gave you what you needed before you knew you needed it. What is stopping you? What is holding you back? As a masterpiece, what story is God asking you to tell? What good works is He calling you to do? What is your first step in heeding that call?

OCTOBER 25

> For you have need of endurance, so that when you have done the will of God you may receive what is promised. Hebrews 10:36

Patient means, "Bearing annoyance, provocation, misfortune, hardship and pain; quietly and steadily persevering. Endurance means, "The ability or strength to continue and last, especially despite stress or adverse conditions." The writer of Hebrews hits us with a double whammy! In order to continue to do God's will, you will need to have the ability to continue and last, quietly and steadily, persevering while managing provocations and hardships. Not much of a sales pitch. Hey, if you commit right now to doing God's will, you will have hardship, misfortune and provocation. But wait, if you commit within the next ten minutes, I promise you will have to dig deep for the strength and ability to see it through. But Jesus Himself said, "If you want to be my disciple, die to self, execute your desires and plans and be prepared; they hated me first, they will hate you also." *Then* you will receive all that He has promised, meaning this one is conditional – rewards in Heaven are influenced by our decisions here on Earth. You will have eternal life; you will have a room in God's house, specially prepared for you by Jesus Himself. In sports, people say, "No pain, no gain." The same goes spiritually, as well. A little pain here on Earth results in great gains eternally. Are you currently walking in a valley, in shadows and darkness? Do you feel the pressure from the enemy to just give up? Is he whispering in your ear, "You can skip church this week, it's not a big deal! You don't need to serve anymore; you've done enough. It's someone else's job now!" If so, don't despair. We are all under attack in our minds and hearts every day. Stay the course, keep praying, keep reading and keep serving. Supernatural endurance is possible for anyone living in His will for his or her life! What area of your life do you need to hand over to God and trust in Him more? What do you need to do to have the strength and ability to continue to do God's will? How can you counteract the pressures from the world and from the enemy?

OCTOBER 26

> When the Philistine (Goliath) arose and came and drew near to meet David, David ran quickly toward the battle line to meet the Philistine.
> 1 Samuel 17:48

When we see trouble coming, what do most people do? Probably turn and run – but what did David do? David saw Goliath approaching, so David *RAN* toward Goliath. Why would David do that? Was it the original *kamikaze* philosophy? Did he have a death wish? Was he high on drugs? None of the above. David was confident in the power of His God! Goliath had blasphemed God's name and David knew that God would not stand for that. God just needed someone who was confident in His Presence to step forward. Neither the king, nor any of his well-trained, well-armed soldiers stepped forward. All were terrified by Goliath's size. David didn't see his size; he saw God's size. David didn't see the strength of Goliath, he only saw the strength of God. So, when the enemy approaches with lies and half-truths, don't run away in fear; run towards them with the power of God. You must be like David, though and trust in the power of God in all aspects and avenues of life. This was not David's first day at the rodeo. He had trusted God in both big and small things to giving him a mature confidence. He had a relationship with God and walked with God through loneliness and against savage animals. If your relationship with God isn't where David's was, it's not too late to start. Read His Word for yourself and listen to songs regarding Him and His love for you. Pray, but be silent in prayer time so you can hear from Him. When the enemy comes, you will have the confidence of David to run quickly towards the Goliath to defeat it. What giant, or Goliath, is in your life? What do you need to do to be more like David and turn the battle over to Him, allowing Him to equip you to defeat the enemy? What is holding you back from going all in, fully trusting God, in to battle?

OCTOBER 27

Heaven and earth will disappear, but my words will never disappear.
Mark 13:31 NLT

Magic has always fascinated me. Even today, as an adult, knowing that there is no such thing as "magic," it still amazes me how people can make the Statue of Liberty "disappear." It really doesn't, because it's a trick played on the mind, but one day Lady Liberty will really disappear along with everything else. I once saw David Copperfield make a Harley Davidson disappear from the stage and appear overhead on a portable catwalk. Now we know that it actually didn't disappear, but it was an illusion. The enemy loves to use illusions to contradict scripture and make us doubt it, but here Jesus, Himself tells us that everything we see and feel may disappear. His Words never will. Buildings are destroyed, cities are vacated to rubble and there are no clues to what happened. Nonetheless, His Words are infinite. Out of His Words, everything was created. We can hold onto the truth of what God has to say to us. It is the only source of truth we can live by, but in order to live by it, we need to be in it – read it, hear it, pray it and meditate on it. We can't let the world's fear come in and overwhelm us. What does His Word say? He will never leave, nor forsake us. Jesus promised that when everything disappears, my *words* will remain forever. So, when He says He "Loves us," that is forever, never changing. When He says that the Father rejoices when one sinner returns to Him, that's forever. He will always rejoice when we return to Him. Unlike coupons we cut out, there is no expiration date on His love, His mercy, His grace, His forgiveness, His holiness, or even His control over all things seen and unseen. We were chosen before the foundations of the worlds were laid. He knitted us together in our mother's wombs. He is our Strong Tower, Provider, Healer, Comforter, Wonderful Counselor, Prince of Peace, Loving Father. As the news reports continue to display despair, believers can choose to tune into hope. While things of this world may look like they are out of control, His promises are not. He is still in control and His promises still hold true. While we may become overwhelmed with news reports, wars, illnesses and violence, He is not taken by surprise, nor has He let go of the wheel; He will always be in control. He still loves us enough to allow us to make choices. When the world overwhelms you, go to the Father to be overwhelmed by His words, His love and His compassion. Spend some time today in His Word, being refreshed and strengthened. So, what Words from Your Father do you need to be reminded of? How much do you believe in how wonderfully and beautifully you were created in His image, on purpose, for a purpose and with a purpose? How can you remind yourself that no matter your choices, He is waiting to rejoice when you return to Him and that it is not too late to do so? What do you need to do to be reminded that you are forgiven and loved?

OCTOBER 28

> Therefore, since we are surrounded by so great a cloud of witnesses, let us also lay aside every weight and sin which clings so closely and let us run with endurance the race that is set before us, Hebrews 12:1

By nature, I do not like slow. I don't just wander around the store. I go, I get, I leave. On the road, please don't be in the passing lane if you are not going to go faster. Here the writer of Hebrews tells us that whatever slows us down, get rid of it. He is not saying being impatient like me on the road is okay; he is saying that what slows us down in our relationship with God, what slows us down from doing His Will and the detours and road bumps we put up need to be taken down. There is a reason there are no speed bumps downtown. We should not build speed bumps when God is calling us to move and if it's a sin issue that is slowing us down, we need to call a spade a spade and deal with it. Life is a marathon and not a sprint, so we need to be smart about how we run it and we need to have the endurance to run it. We cannot afford to take on things that will slow us down or distract us from doing God's Will. Like in a marathon, where there are refreshment stations, we need to partake in rejuvenation as needed. However, like in a marathon, those refreshment stations are on the race course; you can't go off course to be refreshed. Don't detour into temptation alley when you can refresh on the course with what God gives you. When you watch races and marathons, have you ever paid attention to the clothing the runners are wearing? It is very thin, light, almost nothing, including the shoes. It is made of lightweight material so the runner is not bogged down by any unnecessary weight. Just like the Olympics, or an infamous marathon like the Boston Marathon, a lot of people are watching us. Do our words and actions align, or are we carrying the weight of our own hypocrisy? The writer of Hebrews reminds us that, like a marathon runner, strip off every weight that slows you down. The thoughts and lies from the enemy that prevent you or hold you back from doing God's will; it's time to strip those off and throw them away. Low self-esteem, past failures and fears need to be stripped off and thrown away. The writer then goes one step further, adding we need to strip off the *sin that so easily trips us up*. What temptations do you struggle with saying "No" to? Don't place yourself in situations where those temptations occur. What weakness or vulnerability do you have that leads to sin? Strip it off, so it doesn't trip you up and cause you to fall in the race. Set up safeguards around you so when that vulnerability or weakness sneaks in, you have the ability to escape, flee and strip it off, so you can continue the race. Continue with the endurance that the Holy Spirit gives us to see the race through to the end. What affects your endurance with the race that is set before you? What vulnerabilities and weakness toward sin often trips you up? What safeguards can you set up? Who can you ask to help you strip off those temptations, so you can have the endurance that the Holy Spirit wants you to have? What is tripping you up with your walk with God? What do you need to let go of so you can "compete" in this marathon we call "Life"? If your endurance is waning, take time to refresh, but stay on the course. How can you refresh this week, so your endurance is energized?

OCTOBER 29

> But this I call to mind and therefore I have hope: The steadfast love of the LORD never ceases; his mercies never come to an end;
> Lamentations 3:21-22

Corrie Ten Boom once said, "Worry does not empty tomorrow of its sorrow. It empties today of its strength." Worry destroys hope, but Jeremiah states here and reminds us that we need to call to mind God's Word. It is in God's Word that we find hope. Worry is the assassin of hope, one of the many successful weapons of the enemy on Earth. IN Matthew, Mark and Luke, Jesus told us not to worry, "Look at the birds of the air and the lilies of the field, God the Father takes care of them; how much more does He love you and take care of you?" The steadfast love of the Lord never ceases. His love remains steady and strong; it does not waver, nor does it fail, or give up, or quit. His love is a steadfast love that never ceases. The enemy wants us to forget all the times that God has shown Himself to us, all the times that God has answered prayer, all the times God has saved us. But when we remember these little details, we can have hope. While God may be silent in the storm, silent in the trials, it does not mean that He has left us or ignored us. He allows us to go through them for many different purposes: discipline, like in the desert or wilderness, building a deeper relationship through suffering, or developing a better understanding of God and His plan, like Job. We may need to learn a lesson, or He is equipping us for what He knows is coming in the days, weeks, months and years to follow. But His mercies never end, they never cease. He is a shelter in the storms of life and if we take a moment to remember and recall all that He has done in our lives, the current situation we are in will be more bearable because our hope can be restored and refreshed by this. It also creates in us a thankful heart, recalling all of His blessings, His answers of "Yes" and His answers of "No" throughout our lives. Take time today to remember and recall what God has seen you through. What mountains did He move, what waters did He part, what comfort did He bring? What mountains did He *not* move, or waters did He *not* part, or what people or situations did He keep you from that, looking back, you can now recognize as a blessing?

OCTOBER 30

> But the Helper, the Holy Spirit, whom the Father will send in my name, he will teach you all things and bring to your remembrance all that I have said to you. John 14:26

We were not left alone on Earth to try to figure everything out. Jesus promised us that when He ascended into Heaven, He would send us a Helper, a Comforter. The Holy Spirit has always been in existence, is existing and will always be. He is eternal like God the Father and Jesus the Son. He was present at the Creation, He spoke through the prophets of the Old Testament, yet little is taught of Him. He is in the Nicaean and Apostles Creed, yet most books and sermons are focused on the first two personhoods of God. The Holy Spirit tends to be neglected and regulated to creeds and prayers. In 2022, I embarked on a twenty-five-week sermon series on the Holy Spirit, almost half a year's worth of sermons and I probably could do more. My next devotional book will be *90 Days with the Holy Spirit*. Why so much interest and attention on this topic? He was sent to us to teach us God's ways and to unpack what Scripture says. He was sent to bring to mind remembrance of what God said, Jesus did and the life we are called to. So many churches and denominations are deviating from God and dissecting Scripture to make it fit societal agendas. Churches guided and directed by the Holy Spirit would never follow suit; they would only follow the direction and guidance of the Holy Spirit. Holy Spirit-directed churches don't dissect, rather they preach *all* of God's Word, even when society says it's old fashioned and outdated. God's word is Holy and eternal, never changing, nor contradicting. Marriage is between one man and one woman. He created all of creation, male and female. He knitted everyone in the womb. It is Holy Spirit that is active in our lives, even now. Jesus is still in Heaven; the Holy Spirit is with us now! If you research Scripture for references to the Holy Spirit, you will be overwhelmed by the depth and magnitude of the content. My prayer for you is that you get in-tune with the Holy Spirit who is in every believer, sent to help, guide, teach and bring remembrance to all of what God has said and done. He will pray for us when we don't know what to pray for. He inhabits our worship when we worship with our whole hearts. When you need direction and guidance, ask the Holy Spirit. He is able, willing and ready to help; all we have to do is ask. Seek Him and His guidance. How much of a role has the Holy Spirit played in your relationship with God? How active of a role does the Holy Spirit have in your life?

OCTOBER 31

> training us to renounce ungodliness and worldly passions and to live
> self-controlled, upright and godly lives in the present age, Titus 2:12

In 21st century America, when we renounce ungodliness and call sin a *sin*, society attacks us and calls us intolerable. The irony is that they mean it as slander, an attack on our morals and values, but as Christians we are called to not tolerate sin in our lives, nor should we tolerate it anywhere. Does that mean we hate and attack sinners? Absolutely not! Jesus ate with sinners, taught with the sinners and walked with the sinners. Did He do all of this to tolerate their sin or give them a way to escape their sin when they recognize their sin and that it separated them from God? Those to hold to worldly passions and a cosmopolitan worldview try to tell us that Jesus was the most tolerant and nonjudging person; they fail to read further and see that Jesus often tells them, "Now go and *Sin No More*." They tend to forget that part. This reminds us that Jesus was compassionate and loving as He went to those who indulged in ungodly behaviors. Despite the fact they were driven by worldly passions, Christ would teach them, heal them and save them from being stoned to death. Yes, He would forgive them, but also beg them, "Now, go and sin no more." In other words, do not repeat this sin. Jesus whispers to us, too, "Do not continue to desire worldly passions and live an ungodly life; now that you have encountered me, change your mindset, have a mindset set on Me." Like Paul tells Titus, live a self-controlled, upright and a godly life in this present age. In the verse before this, verse 11, Paul says, "For the grace of God has appeared, bringing salvation for all people." It is the salvation to all people and God's grace that gives us the ability to "renounce ungodliness and worldly passions and to live self-controlled, upright and godly lives in the present age." As Christians, we should not follow society, nor allow society to determine what God "really meant" when He said that. God said it, I believe it and that should be good enough for every Christian that reads Scripture for themselves. His Word is not a buffet where we can pick and choose what we want and leave behind what we don't. To live self-controlled, upright, godly lives, we must live by His Word, guided, directed and instructed by the living Holy Spirit in us. In this day and age, we should denounce worldly desires and not go after them. We are not to follow the world's desires, but through prayer and being in the Word, we are to be self-controlled when temptation comes to trap us. Our prayer should be, "Lord, in all my struggles, help me to be self-controlled and not chase after the desires or passions of the world, but help me to live an upright, God-fearing life." How self-controlled are you in general? What worldly desires do you have trouble letting go of? How confident are you in your ability to renounce ungodliness? How do you renounce ungodliness and still love those who do not?

NOVEMBER 1

> For by the grace given to me I say to everyone among you not to think of himself more highly than he ought to think, but to think with sober judgment, each according to the measure of faith that God has assigned. Romans 12:3

Somewhere between me being in school as a student and me being in school as a teacher, the sociology changed from looking at American society as a melting pot. The metaphor described how everything goes in and melts, losing its individual qualities, all the while making the final product stronger, like steel. Now with a diversity-lens we end up comparing America to being a tossed salad, where each individual piece needs to be savored for its unique contributions. The tomato, the carrots, lettuce, etc., all remain individualized and separate. In contrast to this "Look at me, celebrate me" mindset, we see Paul say the exact opposite. No one should think more highly of themselves than another, but with a sober mind, a clear mind with no preconceived ideas, be honest about yourself, in accordance to the amount of faith that God has assigned you. It is believed here that Paul is not talking about the faith of believing in God, but the spiritual power we have been given to use our Spiritual Gifts. Paul, after this verse, takes us into the discussion about Spiritual Gifts and that every believer is part of one body. Because we are all members of one body with different functions, we all have a part to play. But if we allow pride to come in and convince us that we are better than someone else, our spiritual gift means we are a better believer than someone else who does not have that same gift, then we make the Body of Christ unhealthy. We can easily allow corrupt thinking from the enemy to cause illness in the body. Paul says, "by the grace given to me." He basically says, "Let me tell you, if there is someone to boast about, it's me, but I'm telling you, don't think more highly of yourself. We all have a part to play, a function in the body." I would say the opposite is true as well. Don't think any less of yourself than you ought to. You have a purpose and a function in the body. Don't disqualify yourself when it is not us who qualifies or disqualifies, but God qualifies those He calls. In other words, have a right view of yourself; see yourself and others through God's eyes, through the lens of the Holy Spirit. What area of your life has pride puffed you up and you might have a higher view of yourself than you should? What was something God called you to do, but you disqualified yourself from it? What can you do to have a right view, a God's view of your life and yourself?

NOVEMBER 2

> Do not be overcome by evil, but overcome evil with good. Romans 12:21

Just look around – you can see evil infiltrating many aspects of our society, everything from crime to entertainment. Hollywood glorifies violence and even evil, making villains the heroes of the story. Today, we wear our sin on our sleeve like a badge. We raise flags in our yards to show how we celebrate sin, glorify it and are now trying to implement in our elementary schools the very thing God calls evil, sin. We may tend to think that it has only gotten worse, but evil has been oppositional to God since the beginning of time. As Christians, we have a choice to make. We can feel defeated because evil is rampant and hide in our homes, or we can try to choose to ignore it and just go about our daily lives, or as Paul challenges us, we can choose to defeat evil. How do we do that? Paul didn't just leave his message there; he told us how to conquer evil and defeat evil by doing good. Evil cannot stand up to God's work – like darkness is dispelled and pushed away by light, so evil is dispelled by doing good. Good only comes from God, so evil is pushed back and retreats when we do the good that God calls us to do. When you love those who are hurt, help those in need and forgive those who have hurt you, you actually take ground away from the enemy. Don't use empty words; if you say you will pray for someone, pray for them right then and there. Don't wait to help, don't wait to serve and don't hesitate to share God's word. Delay is a tactic the enemy loves, because then dark forces can regroup and detour you. Instead, go forth, do good and boldly do God's will. If you are a Christian, you cannot expect someone else to do God's Will – it takes all of us and we all have a part to play in His Will. So, what are you waiting for? What is God calling you to do that would dispel, conquer and defeat evil? Where can you shine the light of God to dispel the darkness? What good can you do within your life? How can you use your spiritual gifts to bless your neighbor or to dispel evil?

NOVEMBER 3

give thanks in all circumstances; for this is the will of God in Christ Jesus for you. 1 Thessalonians 5:18

Thanksgiving is right around the corner and some Christians have taken to the 30-day thankfulness challenge, which entails, saying or posting something on social media that you are thankful for every day. This is a wonderful idea; it should really be a 365-day challenge. Paul tells his mentee and the church at Thessalonica to be thankful in all circumstances. God wants us to be thankful in all circumstances. Why would that be? The answer is that we have short memories, we tend to only see forward and not remember His protection and provision. The enemy loves to deceive us, making us think our troubles outweigh our blessings. God's Will has always been for us to remember His blessings from the past. Everywhere Abraham went, he built an altar of remembrance. When Joshua led the Israelites into the Promised Land, they built an altar when they crossed the Jordan River. They built these altars to remember the faithfulness and goodness of God. We need to take their example and do the same by keeping a thankfulness or blessing journal. While wandering in the desert for 40 years, they could be thankful that neither their clothes, nor their shoes wore out and they always had food and water. Being thankful in all circumstances is different from being thankful *for* the circumstances. Sometimes we can be thankful for the circumstance, but not always. *Always* we need to be thankful while in the circumstances. What are you thankful for? What will start off your thankfulness list? What is God doing in your circumstances to transform your heart? What can you be thankful for while going through your current circumstance? How can you develop a thankful heart in all circumstances so it becomes who you are, not something you do?

NOVEMBER 4

> "Then the other administrators and high officers began searching for some fault in the way Daniel was handling government affairs, but they couldn't find anything to criticize or condemn. He was faithful, always responsible and completely trustworthy." Daniel 6:4

Have you ever been around people who are always looking for something to be wrong? They are not fun to be around and can drag you down. As Christians, we are not called to do that. In fact, when someone has a fault, we are not supposed to judge them or condemn them. We are called to love and show them grace. We are called to live our lives as Jesus did and when we do that, we will face criticism and people will be looking at us to find fault. But here in the Book of Daniel, we see he lived his life for God; his faith was exemplified in everything from the food he ate to the clothes he wore, to the way he handled his business, to the time he dedicated every day to spending time with God. Because God was with him and blessed him, others tried to find fault in him, but could not. Are we following Daniel's example? As a youth pastor, I would ask my students, "If Christianity became illegal tomorrow, would there be enough evidence to convict you, or would people be surprised you were accused of being a Christian?" We can answer that question better if we take the time to ask ourselves a series of more specific questions, like: What language do you use at work and at play? What music do you listen to? What movies are you into? How do you handle yourself in tough situations and when others attack you? Where does your money go? Upon this deeper introspection, we can learn a lot from Daniel on how to live life according to God's way and how God responds when we do. What is one area in your life you can commit to so your walk with Christ is more in-sync with Him? How can your integrity magnify your relationship with God? What is one area of your life that you need the Holy Spirit's help in being more like the description of Daniel?

NOVEMBER 5

> Even though I walk through the valley of the shadow of death, I will fear no evil, for you are with me; your rod and your staff, they comfort me. Psalm 23:4

Growing up, I was not afraid of heights, but I was afraid of bridges. I would go rock climbing and loved flying, but bridges not only made me uneasy but really scared me, to the point of freezing and turning my stomach in knots with certain ones. Living in Colorado, whenever family from back East would come out to visit, we would always take them to the Royal Gorge Bridge, the world's highest suspension bridge that sways in the wind as multiple vehicles drive over. Putting my trust in the ability of the bridge to hold me up caused fear. Once I deepened my relationship with God beyond religion and into a personal, intimate relationship, bridges don't cause fear anymore because my trust isn't in their ability to remain strong under pressure. Now my trust is in my Good Shepherd, who is walking with me. David writes, "Even though I walk through the valley of the shadow of death, I fear no evil." This could mean the shadow, as in the covering that death seems to cast over people, or it could be referring to the idea that tall objects like mountains and cliffs cast shadows down below. Another interpretation is that robbers, thieves, hunters and predators tend to lie in the shadows waiting to pounce, which can cause fear. But David had the right mindset; he knew that God walked with Him. The Shepherd's rod and staff could be weapons to defend and fight off attackers and predators. His very Presence walking with David provided comfort. Jesus promises to never leave, nor forsake us. The Holy Spirit is with us wherever we go and is ready to act, to supernaturally help us when we ask for it. Why do you fear? Why are the shadows and dark, uncertain areas, such a source of anxiety and concern? Remember, in order for there to be a shadow, there must be a light source. Do we face the shadow or face the light source? Do we believe the lie that we have to be strong enough to walk through the valleys alone, or do we hold onto the truth that the *Paraclete*, the Holy Spirit, who fights back-to-back with us, goes wherever we go and is always there to guide, direct and protect us? What are you holding onto, truth or lies? Is it an individual journey or a guided tour? What causes you fear? How can you let go of that?

NOVEMBER 6

Commit your work to the Lord and your plans will be established.
Proverbs 16:3

Have you ever planned something out and then everything fell apart and you were left there thinking, what happened? This is not how I planned it. Solomon here tells us that if we commit our work to the Lord, He will establish our plans. But first, we must be willing to commit our work to the Lord. We have to allow the Holy Spirit to lead and direct us; then, He will make it succeed. But everything we do, we should do for the Lord and if we do, then we won't have to worry about the plans not working out. It is when we don't commit what we do to work for the Lord or when we decide to take over and think our plans are better than God's plan that we tend to get in trouble or things don't work out the way we thought they should. So, when you are at work, do your job for the Lord so that your attitude, the words you use and your work ethic brings glory to His Kingdom. When you are shopping, shop for the Lord with a positive attitude and positive words, so that your attitude and gratitude show people the goodness of the Lord in you. When you are doing something fun, whether hiking or playing a sport or game, play for the Lord and He will establish you and His plan in you. He will inspire you to have a positive attitude, respecting officials and other players or the environment. When you plan for tomorrow, go to the Lord first, seek the Holy Spirit's direction and plan on whatever it is you are going to do, to do it for the Lord and He will establish the plan for you to follow. What part of your life is not fully committed to the Lord and how can you start to change that? How can you allow the Holy Spirit to direct your path and plans? What area of your life do you need to hand over to Him that you are still trying to control?

NOVEMBER 7

I can do all things through him who strengthens me. Philippians 4:13

Sometimes the struggles we face can be overwhelming. Sometimes failures can become bigger than successes. Sometimes we can be in the mud for so long that we can ask – how can I go on? If we rely on ourselves, we may not be able to, but Paul reminds us with this Scripture how we can go on and get out of the mud or situations we find ourselves in. I can do all things, *everything*, through Him who gives me strength. That means every day we need to connect with our Father; we need to listen to the Holy Spirit speaking to us. While breakfast is said to be the most important meal of the day, I would argue it is our Daily Bread instead. The most important aspect to the start of the day is to be filled with the Holy Spirit and get connected with our Heavenly Father. When we do that, we no longer work on our own strength, but we work on His strength. Our first thought of the day needs to be on Him, His Will for the day. He is the one who can make the struggle bearable. He is the one who reminds us that it is not a failure if we keep moving forward and try again. He is the one who not only lifts us out of the mud and muck, but when He does, we rise clean and washed – no longer wearing the garbage the world has thrown on top of us. As you face struggles and setbacks, invite Him in. Ask for His strength, His presence, His power. When you wake, start first in His Word and feed your soul before your stomach. Dress and prepare your spirit before your body. When you face struggles, what are you looking at, the darkness or what is causing the darkness? If you are looking into the shadows, you are facing the wrong way; turn and face the light. Inscribe this verse on your heart, soul and mind, so that when struggles arrive, you are prepared. When you feel weak, He is your strength. How can you allow Him to be that strength for you? What struggles have you allowed Him to guide you through? What struggle have you been trying to handle that you could turn over to Him and allow Him to be your strength?

NOVEMBER 8

> Oil and perfume make the heart glad and the sweetness of a friend comes from his earnest counsel. Proverbs 27:9

The enemy loves to try convincing us that we should be strong enough on our own. The enemy loves to deceive us into thinking that we would burden others by asking for help. He loves to try to isolate us so he can try to convince us to believe his lies. But just as God said, "It is not good for man to be alone" and He created woman, we need to recognize the lies of the enemy and hold onto the Truth of God; it is not good to be alone. During times of trials and struggles, during the valleys and time in shadows, a heartfelt conversation with a friend can be as pleasing to the soul as a sweet, aromatic perfume. We need to realize that we cannot do life alone and burdens are meant to be shared. Don't try walking through a trial alone. You are more vulnerable to the enemy when alone. If you have to lay your shield down, make sure someone is there to cover you with theirs. Remember, it doesn't take strength or courage to stay home. It takes strength and courage to reach out and ask someone to just listen to you, to talk with you, or to ask them to just sit and be with you. It takes more courage to be vulnerable and ask for help than to suffer in silence. Remember, also, the Holy Spirit is readily available if you take some quiet time to just be still, be quiet and listen. Who do you have to help you in your life when the shadows come in, disappointment hides blessings, the road heads into a valley, or a spiritual attack intensifies? Thank God for these people, but also utilize those that God puts them in your life, so you are not walking it alone. Who can you be that companion to so they do not have to walk life alone?

NOVEMBER 9

"Jabez called upon the God of Israel, saying, 'Oh that you would bless me and enlarge my border and that your hand might be with me and that you would keep me from harm so that it might not bring me pain!' And God granted what he asked." 1 Chronicles 4:10

Jabez had faith and he had no problem calling upon the Lord and believing that the Lord heard him. How many times has someone been talking to you, either while watching TV or doing something else and you don't actually hear them unless they ask, "Are you listening to me?" I have, many times, asked my wife, especially if the TV is on or there is a device in my hand. But luckily for us, God is not like that. He is not distracted by electronics or what's going on down the street, nor is He disinterested. No, He is always listening to us and waiting to listen to us, if we would just talk to Him. Prayer is such a powerful tool, but we treat it like it is a last chance, last-ditch effort, a Hail Mary. When someone is in need, we may even say, "The least we can do is pray for them." No. Prayer is the *most* we can do, especially if we trust in Him. With Veterans Day quickly approaching, please pray for our Veterans. Those who have successfully transitioned back into "normal" society, but also for those who struggle with and have health or mental problems transitioning into a non-combative society or balancing what they saw and dealing with the memories and dreams. Pray for those who continue to have night terrors, suffer from PTSD, or depression. Suicide is highest among active and former military members, more than any other subgroup of our society. Pray for those who are still actively serving to protect our country, our way of life and our freedom. Be thankful for the protection that God has granted us through those who He has called to serve and protect. Who can you be praying for right now, active, reserve, or a veteran? How can you show your appreciation to those who have served or are currently still serving? How can you adjust your prayer life so that you pray for them, not just during Veterans and Memorial Day, but every day?

NOVEMBER 10

> Trust in the Lord with all your heart and do not lean on your own understanding. In all your ways acknowledge him and he will make straight your paths. Proverbs 3:5-6

What do you trust? Or maybe a better question is, *who* do you trust? Why do you have that trust? What had to happen for you to put your trust there? I trust my car to get me from point A to point B. I trust my wife with my heart and dreams. My love for my wife and her love for me is what has allowed me to place my trust in her. I have no reason not to trust my car. But Solomon reminds us here to trust the Lord, not just with our minds, but also with all our hearts. Why is that? If we try to trust Him with our mind and our understanding of how the world works, we will get hurt. He does not work according to societal norms and progress, nor does He allow the world to shape Him. He is the potter, the artist. He shapes us, we do not shape Him. His ways are higher and better than anything, we can possibly conceive of. We need to get our understanding from the Holy Spirit and not try to understand Him or His ways with our own comprehension. Solomon continues within everything we do, acknowledge Him, His working in our life and our reliance on Him and He will keep the road we are on straight. It might be narrow and the world might place exit ramps on it or dig potholes in it, but it is straight. There is no wondering, no question. His path for us is straightforward. Do we take time to see God working in our coworkers? Do we acknowledge His working in our families? When was the last time you just stopped to talk to God in the middle of the day, not during a meal or break time, just intentionally looking for His fingerprints in all avenues and aspects of your life? Solomon reminds us to acknowledge Him in all our ways, in everything we do, everywhere we go. Looking for and being still and quiet enough to hear Him through the hustle and bustle of life, work, family and friends. What do you trust the Lord with? Is it really everything? If He called you to pack up, move and take a lower paying job in a place you never heard of, would you? Or do you only trust God with eternity? How can you trust God with your finances and treasure? How can you trust God with your free time and family? How can you trust God with your talent and profession? What are you holding control of that you can hand over and trust God with?

NOVEMBER 11

> So, if you are offering your gift at the altar and there remember that your brother has something against you, leave your gift there before the altar and go. First be reconciled to your brother and then come and offer your gift. Matthew 5:23-24

There are many verses in the Bible about God loving a cheerful giver, but first and foremost, God wants our hearts. While Jesus was speaking about bringing a tithe to the altar here, I believe He is also speaking about the condition of our hearts when we enter a church service. If church is just a Sunday event or an item on a to-do list, then these verses here will have no application, but... if church is your time to corporately worship and engage God on a deeper level and interact at a deep spiritual level, then I believe that this verse applies to *us* entering worship as well. If you have not forgiven someone of a hurt, can you truly worship God with that unforgiveness in you? When we come to church, it should be with the expectation of experiencing God and there should be some level of anticipation of connecting with or hearing from Him as we prepare to go to church to worship. The anticipation of meeting God and the expectation that something will happen. The expectation is that God will show up and we will leave different, better than when we headed to church and entered the building. Our tithe, our worship is like dirty rags when we come with impure motives or an unclean heart. Before we celebrate communion or the Lord's Supper at church, I ask myself and the church to examine their hearts; is there an unconfessed sin that they need to confess or unforgiveness they need to let go of? I take 1 Corinthians 11 seriously when we take communion, but I think we need to take it seriously for the church as a whole. We must examine ourselves and our hearts and get right with God. Forgiveness is a one-person job, just yours. We are commanded to forgive. Reconciliation is a two-person job. We are not commanded to reconcile, since we cannot control the other person's heart. But forgiveness, yeah, Jesus told us we had to and He suggested we have to do it seventy times seven times. If you feel unchanged or even empty after leaving church, check your heart and examine your deeper motives. Did you come with pure intentions and a pure heart? Did you come refusing to forgive someone? Is there someone you are unwilling to forgive because the hurt is still too real, the wound is still bleeding? Forgive. If you are not ready for reconciliation, that is ok, but forgive. Prepare yourself for worship, repent if you haven't already, forgive if you're holding on. Prepare your heart and truly know that He can do immeasurably more than we can expect and finally come with anticipation and expectation of Him showing up. God forgave you, so what is it that you are unwilling to forgive from someone else? How can you begin the healing process of forgiving someone, whether or not they are still alive? How can you ask God to help you forgive them, even if they know not what they did to harm you?

NOVEMBER 12

> "If you, Israel, will return, then return to me," declares the Lord. "If you put your detestable idols out of my sight and no longer go astray and if in a truthful, just and righteous way you swear, 'As surely as the Lord lives,' then the nations will invoke blessings by him and in him, they will boast." Jeremiah 4:1-2

How can a loving God _____? Fill in the blank. Many people have this question and use this as an excuse to not turn to God, or not follow God. The enemy loves to question people and twist truths about God. He did it in the garden when he asked Eve, "Did God really say you will die? Surely you won't die…" But we see here in the Book of Jeremiah that God calls us to repent several times and warns the nation of Israel. He does the same with us. "Hey you, Joe, yeah you. Do you want Me to bless you and answer your prayers? How about you remove those idols you have put up in My place and actually return to me?" We generally don't have physical idols up in our homes, but how about in our hearts? Careers and financial goals can become an idol if we focus on them more than God. The opinions of others can be more important than God's opinion of us. We may worship sports and recreation. Even technology has become the latest idol in the lives of Christians where we spend more time with these idols, on these idols, than we do with God. Family can become an idol if we are not careful. Just stay with me, walk with me and I will bless you so you can boast. Having the blessings of Heaven poured out onto me is far greater and better than any of the idols I have put up in my life, so why is it so hard to give them up? Like any relationship, it takes time, it takes effort and it takes putting the other person first. With what God did for me, I should put Him first. What idols are active in your life, taking the place of the Father in your life? How can you clear them out to be in right relationship with Jesus Christ? How can you make God actually the first priority in your life?

NOVEMBER 13

> Whatever your hand finds to do, do it with your might, for there is no work or thought or knowledge or wisdom in Sheol, to which you are going. Whatever your hand finds to do, do it with your might, for there is no work or thought or knowledge or wisdom in Sheol, to which you are going. Ecclesiastes 9:10

One of the many things that both my grandfathers and my dad taught me was the concept of hard work, to always give your best and never have any regrets. My dad would say, "If you can look your boss in the eyes and say, 'I gave it my all', that's all they can ask for." The author of Ecclesiastes does not say you have to succeed at whatever your hands find to do, only to do it with all your might. Maybe one of my grandfathers or my dad wrote Ecclesiastes ... well, maybe not, but as Christian men, they lived out this verse and many others in front of my brother, cousins and me. Time is ticking and we are limited to the amount of time we have here on Earth. So, in everything you do, do it with excellence and give it your best effort! If we want to get the best out of life, we have to give it our best. We should not ask God to bless and prosper anything we do halfheartedly; if we don't put our full effort into it, it is not important enough to us, so why would God bless it? Now I am not saying that everything we see as important God will bless, nor am I saying God will bless everything we do with all our might. But the author of Ecclesiastes tells us that whatever we put our hands to, whatever we try to do, we need to give it our all. Life is but a mist, no one is promised tomorrow; so if God is calling us to do it today, we should do it with everything we have. We should work hard to complete whatever we start, because we never know what tomorrow will bring. No matter what God calls us to do, we should give it our all. God gave His all for us, so we should give our all to whatever God calls us to do. What work story is your life leaving as a legacy? How does this verse fit in with your work ethic? How does your work reflect your relationship with the Living God we serve?

NOVEMBER 14

> But to all who did receive him, who believed in his name, he gave the right to become children of God, John 1:12

Why is it that we, as humans, tend to make things more complicated than they need to be? There are many funny memes, as well as serious articles, about making life less complicated, yet we continue to make it complicated. Psychologists say we have an innate complexity bias, that even though we do like simplicity, we feel safe and comfortable in the complex. So as humans, we make things more complicated than they need to be. We even superimpose that on God and His plan to save us and how it all works. God's plan, however, is really quite simple, yet many people make it complicated. There are not a bunch of hoops to jump through or a long list of "to-do" items to check off. But to all who receive Him and believe in His name become His children, children of God. There are no six-week classes to take and no tests to study for and pass. Accept and believe; do that and He gives you the right to become His child, adopted into His family with all the rights and privileges of being a child of the Living God. But, as simple as it is, simple does not mean easy. Once a child of God, He has expectations of us and He warns us, "If you become my child, you will bring burdens on yourself, as well as blessings; attacks come with my acceptance." When you become a child of the king, yes, there is an inheritance that comes with that, but until the time the inheritance is given, we have tasks to do to build His Kingdom and do His will. The devil brings attacks, temptations and hardships, while we respond by dying to self and living for His will, not our own. It is simple, my kids are my kids, whether genetically related or adopted in. They are simply my children, forever and that does not depend on what they can do for me, rather because of who they are. Simple? Yes. Easy? No! I have high expectations for my children, too. They know I care that they study, work hard, love others, give to others and live out their individual faith, not mine. Like with God, being His child is a simple process, but once we realize we are His child, we are called to walk a narrow path that requires His guidance and direction. I am far from perfect, but I tend to use the example of my Heavenly Father to guide my fathering, actions and words. Just like I have disappointed my Father, my God, His love and acceptance of me is not dependent on me, but on Him. It is the same with my kids; while they have disappointed me, it does not change my love for them, because it is not based on what they do or don't do for me, but who they are. What is something God has done, is doing, or wants to do, that you have made or are making more complicated than it needs to be? How can the simplicity of God's plan help you share and live out your faith and relationship with Him? How do you live out being a child of God?

NOVEMBER 15

> O God, you are my God; I earnestly search for you. My soul thirsts for you; my whole body longs for you in this parched and weary land where there is no water. Psalms 63:1 NLT

If you are honest with yourself, where is God on your priority list? To answer that, the first step we have to do every day is to identify who our "god" really is. Notice the lowercase "g." What is most important to us? Is it our job, school, sports, or technology? If we are not careful, they can become the god, the idol we worship and serve. Or is our top priority truly God? While our gut says it's God, what do our actions everyday say? Am I earnestly searching and seeking His Presence and counsel, or as a guy, am I trying to fix it and do it myself? Do I go through life knowing that I have God in my back pocket, just whenever I need Him, because I get to the point where I am stuck and cannot do it myself? Is my soul dying of thirst for a Word from Him? Do I feel incomplete when I do not seek His presence, or do I just meander through the day? The more we become self-reliant, the greater the distance we put between ourselves and God. The more self-reliant we become; our god(s) replace the presence of God. Do we, do I, earnestly desire to feel God's presence in my life, or do we just keep Him in our back pocket for whenever we get in trouble or need something? I ask these questions of you, but also of me, as I struggle the same ways as you. This week my prayer for you and myself, is that this reminder convicts and reminds us to set that time aside and hear from Him. Where in our lives is the time spent seeking Him and being refreshed and refilled by Him? When was the last time we spent time just resting in the Presence of God with no other god to distract us and no list of prayer requests, just being in His presence to be refreshed?

NOVEMBER 16

> "And I heard the voice of the Lord saying, "Whom shall I send and who will go for us?" Then I said, "Here I am! Send me." Isaiah 6:8

Do you remember being in PE class or recess and waiting to be picked for a team? Maybe you were the first, or maybe you were last. For kickball and soccer, I was a captain or one of the first to be picked, but in everything else, I was last. We didn't always get to be on the team we wanted; sometimes, we didn't even get to play. But here, God is asking for a team member. "I need someone to go – who wants to go and talk to my people? Who would be willing to be on my team to share my message with my people?" Isaiah stands up and puts up his hand and calls out, "Lord, Here I am. Send me. Let me go! I want to be on Your team!" What about you? Are you willing to tell God, "Here I am, send me!"? What God was calling Isaiah to do was not easy. He tells Isaiah, I will send you, but they won't listen to you. He was calling Isaiah into a difficult situation that would not be easy, nor successful, but Isaiah wanted to go anyway. Why? For the sole reason that God called him. When was the last time you went *all in*? Was your team in the Super Bowl or the World Series? It is ironic, but we can go all in on things in this world, but when it comes to serving God, we tend to be okay sitting on the sidelines. There was a Bible study series called *Fan or Follower?* – although many people use these terms interchangeably, in fact, they are not the same. Fans tend to jump on and off the bandwagon, but followers tend to do just that, follow wherever their team or band goes. The musical group, *The Grateful Dead*, had followers called *Deadheads* who would travel all over just to hear their band. Isaiah was not a fan of God, but a follower. When the Lord called out, "Whom shall I send?" Isaiah replied, jumping up and down. I imagined Isaiah yelling, "Here I am! Send Me! Send Me! Let me Go!" As a fan, we can become comfortable with assigning God-time to Saturday nights or Sunday mornings, but God doesn't want fans. He wants followers! When there is a need in your community and God asks, "Which of my followers will meet this need?" Are you like Isaiah, ready to roll out and go do anything God asks, or do you assume someone else can take this one for the team? Are you a fan of God? Are you a follower of God? Are you content with just reading and doing Bible Studies, or is your heart aching to be used by God to make a difference, building His Kingdom? How can you train yourself to leave fandom and become a true follower of Christ? How do you respond when God calls you? Do you go back to the bench? Do you leave the field? Do you even show up to the game? See, God is calling us. He has a job for us to do. So, what's holding you back? Is it pride, selfishness? God is trying to pick you to be on His team and you're still standing against the wall. It's time to get in the game and you are asking to join the winning team, so get in it! What will it take for you to say, "Yes, God. I will be on your team!" What more does God have to do for you to be willing to join in on the game?

NOVEMBER 17

> Or do you presume on the riches of his kindness and forbearance and patience, not knowing that God's kindness is meant to lead you to repentance? Romans 2:4

I am sure we have all heard patience is a virtue, but isn't it amazing how few people have patience? Don't we wish everyone around us had more patience! If you don't believe me, try driving at rush hour or going to the store and just sitting back and watching how people go back and forth at the registers looking for the one that will be the quickest. I have to admit, that is me at Walmart, but God is different. God is patient with us. He is tolerant and wonderfully kind, as Paul describes Him here. If He were not tolerant, He would not be so forgiving. He would actually be the kind of god that people try to portray when they make signs and shout, "God hates you," but lucky for us, He does not hate any of His children. Paul originally asked the church in Rome, but here it is also a question for us, "Does this mean nothing to you? He is wonderfully kind; does this mean nothing to you? He is tolerant and patient with you. Does this mean nothing to you?" He is kind, tolerant and patient with us, so that we would run to Him and not let the sin we participate in consume us. It's time that we start treating others the way God treats us. It is better not to judge, nor condemn, people for their sins, rather to be patient and kind. This does not mean we give permission or say sin is okay, because God does not do that with us; it simply means, "I struggle with sin, you struggle with sin, but God, our Heavenly Father, loves us both and He is patiently waiting for us to turn to Him instead of to sin." This week, how can you be more patient and wonderfully kind to others, just like God is with us? How do you personally balance the "hate the sin, love the sinner" thinking? How can you love others and still hold them accountable without judging them? Who in your life is that person for you, non-judging, yet loving you enough to keep you accountable?

NOVEMBER 18

"When you pass through the waters, I will be with you; and through the rivers, they shall not overflow you. When you walk through the fire, you shall not be burned, nor shall the flame scorch you." Isaiah 43:2

Have you ever gotten lost, even for just a moment and panic sets in? Even if only for a second, that panic can be overwhelming. But God says, "When the floodwaters rise, I am with you – there is no need to panic. When you walk through the raging river, I am there with you. The flood, the river, because I am with you, they will not consume you. When the fire comes, I am with you, so you will not be burned." Why, then, do we panic? Why is fear so overwhelming? Do we really trust God to see us through the floods, rivers and fires? Is God the God of all, or just the God of Sundays? For Shadrach, Meshach and Abednego, God was the God of *all* for them. They were willing to die for their faith in Him and their relationship with Him. The king was so enraged that he had them make the furnace hotter. Then he had them thrown into the fiery furnace, a furnace that was so hot that the heat coming off of it killed guards and people stoking the fire. They walked out, not only alive, but also unscorched, unharmed and not even the smell of smoke on them. They trusted God and believed enough to receive an inexplicable miracle. These recent years of pandemics and financial uncertainty have been trying on our country, the world and society. People are wondering where God is in all this. The truth is that God never left; we are the ones who walked away. If we want Him to be with us through the floods, rivers and fires, we need to walk with Him on the sunny, clear days. He needs to be a priority to us. He is immovable, but we tend to wander and stray. Where is He right now? On the Sunday shelf waiting to be taken down or by your side? Is He God of all, or not god at all? How can you implant this Scripture in your heart, so you can have peace when trials come? How can you deepen your relationship with Him now, so that He is God of all in your life?

NOVEMBER 19

He must become greater; I must become less. John 3:30

I am not one for bumper sticker theology, it tends to be shallow, but then there are a few that catch my attention for the good. We've probably all seen bumper stickers or t-shirts that look like $t > i$, but what does it all really mean? My desires, my dreams and my wants must decrease, or be less than, so that in my heart and soul He, God, can increase and be more than. Then His wants, His plans, His desires for my life have room to grow and develop. It is when He becomes bigger than self that we really get a clearer picture of the world and what the real needs are compared to revealing what our wants really are. When God increases and we decrease, we see others' needs as more important than our own desires. We feel constantly connected to the Father like a phone or tablet plugged into its charger, always ready to be used and fully powered up. When He becomes bigger than self, it allows His Peace to settle the storms, His light to shine in the darkness and His grace that picks us up from our failures. We walk in a freedom with a peace that surpasses all understanding. When He becomes bigger than self, addictions are destroyed, chains are broken off, wounds are healed and hurts are easily forgiven. What does your equation look like? Is it $t = i$? Are your desires and plans equal to God's? Or is it $t < i$? Are your desires and wants more important than what God says is important? Does He exist to serve you, or do you live to serve Him? How can your life equation resemble His command to us? What have you seen accomplished when you have decreased so that God could increase? What is He trying to do now in your life?

NOVEMBER 20

> You will seek me and find me, when you seek me with all your heart.
> Jeremiah 29:13

I remember playing hide and seek when my brother and I were kids. All the kids on the block would get together and we would designate the boundaries, like what yards were in, no hiding in vehicles, etc.; then we would run and hide while someone counted and then went to seek the rest of us. Luckily for us, God doesn't play hide and seek; He is always right there for us. Sometimes we act as if we were "it", running around looking for Him, seeking Him, wondering where He is. But in reality, He is really right there, at home base. He never left. God promised His people, Jeremiah and even us today, that if we seek Him wholeheartedly, we will find Him. The key word here is *wholeheartedly*, meaning not just Sunday mornings in church, not Wednesday Bible Studies, not just at meals or bedtime. When we seek Him with our whole heart, with complete sincerity and commitment, we will find Him. But if wholeheartedly means "with sincerity and commitment", most of us need to change our mindset for our daily life. Do you seek His presence with the same tenacity and energy as you do your career, your hobby, sports, or theater tickets? Do you desire to spend time with Him as much as you do on technology or watching sports or movies? Do you start the morning talking and listening to Him? Do you seek Him throughout your day? He shouldn't be just our 9-1-1 or SOS call, but with our whole heart we should seek His Presence. Like in the movie, *Field of Dreams,* "If you build it, they will come," so it is true, "If you seek Him, you will find!" He is not hiding, nor has He walked away. Spend some time today seeking Him with complete sincerity and commitment and see how your day turns out! What does seeking Him wholeheartedly and with complete sincerity look like in your life? What priorities do you have to rearrange in your life to make God higher on that list? What has a higher priority in your heart than God? What are you willing to do to change that?

NOVEMBER 21

> And I am sure of this, that he who began a good work in you will bring
> it to completion at the day of Jesus Christ. Philippians 1:6

I have ADHD, but when I was a child, there was no diagnosis for that. So, I had to develop ways for me to focus, study and complete assignments despite my disability. One of my sons and one of my daughters have it too and it wasn't until they started taking prescription medication that education and follow through actually started to take place without a fight or yelling. Isn't it reassuring that God does not have ADHD – while forming you on a potter's wheel, He did not get distracted and leave you just spinning there alone, or He does not call you to go on a journey or down a certain path and then get distracted and allow you to go off wandering into the unknown alone and unguided? Paul says, "I am sure of this!" There was no doubt in Paul's mind; it was solidified and unshakable knowledge, "He who began a good work in you will bring to completion at the day of Jesus Christ!" In other words, until our last breath escapes our lungs, God is working His masterpiece in us and is not finished, nor does He leave becoming distracted or bored – He finishes every masterpiece He starts. Notice, as well, that Paul does not just say "the work in you," but he specifically says "the *GOOD WORK* in you." No matter what the world may say to you or about you – you are a masterpiece in the making and it is good. Of all of God's Creation, everything was good, except man and humans were *very good*! You are a very good work that is still in the process of becoming whole. Never lose sight that God is always working on you, in you and through you. Allow the Holy Spirit to mold you and craft you in His Image and for His work. Never lose sight that you will always be a work in progress until He calls you home. Until then, there is still time to do something, say something and accomplish something. Never lose sight that He is doing a good work in you. Not good according to your definition of good. Not good according to the world's definition of good. His definition of good is "good work". Are you allowing Him to *work* on you, in you and through you? Do you have a correct view of yourself and the masterpiece of God that you are? How can you walk in the peace and knowledge of God, knowing that God is still at work in you and with you? How are you willing to submit to the Potter's hands to be crafted by Him and not your own desires or wants?

NOVEMBER 22

> I will be filled with joy because of you. I will sing praises to your name, O Most High. Psalm 9:2 NLT

What are some things that bring joy into your life? For a lot of people, they experience joy in getting something they have always wanted. Some people experience joy from being able to go someplace they have always wanted to go. At the same time, others have joy simply spending time with family. Notice that none of these causes of Earthly joy involve God. But here, David says, "I will be filled with joy because of you. Just because of who you are, God, I will be filled with joy. Because of who You are God, I will sing praises to you. I praise you, not because you answered my prayer with 'Yes', not even because life is going good right now; I praise you just because of who you are God. Because of who you are, I have joy and I sing praises." Sometimes when life hits below the belt and we are in mental anguish, emotional distress, or physical pain, we can easily forget the Holiness of God and that He deserves all of our praise. We can easily give praise to Him for answering our prayers, when He gives us what we want, or because He protects us from what we don't want. This removes the holiness from God and regulates Him to more of a servant position; give me what I want and keep me from what I don't want. God's holiness means He deserves praise because of who He is, His holiness and perfectness; it is because He is perfect and holy that He deserves to be praised. How's your thankfulness journal that we discussed at the beginning of the month? If your journal is like mine and like new year's resolutions, you probably did really good for several days (I got to 9 days), but then it fell off your grid and failed to continue. Daily we need to be filled, constantly filled with the Holy Spirit and be seeking His guidance and direction to keep us on track. We need to praise God every day and desire His joy every day. We need to praise God in every situation, because of who He is, regardless of the effects or results. In addition to being thankful, how can you praise God today, just for being who He is – God? How can you have joy despite experiencing trials and suffering? How can you praise Him in the storm?

NOVEMBER 23

> Enter his gates with thanksgiving and his courts with praise! Give thanks to him; bless his name! For the Lord is good; his steadfast love endures forever and his faithfulness to all generations. Psalm 100:4-5

As we approach Thanksgiving, we are reminded that at the root of the celebration it is not just a time to gather with family and indulge in delicious food. Thanksgiving is a state of being for the heart and mind. The online dictionary (dictionary.com) says it is "a noun defined as an act of giving thanks; grateful acknowledgment of benefits or favors, especially to God; a public celebration in acknowledgment of divine favor from God; an expression of thanks, especially to God." It should be a day where we enter His gates, enter His presence with thanksgiving. Do we spend the day consumed with the meal or keeping the central focus that we need to give Him praise, bless His name for all that He is, not just what He has done? The Lord, our God, is good; His love for us endures forever. Even when we doubt, even when we walk away, even when we get mad at Him, it does not affect His love for us. He remains steadfast in His love because of who He is, not depending on what we do for Him. His love for us endures forever and that in and of itself is enough to be in a constant state of thanksgiving. His faithfulness was not just in the past, but it is extended to all generations. Bless His name! Give thanks to Him and not just a 30-second blessing of thanks before your meal on Thursday, but truly give Him thanks. Have a heart of thanksgiving that lasts and endures past the fourth Thursday of November. How can you transform your heart into a *thanksgiving heart* that lasts year-round? How much time do you spend in grateful acknowledgment of the benefits, favors and blessings bestowed on you by God? How do you show thankfulness for the divine favor you receive from God? If a loved one is no longer with us to celebrate Thanksgiving with us, how can you still be thankful and draw close to God?

NOVEMBER 24

> "And when they could not find them, they dragged Jason and some of the brothers before the city authorities, shouting, 'These men who have turned the world upside down have come here also,'" Acts 17:6

Have you ever had a bad situation or been in a bad situation only for God to turn it into good? For instance, my wife was in an accident. A gentleman had a medical issue while driving and he plowed into her at a red light; it destroyed our car that we had only been able to drive for three months. While receiving treatment from that accident, an x-ray revealed a tumor that ended up being thyroid cancer. We were able to catch it in its early phase. Paul was preaching in Thessalonica. The Jews and Gentiles were outraged that this Jew was a member of the Nazarene Sect. They dragged Jason and his brothers into the coliseum when they could not find Paul. "These men have turned the world upside down and have come here also." This was not a positive statement. Jason and his brothers being arrested was not a good thing, but after being released, he was able to send Paul and Silas to Berea where they were better received. The Thessalonians liked the status quo. They did not want their lives to be turned upside down. But Jesus has a way of doing that with the people He met and with us. When He moves in our lives, it can seem as if we are in the ocean's waves and turned upside down. But look at what the Thessalonians were saying – this Jesus is turning the world upside down and his followers are continuing His work; they are messing up our security and our system of controls. I am comfortable and I want to remain comfortable. I want to remain in control. Is that you? Does God want to move in your life, but you are comfortable and in control? Does God have a different story for you? What part of your life are you comfortable and maintaining control over? What area of your life does God want to turn upside down, a blessing in your life? Is God asking you to invite people to church, forgive those who have wronged you, or help those in need? How does God want to use you? Is it like Paul, Silas, or Jason? Whose world does He want you to turn upside down for the sake of the Heavenly Kingdom?

NOVEMBER 25

> "and if he sins against you seven times in the day and turns to you seven times, saying, 'I repent,' you must forgive him." Luke 17:4

This time of the year, we begin to count our blessings and we usually count the material blessings that can be touched or the blessing of good health. How many of us think of the spiritual blessings that we are thankful for? We can be thankful that we are forgiven. God has promised to remove our sin from us as far as the East is from the West. East and West never meet; even when this was written and the world was thought to be flat, East and West never met. Nor in God's eyes does He see us with our sin, because we are forgiven. So, if we are forgiven by Him, how much more should we be *forgivers*, forgiving those who have hurt and wounded us? Peter wanted a limit on how many times we should forgive someone, but Jesus said if in one day someone sins against you and then asks to be forgiven, *YOU MUST FORGIVE HIM!* Jesus doesn't say you should or you need to – He says you *must*. But what about those who don't ask for forgiveness? In another passage, Jesus says we are to forgive them "seventy times seven times"; in another verse, Jesus says, "If a brother sins against us seven times a day and comes and repents, we must forgive." This is probably the hardest group of people to forgive, because when they don't see themselves as doing something wrong, then they can't or won't ask for forgiveness. What about those who have since passed away, but we are left here wounded and still in pain? Yes, we are to forgive them as well. They do not have to be around or even seek forgiveness for us to grant them forgiveness. It is in forgiveness that we break the bondage of the enemy. Forgiveness is more for your spiritual, mental, emotional and physical health than it is for the other person. Forgiveness is a one-person job, while reconciliation is a multi-person job. Who is it that you need to forgive? Why do you think you are withholding forgiveness? How can you work through that in order to forgive? If you are thankful that you are forgiven, forgive someone this week in return. Remember the Lord's prayer, "forgive me my trespasses as I forgive others." How many of your sins would still be forgiven if your grace were measured by the standard set by this prayer?

NOVEMBER 26

> Then Peter came up and said to him, 'Lord, how often will my brother sin against me and I forgive him? As many as seven times?' Jesus said to him, 'I do not say to you seven times, but seventy-seven times.'"
> Matthew 18:21-22

Remember yesterday's devotional where I mentioned that in other verses, Jesus commanded us to forgive? Yeah, this is one of those verses. Why do you think we need so many reminders? It is hard, being human. Why is it hard, especially when we want the same thing from others and from God? We are commanded to forgive. Jesus forgave wholeheartedly. He even forgave His killers as they were driving nails into His wrists. Peter, like most of us, assumed he understood, "Ok, ok, Jesus, I know what You're saying here. Yeah, we have to forgive, but how many times, like seven times seven is a Holy Number; it represents God, so is that a good number of times?" Peter probably thought pretty highly of himself for saying seven, but Jesus replied, "I do not say seven times, but 77 times." 77 is double Holy, double everything, magnified, so never-ending. In other words, you just need to keep on forgiving. Do you want God to stop forgiving you once He hits a certain amount of frustration with your sin? I am pretty sure all of us are past 77. I passed that before going to school! Forgiveness is a one-person job – your job! Forgiveness does not say, "The hurt you caused is okay" or "I am over the hurt," but rather it says, "I am no longer going to hold against you any harm or hurt you caused me." I love this saying that I heard about unforgiveness. "Unforgiveness is like drinking poison and wanting the other person to suffer." I believe everyone has someone they need to forgive, whether alive or already gone from the Earth. We may have someone we need to forgive and maybe for the seventy-eighth time. Who is the Holy Spirit bringing to your mind to forgive? This week, work on forgiveness and receive the freedom that comes from letting go of the hurt. How do you experience the freedom that God gives you? When you pray the Lord's prayer, do you really mean, "forgive me as I have forgiven others," or do you rush through it? How can you pray that line more intentionally?

NOVEMBER 27

> Many are the plans in the mind of a man, but it is the purpose of the LORD that will stand. Proverbs 19:21

I was raised in a blue-collar family with an old fashioned, blue-collar work ethic and planning; after college, the plan was to start a career, stay in that career and retire after thirty years in that career. I had a plan and it was a good plan. Then God showed up. What a rollercoaster ride it became when He did. Now, don't get me wrong, I wouldn't change it, but I have definitely lived out Proverbs 19:21, "Many are the plans in the mind of a man, but it is the purpose of the Lord that will stand." If I am honest with myself and you, the call to ministry started at a very early age. But I desired to have a wife and kids and in the Catholic Church, family and ministry were not possible simultaneously, so I became a teacher. Shortly after that, I was asked to be the youth minister (part-time) at our parish and grew a youth group from next to nothing to a pretty vibrant one, even reaching out to other denominations. After we left the Catholic Church, we joined a Bible teaching/believing nondenominational church and I was called to start a men's ministry there. Within doing men's ministry, I got the call to go to seminary, but after talking to extended family, they all thought I was foolish to leave teaching since I was fully vested in retirement (blue-collar thinking). It wasn't until they finally saw me teach and lead men that they saw God's calling on my life. Long story short, it wasn't until seven years after graduating from seminary that I left teaching (after 25 years) to do fulltime ministry. Throughout the whole path, I had my plans; my wife saw His plan even before the first youth minister job and others saw His calling on my life before I was willing to change my plans. No matter what my opinion was at the time, my calling into ministry was the purpose and plan of the Lord and is still standing. Looking back, I can see all the doors that He opened and closed. The trials, valleys and mountaintops that He led me through to be the pastor that I am today; the hurt and the healing that had to take place so I could better empathize with people going through trials and be willing to be His Hands to help heal and guide. When you are stubborn like me and say "No" two or three times (like Jonah), He brings back around the opportunity for you to get on board with His Will, His purpose. What purpose does God have for your life? Has He been steering you away from plans you made or have? What dreams or plans are you willing to lay aside for His Plan, His purpose for your life? How can you incorporate this verse's message into your prayer life to become aware of His purpose for you?

NOVEMBER 28

> Listen to advice and accept instruction, that you may gain wisdom in the future. Proverbs 19:20

How willing are you to receive advice? I recently had a phone call with my youngest son and he made a comment that when things don't work out the way he wanted and he reevaluates the situation, he will remember what his mom or I told him and he said, "You guys always seem to be right." Jokingly, I told him I never get tired of hearing that; but in all honesty, as a young man, he is trying to figure out life, which comes from trial and error. He now realizes that his mom and I have lived longer and had many more rounds of trials and errors and he is now willing to learn from those and not repeat our errors, but make new ones himself, not experienced by us. He is learning the wisdom Solomon is speaking about here in Proverbs 19:20. Solomon tells us to listen to advice and accept instruction, seek advice and instruction so that we will have knowledge and wisdom to accomplish what God calls us to do. We are created to be in fellowship, not only helping each other, but also instructing each other and sharing successes and failures in life. I've told my kids I'm trying to make the same mistakes my parents made, but to make new ones and hope that when they have kids, they do the same. Don't repeat a mistake; learn from ours and make new ones, because you are trying to be better. I hope my sons are better fathers and better spiritual leaders than I was. They can learn from my mistakes by listening to my advice and utilizing my wisdom, the wisdom I got from my dad, etc. When we think we have all the answers, it can become lonely, as it leaves no room for needing God. He is our ultimate source of wisdom and knowledge. If we don't allow the Holy Spirit to instruct, direct, or guide us, we will surely go off course. We need Him to be our spiritual and emotional compass, keeping us focused on God's Word and God's Will. Fear of the Lord is the beginning of wisdom and knowledge, but if we think we know the answers before the questions are asked, we minimize God and have an inaccurate view of Him, His Power and His Holiness. We can take for granted His omniscience, His divine knowledge over everything. Returning to the opening question, how willing are you to receive advice? When was the last time you sought the advice and guidance of the Holy Spirit? How can you realign your heart to the guidance and instruction of the Holy Spirit? What do you still have unanswered that you can seek the Holy Spirit for advice on? Are you willing to hear it and follow it?

NOVEMBER 29

What is desired in a man is steadfast love and a poor man is better than a liar. Proverbs 19:22

"All God wants is my money." Have you heard that or ever thought like that? Like God's checking account is low and He needs us to spot Him a few hundred dollars. God's true desire is for our hearts. In Hebrew, Solomon talks about loyalty and integrity. Living in love and integrity is what brings happiness. Solomon says that integrity and loyalty are what makes a person attractive. The word that Solomon used for *liar* is used in five other verses in Proverbs and they all relate to lying witnesses and falsely gaining wealth through lies and deception, especially falsely gaining wealth by lying under oath or in court. Rich people tend to lie to protect their wealth; thus, being poor is better than being a liar. Wealthy people tend to be greedy, thus they are the opposite of loyal and loving. When you have integrity, you tend to draw people to you. People are attracted to loyalty, integrity, love and compassion. Thus, it would be better to be poor and keep your integrity, thus attracting people to you, than to be wealthy and alone, whom no one trusts. If God has your heart, then it shows and is demonstrated by your love and compassion for others and your desire to help others is worth far more than someone of wealth promising to help and not following through. How do I get integrity and compassion out of this verse? That is one problem with the poorness of the English language. We have such few words to use in context. In looking at different translations of this verse, you get all of these sayings, but neither the meaning nor the application are contradictory. This proverb is in a long list of proverbs that fall under "the fear of the Lord is the beginning of understanding, the beginning of wisdom." Thus, what is desired of a man who fears the Lord is a steadfast love for God, God's creation and God's children. From that flows compassion, generosity, willingness to help and integrity. Solomon and scholars tend to paint rich, wealthy people with broad strokes, but don't we see this truth even in today's world? Why do we lie to protect our finances? What is the Holy Spirit challenging you with today's verse and application? How can you become more of a Christian defined by Godly integrity, compassion and love? As we head into the Christmas season, how can you better show steadfast love to others?

NOVEMBER 30

> Laughter can conceal a heavy heart, but when the laughter ends, the grief remains. Proverbs 14:13 NLT

Robin Williams is one of my favorite comedic actors. I could never get into his standup because of the foul language, but I loved how he brought characters to life and how funny he was doing interviews, whether it was with Johnny Carson or Jay Leno, etc. His suicide was a shock to the world; his humor was used as a facade, a mask to hide the grief and depression he suffered on the inside. Solomon warns us here, "Laughter can conceal a heavy heart, but when the laughter ends, the grief remains." Like makeup that conceals skin blemishes, laughter just conceals grief. It doesn't fix it, heal it, or remove it; laughter just conceals the heaviness of a heart. The remedy is the Holy Spirit, being honest with Him and allowing Him to comfort and heal us. I don't know about most, but at least for me, as a man, I try to fix everything. I have had to come to the hard understanding that I cannot fix everything. I cannot fix my wife when she is hurting; I cannot fix my kids when they are in trouble. I cannot fix everything about myself. I need help with my flaws. I believe that is why God says marriage completes His image. I believe it is why He created both male and female and within our very DNA He created us to long for fellowship. We are not meant to do life alone. We are created for community. "It takes a village to raise a child" supports that very concept. Laughter is good for the soul. Laughter has been medically proven to be healthy. Laughing releases endorphins in the brain that, in turn, reduce stress in the body. If you have gone to a good comedy show or movie and laughed a lot, you probably felt better because it strengthens the immune system. Laughter is good when it is used as medicine and not as a concealer. We must be honest with ourselves and when we are not emotionally healthy, we must seek professional help. I'll admit I seek humor first, but if that does not have lasting help, then I know to seek other help. God has given us the knowledge to use natural and manmade medicines; it is not a sign of weakness to seek those. With the holiday season approaching, grief and depression tend to invite themselves in. Allow the Holy Spirit to direct and guide you to what your body needs. There is no reason to allow grief to remain, stealing your joy. What do you do when you encounter grief or deal with depression? What helps you the most? Who has the Holy Spirit brought into your life to walk with you through these seasons? How can you allow the Holy Spirit to fulfill His title of the Comforter?

DECEMBER 1

> For in this hope we were saved. Now hope that is seen is not hope. For who hopes for what he sees? Romans 8:24

What is hope? The Oxford dictionary defines it as, "a feeling of expectation and desire for a certain thing to happen," while dictionary.com defines it as, "to look forward to it with desire and reasonable confidence." No matter the worldly definition of *hope*, we can agree that it is future forward looking for something to happen or someone to come through. As we begin the journey towards Christmas, the first theme of Advent is hope. There is a lot of Scripture about hope and Biblical giants of the faith that had hope, but why is it the first theme of Advent? Paul says it here in Romans 8:24, "For in this hope we were saved." Advent is the tradition of expectancy, forward looking to celebrating the birth of Christ. He is our hope and our salvation. Paul continues, "Now hope that is seen is not hope, for who hopes for what he sees?" When we place our faith in Christ, we are saved, but how is He also our hope? Our hope is in His return, which we cannot see. That hope is inspired by the promise of when He returns in His full glory and removes all sin and death. We hope that our loved ones are there in Heaven when we die, waiting to be reunited with us. Our hope is that all pain, all disease and all suffering are gone; as believers, we will be in His Full Presence, eternally worshiping. Again, as we celebrate Advent and look forward to the upcoming Christmas holiday, celebrating the coming of the Christ Child, we have hope. Paul says in verse 25 that while we hope, we patiently wait for it. As a child, I never had patience when it came to Christmas. My brother and I would stay up all night, ready at three, four and five o'clock in the morning to open presents. As an adult, much of that excitement and expectation has died down. Why? Why are we not as excited about Christmas anymore? Where is our hope? What have we placed our hope in? These next four weeks, prepare your heart and your soul for Christmas. Look for the hope that Jesus promises, the hope Jesus brings with His Presence. We find joy when celebrating with excitement and expectations, hope for the presence of the Hope of the World to make His Presence known in His present to *all Believers* – eternal life. Where does your hope lie? What gives you hope? What kills your hope? How can you allow the Holy Spirit to keep a hold of your Hope, so that nothing kills or diminishes it?

DECEMBER 2

> What shall we say then? Are we to continue in sin that grace may abound? By no means! How can we who died to sin still live in it?
> Romans 6:1-2

If your child always wanted a certain, expensive toy, but when you bought it for them, they destroyed it, would you buy it for them again? Let's say that because your child really wanted this toy, you bought them another one and then they ruined the toy again. Would you continue to buy that toy, or any toy, for that child after a while? Paul is asking the same question regarding the gift of grace. The act of forgiveness and grace from God comes from His abundant love for us – a love so strong that He sent His son Jesus to die on the cross so that sin would no longer keep us separate from Him. God did not send Jesus to die for our sins so that we could enjoy a sinful life. The idea that we can keep sinning because of grace and forgiveness shows neither an understanding, nor an appreciation of the gift of grace and forgiveness. This false belief actually denied their identity in Christ. By no means could it be translated, God forbid. God does not permit this and it's not His heart. Grace does not increase when we purposely choose to participate in the same sinful lifestyle. Paul is talking about experiencing no conviction when we sin, no recognition of it separating us from God. This goes beyond failing to deny temptation and committing a sin; this is the idea that because of grace, I can sin as much as I want because God forgives sin. Sin separates us from God. That is why Jesus came and died, to forgive us of our sins and remove that separation from God and us. Just because God loves us and wants to forgive us does not give us permission to keep violating His rules and violating His love for us. Suppose we love God and have a relationship with Him. In that case, we should be avoiding the same temptation, denying selfish desires and living our lives so they are aligned with the life of Christ. We do this by allowing the Holy Spirit to live in us, giving us direction and guidance and instruction. When we are baptized, it symbolizes us dying to the sinful nature and raising back up in a new life, born again of Spirit. How, then, as Paul asks, can we continue to live in sin if we have died to sin? Grace increases when we show our appreciation for *the gift* and use it appropriately. Is there a sin issue that you continue to struggle with? How can you allow the Holy Spirit to free you from those chains? How does the concept of God's Grace impact how you live? Now that you have been given the gift of grace – who is it in your life that you need to extend grace to? How can you help them experience the freedom that comes from living and resting under God's grace?

DECEMBER 3

> For who is the greater, one who reclines at table or one who serves? Is it not the one who reclines at the table? But I am among you as the one who serves. Luke 22:27

I have heard many Christians, pastors and theologians describe God's economy as "an upside-down economy." Why is that? Upside-down just doesn't make sense; but that is why it is the perfect description of God's economy, "it doesn't make sense." According to the world, it doesn't make sense. He doesn't call the qualified. He qualifies those He calls. In Matthew 20:16, Jesus told them, "The first shall be last and the last shall be first." He took twelve ordinary men and turned the world upside down. To do that, God left Heaven and came to Earth and living and leading the kind of life He wants us to live. For who is greater, the one at the table, or the one who serves? Naturally, we would all say the one at the table, the one being served, definitely not the server! Jesus knew how we would answer, "The one at the table?" But Jesus says I am among you, yet I serve, so you must serve others. We are called to live a life contrary or perpendicular to the world, turning worldly wisdom upside down. When we serve, we parallel our lives to reflect the life of Jesus. By doing so, we get to know Him at a deeper level. How can that be? I have never served where I have not been blessed and felt the Holy Spirit's presence within me. You can't do God's Will and be out of His Presence. You can't live your life according to His Will and not be blessed. See, you just can't escape His Presence, most of all, when you are following Him. Yes, we are called to sacrifice and walk down the narrow path of hardship that He walked for us and Jesus said we are storing up for ourselves treasures in Heaven, but He will bless you here, too. We just have to be careful of our definition of *blessings*. While I have not been blessed financially per se, I have been blessed by His Presence almost every time, if not every time. I have been blessed by friendships, deep Christian, loving friendships. Jesus led by example. Jesus served. Jesus served people others thought were unworthy. Who are you called to serve this week? Don't serve for an expected blessing, but serve because of His blessing on your life. Serve because He is calling you to. Is it a neighbor that needs yard work done or a coworker that needs a friend? Pray today and ask Holy Spirit where is God calling you to serve this week? Who is He calling you to serve? How much time are you willing to give the Holy Spirit to direct you in this matter?

DECEMBER 4

"Servants, be subject to your masters with all respect, not only to the good and gentle but also to the unjust." 1 Peter 2:18

Servant is defined as, "A person who serves; serves at the will of someone over them." Here, in America, at least in "polite company," as it's said, "We don't condone slavery," and that is who Peter is talking to. Peter is writing to believers who are in servanthood. While we may not be in the same situation as the first church believers, we are servants, slaves of Christ. Some had good masters and owners, but a lot did not and Peter was writing to both groups. No matter what kind of master or owner you have, this is what you are called to do. Students have classes, so they have teachers over them. Adults have jobs, which means they have employers and bosses over them. No matter who is over us, as Christians, we are called to respect them. It is counter-cultural thinking; the world says respect must be earned, but Peter says that as a child of the Living God, you must give respect. This doesn't mean think about or possibly give respect. You must respect them. Peter, knowing the condition of the human heart, reminds these Believers and us, that we are to respect not only the good and gentle supervisors, but also those who are unjust, mean, or unapproachable. As servants, we should see and look for every opportunity to show that respect. If they need assistance with something, our question should not be, "Should I do this?" but rather, "Why shouldn't I do this?" Going back to the early '90s, we should ask ourselves, "What Would Jesus Do?" Now, this is not a call to be a doormat, but more of a call to be in tune with the Holy Spirit and the battle between flesh and spirit. By asking the second set of questions above, we tune into the Holy Spirit and see if God wants us to serve there. We have to transform our thinking to God's upside-down, counter-cultural economy, so we can be His light shining in a dark world. How can you transform your mind on a daily basis so that the Holy Spirit is the driver and your flesh is in the back seat? In other words, how can you allow the Holy Spirit to be the pilot of your life and you become just the passenger? This week, who are you called to be a servant to and show respect? What is it that God is asking you to do? How will you do God's Will, applying God's Word in your life?

DECEMBER 5

> Now may the Lord of peace himself give you peace at all times in every way. The Lord be with you all. 2 Thessalonians 3:16

What is peace and do you have it? What is your source of peace? Peace is defined as freedom from violent conflict and freedom from the fear of violence. No matter what the situation is, if we walk with the Lord, He will give us His peace, a peace that surpasses all understanding. Paul also states that when He gives us peace, it will be for all times and in every way. He wants us to live in the freedom that comes from His peace. He offers us emotional peace, physical peace, spiritual peace. Emotionally we can live a life free from emotional violence and conflict when our hearts are surrendered to Him. When we are attacked verbally or emotionally, we have the ability to choose conflict or peace, how we react or respond. When you lose a job, a loved one, or get a report from the doctor, you can choose emotional conflict or emotional peace. It all depends on what we set our eyes on. Are you focused on the Holy Spirit? What or who do we have in the crosshairs – the situation or the Savior? If we focus on the situation, we are setting ourselves up for emotional, mental and possibly spiritual conflict. But if we set our focus on the Holy Spirit, we can have emotional, mental and spiritual peace when we face any situation. As we approach the holiday seasons, pandemics coming and going, fears rising, society splitting and allowing hate to reign over our lives, we need to shift the crosshairs off of the situations and onto the Holy Spirit and His Presence in our life. If you are feeling down, seek the presence of the Holy Spirit. If you are overwhelmed, talk with the Holy Spirit. If you are feeling lost, return to, turn back and come back to the very Presence of God and He will give you peace. He will give rest to our souls and ease all our anxieties, if we would just truly seek Him first. May the peace of God that surpasses all understanding be with you today and every day! How do you experience the peace of God? How do you allow the Holy Spirit to fill you with His peace when life gets confusing or hard? How can you turn emotional or spiritual conflict into prayer and peace with the Holy Spirit, allowing God to fight battles for you?

DECEMBER 6

> O Lord, you will ordain peace for us, for you have indeed done for us all our works. Isaiah 26:12

What brings you peace of mind? Is it a certain amount in your bank accounts or stocks and bonds? Is it an insurance policy or retirement fund? Isaiah says the Lord "will ordain for us peace." Peace, true peace, only comes from the Lord. Our future is bright, because salvation belongs only to the Lord. That is what the Study Bible commentary says about this verse. All we have accomplished is really from You God. God allows situations to occur. The Holy Spirit equips us, empowers us and directs us, so we can accomplish God's will. The Holy Spirit gives us peace and provides a path to follow and a light to guide us in the darkness. There is no conflict or hostility within us when we accomplish everything through the Lord, through the Holy Spirit. His Peace settles our minds, which is the battlefield of the enemy. His Peace quiets the conflicts in our spirits. Jesus is the only way – salvation is only found through Him, His ultimate sacrifice. His sacrifice could not be made if He had not come down as man, fully God, but also fully human, to live a perfect life and to die a sinful death so we could have restoration with God, salvation for our souls. He, who knew no sin, committed no sin, became sin so that we could have the righteousness of God, salvation and eternity with Him. As we celebrate Advent, looking forward to the celebration of the manger birth, it's not only the birth of Jesus, but also His Peace that He brings and everything He has accomplished for us. Christmas, Easter and Communion are all tied together – you can't celebrate one without the other two. What has God accomplished in your life? What do you want Him to accomplish this Christmas in your life? What area in your life do you need His Peace to settle into? What can you do this Christmas season to look towards the manger and not to the busyness and demanding side of Christmas?

DECEMBER 7

> And the peace of God, which surpasses all understanding, will guard your hearts and your minds in Christ Jesus. Philippians 4:7

What are you willing to wait for? I remember seeing on TV people lining up outside stores on Thanksgiving afternoon, waiting for Black Friday sales to start. Mervyns had an ad campaign with people waiting outside saying, "Open, Open," like they had magic powers to open the door, they were expectantly waiting for their store to open. Advent, the season we are in, is defined as expectant waiting, the anticipation of the arrival of nobility. Are you waiting on nobility, for nobility, or waiting for the season to be over, or for a tree stuffed at the bottom with presents? We are in the season of Advent, a season of waiting and one of the themes of Advent is Peace. God's Peace, Paul says here, "The peace of God exceeds all understanding." His peace will stand guard over our hearts and minds as we live our lives for our savior Jesus, who we are expectantly waiting for (Christmas being the celebration of His birth). The Prince of Peace? Peace means, "The absence of hostility and violence; no conflict." The more I focus on God and His Presence in my life and walk according to His Will, the conflict and fear that tries to take place in my mind disappears. It is when I walk out of His Hand and try to do things my way that conflict and hostility converge in my mind and bring fear and disturbance. Is it the same for you? As we expectantly await the celebration of the birth of our Savior, Jesus, the real reason for this season, let us focus on the Peace of God, the Prince of Peace, being born. Let us examine our lives. If the peace of God is not residing there, we must evict the fear and hostility and allow God to guide and guard our hearts and minds. What fears do you need to evict or kill with extreme prejudice in your mind? What infiltration from the enemy is occupying space that the Holy Spirit wants to be able to occupy in your mind? What can you do to experience more of the peace of God?

DECEMBER 8

> Peace I leave with you; my peace I give to you. Not as the world gives do I give to you. Let not your hearts be troubled, neither let them be afraid. John 14:27

As we have seen, one of the themes of Advent is Peace. It is a Godly peace and a peace that surpasses all understanding. The Gift of Christmas is *Jesus* Himself. But in John 14:27, Jesus leaves us a gift – the gift of Peace. This is a supernatural gift: Peace of Mind, Peace of Heart, the peace that replaces worry, the peace that replaces fear. God, throughout the Old Testament, told us "Do not be afraid." Jesus echoes that here – "Do not be afraid or troubled. Rest in My Peace." This divine peace is a tranquil state of the soul that fears nothing and is content with whatever they have here on Earth. His Peace allows the mind to maintain its composure during trials and difficult times. His Peace protects our hearts and minds against invasive worldly ideals and fears. Jesus says, "I give not as the world gives." He does not give to cause you to stumble or fail. He does not give out of resistance and being forced to. He gives us His Peace because He loves us. It's been told and posted that God says in the Bible do not be afraid or filled with fear 365 times, a ratio equivalent to a verse for every day of the year. The enemy loves to utilize fear to drive a wedge between God and us; that is why He repeatedly tells us not to be afraid. When we take our eyes off of the Light, we see darkness – that is where fear resides. If we are looking into the shadows, then the light is behind us. All we have to do to not be looking into the darkness, the shadows, is to turn around and face the light. Light casts out and pushes away the darkness. With all the bad news in the world, His Peace is needed even more and how much more do we need His Peace this holiday season? What area of your life is out-of-sorts and needs peace? What is troubling your heart this Christmas? Are you willing to let go of it, hand it over to the Holy Spirit and allow Him to bring you comfort and heal that hurt? How can you experience the gift of His Peace this Advent and Christmas season?

DECEMBER 9

"Every good gift and every perfect gift is from above, coming down from the Father of lights, with whom there is no variation or shadow due to change." James 1:17

Remember that perfect Christmas gift that you wanted? Waiting in expectation of that morning and praying and hoping it was there. My perfect gift didn't fit under the tree and one year my brother and I got that desired gift to share – a dirt bike! The excitement was uncontainable and neither of us slept all Christmas Eve. James reminds us that every good and perfect gift is from above. My brother and I thought my parents got us the perfect gift. As a child, I thought like a child. But the reason we celebrate is because the Father of Lights, who never changes, gave us His Good and perfect gift. He gave us His all – Jesus Christ. Not only was Jesus the only good person to ever live, but He was also the only perfect person to ever live. With God, there is no variation or shadow. His good and perfect gifts never change. We need to take time to slow down, take in the aroma of the season, the music of the season and take in the reason for the season. I believe it's time for me and most of us to share and give away that perfect gift. Give the gift of God's love, God's grace, God's mercy and God's forgiveness. You have one week. Pray about it – ask God to give you the name of someone you could bless this Christmas by giving the gifts of love, mercy, grace and forgiveness to them. As the one giving the gift, you will be more blessed than the one receiving it – that I can promise. How can you focus this Christmas season on sharing the perfect gift of God's Love? What can you do to experience God's gift of grace this Christmas? How can God's gift of mercy affect how you celebrate this Christmas?

DECEMBER 10

> Clap your hands, all peoples! Shout to God with loud songs of joy!
> Psalm 47:1

Worship was really different when we left the Catholic Church and joined a large nondenominational church in town. I struggled with the praise and worship part of the service. I eventually got to where I would clap if others were clapping and raise my hands when others would raise theirs; but then the Holy Spirit started challenging me to do it on my own, not in sync with others and I wrestled with the Holy Spirit over this for a couple of years. It was at youth camp where as an adult sponsor that I finally broke the stronghold of pride that was holding me back. How do you praise God, I mean, actually *praise* Him? Do you make a joyful noise or clap your hands? Do you raise your arms like you are reaching out to Him? In 2 Samuel 6, David was worshiping God with everything he had, dancing and leaping. His wife, Michal, was embarrassed and despised him for it. David replies in verses 21b - 22, "I will celebrate before the Lord, I will make myself more undignified than this, I will be humiliated in my own eyes." David lost himself in the joy of exalting God for all He has done. There is no end to the glories! Look at all that God has done. He stepped out of Heaven, was born of the flesh, to remind us that we were created in His image and we can follow and trust in Him. Then, in the craziest plan ever conceived, He lived a perfect life only to die a sinner's death – for who? He died for those who hated Him then and for those who will hate Him, you and me, throughout all time. Then He rose on Sunday morning, conquering death forever. Doesn't that deserve a shout and a clap? How about inspiring us to raise our hands or make a joyful noise? Worship is not just for the people on the platform leading the songs, but it is a lifestyle we, as Christians, must learn to adopt. How can you magnify your praise to Jesus, to God this Christmas season to change your heart about worship, so it becomes a lifestyle of joyful praise? How does your lifestyle exemplify a life of worship? How much are you willing to be like David and become "more undignified" than this, allowing the Holy Spirit to free you so you can worship freely?

DECEMBER 11

Indeed, all who desire to live a godly life in Christ Jesus will be persecuted, 2 Timothy 3:12

My favorite line I tell students I mentor is, "Jesus never said pick up your recliner and remote control and follow me." Unfortunately, there are some pastors who preach that God wants you to be happy, healthy and wealthy. While God wants us to be happy and more joy filled, He not only warns us, but also commands us to pick up our cross and follow Him. Let us take a serious look at what Jesus meant when He said to "pick up our cross". The cross he is talking about is not the kind we wear around our neck or carry in our pocket. It is not a sticker we put on our bumper or a tattoo we have on our arm or chest. The cross He was talking about, His cross was the death penalty, a symbol of suffering. He is telling us we must daily die to self, die on our cross and allow the Will of God to direct our lives and our decisions. The Will of God and not the will of Joseph should determine what I do, how I do it and who I do it for. Jesus warned us that it would not be easy. Jesus told us that if He were persecuted, we would face it as well. American Christians, I think, tend to equate salvation with blessings and an easy life. We live in a free society and the only persecution we face is being called names, talked bad about, or maybe in the extreme, the loss of a job; but Believers in other countries face persecution as the apostles did, including death, mutilation, or imprisonment. No matter where we live, if we live out our faith, we will face some kind of persecution. Like James' says, we should count it all joy when we are persecuted for our faith. If we are not facing persecution and trials for our faith, do we really have active faith? Are we really living it out? Do others around you know you are a Christian based on your words, actions and decisions? If you do not face persecution or trials of some sort, you need to evaluate how you live out your faith. God has given us other Believers and the Holy Spirit to help us stand tall during these trials and we are never alone. God will never leave us, so we can count on these blessings during our trials and persecutions. I pray for God to bless you and have His Hand of protection on you as you live out your faith. This Advent, this Christmas, how are you living out your faith? What trials are you facing and how can you count them as joy for the Lord?

DECEMBER 12

> Know this, my beloved brothers: let every person be quick to hear, slow to speak, slow to anger; for the anger of man does not produce the righteousness of God. James 1:19-20

Do you have a short fuse? Do you experience triggers that will cause you to shift from a good mood to instantly a bad mood when something is said or done a certain way? For me, it is disrespect; it is just something I struggle to deal with kindly when I see it in others. I can be having a good day, but if I am disrespected, it can set me off and I have to calm down from being disrespected to return to a good mindset… James, while writing to fellow Believers (that includes us), says to be "quick to hear, slow to speak and slow to anger." We need to be able to extinguish any fuse we have before it causes us to explode. Why is that? When we are quick to speak and *quick* to anger, it does nothing to show the presence of the Holy Spirit in us, nor does it produce God's righteousness in us. James continues after that verse to tie unrighteous anger with wickedness, "Therefore put away all filthiness and rampant wickedness and receive with meekness the implanted word, which is able to save your souls. Be doers of the word and not just hearers only, deceiving yourself." When you let unrighteous anger rule in your life, I mean anger controlled by emotion and not the Will of God, then you are not living out your relationship with God, not listening and following the Holy Spirit; you may actually impede the Gospel message! James connects unrighteousness with wickedness and filthiness. When we are quick to speak and quick to anger, we are allowing our emotions to control us instead of us controlling our emotions. When we are quick to speak, we are not really listening to the other person; we react and do not respond. Reacting is out of emotion while responding requires thought, control, facts and not emotions. Responding also takes into account that hurting people will hurt people. If we are quick to speak, we are not taking the time to see where the person is coming from and what is actually behind the words that they are saying. When we are quick to anger, how can anyone possibly see God's love in us? What should cause anger in our lives? How about when God is used as a weapon of hate, or people abuse God's word and gifts or misrepresent God… When we follow Jesus' example of what caused Him to get angry, righteous anger, that does not cause us to sin. We are called to love as God loves us; how is that demonstrated when you are quick to anger? How is that displayed when we are so quick to speak that the other person is not heard or even interrupted? When we do that, we are basically saying, "What I have to say is more important than what you have to say." How does that display the love of God? How does that produce the righteousness of God in our lives? How good are you at being quick to hear and quick to fully listen to what the other person is saying? How well do you do at being slow to speak? How can you improve that so the other person is validated and you can extend the love of God to them by actively listening to them? How well are you at being slow to anger? What can you do to improve this area of your life? How can you learn to respond in love and not react emotionally? How do you see being slow to speak and slow to anger as connected with being a doer of God's Word and not just a hearer of God's word?

DECEMBER 13

> You make known to me the path of life; in your presence there is fullness of joy; at your right hand are pleasures forevermore. Psalm 16:11

When it comes time to pray, do you prepare and specifically set aside time just for being alone with God in prayer? When you pray, do you pray with a list and if so, what does your list look like? It doesn't have to be a selfish list; praying for others is always a good thing. But is the first thing on our list His Presence? David writes here, "Grant me the joy of your presence." What brings you joy? Joy – It's such a simple word. It is also a word that is used a lot in Christianity, as in "Joy to the World," or Love, *joy*, peace, etc. But what is joy? The dictionary definition is "a feeling of great pleasure, to rejoice." If we are honest with ourselves, do we find great pleasure in being in the presence of the Lord? If the answer is yes, then we spend a lot of time being in the presence of the Lord, reading His word, praying, listening, worshiping and even serving Him. But I am a busy person. My ADHD kicks in and I am off chasing something shiny, looking for the source of a noise, or going through a to-do list that does not include prayer. Even still, Jesus is the Way of Life. He said, "I am the way, the truth and the life," so it is in Him we find the Way of Life. I know for me, personally, I need to start my prayer by enjoying being in His Presence and I am starting to. For me, that means I am slowing down, not rushing around and taking time to just sit and enjoy the world that God created. We should enjoy and be thankful for the family and friends that He has brought into our lives. Now that I have rediscovered the joy of being in His presence again when the world throws a trial at me, the joy of His presence carries me through it. So, I ask again, when we pray, or when you pray, what does it look like? A lot of us probably answer family or friends, but Jesus needs to be number one in our hearts and in our lives, not taking second place to anyone, not even our spouses, kids, families, or friends. It's a mixed-up, upside-down plan that does not make a whole lot of sense. But in reality, can we truly love others if we do not love God with all of our strength, in our hearts, minds and souls? Joy should first come from being in His Presence. We need to make Him more of a priority in our lives. When we do, the joy of the Lord can help us overcome any obstacle, barrier, or loss that we could face. It also makes it possible to walk His path, His Way, in His Will for us. Jesus is the Way of Life and joy comes from being in His Presence. What can you do to feel the joy of His presence in your life? What area of your life do you need to free up to rediscover the joy of living in His Presence? What can wait so that you can pray, read, worship and live in the joy of His Presence? How will you make being in His Presence more of a priority?

DECEMBER 14

> "Be kind to one another, tenderhearted, forgiving one another, as God in Christ forgave you." Ephesians 4:32

I don't know about other places in the world, but I know that here in America, as Christians, we can easily forget what life was like without God's forgiveness. We can be a Christian for so long that we forget what it was or is that we are saved from. Paul tells the church at Ephesus and us, that we are to forgive others as Christ forgave us. How did Christ forgive? He did it with everything He had. He held nothing back so that all sins could be forgiven, not just some, or up to a certain number of times to be forgiven. We are called to be kind and tenderhearted. Tenderhearted means, "loving, being moved by compassion." When we go back and read the Gospel accounts and look at how Jesus dealt with the lost and the sinners and then compare it to how He responded to those who were religious and had a righteous air about them, we see how Jesus was moved with compassion to the lost; but with the righteous religious people, He judged with harsh words. Why is that? The religious should have known better. They knew the Word of God and thus should have known the heart of God. The prostitute caught in the act, the woman at the well, the crippled man at the pool, the blind, deaf and mute – Jesus was kind and tenderhearted towards them all. His example to us is ultimately forgiving and loving. Christ appeals to our troubled hearts, "Go and sin no more. I know about everything in your life, but I will still give you living water." He stopped what He was doing to heal hurt and sick people and when people touched Him to be healed, He blessed them instead of reacting defensively or out of anger. The religious he called "a brood of vipers, a decorated tomb, dead on the inside and no knowledge of God, only about God." If anyone should have known the heart of God, it should have been the priests, rabbis and Pharisees who studied and memorized the Word of God. We have to forgive others and allow those who are seeking Him to come to Him as they are; they don't need to change clothes or get their life on the right path before coming to church. We truly need to return to the idea of being a hospital for the sick, not a place for the righteous to gather and pat themselves on the back. The church should not be a place where people compare how better off they are than others. The ground is level at the foot of the cross and we have all fallen short of the glory of God. That is why Jesus had to come save us, because no matter how we try to measure ourselves up to the law, we always fall short. Advent and Christmas are not only perfect times to start inviting friends to church, but also to reevaluate and see if we, ourselves, have lost the first gift of Christmas – Love. "For God so *loved* the World…" Rediscover that first Christmas Gift! Love like God loves you! Who is it that you need to be kind to? Who is the Holy Spirit calling you to be tenderhearted, moved by compassion to? Christmas is the gift of love and because of love, we are forgiven. Who is the Holy Spirit challenging you to forgive?

DECEMBER 15

> I have told you these things so that you will be filled with my joy. Yes, your joy will overflow! John 15:11 NLT

Advent comes from the Latin word *adventus*, meaning "coming," which was translated from the Greek word *Parousia*, meaning "coming" or "arrival." It is the time of the year that we should start to prepare our hearts for the coming or arrival of the Messiah. Peace is one of the themes of Advent. Joy is another theme of Advent, but it is not a worldly definition, meaning "gladness, elation, or cheerfulness." Christ calls us to be filled with His joy and to be filled so much that we are overflowing with His joy. In the previous verses, Jesus tells his disciples that once they are grafted in like a vine, they will bear fruit; but pruning is a necessary task to yielding more high-quality fruits. Pruning allows for healthy plant life and a better, healthy end result. But His joy is not Earthly joy, it is Heavenly joy. When you are in close connection with God and living out God's Will in your life, His joy becomes our joy and our joy will overflow. So, when the pruning process starts, His joy is already within us. It's not about possessions or health or position. It's about walking with the Lord on a daily basis. "The joy of the Lord is our strength." It was joy that gave Him the ability to face the judgment of Pilate, the scourging, the crucifixion. The disciples were filled with His joy to the point of being beaten and they left the beatings rejoicing. Paul was filled so much with the joy of the Lord that when He was in prison and an earthquake shook open the doors and opened the shackles on his hands and feet that he remained in prison singing, overflowing with the joy of the Lord. Ever meet someone whom the world would just seem to pass over, but whose joy was so overflowing that it was overwhelming and contagious? That is the word picture Jesus is trying to paint here. Paul's joy was so overflowing and so contagious that the head of the prison and his entire family came to know Jesus. Yes, there will be trials, but there will also be harvests. Yes, we will have successes, but we will also have droughts. No matter what comes our way, if we are closely walking with Jesus, we can patiently endure and still have joy, because we know whose Hand is holding it all. Are you filled with His Joy? Is His Joy overflowing from you and contagious and overwhelming? How is His joy different from the world's joy? How can you make changes so this describes your walk with the Lord? How can you be more filled with the joy of the Lord?

DECEMBER 16

> For God did not send his Son into the world to condemn the world, but in order that the world might be saved through him. John 3:17

We have all probably seen the signs hanging behind the football goal posts, behind the basket at basketball games on TV, of people holding up signs for John 3:16 – "For God so *LOVED* the world that He gave His only son so that whoever believes in Him shall not perish, but have eternal life." Most Christians probably have that verse memorized and it is a good verse to have memorized, but many don't know the following verse well. "For God did not send His Son into the world to condemn the world, but to save the world and save it through Him." God desires that everyone should be saved, He wants everyone to come home to Heaven, but He will not force them, nor force Himself on them. That is the great thing about free will. He gives us free will as a gift, so we can choose whether or not we love Him, whether or not we go to our Heavenly home. But we must remember – only God is allowed to judge. As Christians, we need to get out of the habit of kicking God out of the judgment seat and sitting in His judgment seat ourselves. There is a difference between holding Believers accountable and judging Believers and Nonbelievers. Gandhi said he likes Christ, but not Christians. He even said, "If it weren't for Christians, I'd be a Christian," when he was turned away upon trying to attend church to learn about Jesus, because he was neither white, nor an upper-class Indian. The church really should be like a hospital for the sick and not a museum for saints. We don't wait until we get better before going to see a doctor, nor should we expect people to get their lives in order before coming to church. They shouldn't have to go get new clothes to come to church. They shouldn't have to conquer their addiction before coming to church. Jesus himself said, "If you are well, you don't need a doctor. I came for the sick." So, especially this time of the year, as we come to celebrate and remember the arrival of our Savior, we need to remember to extend grace and love and invitations and maybe even forgiveness, so no one misses out on the first gift of Christmas – LOVE! Penn, from the famous magicians Penn and Teller, asks a poignant question, "How much do you have to hate someone not to tell them about Jesus?" I would add to that, "How much do we have to hate someone to exclude them from church because of the way they dress or their lifestyle?" This Christmas, whom do you need to share the love of Christ with? What do your words and actions say about your faith, or your relationship with Jesus? This Christmas, how can you extend the love of Christ to others? How can you apply this verse to the Christmas season? How can you apply this verse to your life?

DECEMBER 17

> Instead, seek his kingdom and these things will be added to you.
> Luke 12:31

What do we typically do first each day? Is it taking a shower, brushing our teeth, making coffee, reading the newspaper or watching TV? What do we put our creative energies into? What gets the majority of our attention? Jesus says that if we seek the Kingdom of God above all else, God, our loving Father, will give us all that we need! What is the *Kingdom of God*? It's when we choose to do God's Will. It is allowing Jesus to reside inside us and allowing the Holy Spirit to guide us in our words, actions, thoughts and desires. When we do that, in our jobs, our school work, our social lives, family lives and friends will be better. But let's not forget this second part and ensure we do not misinterpret it. God will give us everything we need, which is not to say that God will give us everything we want. Nor does Jesus say that seeking the Kingdom of God is easy. We need transportation to get to school and work, but does it need to be the newest model car that is fully decked out with all the latest gizmos and toys? We need food, but do we have to eat steak and lobster to be happy? Do we need to eat out and not cook or stay home for meals? God loves us and He wants to bless us, but He also wants us to use those blessings to reach others and above all, He wants a relationship with us and not one of a prayer request vending machine. What He wants from us is a real, honest, growing relationship where we allow Him to also speak to us and when we talk it's not always asking for something, but it is being grateful. This weekend how can you deepen your seeking of the Kingdom of God? What is it in your life that falls under need and not want, that you can be thankful for? Allow God into all aspects of your life, including work, play, friendships, business, family and let Him bless each area of life you allow Him in! Think of it this way, have you ever had something either really important or really needed and couldn't find it? Like maybe your car keys, glasses, or password to your online accounts? It can be frustrating looking for something and not being able to find it. Right? Then, someone points them out or hands them to you and you are good to go! Jesus here tells us, above all else, to seek God and His Kingdom and His Will above all else and He will give us everything we need. He doesn't say "everything we want" – just everything we *need*. This Christmas, are you seeking the Kingdom of God first, or are you too busy with shopping, baking, mailing and wrapping? How much time do you give to God and His Kingdom every day during the day? We need to remember to seek Him first. But remember my example at the beginning? We were seeking something and someone else pointed it out to us. Have you helped anyone seek the Kingdom of God yet? Like when we are frantically looking for something and someone points to them or gives it to us – so should we be helping people find the Kingdom of God, so He can fill those holes in hearts, heal broken spirits and comfort hurting souls. He wants to reveal Himself to everyone, but like the glasses on our head or the car keys on the table, some need help being pointed in the right direction or redirected, realigned to the living and active Kingdom of God. We have 7 days a week to help others seek the Kingdom of God and it can be as simple as paying for the person in front of or behind you in a restaurant line, or having a conversation with the Salvation Army bell ringers or inviting people (friends or strangers) to your Christmas Eve service. All it takes is an initial conversation starter.

DECEMBER 18

Rejoice always, 1 Thessalonians 5:16

Life can be going really good and we can be really thankful and say, "God, thank you for all You've given me. Thank you for all You've done." In those seasons of life, it can be easy to rejoice. But what happens when life doesn't go our way? We do not get the blessing, or we do not get the answer to the prayer we were praying for. Our loved ones die, the job is gone and the health report we were praying against happens anyway. Do you find it easy to rejoice no matter what the circumstances? Can you even rejoice at that moment? Paul says to the church at Thessalonica and us, "Rejoice Always." From Paul, it was not just lip service. In Philippi, Paul and Silas were beaten and thrown in jail. While in jail, in chains, Acts 16:25 says they were praying and singing praises to God until an earthquake not only shook the jail door open, but also the shackles and chains off of Paul and Silas. See, Paul lived it out. Peter and the disciples lived it out. In Acts 5, the disciples were beaten for teaching about Jesus and they left rejoicing. See, *rejoicing* is not necessarily about the circumstances, like in Acts 5, but it could be because God is with you and your deep relationship with Him, like in Acts 16. Paul simply tells us to "rejoice always." During the holiday season, maybe now even more than most times of the year, we may find it hard to follow Paul's advice or his teaching here. But we need to remember to rejoice – when? Always. Why? Because there is a God in Heaven who loves us, a Savior who went to hell and back to redeem us and has prepared a place for us when our mission here is over? Jesus was hated and lied about. His friends betrayed Him. He had friends die. He didn't heal everyone, nor did He convince everyone that He was who He said He was. He was rejected by those who claimed to serve Him, yet He still loved us. He still died while we were still sinners and He rejoices over us. He conquered everything life could throw at Him for us, so that when life throws it at us, we can rejoice knowing whose Holy Hands we are in. No matter what your Christmas season looks like or who is not around your table, how can you still rejoice in the Lord? How can you allow the Holy Spirit to comfort and heal wounds and broken hearts so you can rejoice? What is something you can rejoice about? How do you rejoice over it?

DECEMBER 19

> Therefore the Lord himself will give you a sign. Behold, the virgin shall conceive and bear a son and shall call his name Immanuel. Isaiah 7:14

At this time of year, the holidays can be hard, especially when we have lost someone we love and they are not there to celebrate with us. During times of pandemics and financially uncertain times, it can be magnified even more as a family we would be able to see normally, but we can't. Yet Jesus is Immanuel. Immanuel means God with us. God is with us, even today. He hasn't deserted us, forgotten about us, or left us to our own desires. He is still alive, active and with us. He wants to comfort us when we miss those family members that cannot be with us. He wants to ease our anxiety and worry over pandemics, shutdowns and layoffs. Immanuel, God with us – notice there are no clarifiers on that. *God with us*. It does not mean God with us when we tithe, God with us when we worship, or God with us when we serve. It's an unconditional promise. God is with us where we are right now, no matter our emotional, spiritual, or mental states, GOD IS WITH US! God reigns over pandemics, wars, financial uncertainty and unstable times and He can use them for His good. He used foreign powers to discipline His people when they rejected Him and again to free His people when the time of discipline had come to a close. He used Caesar to get Mary and Joseph to Bethlehem, so His centuries old prophecy was fulfilled. He used Herod to send them to Egypt, so His Will was fulfilled again. He used Pilate to condemn Jesus to be crucified, so He could die for our sins and rise again. So, during the Christmas season, although it may look different than in years past, what will you do to recognize God is with us, *Immanuel*? What do you need to do to readjust your thinking so you can remember *Immanuel* this Christmas? How can you allow *Immanuel* to comfort you with the loss of loved ones and family members? What fears are the enemy using to keep you from the Peace of God? How can you let those go? Take time to prepare not only your heart, but also your soul as for the real reason for the season. How will you do that? God gave the world a sign of what He was going to do and while He was doing it, what sign is He giving you? If you don't know, what are you willing to do to hear from Him more clearly this Christmas?

DECEMBER 20

> For to us a child is born, to us a son is given; and the government shall be upon his shoulder and his name shall be called Wonderful Counselor, Mighty God, Everlasting Father, Prince of Peace. Isaiah 9:6

Before my oldest son was born, his first and last name were already determined. Whoever would be my future wife would have to agree to his first name, although she could determine his middle name. It's tradition. I am Joseph, number six. Lucky for me, my wife agreed. There is a lot to a name. My oldest son is Joseph number seven in a long line of Josephs; we each have a different middle name, but that name ties us together and is more than blood and DNA. Isaiah says that when the Messiah comes, "His name will be Wonderful Counselor, Mighty God, Everlasting Father, Prince of Peace." Now, these were not His actual names, but names that indicate His place in the world, in creation and in the universe and they speak to His character as well. Wonderful Counselor means one who listens to someone in need and guides them to working solutions; how often did Jesus do this? Ironically, He is the solution most often. Mighty God and Everlasting Father speaks about the relationship between Him and God. Jesus often referred to Him and the Father as One, which got Him crucified. Prince of Peace refers to the Heavenly peace that surpasses all understanding. Just like the peace that was with the disciples and apostles when they faced death and were executed. They did so with a peace that is hard to comprehend – no fear, no regret, just peace. This Christmas season, when we are celebrating this Messiah child who is born, this son who is given to us. This Christmas, do you have Peace, or has this season become one of stress and anxiety? Focus on the peace that surpasses all understanding. Draw closer to the Counselor that can lead you in killing the stress, anxiety and sorrow that can keep us from the beauty of the holiday, the reason for the season, our Savior. He wants to be your Prince of Peace, your Wonderful Counselor; all you have to do is embrace Him and allow Him to hold you close. How can you do that this holiday season and allow His peace to flow through you? How do you allow the Holy Spirit to guide your working through situations? What situation or relationship do you need His peace to consume? How can you extend His peace to others this Christmas?

DECEMBER 21

> Greater love has no one than this, that someone lay down his life for his friends. John 15:13

Many people who do not believe ask, "Who is God?" or "What is God?" The simple answer is that *God is love*. The disciple John writes a lot about how God is Love, God is *Agape*. We are approaching Christmas Day, the day that makes this verse relevant. Without Christmas, God being born fully man, fully God, we cannot celebrate Easter. Without Easter, Christmas becomes irrelevant and meaningless. Jesus tells us here why He was born and why He left Heaven to come down. No greater love, no greater *agape* is there than for someone to lay down His life for His friends. Yes, we are friends of Jesus Christ, the living Messiah who saved the world. How does that impact you? Does knowing that Jesus calls you a friend have any impact on you at all? He came down to be born poor, in a stable with no fanfare and no parades, because He calls you friend. He was willing to die for you so that your sin would no longer separate you from God. Only by blood being shed could there be redemption for sin. What sin? All sin. Rape, murder, theft, embezzlement, lying, greed, envy, or putting God anywhere on the list other than the first spot. It is all equal and all sins require the same payment. God loves you, calls you friend and He was willing to die for you so that you would no longer be separated from Him. That is the kind of God He is. While Holy, All-Powerful, All-Knowing and All-Present, He knows you by name and was willing to pay the price so you would be able to be connected to Him again. Some Christians get so caught up in the terms used in the previous sentence that they do not have a personal relationship with God. How can an all-powerful and Holy God have a relationship with me? But you are a friend of God. He calls you friend. So, despite all those descriptions of God being true, this should not prevent you from spending time with Him. Suppose you met Bill Gates or Steve Jobs in high school and college and were good friends with them. After they became billionaires and called you up to go skiing or come over for a cookout, would you choose not to go because of their power and influence? God is more powerful, more influential and more knowledgeable than any human. Before He hung the first star in the cosmos, He knew you by name and He wants to spend time with you. He wants to talk with you and have the ability to speak into your life, not just hear about your life and wants and needs. How does the knowledge of knowing God calls you a friend impact your life? How does God calling you a friend impact your Christmas celebrations? How does knowing that God's love for you allowed your sin to nail Him to the cross so you could have a relationship with Him impact your life? How can you show this devotion and gratitude as you prepare to celebrate your friend, the Savior of the World's birthday?

DECEMBER 22

> So we have come to know and to believe the love that God has for us. God is love and whoever abides in love abides in God and God abides in him. 1 John 4:16

The final theme of Advent is love. How appropriate is that? Right before Christmas, the week's theme is *Agape* Love, God's magnificent Love. God is love and it is because of His love for us that while we were in the process of sinning, He sent His son to die for our sins, so we would not be separated from Him, but have eternal life with Him. John tells us here that if we do not *Agape*, we cannot not and do now know God. It is because God is *Agape*, Love. It is His love for us, His *Agape* for us, that motivated God to leave Heaven and came as a human, fully human, yet fully God. That is what we are preparing to celebrate in a couple of days, Christmas, the birth of Jesus, God incarnate. He came to show us how to live and to live through Him, through His Power. It is not until you have come to know and to believe that love, the *Agape* that God has for us, that you can realize that God is *Agape*. God is Love! When we live in and follow the *Agape* of God, we allow the Holy Spirit to work in us, live in us and abide in us. All we have to do is allow the Holy Spirit to direct, guide and instruct us, within us, so that we follow Him and live through Him. Christmas is not about the love that gives presents, but it is about honoring the *Agape* that brings His Presence. Christmas is not about gifts under the tree, but the Gift in the manger, leading to the ultimate Gift on the Cross. Christmas is about the *Agape* love that God has for you. He loves you, *Agapes* you so much. Do you feel the depths of His love, especially this time of the year, or does stress and being overwhelmed override feelings of His love for you? How can you redirect your efforts to the *Agape* of God? Yes, there are only three days until Christmas and two days until Christmas Eve, but there is still time. There is always time to redirect our compass and our hearts to Reason for this Season. What can you do personally to focus on the *Agape* love of God? What can you do to help your family realign their compasses to the *Agape* of God and the Gift of Christ? What changes can you make? What is something you can do to extend the *Agape* Love of God to those outside your house? How willing are you to allow the God of the upside-down economy to turn your celebration upside-down this Christmas to feel the *Agape* love moving through you? What traditions are you willing to let go of for God's presence to be the present this Christmas? What personal desires are you willing to forgo so that God's *Agape* love is overflowing this Christmas Eve? Christmas Day? Christmas Season? How do you live out *Agape*? How do you *Agape* others, not in your family? How do people know that God, the Holy Spirit abides in you?

DECEMBER 23

> "And Mary said, 'Behold, I am the servant of the Lord; let it be to me according to your word.' And the angel departed from her." Luke 1:38

We all know the beautiful story of the nativity. We have angels singing, wise men with gifts and shepherds as the first visitors to Baby Jesus. Churches have students reenact the story and we all say, "Ahhhh, how adorable." I believe we also gloss over the words of the Nativity Story without thinking of the backdrop or what happens in-between the dialogues. Mary replied to the angel, "I am a servant of the Lord." She recognized her place in His plan and dedicated her life to Him. She was willing to go anywhere once she got her marching orders. She continued, "Let it be to me according to your word." WOW! That is awesome and beautiful, but what does her reply entail? We all know the carrying and birthing of Jesus, but what else? It brought a lifetime of shame. Her shame would affect her father, her mother and her family. Her shame would affect Joseph and his family. She would carry the shame of this pregnancy being outside of marriage and giving Joseph an illegitimate son. Would Joseph even believe her or trust her? The decision to obey and be used by God meant the ridicule, glares and gossip would be lifelong. But Mary did not let any of this or fear stop her from being obedient to the Lord. Mary, a servant of the Lord, knows full well the implications for her, her husband, her child and even any other children she might have. Her firstborn would eventually be arrested, tortured and killed. She had a choice to make, follow the Lord or follow self. She would have to discard and throw away her dreams, her wants, her desires and her life plans. Yet she said, "I am a servant of the Lord, let the Lord's will be done, I am a willing participant in His plan." God did not force her, nor did He trick her. He did not coerce her or brainwash her. Her heart was aligned with God's plan and she wanted to do her part. This Christmas, let's start taking a look at the story behind the story and the implications of God's plan for those who said "Yes" to receiving His gift. Is her story part of your story? Are you willing to give it all up to follow God's will for your life? What does this Christmas look like for you and your family? What are you willing to sacrifice for God to move in your life this Christmas? What's holding you back from experiencing the full blessing of God in your life and do you believe the sacrifice is worth it? Mary did.

DECEMBER 24

> "When Joseph woke from sleep, he did as the angel of the Lord commanded him: he took his wife, but knew her not until she had given birth to a son. And he called his name Jesus." Matthew 1:24-25

Has God ever called you to do something and you thought, "God, that is just too absurd," or "God, that is just too hard!" Jesus' father, Joseph did it many times. Little did he know that by asking Mary to be his bride, he would be getting on a rollercoaster of a journey. Let's imagine what Joseph was going through. He had been betrothed to Mary and soon they would be starting their new life together. He put a lot of time and effort into this relationship, what we call an engagement; for their culture, it lasted almost a year. Now, now she's pregnant and it's not his. He can guarantee that. He must have been thinking, "Have I wasted my time? I love her, but I don't want to have her stoned. I don't want her killed." So, to save his family name, he decided to divorce her quietly. They didn't want a big scene, especially in the small town of Nazareth. But hearing this wild story from Mary, how could it be true? Then an angel of the Lord appeared to Joseph and confirmed everything Mary had said. Now it was decision time. He could go through with the divorce and save his family name or give it up and do life God's way. He would have to give up his dream of having a first-born son to carry on the family name, giving up his family honor since his oldest son will be an illegitimate child. These are just some of the fears Joseph must have had. It would have been easier to avoid the rumors, sneers, people talking as they do in small town gossip. He had saved himself for his wife, lived his life according to the law, kept his body pure for marriage and wanted a family of his own and a son to carry on the name and family tree. He followed all the rules and laws laid out and now – what now? What would you have chosen? He chose to honor God. To raise the Son of God as his own. He chose not to consummate his marriage to Mary until after Jesus was born. Finally, he surrendered his desire to name his first-born son. Joseph was from the line of David, as was Mary; little did they know before they were betrothed what their life would end up looking like. What is it in your life that may not be working out the way you wanted it to? What dream do you have that God is asking you to surrender so that His Will can be done in your life? Following God requires sacrifice; what are you willing to sacrifice for Him? What are you not willing to sacrifice for Him? How can you change your heart to be better aligned with God? What is it this Christmas Season that you need to surrender to God and give up so He can work a mighty, powerful testimony in your life?

DECEMBER 25

> "When the angels went away from them into heaven, the shepherds said to one another, 'Let us go over to Bethlehem and see this thing that has happened, which the Lord has made known to us.'" Luke 2:15

We see how the birth of celebrities or royalty is acknowledged. Makeup artists and hairdressers come in and clean mom up and touch up any blemishes on the baby and the news cameras are all over the place. Journalists fight to get the first pictures or land that interview showing the first glimpse of the celebrity baby. But when the King of the World was born, the first people that were told were shepherds. There probably isn't much of a lower and underappreciated bunch of people in society like shepherds. They were filthy, often eating and sleeping with the animals. Most people avoided shepherds in those days. Unless it was Passover and sacrifice time at the temple, shepherds didn't have much of a social life. Yet, at the moment of birth, they were recipients of the biggest announcement in the history of the world, when the Heavens opened up with an archangel telling the shepherds to go and see the Messiah, the one that everyone had been waiting for. Then a multitude of angels joined in and sang Glory to God. Jesus, King of Kings and Lord of Lords, was not born in a temple, nor was He born in a castle. No maids or servants were waiting on Mary or helping take care of Jesus. No, the Creator of the Universe was born where the animals were kept in a stable. The first people to arrive were not royalty, celebrities, or world leaders; they were the bottom rung on the ladder of career people. Still, they came prepared to worship. They didn't make excuses like, "I'm not dressed for this, I'm not ready, it's not the right time, I have other things to do first, or who will watch these animals?" They didn't care that they were dirty and smelly and they didn't care what the people thought of them. God called them to the manger and they went. They didn't even wonder who would take care of the sheep – they left their livelihood to obey God! What is God calling you to do? Are you one to make excuses, like "I'm not smart enough, I don't know the Bible well enough, or I don't have enough money?" The Creator of the Universe *IS* calling you this Christmas season. What is He calling you to do? What is your response? When God called me, I had to let go of what I thought my parents and family would think. I wouldn't change anything; except I wish I had answered God's call sooner. His path is not easy. The nativity is not easy. The nativity is not pretty. The nativity is dirty and smelly, yet that is where God chose to make His first Earthly appearance. All I am asking of you and myself is to be open to what and where God is calling you this Christmas. As hard as it might be, remember how hard Jesus came into the world, but He did it because He loves you! Is it helping a low-income family have a nice Christmas? Is God challenging you with an end-of-the-year tithe? Is God calling you to sign up to go on a mission trip or to start or join a ministry in your church? What are you willing to leave to go where God is calling you? How can the Good Shepherd inspire you to be more obedient to God?

DECEMBER 26

> "Now after Jesus was born in Bethlehem of Judea in the days of Herod the king, behold, wise men from the east came to Jerusalem, saying, 'Where is he who has been born king of the Jews? For we saw his star when it rose and have come to worship him.'" Matthew 2:1-2

Have you ever worked so hard for something that it was all you ever thought about? Daniel Ruettiger comes to mind. You might know him better as *Rudy* from Notre Dame football. Rudy studied the plays and did everything he could as a walk-on player. He finally earned a spot on the practice squad and helped the varsity players prepare for every game. Finally, in his senior year, in the last game of the season, in the final minutes of the final quarter, the head coach suits up Rudy for three plays. This is what Rudy had prepared for, practiced for and given it all for. He did it. The rest, as they say, is history. The wise men were similar. They had studied and memorized ancient scriptures and were looking for a Heavenly sign of a king being born. Through intense studying and memorization and knowing the current situation in the world, they believed it was the time. They knew the location and then the star came and they followed the star. So, unlike our Christmas pageants, the wise men were not there to see a baby. No, they were actually looking for a 2-year-old sitting on a throne in a castle. When they arrived in Jerusalem and at Herod's castle, needless to say, they were surprised to see an old man on the throne. Herod was caught by surprise too! He was thinking his son was going to take over after him, but when the wise men did not return, Herod ordered all the male children under the age of two in Bethlehem to be slaughtered and hence Jesus' family fled to Egypt. These wise men traveled for two years through the desert, looking for this promised king. Everything they had prepared for was now here. They found Joseph, Mary and Jesus and presented them with the gifts they had prepared. Does He need a gift from me? No. He didn't need the gifts of the Magi either, but these gifts were sacrificed and prepared with a clean heart for the new King. Am I alone, or is anyone else struggling with these questions – or have you ever considered these questions? This question is haunting me and I ask it of you as well, "Am I preparing myself for the birth of Christ like the wise men?" This week I challenge you to wrestle with these questions and the following ones. "Is Christmas just another day on the calendar, or am I excitedly digging into Scripture expecting Him to be there?" and, "Am I actively seeking Him like the wise men, or am I burdened with the holiday of Christmas instead of the historical, supernatural event of Christmas?" What gifts have I thought about and prepared to sacrifice for Him? How can we deepen our worship of Him?

DECEMBER 27

> And Mary said, "My soul magnifies the Lord and my spirit rejoices in God my Savior," Luke 1:46-47

When was the last time you experienced overwhelming joy? What was the situation causing it? Was it a big celebration or a private affair? Can you even recall it? It seems like the more the world turns and revolves, the harder it is to find joy. Nehemiah says, "The Joy of the Lord is our strength." But if that is the case, why do we have difficulty finding joy? Christians can be some of the grumpiest people we meet; why is that? Is not the joy of the Lord their strength? What causes you to rejoice? I mean, really rejoice? Mary rejoiced. Mary knew Nehemiah and knew the joy of the Lord was her strength. She sings in her song, "My soul magnifies the Lord and my spirit rejoices in God my savior." My soul magnifies the Lord – how powerful is that? Such peace and understanding had to be in her heart for her to say that. How deep a relationship she had to have had with the Living God to say such a powerful statement. Magnify, meaning, "to make it larger than it really is." How can you make our Living God bigger, who created the entire universe with His hands? The definition of *magnify* from the time period Mary lived means "to extol or glorify." My soul glorifies the Lord. How many of us have that intimate of a relationship with God that our soul glorifies the Lord? Yes, it should be all of us, but what brings us joy? The Presence of the Lord and the Lord's calling on Mary's life brought her joy. She knew it would be a hard and difficult road, Joseph might divorce her, a lifetime of shame, the pain of the Messiah's death and most likely being there to have to witness it all. Despite it all, the joy of the Lord was her strength; her soul glorified the Lord and her spirit rejoiced that God was calling her to do this. Are you willing to be like Mary, rejoicing when God calls you and magnifying and glorifying Him with your soul? Yes, *magnify* – I believe that in a world that minimizes God and His presence, our soul can magnify and bring Him to full view when we obey and rejoice in His calling on our lives. How do you react when God asks you to do something? Do you hand something out the window to the man or woman on the street corner, tithe to the church, step up and join a ministry, or better yet, step up to lead in a ministry? Do you rejoice and thank God for calling you to serve? Does your soul glorify God with those callings? As we prepare to celebrate the birth of the Messiah and as we have been looking at key members of God's plan and God's story, what are you willing to do this Christmas to make a lifelong change? With all the hate and turmoil in the world, are you willing to listen to the Holy Spirit and do what He is calling you to do? Are you willing to renew your eternal commitment to God?

DECEMBER 28

> Pray without ceasing, 1 Thessalonians 5:17

When I was little, we prayed before every dinner and every night at bedtime we would pray. It was like clockwork; no matter where we were, this schedule persisted. Even as an adult, while it has changed some, my prayer ritual still happens. But now we pray before every meal; my wife and I still pray when we go to bed, but it also happens more frequently. As I have matured in my faith and deepened my relationship with the Holy Spirit, I pray more often throughout the day and for many different reasons. I have stopped saying, "I will pray for you," and started praying for the person right then and there. If I get a text message asking for prayer, I stop what I am doing and pray aloud then and there. While I wish I could say that I "pray without ceasing," as Paul tells us to do here, my ADHD kicks in and I get distracted. Some of my prayers are just thankfulness. "God, thank you for the beautiful sunset. God, you did an amazing job with the clouds today, absolutely amazing. Thank you for the rain. Thank you, God, the tornado missed us. Thank you for stopping me from going when the light turned green. Thank you for allowing me to meet that person." There are so many blessings that I am thankful for. This instruction from Paul, while being few in words, is powerful and important. As we are still celebrating the holidays, how has your prayer life been? We are closing out one year and beginning a new year in a couple of days. Is this an area of spiritual growth that you are willing to work on improving, bettering and increasing? How can we become more aligned with Paul's advice for us here? There are so many things to pray, different ways to pray and opportunities to pray; we should ingrain Paul's message in our hearts and try to pray without ceasing. When you wake up, you start your day in prayer. As your head hits the pillow, is your prayer to God the last thing on your mind? On a scale of one to ten, how reflective is your life of this verse? How can you improve on it? What can you do to change your mindset to start seeing God's fingerprints in all aspects of your life, so you can begin to start praying without ceasing? What is the first goal you are willing to commit to as we start the new year?

DECEMBER 29

> But when you pray, go into your room and shut the door and pray to your Father who is in secret. And your Father who sees in secret will reward you. Matthew 6:6

I have ADHD and I can be easily distracted. My oldest son and youngest daughter have ADHD and they can be easily distracted, too. With the invention of social media, smart technology and streaming services, there is so much out there that competes for our attention. I don't feel like God competes for our attention; He gives us the ability, through the gift of free will, to either choose Him or leave Him. When we do choose Him, He is there, ready and willing to help, listen to and guide us. I have heard that the average time Americans spend just on social media is over five hours a day. Throw in the streaming movie and TV services and it is probably a lot longer. Whether we have ADHD or not, we as a society are easily distracted. How does the time spent with God compare to time on smart devices? Is it even a tenth of the time? I have heard of the late Billy Graham praying, on his knees, for eight hours or more. I am lucky if I get to double digits in *minutes* of prayer. Jesus tells us that when we pray, we are to limit our distractions. "Go into your room and shut the door." He would probably add, "Without your phone, smart watch and tablet" if He were here today. He might specify, "Go into your room with nothing but the clothes on your back, shut the door and in silence pray to your Heavenly Father who is in secret." I get distracted even when I am without my devices to distract me. I start to pray and add in prayers for others, which then reminds me I am meeting with one of them, which reminds me I have to stop at the store on my way to meet them… soon, instead of praying, focusing on the very Presence of the Living Holy Spirit in my life, I am making mental to-do lists and checking my calendar events. I have to be very intentional with my prayer time and if I do not start with asking the Holy Spirit to keep me focused, as I've mentioned previously, I am like the dog from the movie *UP* and I'm off chasing random thoughts. This is a discipline I am still trying to master, conquering the mental distractions that keeps me from staying focused on prayer and being quiet enough to allow God, the Holy Spirit, talk time in my prayer life. I remember being younger and having this ability, but the more time I spent using "smart" technology, the less smart and focused I am. How strong is your prayer life? What would Jesus say to you to create a better prayer time and environment? When was the last time you allowed the Holy Spirit to speak to you? What did He say? What do you have to do to allow Him more time to speak? As you prepare for the new year, what are you willing to commit to so that you can deepen and intensify your prayer life?

DECEMBER 30

> Oh sing to the LORD a new song; sing to the LORD, all the earth!
> Psalm 96:1

Who doesn't like new things? For example, they even sell air fresheners with new car smell. Even if it is only new to you, most people like new clothes and how they make them look. Even new recipes are exciting to try, as we aim to experience new tastes and new flavors. As New Year's Eve approaches, people start planning for the New Year, making resolutions to be a better person, a new person. Who doesn't want to be a new person? The health club, mail order and in person diet programs are counting on people to want to be new and make bold New Year's Resolutions. As Psalm 96 begins, the psalmist calls on us to "sing a new song unto the Lord." For me, I feel like I am called to think back on this previous year and give thanks to God for all He has done; but in doing so, singing a new song, a new praise and a new prayer for this next year. I want to sing a new song of thanksgiving for the blessings and protections God has given me, a new song praising God for who He is and what He will do in my life. I pray, "God create in me a new hunger for Your voice and a new burning desire for Your Word. Holy Spirit, create a new unquenchable thirst for Your Presence in my life." While we should never forget the past, we shouldn't be defined by it, nor be held captive by it, good or bad. The new year is starting and God wants to do something new in our lives. Are we open to it? Singing a new song to the Lord comes in surrender after asking Him these questions: "Lord, what new path are you calling me to? What new ways are You wanting me to utilize to help people? Which new people are you wanting me to help? What new way are You calling me to use the gifts You've given me?" We can also pray, "God create in me a new heart, new desires, a heart that desires that follow you. Holy Spirit, create in me a new hunger for Your Word, a new willingness to follow your direction and a new mind to accept Your guidance and instruction." How willing are you to allow God to bring in someone or something new into your life? How willing are you to get out of your comfort zone to follow the guidance of the Holy Spirit?

DECEMBER 31

> I remember the days of old; I meditate on all that you have done; I ponder the work of your hands. Psalm 143:5

I don't know about you, but have you ever been told to "forget about the past"? The wise old baboon, Rafiki, in *The Lion King* tells Simba, "The past can hurt, but we have two choices: either run from it or learn from it." David calls on us here to remember the past, not to run from it, but to remember all that God has done. David meditates on all that God has done, which, if we do, requires us to remember the hurts and the valleys that we've traveled and dealt with. Now, don't get me wrong. I am not saying God caused the hurt we suffered or led us into those valleys. But it is through the hurt and pain, the learning we get from the valleys, that we can experience the Presence of God at a deeper level. I recently lost my only sibling, my brother Tony. As I sat back and contemplated the past year and meditated on all that God had done, it was in that pain of losing my younger brother that God empowered me. It drove me deeper into my marriage, my relationship with my kids and deeper into my relationship with Him. It brought to life Romans 8:28, that for those who love Christ, love God, all things work for our good. God can use any hurt, any loss, for His good. He doesn't cause the hurt, cause the loss, but if we trust Him, He can use it in our lives for His good. As we prepare to begin a new year, we should do as David did and remember the past year through the lens of God's love. Take time to meditate on all that God has done, all the work God did in our lives and remember all that God has brought us through. Will we take the advice of the wise Rafiki? Will we run from our past, our hurts, or will we learn from them to allow God to use them? Meditate on the good that God has done, as well; remember and bring to mind all the blessings that God has bestowed and answered prayers. Let this meditation help develop a spiritual foundation, an attitude of gratitude and appreciation that can last year-round. Ponder the work God did in your life, recently and afar. Ask the Holy Spirit to bring to mind the person you were on January 1, how different you are now and how better you are now. I truly believe that when you experience the power and Presence of God in your life, you are never the same and you will be better than before. How has God worked in your life this past year? How are you a better person and different from the beginning of the year? What works have you seen God do in the lives of people around you and that you have been praying for? Yesterday's devotional talked about singing a new song to the Lord; what new thing are you willing to do for the Lord? What are you willing to hand over and allow the Holy Spirit to change and make new in your life this next year? How much time daily are you willing to give the Holy Spirit each day this next year, so when December 31st arrives again, you can see the change and difference in your life, because you submitted to the spiritual work and activated the transformational power of the Holy Spirit?

INDEX OF SCRIPTURE
ALPHABETICAL WITH ITS DATE

1 Chronicles 4:10	11/9	2 Corinthians 5:17	1/1
1 Chronicles 16:11	10/5	2 Corinthians 5:21	5/31
1 Corinthians 1:27	6/1	2 Corinthians 6:4	7/23
1 Corinthians 2:9	3/7	2 Corinthians 7:10	6/21
1 Corinthians 4:1-2	4/19	2 Corinthians 9:7	5/23
1 Corinthians 4:20	5/16	2 Corinthians 9:10	6/19
1 Corinthians 6:19-20	7/17	2 Corinthians 10:17-18	8/17
1 Corinthians 8:9	3/18	2 Corinthians 12:9	2/9
1 Corinthians 9:24	7/27	2 John 1:6	3/25
1 Corinthians 9:27	10/20	2 Peter 3:9	1/12
1 Corinthians 10:13	1/19	2 Samuel 22:32–33	8/2
1 Corinthians 13:2	2/10	2 Thessalonians 1:3	3/21
1 Corinthians 13:4-5	2/13	2 Thessalonians 2:2	3/12
1 Corinthians 13:6-7	2/12	2 Thessalonians 3:16	12/5
1 Corinthians 13:8	2/11	2 Timothy 1:7	10/7
1 Corinthians 13:13	2/14	2 Timothy 1:9	3/28
1 Corinthians 14:33a	5/27	2 Timothy 2:22	2/17
1 Corinthians 16:13-14	9/4	2 Timothy 3:12	12/11
1 John 1:5	5/20	2 Timothy 3:16	7/7
1 John 1:9	5/14	2 Timothy 4:3-4	1/15
1 John 3:16	2/18	3 John 1:4	7/21
1 John 3:18	9/21	Acts 1:8	6/5
1 John 4:4	2/2	Acts 17:6	11/24
1 John 4:10	4/5	Acts 20:24	8/29
1 John 4:16	12/22	Colossians 1:10	10/15
1 John 5:3	6/16	Colossians 2:3	4/26
1 John 5:5	8/25	Colossians 2:6	5/2
1 Peter 2:2	3/3	Colossians 3:10	1/5
1 Peter 2:16	7/9	Colossians 3:12	2/19
1 Peter 2:18	12/4	Colossians 3:13	10/3
1 Peter 2:24	6/13	Colossians 3:14	5/12
1 Peter 3:15	4/23	Colossians 3:15	6/11
1 Peter 5:7	5/25	Colossians 3:17	6/3

1 Samuel 16:7	4/12	Daniel 6:4	11/4
1 Samuel 17:45	10/21	Daniel 6:10	2/7
1 Samuel 17:48	10/26	Deuteronomy 6:4-5	2/1
1 Thessalonians 4:7	4/22	Deuteronomy 6:6-9	7/18
1 Thessalonians 5:8	3/31	Deuteronomy 7:9	3/13
1 Thessalonians 5:11	5/28	Deuteronomy 31:6	1/28
1 Thessalonians 5:16	12/18	Deuteronomy 31:8	9/10
1 Thessalonians 5:17	12/28	Ecclesiastes 3:1	10/1
1 Thessalonians 5:18	11/3	Ecclesiastes 3:11	2/26
1 Timothy 1:5	9/3	Ecclesiastes 4:12	7/10
1 Timothy 6:18	4/15	Ecclesiastes 9:10	11/13
2 Chronicles 7:14	5/6	Ephesians 1:7	4/11
2 Corinthians 3:17	7/4	Ephesians 2:10	10/24
2 Corinthians 4:6	1/26	Ephesians 4:2	6/4
2 Corinthians 5:9	4/10	Ephesians 4:15	4/18
2 Corinthians 5:15	8/22	Ephesians 4:29	9/14
Ephesians 4:30	10/8	Isaiah 54:17	6/28
Ephesians 4:32	12/18	Isaiah 57:15b	4/4
Ephesians 5:8	2/25	Isaiah 58:9	1/14
Ephesians 6:10	8/8	Isaiah 59:1-2	8/6
Ephesians 6:11-12	8/9	James 1:2-3	1/21
Ephesians 6:13-14	8/11	James 1:5-6	9/5
Ephesians 6:13-14a	8/10	James 1:12	3/16
Ephesians 6:15	8/12	James 1:17	12/9
Ephesians 6:16	8/13	James 1:19-20	12/12
Ephesians 6:17a	8/14	James 3:13	9/17
Ephesians 6:17b-18	8/15	James 4:7	8/4
Ephesians 6:18b-19a	8/16	James 4:10	1/23
Ephesians 6:4	10/16	James 5:16	1/6
Exodus 14:14	6/30	Jeremiah 1:5	5/15
Exodus 18:18	9/24	Jeremiah 4:1-2	11/12
Galatians 2:14	3/29	Jeremiah 17:7	8/27
Galatians 5:1	7/8	Jeremiah 17:7-8	5/9
Galatians 5:13	1/31	Jeremiah 29:11-12	4/9
Galatians 6:7	3/6	Jeremiah 29:13	11/20
Habakkuk 3:19	9/11	Job 1:21-22	6/27
Hebrews 10:23	5/19	Job 11:18	6/29
Hebrews 10:36	10/25	John 1:12	11/14

Hebrews 11:6	1/20	John 3:16	1/29
Hebrews 12:1	10/28	John 3:17	12/16
Hebrews 13:2	9/25	John 3:30	11/19
Hebrews 13:5	9/18	John 4:4	1/25
Hebrews 2:1	10/18	John 6:26-27	6/15
Hebrews 6:10	3/1	John 8:12	8/19
Hosea 10:12	4/25	John 10:10	2/29
Isaiah 3:10	1/18	John 10:11	6/8
Isaiah 6:8	11/16	John 10:28-30	6/18
Isaiah 7:14	12/19	John 12:46	2/8
Isaiah 9:6	12/20	John 13:35	2/16
Isaiah 12:1	7/16	john 14:23	7/2
Isaiah 12:2	7/31	John 14:26	10/30
Isaiah 26:3	2/6	John 14:27	12/8
Isaiah 26:12	12/6	John 15:11	12/15
Isaiah 30:18	9/15	John 15:13	12/21
Isaiah 40:8	6/22	John 16:33	5/24
Isaiah 40:28	4/3	Joshua 1:9	4/14
Isaiah 40:29	7/5	Joshua 24:15	4/16
Isaiah 40:31	7/1	Lamentations 3:21-22	10/29
Isaiah 41:10	5/17	Lamentations 3:23	3/17
Isaiah 43:2	11/18	Lamentations 3:24	6/26
Isaiah 43:18-19	1/2	Lamentations 3:25	1/27
Isaiah 45:7	4/21	Lamentations 3:25-26	6/20
Isaiah 52:7	9/20	Lamentations 3:39	7/14
Isaiah 54:10	10/14	Luke 1:38	12/23
Luke 1:46-47	12/27	Proverbs 3:3-4	10/11
Luke 6:31	2/4	Proverbs 3:5-6	11/10
Luke 6:37	5/13	Proverbs 3:13	9/8
Luke 7:7-10	7/19	Proverbs 27:9	11/8
Luke 9:23	5/29	Proverbs 27:17	9/12
Luke 9:23-24	6/10	Proverbs 27:19	10/23
Luke 10:40	2/28	Proverbs 11:2	4/20
Luke 12:31	12/17	Proverbs 14:13	11/30
Luke 12:7	9/6	Proverbs 14:30	9/30
Luke 17:4	11/25	Proverbs 15:1	8/7
Luke 2:15	12/25	Proverbs 15:5	9/26
Luke 22:27	12/3	Proverbs 16:3	11/6

Luke 22:42	4/1	Proverbs 16:9	6/2
Malachi 3:6	3/14	Proverbs 16:20	8/24
Mark 13:13	10/27	Proverbs 18:2	9/27
Matthew 1:24-25	12/24	Proverbs 18:10	7/28
Matthew 2:1-2	12/26	Proverbs 19:20	11/28
Matthew 3:8	3/26	Proverbs 19:21	11/27
Matthew 4:4	4/17	Proverbs 19:22	11/29
Matthew 5:14	4/6	Proverbs 20:7	5/4
Matthew 5:15-16	7/15	Proverbs 20:24	2/24
Matthew 5:23-24	11/11	Proverbs 21:21	10/19
Matthew 5:43-44	3/15	Proverbs 22:6	2/22
Matthew 5:44	3/24	Proverbs 23:23-24	10/9
Matthew 6:6	12/29	Proverbs 23:26	7/6
Matthew 6:25	2/3	Proverbs 30:5	8/28
Matthew 6:27	9/1	Proverbs 31:30	7/25
Matthew 6:33	3/19	Psalm 9:2	11/22
Matthew 6:34	2/21	Psalm 16:8	8/20
Matthew 7:13-14	9/28	Psalm 16:11	12/13
Matthew 12:30	1/8	Psalm 18:1-2	3/10
Matthew 12:33	4/8	Psalm 19:14	9/13
Matthew 18:21-22	11/26	Psalm 23:1	4/30
Matthew 20:28	3/30	Psalm 23:3	1/24
Matthew 22:37	3/22	Psalm 23:4	11/5
Micah 6:8	10/22	Psalm 25:7-8	3/27
Numbers 13:30	5/3	Psalm 27:1	5/8
Numbers 23:19	3/2	Psalm 29:2	7/20
Philippians 1:6	11/21	Psalm 31:24	6/24
Philippians 1:9	6/25	Psalm 32:2	1/30
Philippians 1:9-11	5/5	Psalm 32:8	1/4
Philippians 2:3	2/15	Psalm 33:4-5	4/29
Philippians 2:13	9/19	Psalm 33:11	8/3
Philippians 4:4	7/3	Psalm 33:12	7/22
Philippians 4:6	1/13	Psalm 34:3	7/13
Philippians 4:7	12/7	Psalm 34:6	5/11
Philippians 4:8	1/22	Psalm 37:7a	3/11
Philippians 4:13	11/7	Psalm 34:8	9/23
Proverbs 1:8-9	10/13	Psalm 34:18	1/16
Psalm 34:19	2/20	Psalm 130:5	6/7

Psalm 42:11	8/31	Psalm 138:3	5/21
Psalm 43:5	7/26	Psalm 139:23-24	4/24
Psalm 46:10	7/29	Psalm 141:3	9/22
Psalm 47:1	12/10	Psalm 143:5	12/31
Psalm 51:10	1/10	Psalm 145:14	5/30
Psalm 51:12	1/3	Psalm 145:8	5/22
Psalm 56:3-4	7/24	Romans 2:4	11/17
Psalm 57:7	5/18	Romans 3:23-24	6/12
Psalm 62:1	8/1	Romans 4:20-22	7/11
Psalm 62:2	2/23	Romans 5:3	8/23
Psalm 63:1	11/15	Romans 5:8	6/9
Psalm 66:5	10/12	Romans 5:9	8/26
Psalm 71:5	10/4	Romans 6:1-2	12/2
Psalm 73:25-26	4/13	Romans 6:4	8/21
Psalm 91:4	2/27	Romans 8:1	2/5
Psalm 94:19	4/7	Romans 8:6	10/6
Psalm 96:1	12/30	Romans 8:15	9/29
Psalm 97:11	4/28	Romans 8:24	12/1
Psalm 100:4-5	11/23	Romans 8:28	5/7
Psalm 103:8	1/9	Romans 8:32	5/1
Psalm 103:13	10/2	Romans 8:38-39	4/2
Psalm 105:4	8/18	Romans 12:1	6/6
Psalm 111:2	1/17	Romans 12:2	8/30
Psalm 112:7	5/26	Romans 12:3	11/1
Psalm 118:5-6	1/11	Romans 12:9	3/8
Psalm 118:24	6/17	Romans 12:12	6/14
Psalm 119:15-16	8/5	Romans 12:21	11/2
Psalm 119:18	4/27	Romans 13:10	6/23
Psalm 119:45	7/12	Romans 14:17	5/10
Psalm 119:59	9/7	Romans 15:2	9/16
Psalm 119:64	9/2	Romans 15:4	9/9
Psalm 119:114	7/30	Titus 2:7a	3/4
Psalm 119:143	10/10	Titus 2:12	10/31
Psalm 119:147	3/9	Titus 3:1-2	10/17
Psalm 121:1-2	3/5	Zephaniah 3:17b	1/7
Psalm 121:5	3/20	Zechariah 10:2	3/23

Made in the USA
Thornton, CO
01/26/23 09:56:11

ce43e000-9208-4a2d-8215-0ca5ff2442dcR01